Elites and Democratic Consolidation in Latin America and Southern Europe

Employing a framework that focuses on the actions and choices of elites in creating consolidated democracies, a distinguished group of scholars examine in this book the recent transitions to democracy and the prospects for democratic stability in Argentina, Brazil, Chile, the Dominican Republic, Peru, Portugal, Spain, and Uruguay. The role of elites in creating, democratizing, and consolidating the longer-established regimes in Colombia, Costa Rica, Italy, and Venezuela is also assessed, and an analysis of the stable but not very democratic Mexican regime is presented.

Without ignoring the importance of mass publics and institutions, the authors argue that in independent states with long records of political instability and authoritarian rule, democratic consolidation requires consensus on specific democratic institutions and rules of the game, as well as increased integration, among previously hostile elites. Two processes by which this elite configuration can be established are explored in detail: *elite settlements*, in which elites suddenly and deliberately negotiate compromises on their most basic and disruptive disputes, and *elite convergences*, in which a series of tactical decisions by rival elites gradually leads to procedural consensus and increased integration.

This focus on democratic consolidation (rather than on regime transition) and on long-term prospects for stability, as well as the systematic application of a single analytical framework, makes this volume unique in the literature on democratization.

Elites and Democratic Consolidation in Latin America and Southern Europe

Edited by
JOHN HIGLEY AND RICHARD GUNTHER

CAMBRIDGE
UNIVERSITY PRESS

Published by the Press Syndicate of the University of Cambridge
The Pitt Building, Trumpington Street, Cambridge CB2 1RP
40 West 20th Street, New York, NY 10011-4211, USA
10 Stamford Road, Oakleigh, Melbourne 3166, Australia

First published 1992
Reprinted 1995

Printed in the United States of America

Library of Congress Cataloging-in-Publication Data is available

A catalogue record for this book is available from the British Library

ISBN 0-521-41374-5 hardback
ISBN 0-521-42422-4 paperback

Contents

About the contributors

THOMAS BRUNEAU is professor of national security affairs at the U.S. Naval Postgraduate School in Monterey, California. He is the coauthor of *Politics in Contemporary Portugal* (with Alex Macleod) and of *Integration and Change in Brazil's Middle Amazon* (with Rolf Wesche).

MICHAEL BURTON is professor of sociology at Loyola College in Baltimore, Maryland. He has coauthored (with John Higley and G. Lowell Field) a number of articles on elite theory, including two appearing in the *American Sociological Review* and, most recently, "A New Elite Framework for Political Sociology," appearing in *Cahiers Vilfredo Pareto*.

MARCELO CAVAROZZI is professor of political science at the National University of Buenos Aires and a senior researcher at CEDES (Center for the Study of State and Society) in Buenos Aires. He is currently a visiting professor of political science at the Massachusetts Institute of Technology. Among his recent books are *Peronismo y radicalismo: Transiciones y perspectivas en la Argentina* and *Muerte y resurrección: Los Partidos políticos en el autoritarismo y las transiciones en el cono sur* (with Manuel Antonio Garretón).

MAURIZIO COTTA is professor of political science at the University of Siena. He has written extensively on Italian political elites and institutions, and is the coauthor of *Manuale de scienza politica* and coeditor of *Parliament and Democratic Consolidation in Southern Europe*, (with Ulrike Liebert).

HENRY DIETZ is associate professor of government at the University of Texas at Austin. Among his many publications on Peruvian and other Latin American politics is *Poverty and Problem-solving Under Military Rule*. He has most recently coedited *Ethnicity, Integration, and the Military* (with Jerrold Elkin and Maurice Roumani).

CHARLES GUY GILLESPIE was assistant professor of political science at the University of Wisconsin, Madison. Among his publications are *Negotiating Democracy: Party Strategies and the Transition from Authoritarian Military Rule in Uruguay*, *Uruguay y la democracia* (coedited with

Louis Goodman, Juan Rial, and Peter Winn), and numerous articles on politics in the Southern Cone countries of Latin America.

LAWRENCE S. GRAHAM is professor of government at the University of Texas at Austin. His publications include *The State and Policy Outcomes in Latin America, The Political Economy of Brazil: Public Policies in an Era of Transition*, and, most recently, several studies of development policies in Latin America and Southern and Eastern Europe.

RICHARD GUNTHER is professor of political science at the Ohio State University and cochair of the Subcommittee on Southern Europe of the Social Science Research Council. His publications include *Public Policy in a No-Party State, Spain After Franco* (with Giacomo Sani and Goldie Shabad), *Crisis y cambio* (with Juan Linz, José Ramón Montero, Hans-Jürgen Puhla, Giacomo Sani, and Goldie Shabad), and numerous shorter pieces on Spanish and Southern European politics.

JOHN HIGLEY is professor of government and sociology at the University of Texas at Austin. His publications focus primarily on elites and elite theory and include *Elites in Australia* (with Desley Deacon and Don Smart) and *Elitism* (with G. Lowell Field).

ALAN KNIGHT is Annabel Irion Worsham Centennial Professor of History at the University of Texas at Austin. He has written a two-volume study, *The Mexican Revolution*, as well as numerous articles on other aspects of twentieth-century Mexican politics and society.

JOHN A. PEELER is professor of political science at Bucknell University. His writings on Latin American politics include *Latin American Democracies: Colombia, Costa Rica and Venezuela*.

PETER M. SANCHEZ is assistant professor of political science at the U.S. Air Force Academy. His University of Texas doctoral dissertation is entitled "Elite Settlements and Democracy in Latin America: The Dominican Republic and Peru."

Preface

Is another book on democratization really needed? After all, the past five years have seen a flood of writing on the subject, most notably the four volumes edited by Guillermo O'Donnell, Philippe Schmitter, and Laurence Whitehead, *Transitions from Authoritarian Rule* (1986–7) and the still more comprehensive quartet of volumes put together by Larry Diamond, Juan Linz, and Seymour Martin Lipset, *Democracy in Developing Countries* (1988–91). Drawing on the expertise of more than fifty scholars, containing extensive analyses of at least thirty countries, and totaling more than two thousand pages, these eight volumes – augmented by the overview works of John Herz (1982), Julián Santamaría (1982), Guy Hermet (1983), Martin Needler (1987), James Malloy and Mitchell Seligson (1987), Enrique Baloyra (1987), and Giuseppe Di Palma (1990), not to mention a large number of monographic studies – must surely exhaust the subject for now.

Yes and no. Apart from some updating to cover the most recent events, our factual knowledge cannot be extended significantly by another book dealing with democratic transitions in many of the same countries. Justification for such a volume therefore lies at the theoretical and interpretive level. Here, we believe, there is room for further work.

This book is distinct from the existing literature on democratization, in two ways. First, each of the country studies focuses on factors that contribute to the successful *consolidation* of democratic regimes, rather than the transition to democracy per se. Without this focus, another volume of studies of democratic transitions in Southern Europe and Latin America would indeed be redundant. We already know that transitions to democracy may be triggered by a wide variety of events: popular uprisings (Venezuela), defeat in war (Argentina) or the threat of an impending military catastrophe (Greece), the death of an aging dictator (Spain), coups (Portugal and Paraguay), and even the repercussions of a plebescite gone awry (Chile). We also know that the course of transitions may vary considerably from case to case: protracted negotiations among the relevant elites (Brazil and Spain), elite power struggles in the midst of mass mobilizations and revolutionary turmoil (Portugal), solitary decisions by a prominent individual suddenly endowed with emergency powers (Greece), and so forth. And we know that they culminate in regimes that take a variety of institutional forms (see Lijphart, Bruneau, Diamandouros, and Gunther 1988). Unless systematic, cross-national analyses of these transitions are conducted with a specific set of questions in mind, little more can be learned that is of value in building comparative theory.

This volume's second distinctive feature is its single theoretical framework. Each of the case studies applies a common set of concepts dealing with first, the ability of elites to reach agreements that contribute to the consolidation of new democratic regimes and, second, with circumstances that facilitate such agreements. Focusing on the roles played by elites in democratic transitions is, of course, not new. O'Donnell and Schmitter, as well as many of their collaborators, see "elite pacts" as a crucial element in successful transitions from authoritarian rule (O'Donnell and Schmitter 1986, esp. pp. 37–9). Diamond and Linz write that "the skills, values, strategies, and choices of political leaders figure prominently in our explanation of the enormously varied experiences with democracy in Latin America" (Diamond and Linz 1989, p. 14); and Diamond, separately, writes that "if there is any common thread running through the democratic prospects of all ten of the [Asian] countries we examine . . . it is the crucial importance of effective and democratically committed leadership" (Diamond 1989, p. 49). Moreover, many scholars have contended that a disposition toward compromise, flexibility, tolerance, conciliation, moderation, and restraint among elites is a sine qua non of consolidated democracy (Field and Higley 1980; Prewitt and Stone 1973; Putnam 1976). For a democratic system to persist and flourish, elites must engage in "politics-as-bargaining" rather than "politics-as-war" (Sartori 1987, pp. 224–6).

But even though there is broad agreement about this elite precondition for consolidated democracy, there is no similar agreement about how it is created and how it is sustained. The former question goes to the heart of the debate about transitions to democracy; the latter concerns the structure and functioning of elites and their relations with mass publics in consolidated democracies. Do these elite dispositions result from a protodemocratic political culture, from a high level of socioeconomic development, from particular historical experiences, or from particular political and constitutional structures? Do they occur only where ethnic, racial, regional, religious, and other mass cleavages are relatively manageable? Or where mass publics are not divided sharply into antagonistic classes and where inequalities are not excessive? And how are elite dispositions affected by international forces or by specially gifted and charismatic individual leaders?

This volume grapples with these and related questions in the context of recent Latin American and Southern European politics. We advance and explore distinctive explanations for the occurrence and nonoccurrence of democratic consolidation in these countries. We contend that in independent states with long records of political instability and authoritarian rule, distinctive *elite transformations*, carried out by the elites themselves, constitute the main and possibly the only route to democratic consolidation. For consolidation to occur, we argue, elites that had previously been "disunified" must become "consensually unified" in regard to the basic procedures and norms by which politics will henceforth be played.

Such elite transformations from disunity to consensual unity take place in two principal ways. One is through *elite settlements*, in which previously disunified and warring elites suddenly and deliberately reorganize their relations by negotiating compromises on their most basic disagreements, thereby achieving consensual unity and laying the basis for a stable democratic regime. The Glorious Revolution of 1688–9 in England and the constitutional settlement of 1809 in Sweden are striking historical examples of elite settlements that thoroughly transformed politics, created political stability, and allowed a gradual, peaceful evolution to democracy.

Some of the chapters in this book explore the idea that similar elite settlements occurred in 1929 in Mexico, in 1948 in Costa Rica, in 1957–8 in Colombia and Venezuela, and in 1977–9 in Spain, all of which have since had stable political regimes that have, at varying speeds and under varying circumstances, established or moved toward democracy. Additional chapters examine a number of other countries in which elite settlements have been attempted and in which they may even have succeeded: Uruguay, Portugal, Chile, and the Dominican Republic. Why elites in Argentina, Brazil, and Peru have been unable to engineer settlements and the prospects for such agreements in the future are subjects of still other chapters. Finally, we address the question of whether elite settlements and the elite consensual unity that they produced may today be breaking down in Colombia, Mexico, and several other countries.

The other principal route to the consolidation of democracy in already-independent countries is through *elite convergence*. Less sudden than an elite settlement, this process is a series of deliberate, tactical decisions by rival elites that have the cumulative effect, over perhaps a generation, of creating elite consensual unity, thereby laying the basis for consolidated democracy. Two fairly distinct steps in an elite convergence can be discerned. In the first step, some of the warring factions in a disunified national elite enter into sustained, peaceful collaboration in order to mobilize a reliable electoral majority, win elections repeatedly, and thereby dominate government executive power. In the second step, the major elite factions opposing this coalition eventually tire of continuous government by their ideological and programmatic opponents; they conclude that there is no way to challenge their rivals' hegemonic position except to beat them at their own game (i.e., by forming an opposition electoral coalition and abandoning their challenge to the political regime itself). Thus, they decide to compete according to the regime's rules of the game, implicitly or explicitly acknowledging the legitimacy of its institutions. Typically, this is accompanied or followed by a reduction of ideological and programmatic polarization in the party system. Once this second step is taken, a unified elite is created and a consolidated democracy rapidly emerges.

France during the Fifth Republic is a good example of an elite convergence, and we survey this process as it evolved between 1960 and 1986 in Chapter 1. Several subsequent chapters consider the possibility that elite convergences have occurred or are real prospects in Latin America and Southern Europe. In Southern Europe, patterns of elite interaction during the past fifteen to twenty years in Italy and Portugal accord with the convergence process, although the possibility that elite settlements have occurred, or at least have been attempted, in those countries is also entertained. In Latin America, there are grounds for thinking that Uruguayan elites have recently converged and that Peruvian elites may be in the early stages of convergence, despite the dire economic circumstances and political violence confronting Peru. The prospects for elite convergences in Argentina and Brazil are also explored.

By elaborating this elite-centered explanation for the origin of consolidated democracies and by seeing how it fits with their presence or absence in a dozen countries, our aim is to give a sharper focus to the broad shift toward "political" variables in the current discussion of democratic consolidation. In the first chapter, we lay out the essentials of our approach, concentrating on definitions, the relationship between elites and democratic regimes, empirical indicators, and the nature of elite settlements and convergences. We also describe the ways in which elite settlements and convergences contribute to the consolidation of new democratic regimes, and we identify historical, organizational, and social-structural factors that facilitate or impede settlements and convergences in countries undergoing democratic transitions. Later chapters examine these concepts and processes in light of the relevant historical records and current political situations of the principal Latin American and Southern European countries. The final chapter takes stock of our effort and reviews those factors facilitating democratic consolidation by means of elite transformations.

This volume is based on many independent research projects over the past two decades. Collaboration among the volume's contributors stems most directly from a 1987 article by Michael Burton and John Higley entitled "Elite Settlements." In response to this article, Richard N. Adams, director of the Institute of Latin American Studies at the University of Texas at Austin, asked Higley to organize a working group to study elite settlements and democracy in Latin America. With funds provided by the institute and by Robert D. King, dean of the College of Liberal Arts at the University of Texas at Austin, a series of meetings were convened in Austin between May 1987 and December 1988, at which these concepts were discussed and tentatively applied to democratic transition processes in a variety of settings. A second paper by Higley and Burton, "The Elite Variable in Democratic Transitions and Breakdowns," published in 1989, further developed the theoretical perspective. Meanwhile, Richard Gunther had developed an analysis of the transition to democracy in Spain along highly similar theoretical lines. As a National Fellow at the Hoover Institution during a sabbatical year, 1986–7, he was attempting to test various aspects of "the Spanish model" in several Southern European and Latin American settings. In response to an invitation to join the Austin group, it was quickly decided to merge the two efforts. From early in 1988, Higley and Gunther worked jointly and equally to lead the project to completion. Grants from the Tinker Foundation and from the Program for Cultural Cooperation Between Spain's Ministry of Culture and U.S. Universities, together with further assistance from the Institute of Latin American Studies, made possible a final meeting of the group at Lake Atitlán in Guatemala during March 1990. The editors wish to thank these individuals and institutions for their generous support.

We also want to thank a number of scholars who attended the group's meetings and made many valuable suggestions: Arturo Arias, John Booth, Paul Cammack, Michael Conroy, Rodolfo de la Garza, Joe Foweraker, Renee Gannon, Luis Javier Garrido, Richard Graham, Jonathan Hartlyn, Kenneth Maxwell, Luis Milliones, Bryan Roberts, Enrique Semo, Sam Stone, and Torcuato Di Tella. Valuable comments and criticisms were also made by Felipe Agüero, Larry Diamond,

Juan Linz, Anthony Mughan, Kevin O'Brien, Bradley Richardson, and Goldie Shabad, for which we are grateful. Shirley Burleson, a staff member of the Institute of Latin American Studies, helped greatly with the organizational nuts and bolts.

This volume is dedicated to two colleagues and friends. The first is Charles Gillespie, who worked heroically to finish his fine contribution to the volume within weeks of his tragic death in early 1991. One of the most promising Latin Americanists to emerge in recent years, Charlie is sorely missed by all. The other colleague and friend is Richard N. Adams, who initiated our project and supported it over a four-year period. The volume coincides with Rick's retirement after many years of distinguished scholarship on Latin America and on the theory of societal evolution. The editors and authors will be pleased if the volume is seen as a salute to the lasting contributions that Charlie Gillespie and Rick Adams have made.

John Higley and Richard Gunther
July 1991

1

Introduction: elite transformations and democratic regimes

MICHAEL BURTON, RICHARD GUNTHER, AND JOHN HIGLEY

For all the meanings that "democracy" has acquired, there is broad scholarly agreement that it can best be defined and applied in terms of the procedural criteria that Robert Dahl (1971) has specified: a political regime characterized by free and open elections, with relatively low barriers to participation, genuine political competition, and wide protection of civil liberties. Elaborating Dahl's definition, Juan Linz writes that a political system can be regarded as democratic

> when it allows the free formulation of political preferences, through the use of basic freedoms of association, information, and communication, for the purpose of free competition between leaders to validate at regular intervals by non-violent means their claim to rule, . . . without excluding any effective political office from that competition or prohibiting any members of the political community from expressing their preference. (Linz 1975, pp. 182–3)

This procedural conception of democracy is a demanding "ideal type." All of its criteria must be approximated closely before a regime can be called "democratic." Obviously, no real-world regime fits the ideal type perfectly; indeed, many regimes that hold regular elections fall far short. Some regimes tie voting rights to stringent property qualifications, as in most Western countries during the nineteenth century. Some deny the suffrage to whole ethnic categories, as in South Africa or the American South until quite recently. Some outlaw parties that espouse radical ideologies and programs, as has happened to Communist parties in a number of countries. Others marshal majority support for governing parties through corrupt and coercive practices, as the Mexican regime has done for decades. Some regimes sharply limit the effects of democratic procedures by reserving powerful government posts for individuals or bodies that are neither directly nor indirectly responsible to the electorate (e.g., the Portuguese Council of the Revolution between 1976 and 1982). Thus, conceiving of democracy in procedural terms does not lead to a simple distinction between democratic and undemocratic regimes. Between these two poles lie a variety of systems that we will refer to as "limited" and "pseudo" democracies. We can distinguish the more fully democratic regimes from these semidemocratic systems insofar as the former effectively recruit governing elites through free and fair competition among all parties that want to participate – in conformity with democratic rules of the game but irrespective of other aspects of their ideologies or programmatic preferences – and through widespread and unhindered mass participation based on universal suffrage.

The principal alternative to procedural conceptions of democracy is a substantive conception that equates democracy with greater equality in the distribution of national wealth and with "social justice." We have rejected this alternative, for several reasons. First, democracy and economic equality are distinct concepts. For example, under the now-defunct Communist regime of the German Democratic Republic, the distribution of national wealth was more equal than in most Western democracies, and the official ideology endorsed social justice as a main goal, yet the GDR was clearly not democratic. Second, the most common reason for rejecting a procedural conception of democracy (particularly among Latin Americanists) is that democracy is too often little more than a facade behind which a privileged economic elite dominates and exploits the popular classes – through intimidation, electoral corruption, the passivity of unmobilized population sectors, or the outright exclusion of certain political options. But our use of a demanding ideal–typical procedural conception of democracy enables us to deal with such undemocratic practices by classifying the regimes that perpetrate them as limited or pseudo-democracies. Finally, more analytic leverage can be gained by keeping separate the concepts of democracy and economic equality, as one may be temporally and perhaps causally prior to the other. Our rejection of a substantive conception of democracy does not in any way mean that we deny the importance of economic and other equalities (particularly in areas like Latin America, where inequalities are often extreme). We simply think that the concepts of democracy and economic equality are best kept analytically distinct.

This volume is concerned with more than the creation of democratic regimes; it is especially concerned with their stability and prospects for long-term survival. Maintaining stability is often a complex and demanding task in democracies, for by their very nature, they involve the open expression of conflict. Democratic stability requires a careful balance between conflict and consensus. The failure of a democracy to achieve or maintain this balance is manifested in at least three ways (see Gunther and Mughan 1991). The first is a deliberate stifling of democracy through de facto or de jure denial of civil and political rights (preventing significant groups from participating in politics) or through electoral corruption that effectively negates the preferences of a majority of voters, enabling a dominant elite to govern unchecked by electoral accountability. Second, democratic regimes may be unable to keep the expression of conflict within nonviolent bounds. Thus, the occurrence of frequent and widespread political violence is evidence of instability. Finally, efforts to topple the regime itself, through organized coups or mass rebellions, clearly manifest the collapse of democratic stability. Conversely, in stable democracies, civil and political rights are respected; large-scale mass violence does not occur; and coups or other forcible power seizures are essentially unthinkable (Powell 1982; see also Sanders 1981).

During this century, many democratic regimes have come into existence in Latin America, Europe, and elsewhere in which free elections were held, barriers to participation were low, there was meaningful party competition, and civil liberties were not trampled upon. Yet, most of these democratic regimes were either terminated by coups and other violent events, or they gradually gave way to single-party authoritarian regimes. Clearly, a transition to procedural democracy does not guarantee democratic stability. It is necessary to examine both the ways in which democracies are created and the reasons that they do and do not survive.

A key to the stability and survival of democratic regimes is, in our view, the establishment of substantial consensus among elites concerning rules of the democratic political game and the worth of democratic institutions. In Giovanni Sartori's formulation, democratic stability requires that elites perceive politics as "bargaining" rather than "war" and that they see political outcomes as positive- not zero sum (Sartori 1987, pp. 224–6). We regard the establishment of this elite procedural consensus and outlook as the central element in the consolidation of new democratic regimes. By taking the concept of democratic consolidation as our point of departure, we can usefully distinguish several types of democratic regimes.

Consolidated and other democratic regimes

As we define it, a *consolidated democracy* is a regime that meets all the procedural criteria of democracy and also in which all politically significant groups accept established political institutions and adhere to democratic rules of the game. This is, of course, another ideal type, because there is no real-world case in which all political groups fully obey democratic rules of the game and fully acknowledge the legitimacy of the political institutions and principles under which they live – there are always at least some dissident groups in these respects. Because no democratic regime is ever fully consolidated in the ideal-typical sense, democratic consolidation is best regarded as a "process of adaptation/freezing of democratic structures and norms, which come to be accepted as legitimate by part or all of civil society" (Morlino 1986, p. 210). Or again, as Bolivar Lamounier puts it, democratic consolidation is a "process through which democratic forms come to be valued in themselves, even against adverse substantive outcomes" (Lamounier 1988, p. 1).

Analytically, consolidated democracies can be thought of as encompassing specific elite and mass features. First, all important elite groups and factions share a consensus about rules and codes of political conduct and the worth of political institutions, and they are unified structurally by extensive formal and informal networks that enable them to influence decision making and thereby defend and promote their factional interests peacefully (Higley and Moore 1981; Sartori 1987). Second, there is extensive mass participation in the elections and other institutional processes that constitute procedural democracy. No segments of the mass population are arbitrarily excluded or prevented from mobilizing to express discontents, and recourse to various corrupt practices that distort mass participation is minimal. As we shall argue, these elite and mass features of consolidated democracies make them stable and resilient in the face of sometimes severe challenges, with good prospects for long-term survival.

We regard all regimes in Western Europe and North America, together with Japan, Australia, and New Zealand, as consolidated democracies today, although some have only recently achieved this condition. But if consolidation means that all politically significant groups accept democratic rules of the game and acknowledge the legitimacy of existing political institutions, as well as the philosophy that undergirds them, one might question our characterization of Britain and Spain as consolidated. British democracy is not consolidated in Northern Ireland: Irish nationalists deny the legitimacy of the government at Westminster, and they depart frequently from democratic rules of the game in pursuit of their cause; and although Ulster Unionists fiercely defend the Westminster government's legitimacy, their regular resort to violence and repression of minority rights hardly fits with democratic principles. Likewise, in Spain, roughly one quarter of the Basque population supports Basque separatism, and some Basque nationalists have fueled a substantial level of political violence. Although one should not expect perfect conformity with all criteria whenever ideal-type definitions are used, Britain and Spain cannot be regarded as completely consolidated democracies. In both countries, however, all politically significant national-level elites and their organizations (representing an overwhelming majority of citizens in each polity) remain steadfast in support of the existing democratic regime. Hence, we feel comfortable in regarding both countries as consolidated democracies, even though each of them contains a small region in which processes of consolidation are as yet incomplete. What is both theoretically and politically important is that consolidation at the national level has enabled these democratic regimes to withstand serious challenges to their stability and survival, involving the violent deaths of about 2,500 British and 700 Spanish citizens.

The absence or greatly reduced extent of the elite or mass features of consolidated democracies signifies some other regime type. First, where the trappings of procedural democracy exist and there is substantial mass participation, but where there is no real elite consensus about democratic rules of the game and institutions, and where elites are instead disunified in the sense that they distrust and have little traffic with one another, we may speak of an *unconsolidated democracy*. Typically, this follows in the wake of an authoritarian regime's sudden collapse or overthrow. Two classic instances were Weimar Germany, 1919–33, and the Second Spanish Republic, 1931–36, which followed collapses of the German monarchy at the end of World War I and the Primo de Rivera dictatorship, respectively. Both regimes were fully democratic in terms of their constitutions and workings, but both were unstable and extremely precarious. They experienced intense electoral struggles that regularly boiled over into street violence, clashes between paramilitary groups, and, in the case of Spain, civil war. Austria between the two world wars, Italy immediately after World War I, Belgium, Greece, Portugal, and several other European regimes during parts of that critical period were also unconsolidated democracies. Today, the Philippines is a graphic instance of a democracy that remains unconsolidated. After Ferdinand Marcos was overthrown in 1985, democracy was reinstituted, but with a disunified elite, it has been beset by much political violence and several attempted coups. What principally distinguishes unconsolidated from consolidated democracies is, in short, the absence of elite consensual unity.

Where elites share substantial consensus and display structural unity, but where mass participation does not extend much beyond relatively well-off strata owing to a restricted suffrage, and/or where a passive peasantry makes up a large segment of the population, we may speak of *stable limited democracies*. Commonly in such regimes, elections to parliaments or other deliberative bodies are regularly held and publicly contested, and the outcomes of these elections, as well as the decisions of the duly elected deliberative bodies, are binding on the formation and policies of government executives. Government executive power thus passes peacefully between competing political factions and camps who, in effect, take turns governing. At the same time, mass unrest is kept to moderate levels, either because elites actively seek to contain it or because most of the mass population is isolated and uninvolved, and the elites, reflecting their basic consensual unity, do not attempt coups or other irregular power seizures. In short, there is regime stability, but the absence of substantial mass participation means that democracy is limited to such an extent that the requirements of our ideal-type definition of democracy are not met.

Classic examples of stable limited democracies were Britain and Sweden in the nineteenth century. For reasons and in ways detailed later, British and Swedish elites displayed substantial consensual unity by that point in their countries' political development, and those elites operated stable regimes based on principles of representation. But large numbers of adult citizens remained unenfranchised, and occasional outbursts of mass discontent were dealt with harshly (e.g., the Chartist movement in Britain during the 1830s and 1840s). A different, more controversial example of a stable limited democracy is Mexico since 1929. In that year, elites making up the "revolutionary family" achieved substantial consensual unity (see Chapter 4) and, in so doing, set the stage for regular elections to Congress and the presidency, involving peaceful competition for power mainly between factions of the PRI, that now extend over some sixty years. The Mexican regime has been markedly stable and at least outwardly democratic in its workings throughout this period. Most observers agree, however, that mass participation has been seriously fettered by a variety of practices that the PRI has used to maintain its hegemony, so that even today Mexico is, at most, a stable limited democracy.

A fourth, somewhat residual category of democratic regimes must be added to the consolidated, unconsolidated, and stable limited democracies we have distinguished. For want of a better term, we will call them *pseudo-democracies*. We have in mind the large number of regimes that regularly hold elections and proclaim themselves to be "democratic" but in which the elite and mass features of consolidated democracies do not exist to any meaningful extent. Typically, pseudo-democracies are rather tight one-party regimes, de facto if not officially. Elections are held, but they involve so little elite competition and so much mass intimidation that they merely represent perfunctory public ratification of the dominant elite's political choices. Most of the "presidential monarchies" of Africa, the Middle East, and Asia during the past thirty years are examples. Such pseudo-democracies will not concern us in this book, but any typology of democratic regimes requires acknowledging their existence.

On what basis can we classify actual regimes as falling within one or another of the four categories just described? The extent to which a regime is functioning according to the procedural criteria of democracy is rather easily assessed, but how can we tell if it is consolidated? A common temptation is to infer consolidation from observed stability: the regime survives, ergo it must be consolidated. This is, of course, tautological. In an era of mass- and elite-opinion surveys, extensive media coverage of politics, and in-depth interviews with political leaders, however, a variety of measures reflecting the presence or absence of consolidation are available, thus enabling the analyst to collect independent measures of consolidation. The most straightforward of these are found at the time when a constitution (which gives institutional form to a new democracy and helps define its rules of the game) is being drafted and ratified, as this process involves numerous public statements by representative elites, as well as formal votes of ratification by elites and often the electorate. A substantial vote against a constitution motivated by fundamental disagreements signals the absence of consolidation. But it is possible that a sector of society that initially rejected a constitution will later come to regard as acceptable the regime that is built upon it. In such a case, behavioral, elite-interview, or opinion-survey data, in combination with a careful monitoring of public statements made by elites representing the relevant sector, are likely to provide evidence of consolidation.

Antisystem parties with significant and persistent levels of electoral support also indicate a lack of consolidation. The concept of "antisystem party" must be clarified, however. Too often it is used for polemical purposes to stigmatize a democratic party that has no real intention of overthrowing a regime, as the Italian Christian Democrats have done to the Italian Communists. To be regarded as a manifestation of the absence of democratic consolidation, an antisystem party must be unequivocally opposed to the existing regime. Fortunately, from an analytical point of view, most antisystem parties make no bones about their stance: They vote against constitutions or organize boycotts of constitutional referenda; they regularly condemn the regime and articulate their vision of the alternative regime they seek; and they often try to subvert existing institutions, even when elected to serve in them.

Still clearer evidence of the lack of democratic consolidation is the existence of sustained mass mobilization or insurrection against a regime by a large movement demanding radical political change through irregular means. There can be little doubt, for example, that supporters of the Sendero luminoso reject the legitimacy of the Peruvian regime. Given the magnitude of such a movement (in contrast with the much smaller and regionally restricted terrorist movements in Spain and Northern Ireland), the regime cannot be regarded as consolidated and thus likely to survive over the long term without undergoing considerable change.

To conclude, we distinguish four types of democratic regimes: consolidated, unconsolidated, stable limited democracies, and pseudo-democracies. Compared with consolidated democracies, each of the other types lacks elite consensual unity, substantial mass participation in democratic institutions and processes, or (in pseudo-democracies) both. Changes from authoritarian regimes to any of these types of democratic regimes, as well as changes from one to another of the democratic types depend on a variety of circumstances, events, and processes. Understanding these changes and their long-term consequences is the basic purpose of this volume. Let us turn to what we contend is the most crucial variable in such changes: elites.

Elites and democratic regimes

We define *elites* as persons who are able, by virtue of their strategic positions in powerful organizations, to affect national political outcomes regularly and substantially. Elites are the principal decision makers in the largest or most resource-rich political, governmental, economic, military, professional, communications, and cultural organizations and movements in a society (see Burton and Higley 1987b; Dye 1983; Higley, Deacon, and Smart 1979; McDonough 1981; Moyser and Waystaffe 1987; Putnam 1976). This means that they are made up of people who may hold widely varying attitudes toward the existing social, economic, and political order, including the holders of key positions in powerful dissident organizations and movements. Elites in large countries like the United States and the Soviet Union probably number upwards of ten thousand people (see, e.g., Dye 1983; Lane 1988); in somewhat smaller countries like Mexico or Italy, their number is probably somewhere between one thousand and five thousand; whereas in quite small countries like Portugal or

Chile, and most historical cases, elites probably encompass fewer than one thousand persons.

Elites affect political outcomes "regularly" in that their individual points of view and possible actions are seen by other influential persons as important factors to be weighed when assessing the likelihood of continuities and changes in regimes and policies. This does not mean that the typical elite person affects every aspect of regime operation and policy but, rather, that he or she is able to take influential actions on those aspects that are salient to his or her interests and location (Merritt 1970, p. 105). Elites affect political outcomes "substantially" in the sense that without their support or opposition, an outcome salient to their interests and locations would be noticeably different. In addition to their strategic positions in powerful organizations, this ability of elites to affect political outcomes regularly and substantially distinguishes them from other persons and sectors of a society. A lone political assassin can affect outcomes substantially but not regularly, and a citizen casting votes in democratic elections can affect outcomes regularly but not substantially.

Elites relevant to democratic transitions are located within, and in opposition to, authoritarian regimes. Leaders of clandestine labor organizations, political parties, or ethnic, religious, or student movements may be as capable of affecting the course of a democratic transition as is the outgoing authoritarian elite. But whether they are part of an authoritarian regime or of the opposition to it, elites must possess acknowledged authority vis-à-vis an organized sector of society. Not all opposition movements are organized, and therefore, they may lack representative, authoritative elites. (As we shall argue, this is an extremely important variable that greatly affects the prospects for elite transformation and democratic consolidation.) This is not to deny that spontaneous, unstructured, or uncoordinated popular protests and uprisings sometimes have major consequences for regimes. But unless they are directed by acknowledged leaders and are organized, such popular outbursts usually dissipate or are promptly suppressed. The millions of Chinese who demonstrated in May 1989 against the government of Li Peng and, in the final stage, against the PRC regime itself succeeded in bringing to a halt normal life in large parts of the People's Republic and in powerfully voicing their demands for change. But lacking overall organization and thus an acknowledged and coordinated set of elites, they were incapable of formulating and implementing strategies. Even simple decisions, such as to abandon Tienanmen Square on May 30, could not be enforced; instead, the leader of the moment was displaced by those who favored sticking it out to the tragic end.

Even if unorganized popular forces somehow succeed in toppling a regime, they are unlikely to establish a stable democracy. The reason is that democratic stability depends on agreements that can be struck only among elites representing rival organizations and popular groupings. If important and antagonistic sectors of a society are not organized, they cannot be effectively represented in a bargaining process of this kind. Thus, in our analysis, the extent to which social groups are organized and led by elites, and the ability of such elites to reach agreements on divisive issues and subsequently commit their respective groups of followers to the terms of those agreements, are crucial to democratic consolidation and stability.

Types of elites

Recent studies highlight two basic but parallel dimensions in the structure and functioning of elites: the extent of structural integration and the extent of value consensus. Structural integration involves the relative inclusiveness of formal and informal networks of communication and influence among elite persons, groups, and factions (Higley and Moore 1981; Kadushin 1968, 1979). Value consensus involves the relative agreement among elites on formal and informal rules and codes of political conduct and on the legitimacy of existing political institutions (Di Palma 1973; Prewitt and Stone 1973; Putnam 1976). Focusing on these dimensions, we can distinguish three basic types of national elites.

The first is a *disunified elite* in which structural integration and value consensus are minimal. Communication and influence networks do not cross factional lines in any large way, and factions disagree on the rules of political conduct and the worth of existing political institutions. Accordingly, they distrust one another deeply; they perceive political outcomes in "politics as war" or zero-sum terms; and they engage in unrestricted, often violent struggles for dominance. These features make regimes in countries with disunified elites fundamentally unstable, no matter whether they are authoritarian or formally democratic. Lacking the communication and influence networks that might give them a satisfactory amount of access to government decision making and disagreeing on the rules of the game and the worth of existing institutions, most factions in a disunified elite see the existing regime as the vehicle by which a dominant faction promotes its interests. To protect and promote their own interests, therefore, they must destroy or cripple the regime and the elites who operate it. Irregular and forcible power seizures, attempted seizures, or a widespread expectation that such seizures may occur are thus a routine by-product of elite disunity.

We next distinguish a *consensually unified elite* in which structural integration and value consensus are relatively inclusive. Overlapping and interconnected communication and influence networks encompass all or most elite factions; no single faction dominates these networks; and most elites therefore have substantial access to government decision making. Consequently, and in ways that Giovanni Sartori has detailed in his "decision-making theory of democracy," the factions making up a consensually unified elite tend to perceive political outcomes in "positive-sum" or "politics-as-bargaining" terms (Sartori 1987). Although they regularly and publicly oppose one another on ideological and policy questions, all important elite factions share an underlying consensus about rules of the game and the worth of existing political institutions. This underlying consensus is apparent in the "restrained partisanship" with which elites compete for mass support by downplaying or avoiding especially explosive issues and conflicts and by sharply limiting the costs of political defeats (Di Palma 1973).

These features of consensually unified elites make the regimes they operate stable and at least nominally democratic in character. With substantial access, at least informally, to decision making and with agreed rules of competition within a set of similarly agreed political institutions, few elites have incentives to bring down the existing regime by seizing power. Moreover, the competition through restrained partisanship that occurs among the elites means that political institutions function according to principles of political representation. Elite factions and coalitions seek to gain government executive power by appealing for the support of broader segments of the population, promising to represent their interests more effectively. Thus, where there is a consensually unified elite, political institutions are almost certain to be electorally based, although their operation may fall well short of the criteria of procedural democracy. All that one can say in general is that consensually unified elites are associated with stable regimes that exhibit different configurations of representative politics. Whether these regimes approximate consolidated democracies depends, at least in part, on the inclusiveness of elite consensus and unity. If this does not extend beyond a vital core of elites, with other factions remaining disaffected and possibly even disallegiant, then the resulting regime will be a relatively stable but limited democracy.

Finally, although it is irrelevant to the cases examined in this volume, we distinguish an *ideologically unified elite* in which structural integration and value consensus are seemingly monolithic. Communication and influence networks encompass all elite factions, but they run through and are sharply centralized in a dominant faction and the party or movement it leads. Value consensus is uniform in the sense that elites publicly express no deep ideological or policy disagreements, but they instead conform their public utterances to a single, explicit ideology whose changing content and policy implications are officially construed by the uppermost leaders of the dominant faction, party, or movement. The resulting regime is stable in the sense that irregular, forcible seizures of power do not occur, and outwardly at least, executive power is transferred peacefully according to deliberations within some body containing the most senior elite people (though the observer often learns subsequently about ugly power struggles behind the scenes). This body and other political institutions may be formally democratic in their prescribed workings, but the absence of public competition for mass support among elites means that the criteria of procedural democracy are not even remotely approximated. Obviously, we are describing what has frequently been called a "totalitarian" elite and regime configuration.

Disunified, consensually unified, and ideologically unified elites are ideal or pure types that "represent the standards, parameters, or models against which . . . concrete instances can be compared in terms of greater or lesser proximity" (Sartori 1976, p. 145). Thus, elites in different countries can be thought of as clustering around these ideal types. In the disunified cluster, for example, are most European elites from the early modern period until after World War II (see Higley and Burton 1989), all Latin American elites during the nineteenth century and much of this century, and elites in the vast majority of African, Middle Eastern, and Asian countries today (see Diamond, Linz, and Lipset 1988). Countries with elites in the consensually unified cluster range from those with a tenuous consensus and unity (e.g., Malaysia and Tunisia), to those that have recently attained this condition (e.g., France, Italy, Japan), to countries in which elite consensual unity has long been apparent (Britain and the other Anglo-American democracies, the Netherlands, the Scandinavian democracies, and Switzerland). In the ideologically unified cluster are the monolithic Soviet, German, and North Korean elites under Stalin, Hitler, and Kim Il Sung, respectively, as well as the somewhat less unified elites of the Peoples Republic of China, the East European countries from the late 1940s until 1989, Cuba under Castro, and Iran under Khomeni.

Elites of all three types have most commonly originated in the formation of independent nation-states, a process that usually entails much inter-elite violence and that has as its residue deep elite enmities. This was the origin of elite disunity in European countries during the early modern period and in Latin American countries once they broke away from Spain and Portugal in the nineteenth century, and it has been the origin of elite disunity in most African, Middle Eastern, and Asian countries that gained independence during the 1950s and later. But in a small number of countries, the combination of lengthy "home rule" under a colonial power and politically complex independence movements led by local elites has resulted in the creation of elite consensual unity upon attaining national independence – the United States, Canada, Australia, New Zealand, and other countries such as India and Malaysia that eventually broke away from British rule, as well as Tunisia once it broke from French control. In a few countries, ideologically unified elites have been the result of similar struggles for national independence involving wars against colonial or neocolonial regimes in which a doctrinaire elite faction has gotten the upper hand (China after 1949, North Vietnam after 1954, Cuba after 1959).

During the modern era, there has been an overwhelming tendency for the type of elite that emerged in the process of nation-state formation to persist for very long periods, irrespective of the many changes in social structure, socioeconomic fortunes, political culture, and much else that subsequently occurred. And because the great bulk of these elites have been "disunified," what might be called the "modal pattern" of politics in much of the world during the past several hundred years has consisted of regime instability involving irregular, usually violent oscillations between authoritarian and normally short-lived democratic regimes (Higley and Burton 1989). This remains the pattern in most countries of Latin America, Africa, the Middle East, and Asia today.

Modern history thus records relatively few elite transformations from one basic type to another. Such elite transformations appear to occur only in rare circumstances, and they take only a few forms. Because of our interest in the emergence of consolidated democracies, we are mainly concerned with elite transformations from disunity to consensual unity, which is a key feature of such democracies. How do elite transformations from disunity to consensual unity occur? What are the roles played by elites and mass publics in these processes? We contend that transformations from elite disunity to consensual unity take two principal forms: settlement and convergence. We shall describe each in some detail.

Elite settlement

Elite settlements are relatively rare events in which warring elite factions suddenly and deliberately reorganize their relations by negotiating compromises on their most basic disagreements (Burton and

Higley 1987a). Such settlements have two main consequences. First, they create patterns of open but peaceful competition among major elite factions, the result of which has historically been a stable limited democracy. Second, they can facilitate the eventual emergence of (though they do not guarantee) a consolidated democracy. Because they have such watershed effects, elite settlements are as consequential as social revolutions. Curiously, they have not received anything like the scholarly attention they deserve.

Four especially clear-cut instances of elite settlements are England in 1688–9, Sweden in 1809, Colombia in 1957–8, and Venezuela in 1958. Subsequent chapters in this volume explore settlements that occurred in Mexico in 1929, Costa Rica in 1948, Spain and the Dominican Republic in the late 1970s, and the contemporary legacies of the Colombian and Venezuelan settlements are also assessed. Here, we concentrate on the original English, Swedish, Colombian, and Venezuelan cases in order to illustrate the ways in which elite settlements can take place, and we examine how relationships between elites and mass publics facilitated or hindered them.

Two sets of circumstances appear to have fostered elite settlements. The first was the prior occurrence of a conflict in which all factions suffered heavy losses. In the wake of such conflicts, deeply divided elites tended to be more disposed to seek compromises than they otherwise would have been. The English civil wars of the 1640s, which entailed considerable elite fratricide but had no clear victor, and the wave of violence that began in Colombia in 1948, in which no elite faction clearly triumphed, are examples. Bloodied but not wholly bowed, the English Tories and Whigs and the Colombian Conservatives and Liberals had, for the moment at least, little desire for more fighting (Schwoerer 1981; Wilde 1978). Moreover, social leveling tendencies that surfaced in both conflagrations made the English and Colombian elites keenly aware that renewed fighting might well cost all of them their elite positions. Although no similar civil war preceded the elite settlements in Sweden and Venezuela, in both countries the elites had experienced several decades of intense but inconclusive struggles for factional ascendancy, also accompanied by indications of the potential for leveling tendencies to take control: a peasant uprising and march on Stockholm in 1743 during the ongoing conflict between the Hat and Cap elite factions; and in Venezuela, mass protests against the dictatorship of Marcos Pérez Jiménez during 1956–7, combined with an increasingly mobilized working class and peasantry.

The second circumstance that triggered settlements was a major crisis that threatened the resumption of widespread violence. Such crises typically centered on the incumbent head of state and were the culmination of his or her policy failures, power abuses, and demonstrated personal weaknesses, made manifest by a particular action or event that brought elite discontents to a boil. In England this was the news that King James II would have a Catholic heir, a development that climaxed bitter resistance on the part of predominantly Protestant elites to James's aggressively pro-Catholic policies and that occurred in the context of growing elite alarm about the possibility of an alliance between the Catholic kings of England and France. The Swedish crisis involved the loss of Finland to Russia in 1808, impending Russian and Danish–French invasions of Sweden proper, and economic disarray, all of which were viewed by elites as outcomes of King Gustav IV Adolf's ill-considered policies and personal failings. The crises in Colombia and Venezuela were sharp economic downturns punctuated by efforts of the military dictators Rojas Pinilla and Pérez Jiménez, respectively, to extend their tenures. In short, a crisis partly brought about and made intolerable by the incumbent ruler's blunders and ambitions motivated elites in each country not only to remove him and his entourage, but, more important, to reduce drastically the elite enmities that produced the situation.

If these or similar sets of circumstances inclined elites toward a settlement, the ensuing processes had several distinct features. One was speed. It appears that elite settlements are accomplished quickly or not at all (see Share 1987). Facing a serious political crisis that threatens renewed elite warfare, a settlement involves intensive efforts to find a way out. Fear of the consequences of not doing so loosens the fixed positions and principles of various factions and disposes them to consider concessions that they would not countenance in other circumstances. Thus, the coming together of Tory and Whig factions in England began in earnest during the first half of 1688 with a conspiracy among key faction leaders and the Dutch *stadholder*, Prince William of Orange, to unseat King James II. The key components of the settlement were agreed to by the major factions less than a year later, in February 1689. The Swedish settlement was even more rapid, involving a similar elite conspiracy against the king during the winter of 1808–9, followed by the drafting and acceptance of a new constitution during May and June 1809. In Colombia, the overthrow of Rojas Pinilla was orchestrated by a coalition of Liberal and Conservative party leaders between July 1956 and the following May. The constitutional components of the Colombian settlement were negotiated by the same coalition from July to October 1957 and overwhelmingly approved in a plebiscite two months later. The Venezuelan settlement got under way with a meeting of the heads of the three major parties and two business leaders in New York City in December 1957; the settlement agreements were made final exactly a year later.

This does not mean that elite settlements became complete and irreversible in such brief periods but only that their basic components were put together rapidly. It is important to distinguish between the initial settlement and a subsequent broadening of the scope of elite consensual unity. Factions seeking to undercut a settlement were usually present: Jacobites who wanted to return the Stuarts to the English throne; embittered supporters of the ousted Swedish king and of Rojas Pinilla in Colombia who attempted subsequent coups; a leftist guerrilla insurgency in Venezuela during the early 1960s. Extending over several years, even a generation, the sudden and deliberate elite cooperation that made settlements possible had to be sustained to thwart such challenges, and elites that were not part of the original settlement had to be incorporated. Success along these lines served to solidify the consensually unified elite structure.

A second feature of the settlement process was face-to-face, largely secret, negotiations among leaders of the major elite factions. Through a combination of skill, desperation, and accident, impasses were broken and crucial compromises were struck. The number of negotiating sessions involved in elite settlements was probably in the hundreds, as they required not only compromises between major factions but also agreements within them. After William's engineered invasion of England in November 1688, for example, secret meetings among the principal Tory and Whig leaders produced the decision to hold a special parliamentary convention to address unresolved issues. This three-week convention, itself a flurry of secret meetings, resulted in the Declaration of Rights, the formal expression of the English elite settlement, which William and Mary accepted along with the crown on February 13, 1689. In Sweden, two weeks of intensive, secret deliberations among a fifteen-man committee, plus its pivotal secretary Hans Jarta, produced the concessions and draft constitution that were then ratified in three more weeks of discussion by the estates of nobles, clergy, merchants, and free farmers. One of the earliest important meetings in the Colombian settlement occurred in Spain in July 1956 between just two people: Laureano Gómez, the exiled former president who remained leader of a major Conservative party faction, and Alberto Lleras, a former president and leader of the Liberal party. The two met again in Spain in July 1957 and signed the Pact of Sitges, which set the framework for a succession of talks between and within party factions from July to October 1957. The result was the National Front platform for constitutional reform, which was overwhelmingly approved in the December 1957 plebescite. Similarly, the broad outlines of the Venezuelan settlement were shaped in the New York City meeting of December 1957, among five party and business leaders, and the written expressions of the settlement – the Pact of Punto Fijo and the Statement of Principles and Minimum Program of Government – were fashioned in meetings at the home of a party leader, Rafael Caldera of the Christian Social party, during the fall of 1958.

Such formal, written agreements constituted another feature of elite settlements. Written agreements committed elite factions publicly to the concessions and guarantees made privately. But formal agreements and constitutions by themselves hardly sufficed to produce common elite acceptance of a new code of political conduct, which was the most fundamental and lasting consequence of the elite settlement. Behind such agreements there must be a great deal of forbearance and conciliatory behavior among the most central elite actors. By their nature, such subtle retreats from intransigence and enmity are sometimes difficult for outside observers to detect. Nevertheless, some observable behavioral patterns indicate the sea change in elite conduct that these settlements involved.

As the newly crowned king of England, for example, William could have ignored the restrictions that the Declaration of Rights placed on his authority. Yet he honored them and acquiesced to further restrictions in late 1689. Very importantly, he also distributed offices so as to achieve a balance between Tories and Whigs. Continuing to act in the spirit of the settlement, William accepted additional restrictions during his reign: Annual parliamentary sessions became the norm, even though not required by law, and the House of Commons gradually assumed a significant role in foreign policy, though this was traditionally the Crown's prerogative. Similarly, in Sweden the interim king regent, Karl XIII, uncle of the deposed Gustav IV Adolf, refused to support efforts to organize a royalist countercoup in 1810, thereby giving leaders of the 1809 settlement vital time to consolidate the new regime. And the crown prince, Bernadotte, recruited from France to become Sweden's new king, agreed to delay his ascent to the throne for a full eight years so as to ensure a gradual and peaceful transition from the old order to the new. In Colombia, the pressing question of whether the Liberal–Conservative coalition, which had agreed to a fifty–fifty split of all government offices for sixteen years, should have a Conservative or a Liberal as its presidential candidate was resolved through informal agreements among the factions just ten days before the 1958 election. In Venezuela, almost three years passed before the terms of the elite settlement were given legal status in the constitution. But though not legally bound to do so, Rómulo Betancourt, the new president, immediately showed his commitment to power sharing by appointing members of the two major opposition parties to his cabinet, and he moved in other ways to create a climate favorable to those parties.

Another notable feature of past elite settlements was the predominance of experienced political leaders; "new men" played only peripheral roles. In the English case, for example, the instigators of Prince William's invasion, the members of the parliamentary rights committees, and William and his advisers all were political veterans. In Sweden, Hans Jarta and the members of the fifteen-man constitutional committee had been politically active for several decades. In Colombia, both the leading negotiators of the settlement, Laureano Gómez and Alberto Lleras, were former presidents; they and most other principal actors had been involved in the failed effort to form a Liberal–Conservative coalition a decade earlier. In Venezuela, the central negotiators were the Democratic Action, Christian Social, and Democratic Republican Union party leaders, each with at least twenty years of political experience and standing.

This predominance of experienced leaders in settlements was probably a key to their success. Usually, it is only established leaders who have the skill and standing to impose unpalatable concessions and compromises on their followers. Their superior knowledge of issues and of how politics are played enables them to see what has to be done and how to do it. Moreover, long political experience often entails political learning: Recollections of costly previous conflicts appear to have induced leaders in the cases we are considering to avoid the risks inherent in a resumption of unrestrained conflict (Levine 1978).

In addition to these procedural features of elite settlements – speed, face-to-face secret negotiations, formal agreements, and informal forbearance among experienced leaders – did previous elite settlements display structural similarities? It may be significant that at the time English, Swedish, Colombian, and Venezuelan elites achieved settlements, each of their countries was at a relatively low level of socioeconomic development. England and Sweden were predominantly agrarian societies. Although Colombia and Venezuela were substantially more urbanized by the time of their settlements in the 1950s, neither was highly industrialized. This suggests that all four national elites enjoyed considerable autonomy from mass followings and pressures. Elite factions and leaders could compromise on questions of principle without strong pressures to stand firm. Members of traditional oligarchies rather than leaders of large and complex mass organizations and movements, the four elites were comparatively free to make the concessions and deals that settlements require.

Outwardly at least, Colombian and Venezuelan elites seem to have possessed less autonomy than did the elites of preindustrial England and Sweden. Most key Colombian and Venezuelan actors led organized political parties, and they were presumably constrained by calculations of electoral costs, party splits, and the like. Yet, under the dictatorial regimes of both countries during the 1950s, those parties were hardly vital, full-bodied mass organizations. Indeed, several party leaders were in exile at the time, and it is probably of no small consequence that some of the meetings that produced the Colombian and Venezuelan settlements took place abroad – in Spain, in Puerto Rico, in New York City. In short, the absence of full-scale industrialization in Colombia and Venezuela, combined with the partially repressed situation of parties and other mass organizations in those countries, meant that like their English and Swedish counterparts of an earlier period, elites in Colombia and Venezuela enjoyed substantial autonomy. The importance of elite autonomy in fashioning settlements can also be seen in the secrecy of the negotiations they involve; settlements, it would appear, cannot be arranged in a democratic or mass-media fishbowl.

This does not mean, however, that elite settlements unfold without regard to mass publics. We have already mentioned elite fears of leveling sentiments as a spur to quick action. In addition, a degree of mass mobilization may be necessary to bring down a ruling clique and to defend particular positions as elites jockey toward compromises on their most basic disputes. Even in their day, the English elites who plotted William's invasion and subsequently worked out the rules under which he would be king felt compelled to mount a public relations campaign announcing and defending their actions. Their opponents, the royalist faction around James II, responded with their own campaign for public support. Public discussion of the settlement process was further informed by leaks about who took what position. Similar patterns appear in the other settlements we have summarized. This public aspect of elite settlements is also seen in the promulgation of eminently public documents, especially constitutions, in all four countries. In short, although settlements are primarily the result of private negotiations among relatively autonomous elites, they have an important public, or mass, aspect. The significance of this aspect has probably increased with the expansion of information about elite activities disseminated by the modern news media and with the development of opinion polling.

But mass involvement presents a tricky problem for elites who would fashion a settlement. On one hand, it is essential that compromising moderates be able to mobilize mass support against intransigent leaders and factions. On the other hand, these compromisers run the risk of losing mass support if they are perceived as selling out their followers. Their leadership positions must be sufficiently strong that they can negotiate away important concessions to traditional enemies without being ousted. Taken with the other features we have noted, this delicate balancing act helps explain why elite settlements have been so rare in modern history and in the contemporary world. The triggering circumstances, subsequent processes, elite autonomy, and limited mass mobilization that appear to have been crucial are rarely all present. This is an important reason that disunified elites and unstable political regimes are such persistent features of today's developing countries, no matter how much change occurs in other aspects of their social structures or in their economic and international situations.

Elite settlements and democratic consolidation

Stable limited democracies have historically been the direct and fairly immediate result of elite settlements. Thus, the direct result of the English settlement of 1688–9 was an accepted set of representative parliamentary and competitive-partisan institutions. Parliament quickly became the arena in which political conflicts were played out according to detailed rules governing factional competition, and it became the principal locus of governmental authority. Nonetheless, given the sharp restrictions on the suffrage that persisted for another two hundred years, the English regime only much later began to approximate a consolidated democracy. Likewise in Sweden, an entire century passed between the creation of a stable, basically representative political regime (the immediate product of the 1809 settlement) and the flowering of democracy. Thus in history, elite settlements stabilized political environments and regulated conflicts between rival elites, but they did not produce full-blown democratic regimes in any immediate way.

It is important to examine the time lags between elite settlements and consolidated democracies because they reveal the linkages between mass- and elite-level elements in our theoretical perspective. Social scientists have long noted a strong correlation between a society's level of socioeconomic development and the extent of mass participation in democratic politics (e.g., Almond and Verba 1963; Deutsch 1953; Lerner 1958; Lipset 1960, 1981). Subsistence economies are normally associated with populations that are illiterate, geographically isolated, deferential to local elites, and uninvolved in national politics. None of these features is conducive to the independent but restrained mass participation in politics that characterizes democracies. As societies modernize economically, however, populations become politically "mobilized" in terms of participatory values and expectations, and they play larger roles in national politics.

Mass mobilization and demands for participation constitute an important variable that may intervene between elite settlements and the attainment of consolidated democracies. Where settlements precede industrialization and modernization, the manner in which newly mobilized mass publics are subsequently incorporated into politics is crucial. As the English and Swedish cases illustrate, consensually unified elites that are formed in settlements may gradually include and coopt the elites that later emerge from the mass parties and movements spawned by industrialization and modernization. Progressive extensions of the suffrage to the mass public may go hand in hand with this process of elite inclusion and cooptation. In England and Sweden, consolidated democracies were the long-term result.

What would have happened if the elites that made those settlements had decided instead to block effective participation by newly mobilized mass publics and their elites? The fledgling representative regimes of Southern Europe in the late nineteenth century suggest an answer. In Spain, a pact in 1876 between Cánovas, the Conservative party leader, and Sagasta, the Liberal party leader, provided for a regular alternation in government between the two parties. But after the introduction of universal male suffrage in 1889, the electoral outcomes that had been carefully orchestrated in this "Turno pacífico" elite pact could be achieved only through the intercession of local notables (*caciques*), who used their positions of power and influence to induce voters in their districts to support Conservatives or Liberals, while denying support to emerging groups such as the Socialists. This reliance on *caciquil* domination of a dependent peasantry, as well as the use of outright corruption and intimidation, enabled Conservative and Liberal elites to maintain parliamentary majorities for four decades, but the result was an unconsolidated rather than a consolidated democracy. In 1923, the Spanish regime was easily toppled by a military coup. Our point is that the pact between Cánovas and Sagasta in 1876 fell short of an elite settlement and was instead a convenient device by which two entrenched elites sought to prevent emerging elites from displacing them. But by making this arrangement and enforcing it over several decades, Conservative and Liberal elites succeeded only in ensuring the regime's rejection by the excluded elites and the increasingly mobilized mass publics they led. As the analysis of Italy in Chapter 5 shows, an altogether similar pattern, with the same result, occurred in that country between 1876 and 1922. Moreover, something like this pattern has unfolded in Colombia during the past ten to fifteen years, and it suggests a reversal of the democratic consolidation that began with the Colombian elite settlement in 1956–7 (see Chapter 3).

The maintenance of elite settlements over time requires adaptability on the part of founding elites and the institutions they create. Insofar as social change mobilizes new groups for active participation in politics, those groups must be brought under the umbrella of the settlement and accepted as full participants in the democratic game of politics. This suggests a causal ordering among the key concepts in our theory to account for two different kinds of outcome, as summarized in Figure 1.1.

Figure 1.1. Elite settlement precedes modernization

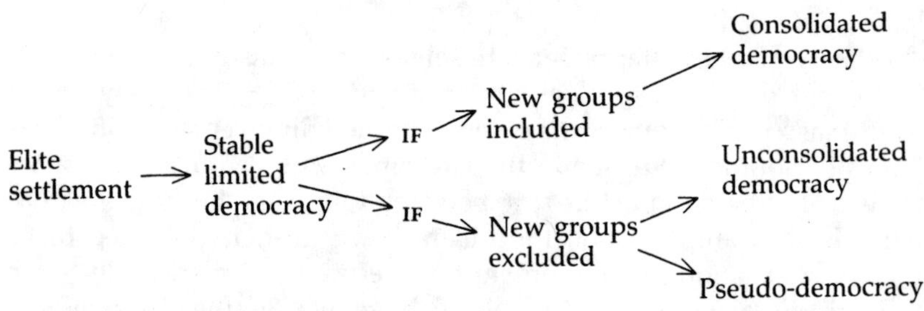

Most countries have by now crossed the modernization threshold necessary for mass participation. Hence, the model based on the British, Swedish, and other earlier examples may no longer be applicable. Nonetheless, the pervasiveness of elite disunity and regime instability in today's developing countries, together with spreading mass-level violence in them, make elite settlements more important than ever. Thus, a second diagram, in which a settlement occurs in the course of a regime transition from authoritarian to democratic rule within an already politically mobilized society, is needed (Figure 1.2).

Figure 1.2. Democratic transitions with/without elite settlements

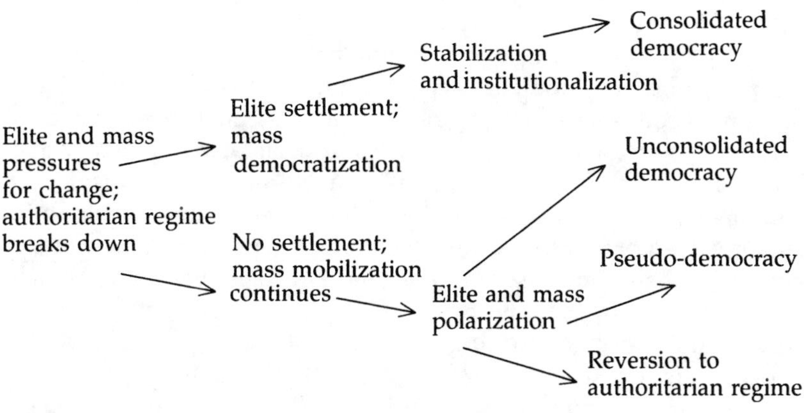

The collapse or impending collapse of an authoritarian regime is most commonly accompanied by frequent and often large-scale mass mobilizations. However, as O'Donnell and Schmitter have observed, although "an active, militant and highly mobilized popular upsurge may be an efficacious instrument for bringing down a dictatorship, [it] may make subsequent democratic consolidation difficult, and under some circumstances may provide an important motive of regression to an even more brutal form of authoritarian rule" (1986, p. 65). This typically involves a self-reinforcing cycle of mass action and state reaction, in which street mobilizations provoke repressive regime responses that, in turn, generate even more bitter mobilizations and protests. The resulting dialectic of rocks, clubs, and tear gas exacerbates antagonisms and further polarizes groups. Relations among elites are characterized by hatred and distrust, and they engage in a no-holds-barred struggle for power. The sequence depicted in the lower part of Figure 1.2 is therefore all too likely.

The sequence depicted in the upper part of Figure 1.2 is more favorable for democratic consolidation. In this instance, there is a settlement that, as we have argued, serves to stabilize the political environment by establishing a procedural consensus, institutionalizing behavioral norms that restrain expressions of conflict, and encouraging patterns of elite interaction that reduce animosities across traditionally divisive lines of cleavage. In addition, elites demobilize their supporters, thereby reducing the possibility that polarizing incidents of mass violence will break out. Democratic transitions in Spain at the end of the 1970s (see Chapter 2), Costa Rica in 1948, and

Venezuela in 1958 (see Chapter 3) followed this pattern rather closely, and Uruguay's democratic transition in the mid-1980s also displayed some of its features (see Chapter 6).

Engineering elite settlements in contemporary societies is a daunting task, however, and the fact that they have occurred in a mere handful of countries is not surprising. Yet, settlements may well constitute the only direct and rapid route to consolidated democracy that is available in today's world. Key factions in a number of disunified national elites appear to sense this. Chile's democratic transition in 1989 involved protracted, secret negotiations aimed at forging a broad elite front that would reassure the Pinochet regime while marginalizing elites on the extreme right and left (see Chapter 7). In South Africa, the release of Nelson Mandela and the legalization of the African National Congress followed lengthy behind-the-scenes discussions among opposing elites and led to the opening of previously unthinkable negotiations between white and black leaders. In Poland and some other East European countries, a "roundtable" model was adopted that facilitated private discussions between elites representing the old communist regimes and elites leading popular forces. These and similar attempts at settlements may fail because the process is very difficult, but they attest to the perceived relevance and importance of settlement-like negotiations among elites during democratic transitions today.

Elite convergence

A second kind of elite transformation from disunity to consensual unity is what we call an *elite convergence*. It is a fundamental change that takes place within unconsolidated democracies, and it is initiated when some of the opposing factions in the disunified elites that characterize such democracies discover that by forming a broad electoral coalition they can mobilize a reliable majority of voters, win elections repeatedly, and thereby protect their interests by dominating government executive power. The elite convergence continues once successive electoral defeats convince major dissident and hostile elites that to avoid permanent exclusion from executive office they must beat the newly formed dominant coalition at its own electoral game. This requires that they acknowledge the legitimacy of existing democratic institutions and promise adherence to democratic rules of the game. In short, it requires that opposition groups abandon antisystem or semiloyal stances and become trustworthy competitors for electoral support. The completion of an elite convergence is most clearly signaled by the electoral victory of the previously dissident elite or elites, followed by their governing in a way that is fully respectful of established institutions and the rules of the game. As in the case of elite settlements, elite consensual unity is achieved, consolidating the democratic system.

In most modern societies (whose electorates are usually characterized by low levels of ideological or class polarization), an elite convergence commonly involves an additional change. In order to compete more effectively for support from predominantly centrist voters, polarized elites must moderate their distinctive ideological and policy positions (see Dahl 1966, p. 373; Downs 1959; Gunther, Sani, and Shabad 1986, chaps. 4, 8). This moderation gradually bridges the deep ideological chasms that mark elite disunity, and it narrows the scope and intensity of conflict over government policy, further reinforcing regime stability.

The paradigmatic case of an elite convergence is probably France, beginning with the founding of the Fifth Republic and culminating in the successful 1986–8 "cohabitation" between rival factions that at the outset of the convergence had been deeply and bitterly opposed. Other elite convergences can be seen in the gradual coming together of socialist and nonsocialist elites in Norway and Denmark during the first third of this century (see Higley, Field, and Groholt 1976) and in the gradual diminution of elite antagonisms in Italy, Japan, and Greece over the last decade or two. The way in which the Italian convergence took place between about 1960 and the early 1980s is described in Chapter 5. Here we can best bring out the main features of elite convergences by summarizing the French case.

Disunity was the condition of French elites throughout France's modern history. Fueled by bitter memories of the Revolution, which itself originated in and manifested deep elite disunity, incessant power struggles among French elites caused several regime upsets during the nineteenth century and made the long-lasting Third Republic a very precarious affair until its downfall in 1940. The disunity of French elites persisted during the Fourth Republic after World War II, as indicated by the existence of important and powerful antisystem parties and movements at both ends of the political spectrum. Conservatives supporting General Charles de Gaulle withheld support from the Fourth Republic on the grounds that the weakness and division inherent in its "assembly government" betrayed the basic interests of the French nation by denying it strong leadership. They favored replacing the Fourth Republic with a new regime along lines articulated by de Gaulle in 1946 (see Harrison 1969, pp. 24–8). A second antisystem movement on the right burst forth in the form of a "flash party" in 1956: the Poujadist movement, which combined "hostility to the wealthy with anti-industrialism, anti-parliamentarism and anti-Semitism" (Safran 1985, p. 68), received 12 percent of the vote and elected fifty-three deputies to the last parliament of the Fourth Republic. And on the other end of the spectrum was the Stalinist Parti communiste français (PCF), which regularly received over a quarter of the votes cast in Fourth Republic elections.

Nearly half of all seats in the National Assembly during the 1950s were occupied by representatives of these and other antisystem parties. This meant that governing majorities could be formed only by coalitions of virtually all the other parties in the assembly – ranging from the Marxist Section française de l'internationale ouvrière (SFIO) on the left to Conservatives on the right, and from the anticlerical Radical Socialists to the Catholic Mouvement républicain populaire. These ideological and programmatic differences, combined with partisan fragmentation within various *tendances* and with the unrestrained pursuit of personal ambitions by many deputies meant that the average government would not survive for more than about eight months.

The Algerian crisis of 1958 was a turning point for French elites. Its outcome was de Gaulle's return to power under circumstances that facilitated the consolidation of what had previously been only a de facto, disorganized alignment of right-wing and centrist elite factions. Upon becoming prime minister in 1958, de Gaulle promptly set about replacing the regime with the semipresidential Fifth Republic, along the lines he had envisioned a decade earlier and in which he, as president, would occupy a dominant position. At the same time, his associates rapidly organized a wide-ranging political party, the Union pour la nouvelle république (UNR), to support him. During the next few years he took important steps toward strengthening the new regime, most significantly by resolving the Algerian decolonization crisis that had triggered the Fourth Republic's collapse and by subduing rebellious segments of the French military.

The period between de Gaulle's return to power in June 1958 and the winning of an absolute majority by the pro-Gaullist coalition in the National Assembly elections of November 1962 should be seen as the time when the French elite convergence began. During those years, right-wing and centrist elite factions that had previously been at odds became persuaded that their interests could best be protected through electoral cooperation against the left. The center–right elite coalition that dominated French politics for the next twenty years took shape.

From the early 1960s, therefore, French elites were increasingly divided into two broad camps. On the one side was the electorally dominant coalition of centrist and right-wing factions who defended the new regime, as well as an essentially capitalist economic system. For some time, they occupied most of the powerful positions in politics and society: They held the key posts in cabinets, the higher civil service, business firms and associations, and in a variety of public bodies such as the bourgeois parties, the church and its affiliated organizations, the media, and some trade unions. Arrayed against this coalition were Communist and Socialist party leaders, most trade union officials, as well as many prominent intellectuals and celebrities affiliated with the Communist and Socialist parties and movements. This camp held a basically Marxist perspective on economic and social matters, as well as a weak opposition status in the political system.

Over the next twenty years, the parties on the left underwent substantial changes that opened the way to the consensual unification of all major elite factions. From the perspective of democratic consolidation, the Communist elite underwent the most significant change. By the late 1960s, it had begun to abandon many of the tenets of Marxism-Leninism, replacing them with an inconsistent but predominantly Eurocommunist orientation. In repudiating the concept of the "dictatorship of the proletariat" and in agreeing with the Socialists to share posts in a future leftist government, the Communist elite abandoned its antisystem stance and committed itself to working within established institutions and to playing the game of politics according to the rules laid down by the elites who established and dominated the Fifth Republic. This commitment was formalized in the Common Governmental Program of 1972, in which the Communists explicitly endorsed the concept of a multiparty system, the sovereignty of the suffrage and alternations of power, as well as the protection of basic individual liberties. It is important to note that this major shift was motivated largely by the logic of the ongoing elite convergence: Realizing the impossibility of coming to power by "storming the Winter Palace" and tiring of the futility of opposition to the ensconced Gaullist majority, the Communist leaders concluded that only an explicit break with their previous antisystem stance would give a majority of French voters sufficient confidence to support a Socialist–Communist electoral coalition.

The socialist bloc also underwent a significant change. Several formerly independent socialist factions merged with the old and organizationally inadequate SFIO to form a new Socialist party. Party institutions were rebuilt so as to pose a more credible electoral challenge to the dominant center–right coalition. In the course of bargaining with the Communists over the Common Governmental Program, the Socialists modified many of their policies to make them compatible with those of the Communists. This amounted to a shift to the left by the Socialists. But by 1978, when the Communists withdrew from the Common Governmental Program, the Socialists had become the major opposition party.

The successful transformation of the Socialist party was registered in its great electoral victories of 1981, in which it won both the presidency and an absolute majority in the National Assembly. These triumphs enabled François Mitterrand's first government to implement many of the Socialists' policies, particularly the nationalizations of a significant number of banks and industrial conglomerates, as well as the use of stimulative fiscal measures to halt an economic recession. Within two years, however, these policies had clearly failed: The reflationary fiscal measures did not stave off recession and instead contributed to the collapse of the franc, and the nationalizations proved to be much more costly than originally anticipated. In order to avoid a devastating defeat in the 1984 elections, the Socialist government made an abrupt about-face in economic policy, abandoning maximalist socialism for moderate social democratic policies that have characterized the Socialists ever since.

Over a period of twenty-five years, then, French elites underwent substantial convergence. Partial elite unification first occurred on the right. The formerly antisystem Gaullists used the Algerian crisis of 1958 to dismantle the Fourth Republic and create in its place a regime they could support. This was accompanied by the construction of a strong and durable coalition among previously feuding centrist and right-wing factions. The electoral dominance of this coalition gradually forced the leftist elites to reexamine their strategies, policies, and ideologies. The Communist party's abandonment of its previously antisystem stance, made explicit in the 1972 Common Governmental Program with the Socialists, meant that the new Fifth Republic would not be seriously challenged by a major elite grouping on the left. Consensual unity among all important elites was from that point at least a tacit feature of French politics. This was followed by an ideological and programmatic convergence, as the PCF was displaced by the Socialists as the largest party on the left and, more directly, by the pronounced moderation of the Socialists from that time on. (It is interesting to note that the French Socialists reversed the usual order in which socialist ideologies are moderated and government posts are won. More typical are the cases of the Spanish Partido socialista obrero espãnol [PSOE] and the West German Sozialdemokratische Partei Deutschlands [SPD], in which a dramatic party congress – a "Bad Godesberg" – usually moderates the party's basic stands well before the party is perceived as acceptable by a majority of voters, and is thereby able to win a victory at the polls.)

The consensual unity of French elites was evident in the comparative ease with which they managed the "cohabitation" of 1986–8 when prime ministerial and cabinet positions were held by center–right leaders and the presidency was still occupied by Mitterrand. At any other time in French history, the opportunities that this awkward circumstance presented for undermining opponents and inciting a regime crisis would have been eagerly seized by antagonistic elites. But the cohabitation of a Socialist president and a conservative government unfolded without any major crisis. Still further evidence of the consensus and unity that now characterize French elites can be found in the formation of a Socialist–centrist coalition government after the 1988 elections. In the view of Stanley Hoffmann, the 1980s thus witnessed the consolidation of the Fifth Republic, a meltdown of the Communist left, the transformation of the Socialists into garden-variety social democrats, and electoral contests that have centered on policy differences of degree, not of kind (Hoffmann 1987, pp. 347–9). France has become a consolidated democracy as a consequence of the elite convergence we have described.

Because elite convergences may be taking place in several unconsolidated democracies today, it is worth abstracting from the French case what appear to be key facilitating circumstances. One, already noted, is the achievement of a relatively high level of socioeconomic development. Economic prosperity must be sufficiently widespread that an electoral majority prepared to support appeals to defend established institutions – essentially the status quo – is at least latent. This makes possible the formation of a winning center–right elite coalition whose repeated electoral victories eventually force dissident elites to emulate its appeals and to accept established institutions and procedures. A fairly large number of countries in Latin America, Southern Europe, and East Asia have achieved this development level, and although their elites remain disunified and their democratic regimes unconsolidated, they are candidates for the convergence process. However, a successful convergence may also depend on the appearance of a dynamic, popular leader analogous to General de Gaulle, who alone is able to forge a winning coalition among previously feuding center–right elites. The emergence of such a leader is not inevitable, of course, and his or her success may in turn depend on the occurrence of some dire crisis, such as France experienced in 1958. Finally, even where a latent electoral majority is available for center–right mobilization and a leader able to fashion the requisite electoral coalition appears, a considerable measure of good fortune, economic and otherwise, may also be necessary: Mass- and elite-level moderation were certainly facilitated in France, Italy, and Japan by highly favorable economic conditions. Whether countries in less fortunate circumstances can undergo elite convergences thus remains an open question, to be addressed in analyses of Argentina, Peru, and Brazil (Chapters 7, 8, and 9).

Some concluding observations

A central argument in this chapter has been that the stability and long-term prospects for survival of democratic regimes are greatly enhanced when consolidation has been achieved – that is, when broad elite consensual unity exists within a regime that is fully democratic. We have described the two principal ways in which consensual unity can be achieved in the contemporary world – elite settlements and convergences. Let us conclude by summarizing the relationship between consolidation and stability and by contrasting our analysis with some similar approaches.

Democratic consolidation is conducive to long-term stability for several reasons. First, acknowledging the legitimacy of democratic institutions and respecting rules of democratic procedure discourage governing elites in new democracies from trampling on the rights of opposition groups. A lack of such commitment, on the other hand, could be compatible with a progressive abridgment of democracy that might ultimately culminate in its transformation into a limited democracy or an authoritarian regime. In short, because governing elites share the consensus supporting a democratic regime, respect for its norms and institutions serves as a check on abuses of executive power.

Democratic consolidation also contributes to stability by reducing the intensity of the expression of conflict and by restricting conflict to peaceful institutionalized channels. Acknowledgment of a common set of democratic norms of behavior reduces uncertainty about what constitutes proper or improper political behavior and contributes to the routinization of nonviolent and mutually respectful expressions of political conflict. Insofar as these norms eschew violence, intimidation, and the like, their widespread acceptance reduces mutual fears and suspicions. And insofar as losing in a political conflict is not usually perceived as posing a direct threat to the physical or material well-being of either side, the intensity of the conflict is mitigated, and incumbents who lose an election are more willing to step down, confident that they will survive and perhaps return to power at some point in the future. Acknowledgment of the legitimacy of governmental institutions in a new democracy, moreover, also increases the probability that conflict will be channeled as a matter of choice through democratic, representative institutions, rather than into unregulated extraparliamentary arenas.

The dynamics of political conflict in unconsolidated democratic regimes are qualitatively different. Important and powerful elites deny the legitimacy of the existing regime, and they seek to overthrow it. Challenges to regime legitimacy and the absence of consensual acceptance of democratic norms of behavior also contribute a tenuous, conditional, and mutually suspicious quality to expressions of political conflict. Few political actors are prepared to stake their futures on the workings of democratic institutions; they look for other, frequently illegal and antidemocratic ways to shore up their positions, engaging in democratic processes only as long as their interests are not threatened thereby. And because they also perceive rival political parties as conditional in their support for democracy and equivocal in their commitment to democratic rules of the game, political competition and conflict are fraught with suspicion and distrust. Insofar as mass mobilizations in the streets take the place of bargaining among representative elites as the principal form of "dialogue" between government and opposition (or even between rival opposition groups), a self-reinforcing cycle of protest–repression–protest may be set in motion that progressively polarizes relations among groups and raises the overall level of violence within the polity. It is therefore unlikely that the existing regime will survive the next serious political crisis.

In sum, democratic consolidation – elite consensual unity within a fully democratic system – contributes greatly to regime stability. We further contend that a stable limited democracy – a regime that is generally representative but not widely democratic, in which elite consensual unity has been established – can set the stage for a progressive expansion of the suffrage and expansion of the scope of elite consensual unity (incorporating newly emerging elites) that culminates in a consolidated and stable democratic regime.

A number of scholars have recognized the general importance of elite accommodation and consensus in the functioning of stable democratic regimes. In particular, Arend Lijphart's concept of consociationalism shares with our theoretical perspective an appreciation of the importance of relatively inclusive, behind-the-scenes negotiations among competing elites (Lijphart 1968, 1977). Lijphart also shares our contention that elite awareness of the potential for destructive political conflict, usually motivated by memories of past conflicts, is an important factor that induces elites to take extraordinary steps to restrain current and future conflicts. He observes that "the essential characteristic of consociational democracy is not so much any particular institutional arrangement as the deliberate joint effort by the elites to stabilize the system" (Lijphart 1969, p. 213). Nevertheless, most analyses of consociational democracies pay relatively little attention to the elite bargaining that initiates and underlies them, and they instead concentrate on the consociational pattern of governance in which political inputs and outputs are distributed proportionately among culturally distinct elites and the population segments they lead. A protracted debate over the workings and merits of "majoritarian" and "consociational" institutional arrangements has resulted (see especially, Lijphart 1984; Sartori 1987).

By contrast, the focus of this chapter and volume is on elite interactions per se in democratic transitions and consolidations. We are interested in how national elites sometimes transcend their disunity through settlements and convergences, and we regard the specific institutional arrangements that follow these events as secondary matters. What is most important, we argue, is to understand the circumstances and processes that foster elite transformations from disunity to consensual unity. If such transformations occur, a stable limited democracy can be established, and the emergence of a consolidated democracy is greatly facilitated, irrespective of the specific institutional arrangements that may be adopted. Indeed, the British elite settlement of 1688 culminated in establishment of what Lijphart regards as the model "majoritarian" system. Although an elite settlement may lead to a consociational form of government, such an outcome is not required by our concept.

Another difference between the concept of consociational democracy and our concepts of elite settlement and convergence is that the former has a substantive component, whereas the latter may be entirely procedural. Consociational democracy is conceived as an arrangement for sharing material goods and other substantive benefits among all sectors of a society on a proportional basis, and it uses a procedural mechanism – the mutual veto – for ensuring this. Elite settlements and convergences, by contrast, are concerned mainly with establishing political institutions and rules of the game that elites can live with. Whether broader population categories benefit substantively from settlements and convergences is not part of their conceptualization. In most historic instances, indeed, it is doubtful that anyone other than elites and their close associates derived immediate substantive benefits.

Our approach also differs from Lijphart's consociational concept in that it applies to a much wider range of societies. Consociational democracy requires a society's clear segmentation into culturally defined groups whose identities, mores, and folkways are distinct, and in which, furthermore, no single group is overwhelmingly dominant. By contrast, our concepts can be applied to all modern and modernizing societies, not just those that are highly segmented. Settlements and convergences do require a degree of hierarchical organization in a society (without which there would be no elites with acknowledged authority to bargain on behalf of specific clienteles), but there is a significant difference between our concept and Lijphart's concerning the extent to which this organization represents a compartmentalization of society.

The concept of "elite pacts" is also closely similar to our concepts of elite settlements and convergences. As defined by O'Donnell and Schmitter, an elite pact is "an explicit, but not always publicly explicated or justified, agreement among a select set of actors which seeks to define (or, better, to redefine) rules governing the exercise of power on the basis of mutual guarantees for the 'vital interests' of those entering into it" (1986, p. 37). They argue that pacts play an important role in the establishment of stable democracies, and they note that two of the three Latin American democracies that survived the wave of authoritarianism that swept the continent during the 1960s and 1970s – Colombia and Venezuela – originated in pacts. They treat Costa Rica, the third democracy that survived, as simply anomalous because no pact occurred at its outset in 1948. In our perspective, by contrast, all three of those democracies originated in elite settlements or partial settlements. The contention that the Mexican regime originated in an elite settlement also helps account for that regime's survival during the turbulent 1960s and 1970s.

Elite settlements differ from pacts in several important ways. First, pacts are more specific and less inclusive of all major elites. Drawing on Antonio Gramsci, Schmitter and O'Donnell (1986) contend that democratic transitions involve a "military moment," a "political moment," and an "economic moment" and that there should be a different pact for each moment. Similarly, Karl argues that a "foundational pact . . . necessarily includes an agreement between the military and civilians over the conditions for establishing civilian rule, . . . and a 'social contract' between state agencies, business associations and trade unions regarding property rights, market arrangements and the distribution of benefits" (1990, p. 11). By contrast, our concept of elite settlements focuses on the so-called political moment. We do not share the idea that economic and military pacts are essential components of all successful regime transitions. In some instances, a civilian–military pact my play an important role in getting a military regime to step aside (e.g., Uruguay, see Chapter 6; Peru, see Chapter

8). In other instances, economic agreements may figure prominently in a democratic transition (e.g., Venezuela, see Chapter 3). But these are not necessary components of elite settlements.

Elite pacts and elite settlements also differ in their practical and normative implications. Pacts are often a means by which economic elites continue their domination and exploitation of the "popular classes." Thus, Karl argues that foundational pacts

> are antidemocratic mechanisms, bargained by elites, which seek to create a deliberate socioeconomic and political contract that demobilizes emerging mass actors while delineating the extent to which all actors can participate or wield power in the future. They may accomplish this task by restricting contestation..., by restricting the policy agenda itself..., or by restricting the franchise.... Regardless of which strategic option is chosen, the net effect of these options is the same: the nature and parameters of the initial democracy that results is markedly circumscribed. (Karl 1990, pp. 11–12)

In an earlier analysis, Karl added that such pacts can "institutionalize a conservative bias into the polity, creating a new status quo which can block further progress toward political, social and economic democracy" and that "this is a logical outcome since pact-making among elites, often conducted in secrecy, represents the construction of democracy by antidemocratic means" (Karl 1986, p. 198). Our approach differs in two respects. First, only the concept of "direct democracy" requires that decisions be made in public forums. If a procedural conception of democracy is adopted, private negotiations among elites are an acceptable, even routine feature of democratic governance, as long as the elites involved are held publicly accountable through the elections and other processes that the procedural conception specifies. Second, to the extent that "pacts" deliberately exclude and seek to marginalize important elites and social groups, they are anti-democratic in their thrust; in our terminology, they culminate in the creation of "limited democracies" or pseudo-democracies. But not all elite agreements are so exclusionary or restrictive. It is important to recognize the occurrence of much more comprehensive elite settlements which, as in the case of Spain (see Chapter 2), can lead directly to a consolidated democracy or, as in the cases of Sweden and Britain, establish stable limited democracies that eventually evolve into consolidated democracies. Our main claim about elite settlements is that by virtue of their breadth and the procedural guarantees of security that they give to all important elites, they can open the way to consolidated democracies. To borrow some formulations from Adam Przeworski, we regard an elite settlement as "a contingent institutional comprise," whereas an elite pact may well be a "substantive compromise"; only the former, he argues, is consistent with democracy (Przeworski 1986, pp. 59–60).

The following case studies focus on our contention that the key to the consolidation of new democratic regimes lies in the transformation of political elites from disunity to consensual unity via elite settlements or elite convergences. Which of the recent democratic transitions in Latin America and Southern Europe involved such transformations? How did they occur? And what have been the consequences for democratic consolidation so far? And in those countries where there was no elite transformation, what prevented it, and what are the prospects for the survival of their democratic regimes? In the final chapter, we will assess the extent to which the answers that emerge from the case studies bear out our theoretical propositions.

References

Almond, Gabriel, and Sidney Verba. 1963. *The Civic Culture: Political Attitudes and Democracy in Five Nations*. Princeton, NJ: Princeton University Press.

Burton, Michael G., and John Higley. 1987a. "Elite Settlements." *American Sociological Review* 52:295–307.

1987b. "Invitation to Elite Theory." In *Power Elites and Organizations*, ed. G. William Domhoff and Thomas R. Dye. Newbury Park, CA: Sage.

Dahl, Robert A. 1966. "Some Explanations." In *Political Oppositions in Western Democracies*, ed. Robert A. Dahl. New Haven, CT: Yale University Press.

1971. *Polyarchy: Participation and Opposition*. New Haven, CT: Yale University Press.

Deutsch, Karl. 1953. *Nationalism and Social Communication*. Cambridge, MA: MIT Press.

Diamond, Larry. 1989. "Introduction: Persistence, Erosion, Breakdown, and Renewal." In *Democracy in Developing Countries: Asia*, vol. 3, ed. Larry Diamond, Juan J. Linz, and Seymour Martin Lipset. Boulder, CO: Lynne Rienner.

Diamond, Larry, and Juan J. Linz. 1989. "Introduction: Politics, Society, and Democracy in Latin America." In *Democracy in Developing Countries: Latin America*, vol. 4, ed. Larry Diamond, Juan J. Linz, and Seymour Martin Lipset. Boulder, CO: Lynne Rienner.

Diamond, Larry, Juan Linz, and Seymour Martin Lipset, eds. 1988. *Democracy in Developing Countries: Africa*. Vol. 2. Boulder, CO: Lynne Rienner.

1989a. *Democracy in Developing Countries: Asia*. Vol. 3. Boulder, CO: Lynne Rienner.

1989b. *Democracy in Developing Countries: Latin America*. Vol 4. Boulder, CO: Lynne Rienner.

Di Palma, Giuseppe. 1973. *The Study of Conflict in Western Societies: A Critique of the End of Ideology*. Morristown, NJ: General Learning Press.

1990. *To Craft Democracies: An Essay on Democratic Transitions*. Berkeley and Los Angeles: University of California Press.

Downs, Anthony. 1959. *An Economic Theory of Democracy*. New York: Harper Bros.

Dye, Thomas R. 1983. *Who's Running America: The Reagan Years*. 3rd ed. Englewood Cliffs, NJ: Prentice-Hall.

Field, G. Lowell, and John Higley. 1978. "Imperfectly Unified Elites: The Cases of Italy and France." In *Comparative Studies in Sociology*, ed. R. Tomasson. Greenwich, CT: JAI Press.

Field, G. Lowell, and John Higley. 1980. *Elitism*. London: Routledge & Kegan Paul.

Field, G. Lowell, John Higley, and Michael G. Burton. 1990. "A New Elite Framework for Political Sociology." In *Revue européenne des sciences sociales* 28: 149–82.

Gunther, Richard, and Anthony Mughan. 1991. "The Separation of Powers and Conflict Management." In *Do Institutions Matter? Policymaking in Presidential and Parliamentary Systems*, eds. Bert Rockman and R. Kent Weaver. Washington, DC: Brookings Institution.

Gunther, Richard, Giacomo Sani, and Goldie Shabad. 1986. *Spain After Franco: The Making of a Competitive Party System*. Berkeley and Los Angeles: University of California Press.

Harrison, Martin, ed. 1969. *French Politics*. Lexington, MA: Heath.

Higley, John, and Michael G. Burton. 1989. "The Elite Variable in Democratic Transitions and Breakdowns." *American Sociological Review* 54:17–32.

Higley, John, Desley Deacon, and Don Smart. 1979. *Elites in Australia*. London: Routledge & Kegan Paul.

Higley, John, G. Lowell Field, and Knut Groholt. 1976. *Elite Structure and Ideology*. New York: Columbia University Press.

Higley, John, and Gwen Moore. 1981. "Elite Integration in the United States and Australia." *American Political Science Review* 75:581–97.

Hoffmann, Stanley. 1987. "Conclusion: Paradoxes and Discontinuities." In *The Mitterrand Experiment*, eds. G. Ross, S. Hoffmann, and S. Malzzcher. New York: Oxford University Press.

Kadushin, Charles. 1968. "Power, Influence and Social Circles: A New Methodology for Studying Opinion Makers." *American Sociological Review* 33:685–99.

1979. "Power Circles and Legitimacy in Developed Societies. In *Legitimation of Regimes*, ed. Bogdan Denitch. Beverly Hills, CA: Sage.

Karl, Terry. 1986. "Petroleum and Political Pacts: The Transition to Democracy in Venezuela." In *Transitions from Authoritarian Rule: Latin America*, ed. Guillermo O'Donnell, Philippe C. Schmitter, and Laurence Whitehead. Baltimore: Johns Hopkins University Press.

1990. "Dilemmas of Democratization in Latin America." *Comparative Politics* 23:1–21.

Lamounier, Bolivar. 1988. "Challenges to Democratic Transition in Brazil." Notes prepared for the panel "After the Transition: The Consolidation of New Democratic Regimes," American Political Science Association annual meeting, Washington, DC: September 1988.

Lane, David. 1988. *Elites and Political Power in the USSR*. Brookfield, VT: Edward Elgar.

Lerner, Daniel. 1958. *The Passing of Traditional Society*. New York: Free Press.

Levine, Daniel H. 1978. "Venezuela Since 1958: The Consolidation of Democratic Politics." In *The Breakdown of Democratic Regimes: Latin America*, ed. Juan J. Linz and Alfred Stepan. Baltimore: Johns Hopkins University Press.

Lijphart, Arend. 1968. *The Politics of Accommodation: Pluralism and Democracy in the Netherlands*. Berkeley and Los Angeles: University of California Press.

1969. "Consociational Democracy." *World Politics*, 21:207–25.

1977. *Democracy in Plural Societies: A Comparative Exploration*. New Haven, CT: Yale University Press.

1984. *Democracies*. New Haven, CT: Yale University Press.

Lijphart, Arend, Thomas C. Bruneau, P. Nikiforos Diamandouros, and Richard Gunther. 1988. "A Mediterranean Model of Democracy? The Southern European Democracies in Comparative Perspective." *West European Politics* 11 (January): 7–25.

Linz, Juan. 1975. "Totalitarian and Authoritarian Regimes." In *Handbook of Political*

Science, vol. 3, ed. Fred I. Greenstein and Nelson W. Polsby. Reading, MA: Addison-Wesley.

Lipset, Seymour Martin. 1960. *Political Man*. New York: Doubleday.

1981. *Political Man*, expanded and updated ed. Baltimore: Johns Hopkins University Press.

McDonough, Peter. 1981. *Power and Ideology in Brazil*. Princeton, NJ: Princeton University Press.

Merritt, Richard L. 1970. *Systematic Approaches to Comparative Politics*. Chicago: Rand McNally.

Morlino, Leonardo. 1986. "Consolidamento democratico: Definizione e modelli." *Rivista italiana di scienza politica* 2 (August).

Moyser, George, and Margaret Wagstaffe, eds. 1987. *Research Methods for Elite Studies*. Boston: Allen & Unwin.

O'Donnell, Guillermo, and Philippe C. Schmitter. 1986. *Transitions from Authoritarian Rule: Tentative Conclusions About Uncertain Democracies*. Baltimore: Johns Hopkins University Press.

Powell, G. Bingham. 1982. *Contemporary Democracies: Participation, Stability and Violence*. Cambridge, MA: Harvard University Press.

Prewitt, Kenneth, and Alan Stone. 1973. *The Ruling Elites: Elite Theory, Power, and American Democracy*. New York: Harper & Row.

Pridham, Geoffrey, ed. 1990. *Securing Democracy: Political Parties and Democratic Consolidation in Southern Europe*. London: Routledge & Kegan Paul.

Przeworski, Adam. 1986. "Problems in the Study of Transition to Democracy." In *Transitions from Authoritarian Rule: Comparative Perspectives*, ed. Guillermo O'Donnell, Philippe C. Schmitter, and Laurence Whitehead. Baltimore: Johns Hopkins University Press.

Putnam, Robert D. 1976. *The Comparative Study of Political Elites*. Englewood Cliffs, NJ: Prentice-Hall.

Rustow, Dankwart. 1970. "Transitions to Democracy: Toward a Dynamic Model." *Comparative Politics* (April):337–63.

Safran, William. 1985. *The French Polity*, 2nd ed. New York: Longman.

Sanders, David. 1981. *Patterns of Political Instability*. London: Macmillan.

Sartori, Giovanni. 1976. *Parties and Party Systems*. Cambridge: Cambridge University Press.

1987. *The Theory of Democracy Revisited, Part One: The Contemporary Debate*. Chatham, NJ: Chatham House Publishers.

Schwoerer, Lois. 1981. *The Declaration of Rights, 1689*. Baltimore: Johns Hopkins University Press.

Share, Donald. 1987. "Transitions to Democracy and Transition Through Transaction." *Comparative Political Studies*, 19:525–48.

Wilde, Alexander W. 1978. "Conversations Among Gentlemen: Oligarchical Democracy in Colombia." In *The Breakdown of Democratic Regimes: Latin America*, ed. Juan J. Linz and Alfred Stepan. Baltimore: Johns Hopkins University Press.

2

Spain: the very model of the modern elite settlement

RICHARD GUNTHER

The Spanish constitutional monarchy is today a consolidated democracy. Only in the Basque provinces (Euskadi) is there any significant challenge to the legitimacy of the regime. In that region, about one quarter of the population still regard the Spanish state as an illegitimate imposition on the Basque nation. Some Basque parties have maintained (at least until very recently) a semiloyal stance vis-à-vis the regime, and one has functioned unequivocally as an antisystem party. That party, Herri Batasuna, has consistently received about one sixth of the vote in regional and national elections over the past decade and a half. It has also supported an organization, Euskadi ta Askatasuna (ETA), that has used terrorist violence in its campaign for Basque independence – a clear violation of the democratic rules of the game.

But there can be no doubt that the present democratic regime is sufficiently consolidated to have survived even this dramatic challenge. Despite the terrorist violence that has claimed over seven hundred lives, support for the system has remained solid. Public opinion polls have revealed widespread popular support for this democratic regime and no significant rejection of existing institutions or practices.[1] No nationwide party maintains a semiloyal or antisystem

1 A 1986 Eurobarometer poll, for example, revealed that 56 percent of Spaniards claimed that they were "very satisfied" or "fairly satisfied" with the way that democracy works in Spain. This level of system satisfaction is superior to those found in Italy (25 percent) and Ireland (44 percent), although it lags somewhat behind that of West Germany (71 percent) (Moxon-Browne, 1989, p. 19). Morlino and Montero (1990) concluded from an extensive body of survey data (collected as part of a systematic four-nation survey of popular support for democratic regimes in Southern Europe) that the Spanish regime is regarded as fully legitimate by an overwhelming majority of its citizens. They also found that Spaniards' scores on questionnaire items measuring a variety of "system-support" attitudes were generally higher than those

stance, and all unequivocally support the constitution (ratified overwhelmingly, except in Euskadi, by a popular referendum in 1978). Behavioral conformity with democratic rules of the game (except in Euskadi) is as extensive as in other consolidated democracies.

What is most remarkable is that system support has remained unshaken despite several severe tests, apart from ETA's terrorist campaign. An attempted coup in February 1981 achieved an immediate tactical success – including the capture at gunpoint of the entire elected leadership of Spain's government and all nationwide political parties, coupled with military mobilization and a proclamation of martial law in one populous region – and yet the coup failed to attract support from other military units, significant sectors of public opinion, or political parties. Instead, in the aftermath of the coup's failure there was a significant expansion in the scope of elite consensual unity, as those military officers previously ambiguous in their commitment to the new democratic regime abandoned all expectations that an alternative form of government was possible or desirable. One important study (Agüero 1991) concludes that consolidation of the Spanish constitutional monarchy was secured at that time, as virtually the entire military hierarchy joined the procedural consensus in support of the system. That same study, however, also highlights the importance of developments that had occurred two years earlier (which will be the principal focus of this analysis) – the establishment of consensual unity among national-level party leaders in the course of the constituent process.[2]

One cannot argue that democratic consolidation in Spain between 1978 and 1982 was facilitated by favorable economic, social, or political conditions: The new regime's worst political crisis (the decomposition of its governing party) coincided with a severe drought, a disastrous decline of several key industrial sectors, and rates of unemployment that eventually reached 22 percent of the labor force (see Rodríguez

found in Italy, a democracy whose legitimacy would be questioned by few serious scholars today.

2 Agüero argues that one of the most important factors in securing the supremacy of civilian political elites over the military in democratic transitions is the absence of semiloyal or antisystem political party elites who call upon the military for support in the course of partisan conflicts. Instead, the attempted coup of 1981 met with solid opposition from all political parties. This was most clearly symbolized in the course of the coup when the leader of the right-wing Alianza popular and former Franquist minister Manuel Fraga Iribarne melodramatically stood up in the Cortes and dared his captors to begin by shooting him if they were serious about overthrowing Spanish democracy. The complete loyalty to the new regime of Alianza popular denied the conspirators of the kind of civilian allies often necessary for the overthrow of democratic regimes.

Díaz 1989). And yet support for the system among the general public, key national elites, secondary organizations, and political parties remained solid. No serious observer of Spanish politics today acknowledges even a remote possibility of a military coup or return to authoritarianism by some other means.

In this chapter, I will argue that successful democratic consolidation in Spain was primarily the product of a profound transformation of Spain's political elites from disunity into consensual unity. For the most part, this transformation involved the processes of an elite settlement. All significant nationwide political parties were induced to acknowledge the legitimacy of the regime's institutions and respect for its behavioral norms through extensive rounds of negotiations from the second half of 1976 through the end of 1978, culminating in the overwhelming endorsement of the new constitution in the December 1978 referendum. This elite settlement also helped forge a high and unprecedented level of structural integration among national elites. Mutual respect for political opponents is, for the first time in modern Spanish history, virtually universal among elites at the core of the political system in Madrid. Bonds of personal friendship, established through the settlement process and reinforced by more than a decade of restrained partisan conflict, have transcended formerly divisive political and social cleavages.

Elements of an "elite convergence" can also be seen, although its contribution to regime consolidation has not been as decisive. The most marked convergence has been a narrowing of ideological and programmatic differences among the major nationwide parties. In order to challenge the initial electoral dominance of the Unión de centro democrático (UCD – which led single-party minority governments from June 1977 through October 1982), parties on both its left and right moderated their ideologies, programs, and behavioral styles so as to be more acceptable to the modal center–left Spanish voter. The conservative Alianza popular (AP), established by seven prominent figures from the Franquist regime, has abandoned all vestiges of the corporatism, integral Spanish nationalism, and ambiguous embrace of democratic principles inherent in the stands taken by its founding elite. From 1979 until the retirement of its leader, Manuel Fraga, in 1989, the party presented itself as a conservative but democratic party, whose policies were often modeled after those of Margaret Thatcher and Ronald Reagan. Under the leadership of José María Aznar, the party may be moving even further toward the center of the political spectrum.

At the other end of the left–right continuum, the Partido comunista de España (PCE) transformed itself into a Eurocommunist party, loyal to democratic institutions and practices since the first elections of 1977 and relatively moderate and pragmatic in its electoral programs. Although this change had its origins in developments preceding the transition to democracy, it reached a high point with the ninth party congress of 1978 and the 1979 election campaign – convened in the immediate aftermath of the successful constitutional referendum. During this period, interviews with PCE leaders[3] clearly revealed that broadening the party's electoral appeal was a significant motive for change, in accord with the logic of "elite convergence," as described in Chapter 1. The most remarkable example of convergence, however, is that of the Socialist PSOE (Partido socialista obrero español), which initially emerged from clandestinity in 1976 as a "Marxist" party (adopting that self-designation for the first time in the party's history) advocating radical proposals, including extensive nationalizations of private business firms, elimination of the religious sector of education, and recognition of the right to "self-determination" by the various regions of Spain. And yet by the time it came to power in 1982, it had become perhaps the most conservative "socialist" party in Europe, adopting more restrictive economic and fiscal policies than the preceding center–right UCD governments and privatizing an extensive array of parastate industries. Although an analysis of these programmatic changes is clearly beyond the scope of this chapter (see Gillespie 1989; Gunther 1986a and 1986b; and Gunther, Sani, and Shabad 1986; and Share 1989), and is not as crucial to the consolidation of democracy as are other aspects of elite transformation, the narrowing of ideological and programmatic differences among Spain's major political parties is another element that has contributed to long-term democratic stability.

An unusual form of elite convergence may eventually bring about the extension of consensual unity to the Basque elites. Following a party schism that became apparent in December 1984 (culminating in the formation of a rival center–left/Basque nationalist party, Eusko Alkartasuna), the Partido nacionalista vasco (PNV) lost its majority in the Basque parliament and therefore faced the prospect of having to relinquish control of the regional government for the first time since 1980. Given the lack of alternatives, the PNV formed a coalition

3 Between 1977 and 1984, I conducted over three hundred hours of interviews with leaders of the UCD, PSOE, PCE, AP, PNV, Euskadiko ezkerra, Convergència democràtica de Catalunya, and Esquerra republicana de Catalunya, including over twelve hours of interviews with all three of Spain's democratic prime ministers. I conducted an additional two hundred hours of interviews with Franquist elites between January 1974 and March 1975. Much of the following analysis is based on the verbatim transcripts of these interviews.

with the PSOE, the party of government in Madrid and previously its principal adversary. But in return for its support in the regional parliament, the PSOE demanded that the PNV sign a legislative pact, according to which it would have to abandon many of its previous manifestations of a "semiloyal" stance toward the Spanish democratic regime. This included a pledge of "willingness to carry out the Constitution, the Statute of Autonomy and other related laws, including decisions handed down by the courts," as well as to cooperate in the struggle against terrorism (Shabad 1986, p. 144). This pact (motivated by the desire to achieve a governing majority – the driving force behind elite convergences) has significantly affected relations between the largest Basque nationalist party and Madrid (previously marked by disturbingly rancorous outbursts), has led to considerable success in the fight against terrorism, and has contributed to an altered climate of opinion in Euskadi, which is now much less sympathetic toward ETA. Finally, in January 1990, the PSOE used its bargaining leverage to extract an even more explicit commitment to the regime by the PNV: It threatened to quit the coalition unless the PNV would sign a document unequivocally committing itself to obey and respect the Spanish Constitution (*El País*, January 15, 1990). If this agreement is followed by PNV behavior confirming abandonment of its former semiloyal stance, this will represent a significant step toward democratic consolidation in Euskadi.

Given the relatively minor contribution to democratic consolidation made by these aspects of elite convergence, this chapter will concentrate on the elite settlement of 1977–9. Testing many of the causal claims set forth in Chapter 1 is enhanced by the fact that Spain provides us with several opportunities for comparative analysis. Because the country has undergone two democratic transitions in this century – one in 1931 and the other after the death of Francisco Franco, the first unsuccessful and the second successful – the importance of the various aspects of elite settlements can be weighed by comparing the two democratic transitions. Moreover, because democratic consolidation in Euskadi has so far been incomplete, compared with the rest of Spain, juxtaposing the Basque situation with that of the rest of the political system also illuminates important aspects of elite settlements, such as inclusiveness of all politically significant groups, secrecy, and speed. This chapter will also attempt to explore systematically the possible prerequisites for the attainment of a successful elite settlement and will therefore examine the degree of organization and absence of fragmentation of the opposing forces, the institutional setting within which the transition unfolded, as well as certain personal characteristics of the relevant elites.

Although I emphasize the role played by elites in laying to rest traditionally divisive issues and in founding and consolidating a new democratic regime, the importance of certain nonelite factors must not go unnoticed. The higher level of socioeconomic modernization that Spain had reached by the 1970s, with substantial literacy and affluence and reduced class tensions, certainly differed from the situation of the 1930s. Depoliticization of the general public and the lack of credible nondemocratic models for emulation also distinguish the 1970s from the 1930s, when Fascist Italy, Nazi Germany, and a Stalinist Soviet Union had their respective groups of admirers. In the 1970s, a widespread desire to "join Europe" reinforced democratizing tendencies, made neighboring democracies models to emulate, and, in some instances, led to infrastructural support for newly emerging political parties and trade unions (see Whitehead 1986). Moreover, Vatican Council II had transformed the behavior and popular image of the Catholic church which, in combination with the marked secularization of Spanish society, made the religious cleavage somewhat less divisive than four decades earlier. Finally, the passage of time and the gradual disappearance of generations directly responsible for the civil war and the early, repressive years of the Franquist regime helped Spaniards forgive, or at least coexist with, former enemies. All of these factors have been analyzed elsewhere (Gunther and Blough 1981; Gunther, Sani, and Shabad 1986; Linz et al., 1981), and so they will not be dealt with here. It is important to note, however, that those earlier studies concluded that although mass-level, social structural, international, and temporal factors all contributed to the successful consolidation of Spanish democracy in the 1970s and early 1980s, they were less decisive than were the actions of political elites.

From elite disunity to democratic consolidation

Throughout the nineteenth and early twentieth centuries, Spanish politics was characterized by elite disunity, deep social and political conflicts, and endemic regime instability. Moreover, rather than evolving through incremental reforms that become embedded in institutions and in the political culture, political changes often took the form of drastic swings of the pendulum from one extreme to the other. Over nearly two centuries, Spain swung back and forth between monarchy and republic, democracy and authoritarianism, rigid centralism and regional autonomy, confessionalism and anticlericalism. Juan Linz concludes in his brilliant survey of Spanish history and political culture:

> In Spain, there has been no continuous flow of tradition, no continuous transmission of a cultural heritage, no continuous process of selection of the past to be shared and incorporated into the present. The history of few countries is perceived in such conflictual terms as by the Spaniards who talk about "two Spains" in permanent struggle, or as a genuine Spain and an "anti-Spain" that needs to be destroyed to save the true essence of the nation. ... Intellectuals have confronted Spaniards with the choice to approve or reject in toto long periods of their history, to choose sides for or against almost any of the great decisions that affected its development. (Linz 1972, pp. 2, 66)

Francisco Franco founded his regime in a manner that represented a pendular reaction against what were regarded as weaknesses in the institutions and policies of the Second Republic. In creating a new regime after the collapse of the Republic in the civil war of 1936–9, the Franquist elite was reversing most of the reforms undertaken by that unstable democracy and creating institutions that would be perceived as anachronistic in the context of the urbanized, industrialized Spain of the 1970s. Accordingly, many aspects of the Franquist regime were regarded by the architects of Spain's current regime as an implicit agenda for change. Among those were the Franquist regime's authoritarianism (specifically, its prohibition of competitive political parties and the absence of basic civil and political rights), its confessionalism, its corporatist or "vertical" system of labor organization, and its extreme centralization of decision making. The monarchy installed by the aged generalísimo in 1967 was also subject to challenge on the grounds that it was an inheritance from the authoritarian past. Although there was a vague but widespread belief among the general public concerning the desirability of some form of political evolution toward the kinds of democratic systems that existed in neighboring West European countries, there was no consensus concerning how such a regime would come into existence, what form it should take,[4] and whether it would be successful in regulating conflicts over traditionally divisive issues that had destabilized and eventually destroyed Spain's previous experiment with democracy.

In founding a new democratic system, Spain's political elites had to confront issues over which they, and Spanish society, were polarized and divided. Determining the basic political institutions of the post-Franco political order pitted left against right, incumbents against their clandestine opponents, center against periphery, monarchists against republicans. The selection of an electoral law had an imme-

4 As an example of the extent to which there was a lack of consensus regarding the direction of political change, only 37 percent of those polled in 1975 said that they favored legalization of multiple political parties (see Linz et al., 1981, p. 10).

diate and lasting impact on each group's chances of coming to power through electoral means. Legalization of the Communist party was vigorously opposed by conservatives, but exclusion of the largest party of opposition to Franco from participating in the institutions of a new regime would almost certainly lead to an immediate challenge to its legitimacy.

The position of Juan Carlos – Franco's successor as head of state – was also an object of conflict. Several political parties, most importantly the two large parties of the left, the Socialist PSOE and the Communist PCE, were by tradition opposed to all forms of monarchy, and many of their leaders believed, as stated by a Socialist deputy in 1978, that "in Spain, liberty and democracy have come to have only one name: Republic!" (Gómez Llorente 1978, p. 2197). PCE leader Santiago Carrillo went so far as to predict that historians would refer to Juan Carlos as "Juan the Brief." Rejection of the monarchy, however, would at least partly preclude an evolutionary path to democracy and could needlessly alienate significant sectors of Spanish society, as had occurred in 1931 (see Mori 1933, pp. 350–3). Reflecting the initial polarization of party elites over this issue, supporters of rival parties were sharply divided. A poll taken in 1979 (several months after an elite-level compromise had been secured over this issue) showed that Communist voters who preferred a "republic" outnumbered those favoring a "monarchy," by 65 percent to 14 percent. At the other end of the political spectrum, the opinions of AP voters were almost a perfect mirror image of Communist party supporters on this issue: They favored a "monarchy" over "republic" by a margin of 68 percent to 7 percent.[5]

Several decisions also had to be made concerning the constitution's treatment of economic and social issues. Perhaps none of these was as potentially divisive as a redefinition of the role of the Catholic church in Spanish society and its relationship with the post-Franco state. Indeed, the manner in which the Spanish constituent elites of 1931 dealt with this issue directly contributed to the collapse of the Second Republic. Adoption of an anticlerical constitution led significant sectors of Spanish society to reject that regime as a partisan imposition on the rest of society of the values of a temporary majority. The legitimacy of the Second Republic was thus challenged from the very moment of its birth (see Gunther and Blough 1981).

5 The source is the 1979 postelection poll of 5,439 Spanish citizens by DATA, S.A., conducted for Richard Gunther, Giacomo Sani, and Goldie Shabad. Generous financial support for this study was provided by the National Science Foundation under grant no. SOC77–16451.

The Spanish Nationalist forces that toppled the regime in 1936 channeled this disaffection against what they portrayed as a godless cabal of Socialists, Communists, and Freemasons. Under the Franquist regime, the church enjoyed a powerful and privileged position. In reaction to the anticlerical policies and constitution of the Second Republic and as a reward for the support of religious Spaniards and the church during the civil war, Franco reestablished Catholicism as the official state religion, restored state subsidies to the church, granted church officials a dominant position in the education system, and outlawed divorce. In return, Franco was given an important role in appointing bishops. Not only were certain facets of this relationship objectionable to significant members of the constituent elite, but even church officials felt uncomfortable with their close ties to the state and, as early as 1971, began to issue calls for more autonomy (see Payne 1984). There was great concern, however, that this process of disestablishment not be permitted to go so far as to alienate religious Spaniards from the new regime, as had occurred in founding the Second Republic in 1931. This was particularly troubling insofar as the alignment of partisan forces that emerged from the first election in 1977 clearly reflected the clerical–anticlerical division in Spanish society. Our 1979 poll of Spanish citizens (again, conducted nearly one year after an elite level agreement over this issue) revealed that 64 percent of Communist voters regarded the influence of the church on Spanish society as detrimental, but that only 9 percent of UCD voters did so. Similarly, 78 percent of Communist and 66 percent of Socialist party supporters polled in 1979 opposed the continuation of state subsidies to private (mostly religious) schools, whereas over two thirds of UCD and AP voters favored those subsidies.

Clearly the most difficult political–institutional issue confronting the architects of the new regime concerned demands for political and administrative autonomy or independence by regionalist and micro-nationalist parties. In the late nineteenth century, micro-nationalist movements emerged in several regions with distinct languages and cultures. By 1936, they were strong enough to secure charters of regional autonomy for Catalunya and Euskadi, as well as a commitment by the last Republican government to grant autonomy to Galicia. The Spanish Nationalist regime of General Franco, however, was implacably opposed to what it perceived as the dismemberment of the Spanish nation under the republic, and it abrogated those agreements. All vestiges of regional administrative and political autonomy, except in two provinces that had supported Franco in the civil war, were eliminated. The reemergence of micro-nationalist political organizations and some political violence, including the assassination of the prime minister, Luis Carrero Blanco, in the final years of the Franquist regime, made it clear that demands for restructuring the Spanish state would have to be addressed. But it was also obvious that it would be exceedingly difficult to reach a compromise satisfactory to both Basque nationalists favoring complete independence from Spain, on the one hand, and Spanish nationalists in such key institutions as the army, on the other. Not only did this question divide the Spanish center from the micro-nationalist periphery, but it also led to considerable fragmentation within some regions, especially Euskadi. Seventeen percent of the respondents to our 1979 survey who resided in Euskadi favored continuation of the highly centralized Spanish state, and one quarter favored outright independence.

Thus, in constructing a new regime the post-Franco elites of Spain and its various regions faced several traditionally divisive issues, some of which had directly contributed in the past to democratic instability, regime collapse, and civil war. Although class conflicts and the degree of polarization along the left–right continuum had been softened considerably by rapid economic growth during the 1960s and early 1970s and by the explicit efforts of the Franco regime to depoliticize Spanish society, there remained many questions over which Spaniards were badly divided. Given the extent of mass-level polarization over some of these issues, moreover, successful conflict regulation would require initiatives at the elite level to forge a new consensus.

The transition

For nearly a year following the death of Francisco Franco (in November 1975), it was entirely unclear how (or even if) a successful transition to democracy could be achieved. The first question to be addressed was whether it would be possible to establish a democratic regime through an evolutionary process or whether the old regime could be dislodged only through a more abrupt and tumultuous *ruptura*, forced by mass mobilizations.

The lack of significant progress toward democratization under the second Arias Navarro government (December 1975 through June 1976), coupled with the existence of institutional obstacles to reform set in place before Franco's death (e.g., the corporatist Cortes and the Council of the Realm), gave rise to pessimism over the prospects for peaceful change. Assuming that change could only be brought about through a *ruptura democrática*, most major parties of the clandestine opposition (the largest of which, by far, being the Communist party) formed broad-based coordinating councils and began to collaborate with one another in their efforts to topple the regime. They demanded total amnesty for and immediate release of all political prisoners, prompt legalization of all political parties, formation of a provisional government, and immediate elections to a constituent assembly (see Carr and Fusi 1979; Maravall 1981; Oneto 1985; Powell 1989 and 1991; Preston 1986; and Sinova 1984). In support of their demands and in frustration over the complete lack of progress toward reform under Carlos Arias Navarro, they organized an ever-increasing number of public demonstrations and strikes. Their success in organizing politically motivated strikes by workers was impressive: Maravall calculates that the number of strikes grew from 931 in 1973, to 2,290 in 1974, to 3,156 in 1975, and to 17,731 in 1976 and that the number of man hours lost through such activities increased more than tenfold, from 14.5 million in 1975 to 150 million in 1976 (Maravall 1981, p. 27). In short, a significant mass mobilization of opposition forces was taking place, and a showdown with defenders of the Franquist state seemed inevitable. Even though most Spaniards preferred evolutionary reforms over abrupt change, 79 percent of a sample of workers polled in early 1977 concluded that "the egoism of the powerful will make any reform impossible" (Maravall 1981, p. 33).

Instead, there was rapid progress toward democratization following the king's dismissal of Arias Navarro and the appointment of a new government in July 1976. The key to this reform process was the leadership of Adolfo Suárez, a young and relatively unknown product of the Movimiento nacional (uncharitably described by the second-ranking Socialist leader, Alfonso Guerra, as "a creature who crawled from the sewers of fascism"), who had previously served under Franco as director general of the state-run television network and, in the first post-Franco government, as minister of the Movimiento. In an impressive display of political skill (and in close collaboration with the king and Torcuato Fernández-Miranda, president of the Cortes and of the Council of the Realm), Suárez persuaded the corporatist Cortes to commit institutional suicide by approving the Law for Political Reform in October 1976, which established procedures for future political reforms to be undertaken by a new, democratically elected Cortes. In rapid succession other crucial reforms were enacted: Hundreds of political prisoners were granted pardons in July 1976 and March 1977; the Movimiento was disbanded and political parties were legalized; the vertical labor syndicates were abolished and replaced by independent trade unions; an electoral law that set the rules for electoral competition was passed that was regarded as acceptable by both left-wing and right-wing political parties; despite fierce opposition from certain sectors of the military, the PCE was admitted as a legitimate contender in the new political arena; and democratic elections were scheduled for June 1977.

In the first stage of the transition, key decisions were made by Adolfo Suárez and enacted by decree (except for the Political Reform Law, approved by the Cortes and ratified in a popular referendum). Initially, Suárez consulted with the king and his close advisers, but not with opposition elites. Indeed, Socialist leader Felipe González reported (in a 1984 interview) that throughout July 1976, the first eleven or twelve attempts by Suárez to begin a face-to-face dialogue were rejected by the PSOE. Thus, the first few steps in the transition (the July 1976 amnesty and drafting of the Political Reform Law) were largely unilateral. But beginning in August 1976, extensive consultations with elites on both the left and the right got under way. By this time, the Socialist elite had concluded that Suárez was serious in his reform efforts, and it therefore permitted González to enter into an extended dialogue with the prime minister (although some in the party leadership criticized González for these contacts with a former leader of the Movimiento). In retrospect, Suárez's initial, unilateral steps can be seen to have been crucial to creating a level of confidence among opposition forces that significant reform was possible.

Consultations with representatives of the right (especially those members of the Cortes who had just formed the first political party, Alianza popular) were particularly intensive during Cortes deliberations over the Political Reform Law. In some respects, this represented a vigorous lobbying effort necessary to secure Cortes passage of the reform law, without which evolutionary reform would have been impossible. But it also represented the first instance of formal bargaining with elites of other parties. In exchange for their support of the reform law, AP elites demanded a pledge concerning the introduction of "correctives" into a future electoral law. It is clear that one of the pivotal factors inducing many members of the Cortes to support the reform law was the expectation that Alianza popular could win (or at least do quite well) in any future election.[6]

Following approval of the Political Reform Law, formal contacts between Suárez and representatives of opposition groups began in

6 Powell also claims that "negotiations" of a very different kind also took place: "Some procuradores were threatened with scandals of an economic and sexual nature in order to guarantee their support for the government" (1991, p. 200). Perhaps the most important aspect of the strategy was enlistment as speakers in favor of the reform law of prominent figures in the Cortes (such as Miguel Primo de Rivera, whose late brother had founded the Falange española, which later became the Movimiento nacional) who were regarded by many as very influential and who had extensive clientelistic networks within that body.

earnest. A nine-member negotiating committee[7] was created to articulate the opposition's demands concerning legalization of political parties, the shape of the electoral law, liquidation of the Movimiento nacional and the vertical *sindicatos,* and grants of amnesty to additional political prisoners (including Basque nationalists accused of violent crimes). For the most part, these contacts did not constitute formal negotiations. Instead, as described by Felipe González in a 1984 interview, Suárez listened to the appeals of the various parties and "skillfully translated our demands into the terms of the decree laws."

In one instance, however, Suárez did engage in a bargaining process – but with a third party rather than with the elites who thought they were involved in negotiations. In his meeting with the Consejos superiores de los ejércitos (virtually all of the highest-ranking officers in the army, navy, and air force) on September 8, 1976, at which he "informed" them of his plans for reform, he stated, in response to their expressions of concern, that he could not legalize the Communist party, given its current statutes. Some military officers concluded from this statement that Suárez would heed their wishes and continue to ban the PCE. Instead, he took advantage of the ambiguity of this statement and used it as leverage to induce the Communist party to modify several of its traditional stands. In the end, in exchange for legalization, the PCE dropped its opposition to the monarchy and committed itself to Suárez's reform effort as a potentially viable path to democracy. With this bold decision to legalize the Communist party (announced during the Easter week vacation, when most of the key military officers were away), Suárez accomplished two objectives: Through negotiations with Communist elites, he reinforced the moderating tendencies within the PCE initiated previously by party leader Santiago Carrillo, and by legalizing the largest party of opposition he enlisted into the reform process a crucial organization that otherwise would almost certainly have posed a challenge to the legitimacy of the emerging regime. Suárez claims that this was his main reason for legalizing the Communist party and that a continued ban on the party would not only have destroyed the credibility of his reform process but also would have produced a backlash that might have increased support for the party. (It is interesting to note that he also "undertook many public opinion polls at that time" and that on this basis concluded that the PCE could not pose a significant electoral threat, while

7 This committee included representatives of the Socialist, Social Democratic, Communist, Liberal, and Christian Democratic parties; the three largest trade unions; and moderate Basque, Gallego, and Catalán groups.

at the same time its continued exclusion from the political process would be unpopular with the general public.)

In addition to legalization of all political parties and trade unions, the drafting of an electoral law was a critical act during this stage of the transition. The design of an electoral system in advance of a first democratic election is of considerable importance from the standpoint of regime legitimacy and viability. A difficult balance must be struck between the need to create a party system conducive to stable government and the representation of the interests of significant political and social groups. On the one hand, excessive fragmentation of the new party system had to be avoided in order to facilitate the formation of a government able to enact and implement legislation. (This was a particularly salient concern in Spain in early 1977, when over one hundred political parties came into existence, seventy-eight of which fielded candidates and received votes in the June 15 election.) On the other hand, exclusion of significant political forces from a constituent parliament could threaten the legitimacy of the new regime. These choices were also complicated by calculations of partisan self-interest, with each party pushing for an electoral system that it regarded as maximizing its share of parliamentary representation.

The electoral law enacted by the Suárez government in March 1977 represented a compromise (ultimately accepted by all significant parties, although with predictable grumbling from time to time) among the conflicting demands of the various parties. In accord with Suárez's own wishes and the demands of the Socialists and Communists, proportional representation principles were adopted. However, in order to gain their support for Cortes passage of the Political Reform law, Suárez promised AP *procuradores* that the law would include certain "correctives," which would somewhat overrepresent the two largest parties in most districts. These were intended to reduce party-system fragmentation and facilitate governance in the new democracy. (The AP was also motivated to push for these correctives because in the autumn of 1976, its leaders believed that it would be one of the two largest parties and would therefore gain a partisan advantage.) The electoral system enacted in March 1977 has proved to be successful in several respects. By reducing party-system fragmentation and overrepresenting the two largest parties, it has facilitated the formation of stable governments. But it has done so without excluding important groups from parliament or grossly distorting the representation of public opinion, both of which were of great importance in the constituent period of 1977–9 (see Gunther 1989).

The critical stage of the transition to a new democratic regime, which lasted from July 1976 until the first free elections in June 1977, was thus guided by the bold initiatives and good judgment of Adolfo Suárez, who relied heavily on extensive personal contacts with party elites. This process, however, is better regarded as involving "dialogues" rather than "negotiations" among key elites. In the end, Suárez acceded to the demands of the opposition with regard to the legalization of all parties (including the PCE), an additional round of amnesties for political prisoners, and many aspects of the electoral law. But he remained steadfast in his refusal to appoint a provisional government and immediately hold elections to a constituent assembly. Instead, he insisted on an evolutionary process within the existing institutional framework, and in particular, he insisted on (and repeatedly negotiated for) acceptance of the monarchy by traditionally republican parties.[8]

The evolutionary nature of this transition was, for several reasons, of great political significance. It contributed to the legitimacy of the new regime in the eyes of many Franquistas by initiating political change legitimized by a head of state personally appointed by Franco and using institutions established by the Franquist regime itself. Thus, important sectors of the former regime would play active roles in the reform process, rather than sitting on the sidelines as embittered opponents of change or as vengeful victims of a political purge. The institutional discontinuity resulting from an abrupt break from the past would have made impossible a formally legal transition to democracy, thereby precluding a "backward legitimation" of the transitional government (see Di Palma 1980).

The evolutionary nature of the transition also ensured that change would take place within a relatively stable political and institutional environment, and not within a chaotic political vacuum. The Catalán Communist (now Socialist) leader Jordi Solé Tura points out that by way of comparison,

> the three great constituent moments of a democratic variety in our constitutional history [1812, 1869, and 1931] took place within a common situation of an institutional vacuum, a radical break with dynastic power, a sudden irruption of important sectors of the populace into the political scene, a military crisis, and a correlation of forces favorable to those groups with the most radical transformative desires. (Solé Tura 1978, pp. 19–20)

8 As argued, acceptance of the monarchy was one of the demands made by Suárez in exchange for legalizing the PCE. In addition, Powell (1991, pp. 240–4) claims that in return for its "preautonomy statute," the Catalán Generalitat (government, then in exile) had to pledge to support the monarchy and respect the unity of Spain.

Another transition under such circumstances would have heightened the anxieties of those fearing an impending collapse of law and order and might have played into the hands of those few (but strategically placed) elites in the "bunker" who wished to return to an authoritarian regime. Indeed, as I will argue later in this chapter, institutional continuity played an important role in thwarting the attempted coup in February 1981.

An additional difference between the Spanish transition and those initiated by the abrupt collapse of an authoritarian regime is that steady, gradual steps toward the first democratic election enabled parties representing virtually every conceivable social group or ideological orientation to organize and compete in forming a constituent assembly. An election convened too hastily can distort the representation of public opinion in parliament in two ways: First, it can give a significant organizational advantage to those groups that have been active in clandestinity (such as the Communist party), resulting in the underrepresentation of social interests and ideological families not organized at the time the parties are first legalized. Second, the political atmosphere surrounding the abrupt collapse of an authoritarian regime is usually charged with emotions and attitudes not typical of a society under normal circumstances. In 1931, for example, the abrupt abdication of King Alfonso XIII was accompanied by an upsurge of republican and anticlerical sentiments, and the elections to a constituent assembly convened immediately thereafter effectively overrepresented those opinions. This (along with the distorting influence of the Second Republic's electoral law) contributed to the impression of an overwhelming mandate for the victorious coalition and a belief that compromise with other groups was unnecessary. In contrast, the balance of partisan forces present within the constituent Cortes of 1977 more accurately reflected the moderate, center–left orientation of most Spanish voters.

Constructing a new regime

By the time the first democratically elected Cortes convened in July 1977, several significant political changes had taken place. Many of the institutions of the Franquist regime had been or were in the process of being dismantled (the largely unelected Cortes, the corporatist *sindicatos*, the Movimiento) and democratic or pluralistic institutions had taken their place (an elected Cortes, class-based trade unions, and a multiparty system). Other less visible but highly significant changes were also under way.

One of the most important of these changes was a substantial increase in the structural integration of Spain's elites. Elite disunity had characterized Spanish politics throughout the twentieth century, and it took a variety of forms. Under the Republic, ideological polarization among party elites was accompanied by a highly rancorous behavioral style (Payne 1970, p. 91), and other key elites (especially in the military and the church) were alienated from the regime altogether. Disunity reached an extreme during the civil war, with violent clashes not only between the Nationalist and Republican camps but within the Republican camp as well (e.g., the bloody purge of anarchists and anarchosyndicalists by the Communists). Under Franco, conflict was suppressed and ideological polarization was reduced, but this meant repression of the vanquished by a victorious coalition, followed by sullen resignation to the impossibility of overturning the existing system. Although behavioral manifestations of conflict between elites were infrequent under Franco, the dividing line between elites supporting the regime and those leaning toward the opposition was extreme, with only one partial exception. That exception was within the rapidly expanding university system, in which friendly personal relations among colleagues, and between professors and students, often crossed over former ideological divisions. Because the leadership of each of the nationwide parties included a sizable contingent of university professors and graduates, these personal ties facilitated the subsequent structural integration of Spain's political elites.

But the real advances in structural integration began in late 1976 with the first rounds of face-to-face contacts between Suárez and various opposition leaders. By all published accounts (confirmed through personal observations and extensive in-depth interviews), relations between Suárez and the two leading opposition leaders, Santiago Carrillo (PCE) and Felipe González (PSOE) were cordial and open. Friendly interpersonal relations across party lines extended to a much broader array of elites in negotiations over the constitution and regional autonomy statutes during the following two years, as we shall see.

Elite structural integration was further reinforced through two important confidence-building exercises in 1977. The first was a formal reconciliation with Josep Tarradellas, exiled president of the Generalitat (the Catalán regional government), accompanied by the granting to Catalunya of a preautonomy statute. Though largely symbolic, these steps were important in demonstrating the Spanish government's willingness to reach an accommodation with formerly alienated Cataláns and in bringing Catalán political elites into the transition process as active collaborators (see Powell 1991, pp. 240–4). (It is interesting to note that a similar effort to extend a preautonomy statute to Euskadi may have backfired, thereby exacerbating relations among key elites. Due largely to the fragmentation of the Basque party system, the first president of a preautonomy government in Euskadi was a member of the PSOE, Ramón Rubial, not of the Basque nationalist PNV.)

The second confidence-building exercise of 1977 was successful negotiation of the Pacts of Moncloa. These agreements were prompted by a growing economic crisis that in 1977 pushed the rate of inflation in the consumer price index to 26.4 percent. In response, trade unions asked for large increases in labor-contract negotiations and backed up their demands with increased strike activity. This greatly alarmed the finance minister, Francisco Fernández Ordóñez, and the vice-president for economic affairs, Enrique Fuentes Quintana, and led to the convening of high-level talks at the prime minister's residence (the Moncloa Palace) that included leaders of the Socialist and Communist parties. The resulting Pacts of Moncloa pledged the government to a continuing program of reforms of political institutions, the social security system, and the regressive taxation system inherited from the Franquist regime; to government controls on price increases; to democratization of the education system; and to certain other policy changes (see Rodríguez Díaz 1989). In exchange, the Socialist and Communist parties promised to induce those trade unions over which they had influence to refrain from excessive strike activity, to limit demands for pay increases to 22 percent, and to accept more restrictive monetary and expenditure policies.

The economic consequences of the Pacts of Moncloa are debatable, but from the standpoint of regime legitimacy and stability, the political impact of these negotiations was unambiguously positive. Labor relations were immediately stabilized, and both government and opposition received and extended gestures of good faith. Of greater political significance were the further strengthening of elite structural integration (especially that resulting from the extremely cordial and productive interactions between PCE and government elites) and the dramatic legitimization of the role of the Communist party in Spanish society. There could be no greater symbol of political change than that of Santiago Carrillo (who, less than one year earlier, had been arrested and jailed on returning to Spain) emerging from the presidential palace after deliberations over a wide range of government policies. The pacts were, as described by Santiago Carrillo in a speech to the Cortes, "an act of national responsibility in order to restore democracy" (ABC, November 3, 1977).

From the standpoint of theory building, two points are worth mentioning at this juncture. The first is that the Pacts of Moncloa did not represent permanent substantive commitments by the newly emerging regime. The terms of the agreements were strictly limited in scope and duration. They were an attempt to address the economic crisis through short-term economic and political arrangements and did not impose limits on the capacity of future governments to enact whatever economic or social policy they might regard as desirable. Indeed, all the Suárez government committed itself to was to carry through with policies it intended to implement anyway – continued political reform, as well as changes in the social security and taxation systems that had been initiated under the Franquist regime (when Fuentes Quintana was director of the Instituto de estudios fiscales and Fernández Ordóñez was general technical secretary in the Ministry of Finance) (see Gunther 1980). In this respect, the Pacts of Moncloa differed from the kind of substantively restrictive pact described by Karl and discussed in the Introduction (Karl 1986).

The second aspect of the Moncloa pacts that is of theoretical interest derives from Felipe González's observation that the most enthusiastic advocates of this agreement (even more than Suárez) were two of the PCE's representatives in the talks, Santiago Carrillo and Ramón Tamames. Tamames, in particular, was apparently quite passionate in arguing that this social pact was the only means by which inflation rates could be reduced. What is interesting about this is that Tamames is one of Spain's most noted economists. One is led to hypothesize that the inclusion in bargaining teams of cognitively complex technocrats may help alter perceptions of what otherwise might be regarded as zero-sum class conflicts. Insofar as a Communist stance in these deliberations might otherwise have been a rigid defense of the short-term economic interests of the working class (by opposing wage restraints), the technocratic translation of this economic issue into expanding-sum terms (i.e., that everybody would benefit over the long term from lower inflation), may have helped lead to an important concession by the PCE. In addition, cognitively complex individuals are more likely to perceive gains secured in other sectors in return for concessions on such issues as wage restrictions.

Thus, by autumn 1977, the former regime had been largely dismantled; democratic institutions had begun to emerge; the extent of structural integration among Spanish and Catalán elites had increased; and the political atmosphere had been stabilized through the demobilization of opposition supporters and a marked reduction in strike activity. But important obstacles still had to be overcome. A new constitution – giving institutional form to the new democracy, regulating such traditionally divisive issues as church–state relations, and decentralizing the Spanish state – still had to be written.

Constitutional negotiations. The Cortes that assembled in July 1977 to write a new constitution consisted of a Congress of Deputies and a Senate. In the Congress, where the constitutional deliberations began, was a broadly representative array of political parties, two of which (the center–right UCD and the Socialist PSOE, with 165 and 118 seats, respectively) were slightly overrepresented as a result of the biases inherent in the electoral law. Two other nationwide parties also had significant representation, the Communist PCE and the right-wing AP, with 20 and 16 seats each. Several regional and micro-nationalist parties were also present, the largest being the Catalán group, with 11 deputies, and the 8 representatives of the Basque nationalist PNV. The UCD was 11 seats short of an absolute majority in the 350-seat Congress but was able to form a single-party minority government.

The composition of the Congress meant that conflicting positions would be articulated vis-à-vis each of the basic cleavages that traditionally divided Spanish society. Economic and labor-related articles of the constitution would pit the leftist PCE and PSOE, which had their own trade unions, against the other four major parties, each of which received some electoral support from business groups. Concerning church–state relations and the monarchy, the traditionally anticlerical and republican PCE and PSOE initially opposed the preferences of the other parties, although the PCE quickly adopted nonconflictual stands on both issues, leaving the Socialists alone in opposing the strongly promonarchical and clerical positions of the AP and UCD. Center–periphery conflicts arrayed the Basque and Catalán nationalist parties against the UCD and the intensely Spanish-nationalist AP, with the Socialists and Communists shifting positions from one relevant constitutional article to the next.

The formal parliamentary phase of the constituent process began with the appointment of a seven-man *ponencia* (drafting subcommittee). The governing UCD had three representatives on the *ponencia,* with one representative each for the PSOE, the AP, the PCE, and the Catalán nationalist Convergència democràtica de Catalunya. The designation of this broadly representative subcommittee was forced on Suárez as the result of pressure from the Socialists. In one of his few lapses of good judgment during the transition, Suárez initially proposed appointing a committee of experts to draft a constitutional text. PSOE leaders argued against this, claiming that it was essential that the drafting of a new constitution include the direct participation of democratically responsible party leaders (see Peces-Barba 1988, pp. 17–22). The Socialists were particularly concerned that this effort include "the presence of the right of Franquist origin on the *ponencia*" (Peces-Barba 1988, p. 20). Even after acceding to the PSOE's demands concerning the appointment of a politically representative committee, it took the form just described only after an important concession by the Socialists. In order to give the Cataláns representation on the *ponencia*, the PSOE gave up one of the two seats initially allocated to it. In the end, the subcommittee still excluded representation of the Basques, an exclusion that had important consequences.

The first round of deliberations by the *ponencia* lasted from late August until mid December. In accord with a proposal made by Miguel Roca, these deliberations were entirely confidential. The importance of this privacy is underscored by the Socialist representative Gregorio Peces-Barba:

> The passage of time has confirmed that this was a wise decision. We could work quietly, with neither interference nor pressures. . . . Thanks to this confidentiality, we were able to write a first draft that, for better or worse, required the agreement of only seven persons. In this respect, it was very important to act with autonomy. (Peces-Barba 1988, p. 33)

High-ranking party officials were usually kept informed of these deliberations and conveyed general guidelines to their representatives, but during this first round of deliberations there was no overt interference. This isolation of the *ponencia* ended in late November, when a draft of the constitution was leaked to the press (by a Socialist deputy, Peces-Barba believes). At that point (in his words), "the problems began." Church dissatisfaction with portions of that draft led to the first instance of interest-group pressures being exerted in the constituent process and ultimately induced the *ponentes* to modify their initial wording.

Interest groups and other political parties were brought more fully into the process in January 1978, following publication of the initial draft. All parties (even those without parliamentary representation) were invited to submit amendments during a twenty-day period, by the end of which well over one thousand amendments had been proposed. The *ponencia* then reconvened to consider those amendments, although one *ponente* later admitted that only about one hundred of them were given serious consideration. During this second round of *ponencia* deliberations, following the mobilization of interest groups and party factions – especially within the UCD – a more conflictual pattern of decision making emerged. The more conservative sectors of the UCD pushed for an informal alliance with Manuel Fraga in introducing a series of amendments (primarily concerning church–state relations) regarded as objectionable by the Socialists. In protest, the Socialist representative walked out and thenceforth boycotted the *ponencia* meetings. He did, however, return in late March to sign the final document produced by the *ponencia*, although he made it clear that portions of the constitutional text were unacceptable. One *ponente* (Manuel Fraga) estimated that by the time the *ponencia* had finished its work, full interparty agreement had been reached concerning about 80 percent of the text. Important differences, however – concerning such matters as divorce, abortion, the death penalty, the electoral law, labor relations, regional autonomy and the role of the church in the education system – remained unresolved.

Prospects for satisfactory resolution of those conflicts did not appear bright when public debate over the constitution began in May in the constitutional committee of the Congress of Deputies. Rather than securing broad agreement among all or most of the significant parties concerning these basic issues, direct conflicts between left and right were decided in the initial deliberations by relatively close votes, in accord with winner-take-all majoritarian principles. As the Communist representative on the *ponencia* explained in an interview:

> At that moment a consensus was very difficult [to achieve] precisely because an open battle had broken out when we entered the public phase. In the first articles of the constitution, we observed with great alarm that the UCD was inclined to make pacts with Alianza popular, and this threatened to tear down everything that we had constructed.

Clearly, enactment of a constitution with the support of a narrow "mechanical majority" of UCD and AP deputies and without the approval of the regionalist or leftist parties would have grave implications for the legitimacy of the new regime. Moreover, the increasingly rancorous tone of the Cortes debate and the disturbingly slow pace of passage of the first two dozen articles (about one a day, which, if maintained throughout all subsequent stages of deliberation in the Congress and Senate, would have required about two years to complete the constituent process), meant that a consensual constitutional document apparently would not be adopted.

A new decision-making style was initiated on May 22, the eve of the committee's deliberations over the potentially explosive article governing the education system. On that night four UCD representatives met with four Socialist deputies at a Madrid restaurant to attempt to resolve their outstanding differences. By the next morning they had reached compromise agreements concerning all the major religious issues (disestablishment, education, divorce, and abortion), labor relations, conscientious objection to military service, and constitutional principles governing the proper role of the state in the economy. Although the Communists and Cataláns did not play direct roles in the negotiations of May 22, they had previously consulted with the UCD and had given their approval to this private bilateral negotiation. As the Communist *ponente*, Jordi Solé Tura, explained, "faced with the danger of a breakdown, we preferred at that moment to enter into the game of nocturnal consensus."

In light of the success of "the night of José Luis" (the name of the restaurant), all serious differences among Socialists, Communists, Centrists, and Catalàns, and, at times, the Basques were dealt with subsequently in private negotiations among party leaders. Thenceforth, floor debates in the Congress and Senate among those parties were brief and perfunctory, and rancorous exchanges were generally avoided. Only the deputies of the Alianza popular and of parties represented by only one or two elected officials were systematically excluded from the so-called politics of consensus. And only the issue of regional autonomy for Euskadi resisted attempts at resolution through this procedure.

In the Senate (where the UCD enjoyed an absolute majority), however, even these agreements began to come unglued. Because of a lapse of UCD party discipline and the totally undisciplined behavior of some the unelected Senators by Royal Designation, nearly all of the first twenty-two articles were altered by the constitutional committee of the Senate. In some instances these changes represented frivolous tinkering with carefully negotiated compromise language. One royal senator, the Nobel Prize–winning novelist José Cela, introduced a series of amendments designed to improve the literary style of the constitution. One of these motions, for example, removed from the list of fundamental principles in Article 1 the phrase "political pluralism"; this was, as Cela explained, "simply because I didn't like it" (*Informaciones*, August 19, 1978). Other changes had more serious implications: Conservative Christian Democrats in the UCD took advantage of their party's lax discipline in the Senate to introduce amendments that reversed the compromise reached with the PSOE on religious issues on May 22. If adopted, these changes could have provoked a rejection of the constitution by the country's second largest party. Fortunately, UCD leaders recognized this danger; they resumed private discussions among the relevant party leaders and imposed greater discipline on their Senate delegation, forcing them to withdraw their amendments. A potential disaster was averted, and the fragile consensus forged in the Congress of Deputies emerged intact.

Outside Euskadi, only a few extremists opposed endorsement of the constitution. Nine right-wing bishops (out of a total of about eighty) spoke out against the constitution, but they were reportedly voted down in the Episcopal Conference by a margin of about seven to one,[9] and the church decided to permit individuals to make up their own minds about accepting it. Five members of the AP delegation in the Congress voted against the constitution and three more abstained, but any negative consequences resulting from this stand affected them as individuals, rather than the political system as a whole. Their opinions clashed directly with those of party leader Manuel Fraga, who secured endorsement of the constitution by the executive committee of the Alianza popular and committed the AP to an active campaign for its ratification in the December referendum. The right-wing dissidents withdrew from the AP, thereby consigning themselves to political oblivion. This schism effectively converted the party to an unambiguously democratic force, committed to playing the game of politics according to the regime's rules. Over the long term, it also played a decisive role in converting former supporters of the Franquist regime into loyal democrats.

The role (or nonrole) of the military in deliberations is worthy of mention. In keeping with precedents excluding the military from an active decision-making role established earlier, they were not consulted during the constituent process. This is not to say that their basic concerns were ignored in drafting the constitutional text. Indeed, Adolfo Suárez consulted with his close collaborator and vice-president, General Manuel Gutiérrez-Mellado, concerning the phrasing of key constitutional articles, with the intention of avoiding language that might provoke an otherwise avoidable negative reaction by the military. Nevertheless, in contrast with the transitions to democracy in Portugal, Brazil, Peru, and Chile, the military in Spain played no institutional role in writing a constitution (see Agüero 1991).

The constitutional agreement of 1978 represented an elite settlement among all politically significant parties outside of Euskadi. No party could claim that it was entirely satisfied with the constitutional text passed by the Cortes on October 31, 1978. Each of the principal protagonists had to give up something during the fifteen months of negotiations, but in the end this crucial document was endorsed by leaders of all except the Basque nationalist parties. This agreement

9 *Informaciones*, November 29, 1978, p. 35.

not only set up representative and governing institutions regarded as legitimate by all significant political elites and their supporting groups, but it also laid to rest many historically divisive issues. All conflicts were resolved concerning the status of the monarchy, and compromises concerning articles dealing with church–state relations, labor relations, the role of the state in the economy, and many others meant that future conflicts over these issues (inevitable in any democracy) could easily be regulated and contained in established institutional channels. In the end, a full procedural consensus was forged among all nationwide parties, from the Communists to the Alianza popular, and among Catalán party elites as well. Only the Basque problem resisted resolution.

The largest Basque nationalist party, the PNV, abstained from the Cortes vote on the constitution, even though (as the leader of the PNV parliamentary delegation, Xabier Arzallus, admitted) the PNV got almost everything it asked for in the course of the negotiations (*Informaciones*, July 24, 1978) The PNV's specific objection to the constitution concerned an "additional disposition" relating to restoration of Basque *fueros* (historic rights). That provision expressed "respect for the historic rights of the [*foral*] territories," whose realization "will be accomplished . . . within the framework of the constitution and the statutes of autonomy." The PNV was particularly opposed to the phrase "within the framework of the constitution," arguing that the *fueros* were historic rights that took precedence over the constitution and that the present constituent elites even lacked the authority to "concede" the restoration of those rights. The UCD was equally vehement in opposing an unmitigated restoration of the *fueros*, because historically they included an implicit acknowledgment of the right to self-determination. This understanding of the *fueros* was shared by many Basque nationalists. As party leader Xabier Arzallus stated at a party rally: "Ancient Basques lived within an ensemble of kingdoms that were later called Spain . . . and as a guarantee that its way of life would be respected, the right of secession was always reserved. We also reserve [that right], be it or not in the constitution" (*Informaciones*, August 9, 1978). These differences could not be resolved. The PNV delegation walked out of the Congress of Deputies just before that body approved the constitution and abstained from the final Cortes votes ratifying that document, and the party campaigned for abstention in the constitutional referendum.

A more radical Basque nationalist alternative was also represented in the Congress of Deputies. Euskadiko Ezkerra Deputy Francisco Letamendía voted against the constitution, and his party campaigned against its ratification in the referendum. "The right to self-determination," Letamendía argued, "is a fundamental democratic right, without which the constitution has no meaning for us. If the Basque people, someday, were to face this alternative, you can be sure that Euskadiko Ezkerra would vote for independence. . . . Euskadi is not a region but, rather, a nation divided into two halves" (Letamendía 1978, p. 2084).

As a result of the "semiloyal" stance of the PNV elite and the antisystem opposition of Euskadiko Ezkerra, less than half of the Basque electorate voted in the December 1978 constitutional referendum (46 percent, compared with a turnout of 68 percent throughout Spain). Only 68.8 percent of those who voted, moreover, cast favorable ballots – some 20 percent less than the national average. In Catalunya, by comparison, the turnout was 68 percent, and the affirmative vote (90.4 percent) exceeded the national average. The PNV's ambiguity toward the new regime and the outright hostility of more extreme Basque nationalists posed a regional challenge to the legitimacy of the new regime. This contributed, in turn, to an atmosphere of increasing tension, violence and uncertainty about the regime's stability.

Spanish and Basque elites had a second opportunity to reconcile their differences during the following year's deliberations over a Basque statute of autonomy. The process of drafting this statute bore a remarkable resemblance to the procedures in writing the Spanish constitution. A draft of this document was first prepared by the assembly of Basque parliamentarians (Euskadi's Cortes delegation). The text that was subsequently submitted to the Cortes was drafted primarily by the PNV and PSOE representatives in that delegation (see Bordegarai and Pastor 1979). Following its presentation to the constitutional committee of the Congress of Deputies, other parties were given the opportunity to file amendments. The most serious threats to the Basque draft were posed by amendments submitted by the UCD, which, as the governing party, was to play the role of defender of the interests of the Spanish state. The UCD's opposition to key provisions gave rise to much pessimism and considerable doubt as to whether a compromise could ever be reached.

In order to make an agreement easier, the UCD returned immediately to the decision-making style that had helped secure consensual support for the constitution the year before: Seemingly interminable rounds of private negotiations were held between the top leaders of the UCD and the PNV at the prime minister's residence. During decisive stages of those discussions, the prime minister, Suárez, and the PNV party head, Carlos Garaicoechea, would themselves conduct negotiations without the attendance of their respective advisers.

These private discussions were held simultaneously with the public deliberations of the constitutional committee of the Congress. Following the opening sessions of that committee, however, no efforts were made to conduct serious negotiations in that open forum: Debate was often intentionally delayed while deputies awaited the arrival of the latest package of agreements from the Moncloa Palace. The end result of this procedure was an agreement between the UCD and the PNV that (despite some grumbling about having been left out of the deliberations) was accepted by all the major parliamentary parties. Even Euskadiko Ezkerra (which by this time had undergone a schism) endorsed the statute and urged a yes vote in the referendum to follow. Only the more extremist Herri Batasuna (much of whose leadership had splintered off from Euskadiko Ezkerra) continued its opposition to all agreements with the Spanish state that did not recognize the right to self-determination, complete amnesty for ETA prisoners, and the immediate removal of Spanish police from the region.

Since enactment of the Basque autonomy statute in 1979, the three Basque nationalist parties have taken three distinctly different stands. Euskadiko Ezkerra has become a loyal competitor in the Spanish democratic regime. One of the party's top leaders stated in a 1983 interview that the EE's endorsement of the autonomy statute implied endorsement of the Spanish constitution, to which the party's representatives swear loyalty. Euskadiko Ezkerra has consistently supported Basque and Spanish government institutions and has conformed with the democratic rules of the game. The most important manifestation of this is its renunciation of terrorist violence. Even though many of the party's elite had been involved with ETA activities in the past (particularly with the political–military faction, ETAp-m), they unequivocally concluded that with the securing of a reasonable statute of autonomy, all terrorist violence should cease. Before securing autonomy, one party leader explained, in an 1983 interview, that ETA's violence played a useful role in inducing the Spanish state to make concessions: "But once the majority of the Basque people demonstrated their desire to accept new rules of the game, [ETA] lost its *raison d'être* and now has no role to perform." In addition, the structural integration of EE elites with their Spanish counterparts increased significantly, as revealed in the merger of the EE with a large segment defecting from the Spanish Communist party.

Herri Batasuna maintains an antisystem stance, and supports ETA's paramilitary efforts to secure independence from Spain. It rejected both the Spanish constitution and the Basque autonomy statute and, until 1989, refused to permit its elected deputies to take their seats in the Madrid parliament. It refused to accept the legitimacy of the constitutional monarchy. One party leader (one of the more moderate members of the party elite!) stated in a 1983 interview that the only political changes that have taken place in Madrid since the death of Franco was a "democratization of fascism – the same fascism as before." Structural integration with Spanish elites is nonexistent, and extreme animosity and suspicion characterize the HB's attitudes toward the Spanish state. One HB official even contended, in a 1983 interview, that the Spanish bourgeoisie was peddling hard drugs to Basque youth as a means of diverting them from involvement in politics. Another claimed that Spanish politicians rejoiced over the devastating floods of 1983, because they weakened the resolve of Basque workers to oppose the government's industrial policies.

The PNV has maintained a semiloyal stance, although its antagonism toward the Spanish state has softened since 1985. The party's elite claims that it "obeys" the Spanish constitution, as its deputies must swear before taking their seats at the beginning of each parliamentary session in Madrid, but denies that this represents an endorsement of that document. (As described by an Herri Batasuna leader, "The PNV says that it does so for tactical reasons – that it swears to obey a constitution that it, itself, rejects. We don't obey the constitution, nor do we swear to do so.") The party's president rejected a suggestion, in a 1983 interview, that the PNV's endorsement of the autonomy statute implied endorsement of the constitution. And a PNV deputy flatly stated that the party would never support the Spanish constitution "because it is a Spanish constitution." The party's ambiguous stand on the constitution is also reflected in a studied ambiguity regarding independence from Spain. As a high-ranking party leader "explained" in a 1983 interview:

> I would say that my people are *independentistas*, and the thesis of my party is that of forming a Basque state. Well, this happens all the time – everybody also aspires to be rich. One can aspire to many other things in life. But I think my people are very realistic. I have no intention of forming a Basque state . . . I think people are reasonable about this. Now, if I were to say "I am a Spaniard and I renounce Basque independence," they'd throw me out of the party.

This tortuous ambiguity has occasionally been accompanied by semiloyal behavior. The PNV boycotted all sessions of the Cortes from January until September 1980 in a dispute with the government over the transfer of governmental functions from central to regional government institutions. And until the late 1980s, it refused to condemn ETA's use of violence. When I used the word "terrorism" in an interview with a PNV leader in 1979, he angrily shot back: "I perfectly remember French patriots who fought against Pétain. Then, they were called terrorists. Well, the Vichy government called them terrorists. Today they are patriots. Hence, everything is relative. They speak of the terrorists of ETA, but I would never speak of ETA terrorism."

Since 1985 there has been evidence of a gradual shift on the part of the PNV. As suggested earlier in this chapter, it is likely that formation of a regional coalition government with the PSOE, beginning in January 1985, has initiated a process of "elite convergence." Whatever may be the cause, it is notable that the Basque government condemned ETA for a terrorist attack, for the first time, just two months after the coalition's formation. Since then, rancorous exchanges between Basque and Spanish political leaders have become less frequent, and cooperation between the two governments against ETA violence has increased (see Shabad 1986). Whether the signing of a document in January 1990, pledging respect for the constitution, represents an abandonment of the party's former semiloyal stance remains to be seen.

Explaining the two Spanish cases

Before an elite settlement can take place, there must exist recognizable elites with the authority to make binding commitments on behalf of their respective clienteles and supportive organizations. The essence of an elite settlement is a bargain among elites that their respective supporters will accept. In this respect, some minimal level of organization of groups opposing an authoritarian regime is a prerequisite for successful democratic consolidation.

The uneven authoritarianism that characterized the final decade of the Franquist regime, coupled with the widely anticipated demise of the aged dictator, facilitated both the transition to democracy and the elite transformations that consolidated it. During the late 1960s and early 1970s, clandestine trade union organizations were formed on shop floors, and clusters of student activists organized various opposition protoparties in anticipation of a post-Franco era. The largest trade union and the largest clandestine political party were Communist, and both had established leadership structures. The degree of institutionalization of the PCE and its trade union ally, the Comisiones obreras, was of considerable importance during the course of the transition. The discipline of the party's militants meant that just as the party's leaders had mobilized them in opposition to the regime, so too could they demobilize them to give Suárez's efforts at democratization a chance. Similarly, the authority of the Comisiones obreras leaders enabled them to implement effectively the terms of the Pacts of Moncloa, at a time when economic destabilization could have placed considerable stress on the political system and when the establishment of trust and mutual confidence among rival elites was crucial. The Socialist party and its affiliated trade union, the UGT, more hastily attempted to reorganize themselves as the death of Franco approached, resulting in internal instability that undermined Felipe González's leadership position from time to time (see Gunther 1986b; Share 1989). Nevertheless, González was able to "deliver the goods," in part because of his personal charisma, in part because of the party's status and legitimacy stemming from its century-long tradition, and in part because the PCE's moderation meant that he could engage in negotiations with the UCD without being threatened by "outbidding" from a party on his left flank. In short, the emergence of two large opposition parties in the final days of the Franquist regime greatly facilitated the bargaining processes that followed, making it possible to demobilize activists in order to stabilize the political environment.

In contrast, both the Second Republic and Euskadi in the 1970s were characterized by fragmented and unstable elite structures. In the Second Republic, more than twenty parties obtained parliamentary representation in each of its three legislatures, with at least eleven parties in each session having ten or more seats. In none of those legislatures did a single party control more than 23 percent of the seats. This extreme fragmentation led to government instability and reinforced the intransigence so characteristic of important Republican elites. Sartori has argued that "beyond a certain limit, the more the number of parties increases, the more their identification becomes a problem; and the remedy to which each party has recourse in order to be perceived as distinct is a punctilious ideological and principled rigidity" (Sartori 1972, p. 159). This proposition describes the rancorous and inflexible interactions among contending elites in the Second Republic. It also fits the Basque political system in recent years, in which elites have been fragmented along several lines: Basque nationalist versus nationwide Spanish parties, left versus right, and parliamentary versus clandestine revolutionary groups. No single set of Basque elites has had the authority necessary to make binding commitments, and Basque elites contemplating concessions to the Spanish state have risked being "outbid" by more extreme groups, thus endangering their leadership positions (as shown in the preceding interview excerpt). Thus, one important variable affecting prospects for successful democratic consolidation appears to be the recognized and secure leadership of a relatively cohesive (or at least not excessively fragmented) opposition.

This crucial difference between Basque elites and their Spanish counterparts produced an entirely different set of political dynamics in Euskadi throughout the transition (see Malefakis 1982). At the national level, the democratization process following the appointment of Suárez as prime minister in July 1976 was characterized by restrained partisanship and private negotiations at the elite level, concomitant with demobilization at the mass level. The late-Franquist and post-Franco periods in Euskadi, in contrast, involved extraordinarily high levels of mass mobilization over an extended period of time: Our 1979 survey data revealed that an astounding 40 percent of Basque respondents had personally participated in protest demonstrations. The principal arena for "dialogue" between government and opposition was the streets. The progressive fragmentation and polarization of elite structures (with Basque nationalist parties experiencing repeated schisms and with ETA itself dividing and subdividing throughout this period) meant that no single set of Basque leaders had the ability to make binding agreements on behalf of all politically active Basque nationalists. In marked contrast with the "politics of consensus" in Madrid, the ultimate consequence of the dialectic of rocks, clubs, and tear gas that dominated the transition process in Euskadi was extreme polarization. Between 1976 and 1979, the portion of the Basque electorate placing itself near the center of the political spectrum fell from 39 percent to 20 percent; the level of class consciousness and polarization increased;[10] electoral support for the most extreme revolutionary-nationalist party, Herri Batasuna, steadily increased, and HB voters became more exclusionary in their national self-identification and more uniform in their support for Basque independence. Likewise, hostility toward the army, the police, and "big business" (all symbols of the Spanish capitalist order) was much greater in Euskadi than in any other part of Spain (see Linz 1986). Although one might speculate that the increasing Basque hostility toward ETA in the late 1980s augured well for an ultimate decrease in support for terrorist violence, the fact that expressions of support for independence among Basque survey respondents more than doubled between 1976 and 1979 and have remained more or less stable at about 25 percent of the population since then suggests that this divisive regional conflict is far from over. In addition, there is

10 The percentage of Basque respondents stating that they consciously identified with a social class increased from 48 percent in our 1979 survey to 63 percent in 1982, which is the highest level of any region in Spain. Our 1982 survey of 5,469 Spaniards was conducted by DATA, S.A., according to an identical sample design as that used in 1979. This survey was made possible through generous financial support from the Stiftung Volkswagenwerk and National Science Foundation grant no. SES–8309162.

evidence that acceptance of violence as a legitimate form of political activity has become a distinguishing and possibly durable feature of Basque political culture.[11]

Why did the Basque region follow such a drastically different transition trajectory from that of the rest of Spain? One study of Basque politics (Clark 1984) concludes that this cannot be attributed to any mass-level political–cultural variables and argues, instead, that patterns of interaction between the Basques and the Spanish state were the principal cause. The study contends that polarization and violence in Euskadi were responses to the previous repression of Basques (especially the Basque language and cultural symbols) under the Franquist regime, as well as reactions to the police repression of Basque nationalists during the transition to democracy. I would add that police repression is a predictable response to pressure for political change exerted largely through popular mobilization accompanied by high levels of political violence. Such processes set in motion a self-reinforcing cycle of violence, in which action by one side engenders desires for revenge by the other. It is noteworthy that this was clearly acknowledged by ETA tacticians, who regarded it as an officially endorsed strategic option at various stages in the struggle against their Spanish state. According to the "action–repression–action spiral" strategy, each repressive act by Madrid had to be answered by an even more provocative act, eventually producing a massive conflagration in the course of which prospects for secession would be increased. Functioning as an agent provocateur, ETA pushed the transition to democracy in Euskadi along a path markedly different from that followed in the rest of Spain. I agree with Clark's depressing conclusion: This process may have been initiated by the independent acts of political elites, but once set in motion, it was probably no longer under their control. Consequently, "ETA is caught in the grip of forces that are created by insurgent violence itself and that tend to make the violence self-sustaining, almost apart from the wishes of the participants or the objective conditions that led to the insurgency" (Clark 1984, p. 278).

This important set of variables thus requires the structuring of opposition elites. We must also take into consideration the elite configurations within the outgoing authoritarian regime. Here, again, we

11 A 1984 DATA study of Spanish young people, for example, found that in Euskadi fully 44 percent of those interviewed stated that the use of violence was an acceptable means of defending Basque national interests, and 48 percent stated that it was a legitimate means of addressing labor disputes; only 16 percent and 12 percent, respectively, denied its acceptability as a means of addressing these issues. See Francisco Orizo et al., *Juventud Española 1984* (Madrid: Ediciones SM, 1985), p. 406.

find that uneven authoritarianism under Franco facilitated the emergence within the regime itself of elite dispositions conducive to an eventual elite settlement. Because there was no clearly defined regime ideology, the apparatus of the state could be infiltrated by individuals holding a variety of values and political objectives. The emergence of an Adolfo Suárez or Manuel Fraga or Fernando Abril meant that individuals with reformist intentions were positioned to negotiate the regime out of existence. An ideologically unified elite, in contrast, might well have had no intention of democratizing and thereby would have to be displaced through force. Instead, the "limited pluralism" of the Franquist regime made possible an evolutionary path to democracy (see Linz 1970).

Procedural variables

The processes through which negotiations were undertaken were also significant. Other things being equal, private negotiations among a relatively small number of elites, but including all politically significant factions, are most conducive to acceptable compromise agreements. Decision making is easier when the number of participants is reasonably small. This has been demonstrated by numerous experiments in social psychology, in which the number of participants per se has a significant impact on the capacity of groups to make decisions. The optimum size for reaching collective decisions appears to be about six.[12] Larger groups tend to dissolve into debating societies and reach decisions only with great difficulty. Thus, the small numbers of negotiators at crucial stages in the Spanish constituent process (the seven-member *ponençia*, the eight-man dinner party on "the night of José Luis," and the several small teams of negotiators in the Moncloa Palace deliberations over the Basque autonomy statute) appear to have been propitious.

The number of potential participants in such negotiations is partly a function of political-group organization in the final stages of an authoritarian regime, but it is also a function of electoral laws that translate popular support for groups into representative delegations in Parliament. Electoral systems that excessively fragment party systems may impede negotiation efforts by putting too many cooks in the kitchen. But at the other extreme, electoral systems that manufacture "artificial majorities" may contribute to the belief that com-

12 See B. P. Indik, "Organization Size and Member Participation," paper presented at the meeting of the American Psychological Association, New York City, September 1961; A. P. Hare, "A Study of Interaction and Consensus in Different Sized Groups," *American Psychological Review*, no. 17 (1985): 261–7; and R. Marriot, "Size of Working Groups and Output," *Occupational Psychology*, no. 23 (1949): 47–57.

promise is unnecessary, enabling elites to impose their preferences on opponents in a majoritarian, winner-take-all fashion, even though they represent only a small plurality of the population. This occurred under the Second Republic, whose electoral law so distorted public opinion in allocating parliamentary seats that it created the illusion within the Cortes of an overwhelming mandate in favor of the policy proposals of the victorious coalition, when, in fact, that coalition had received only a bare plurality of the popular vote. In this respect, the electoral law of Spain's current democracy appears to be optimal, insofar as it somewhat overrepresents the two largest groups nationwide and eliminates the smallest groups, but it does so without grossly distorting the distribution of opinion among the Spanish electorate. Adolfo Suárez was well aware of the dangers inherent in an artificial majority, and he expressed his appreciation for the existing electoral law in a 1983 interview: "If I had had an absolute majority in the Parliament, I probably would not have succeeded in writing the constitution I wanted – a constitution regarded as valid by everybody. There was a dogmatic attempt inside my own party to impose" a more partisan and one-sided constitution on Spanish society.

Privacy was also an important ingredient in the largely successful deliberations over the Spanish constitution and the Basque autonomy statute. Other things being equal, discussion in public rather than private forums contributes to the unwillingness of participants to make concessions. Because a principal function of party elites is to articulate the conflicting demands of their supporters, any abandonment of those demands in public may alienate the elites' respective clienteles and lead them to withdraw their support. Fearing this, party leaders engaged in public negotiations will be inclined toward intransigence, thus precluding the possibility of effective compromise. Deliberations in public forums may, in fact, provide incentives for individuals to engage in demagogic posturing as a means of attracting supporters or advancing their own personal careers. Indeed, in each of the phases of the constituent deliberations of 1977–9 that took place behind closed doors, progress was made toward establishing consensus; and on every occasion when real decisions were being made in open forums (e.g., in the *ponencia* following publication of the constitutional text and mobilization of party factions, in the constitutional committee hearings of May 1978, in the Senate deliberations of August 1978, and in the Cortes deliberations over the Basque autonomy statute in 1979), agreements tended to come unglued; majoritarian principles displaced consensualism; and a polarization between opposing camps became apparent. This was also true of the 1931 deliberations over the constitution of the Second Republic, when decision making in public culminated in the enactment of a partisan constitution whose legitimacy was immediately challenged by the losing side. As one participant described it, "The parliamentary committees went beyond the proposals of the government, and the plenary sessions of the Cortes accentuated the sectarianism of the committees. . . . In [the decisive] session of the constituent Cortes, the seed of discord was sown, which would end in a confrontation between brothers with weapons in their hands" (Gil Robles 1968, pp. 45, 54).

Including representatives of all "politically significant" groups in the negotiating arena also appears to be important for several reasons:

1. All demands coming from significant groups must be adequately articulated, so that they can be taken into consideration in reaching a compromise. Exclusion of any important group may artificially shift the decision away from the true center of gravity of preferences concerning important issues.
2. Participation in group negotiations serves to convince representatives of the relevant groups that a compromise solution is the only way to attain even some of their initial demands without incurring significant long-term costs.
3. Direct involvement in face-to-face negotiations that are even partially successful socializes the participants into adopting more favorable attitudes toward the group and the outcome of the group process. This provides an important opportunity for forging structural integration among once-antagonistic elites. Moreover, as a result of pressures toward cognitive consistency, active participation in the group process predisposes individuals to defend more vigorously those agreements reached by the group, thus making more likely the endorsement of these agreements by their respective followers (see Abelson et al., 1968).
4. Perhaps most important, the inclusion of all significant elites in the decision-making process disposes them to believe that they have a stake in the new political system. Conversely, exclusion leads groups to deny the legitimacy of the system and to reject its decisions.

In accord with these propositions, it is important to note that the only significant blocs of deputies who did not vote in favor of the constitution were those of the PNV (which had not been represented in the *ponencia)* and about half those of Alianza popular (which had been excluded from all the nocturnal negotiations of the "politics of consensus"). PNV Deputy Kepa Sodupe said about the lack of Basque support for the constitution: "Most of the difficulties that appear now resulted from the exclusion of the PNV during the ten months in which the constitution was elaborated, whereas all the other groups had more opportunities to make themselves heard, to participate in the consensus and to decide by voting" (*Informaciones*, June 20, 1978).

In addition, involvement in face-to-face negotiations of this kind may forge friendships among individuals previously suspicious of and hostile toward one another. All of those *ponentes* I have interviewed or who have published memoirs (five of the seven) and several of the individuals participating in the "José Luis" negotiations agreed that warm, close personal relations were an unanticipated consequence of their months of work on the constitution. This contributed to greater "structural integration" among Spanish elites at the national level, contributing to restrained partisanship ever since.

The principle of inclusiveness, however, clashes somewhat with the principles of privacy and small group size in negotiations. If virtually all groups are represented in the negotiations, the number of participants can easily swell to unmanageable proportions. Hence, the awkward phrase "all politically significant groups" may be a necessary component of our theoretical formulation, even though it represents an imprecise "fudge factor." However, given that by their very nature, ideal types are so demanding that no real-world cases fully meet all of their criteria, this lack of precision is methodologically defensible.

Inclusion of all politically significant groups in negotiations may be impossible, even undesirable, for other reasons as well. Relations between civilian politicians and the military pose a particular dilemma in this regard. In a democratic system, according to our ideal-type definition, there should be no privileged elite that is not electorally responsible that possesses reserved powers or that can veto policy decisions made by elected officials. Indeed, Agüero (1990) and others argue persuasively that one of the most crucial tasks to be performed in democratic transitions (especially in Latin America) is the extrication of the military from civilian politics. In a true democracy, the policymaking role of the military should be unequivocally restricted to the defense and national-security sectors, and even there, the supremacy of civilian government ministers must be respected. Paradoxically, Francisco Franco contributed to the success of the democratic transition by gradually extricating the Spanish military from domestic politics: Whereas in the early years of the Franquist regime, a substantial number of civilian ministries were headed by military officers, by the 1970s only the defense ministries had military ministers (see Gunther 1980, pp. 20–3; Linz 1970, p. 267; de Miguel 1975). At the outset of the transition, Suárez and his collaborators thus confronted an awkward choice. As we have argued, inclusion of elites in negotiations over democratic transitions can coopt the participants in those talks and help secure their loyalty to the new regime. But at the same time, inclusion of military elites in negotiations regarding the structure of a civilian democratic regime would imply that the military had a legitimate role to play in domestic politics. In short, such inclusion might have implicitly redefined the role of the military, increasing its involvement in domestic politics in the future and undoing the good deed that Franco had inadvertently performed on behalf of the new regime.

In the most exhaustive study of the Spanish military during the transition, Agüero (1991) contends that at no point during the transition was the military permitted to enter into real negotiations regarding the course of important political developments. At most, they were merely "informed" by Suárez of his intentions, and much of the time found themselves reacting to *faits accomplis*. This fits with statements by Suárez in a 1983 interview, clearly indicating that in his view, the role of military officers was to obey, not to become active participants in political decision-making processes. Through his own behavior and that of Vice-President General Gutiérrez Mellado, this restricted role for the military was institutionalized. Under Suárez's presidency, the single exception to this principle of not acquiescing to military demands regarding political matters was the noninclusion under the terms of a general amnesty of military officers convicted of belonging to a clandestine organization (the Unión militar democrática) – and this, in some respects, may be regarded as an internal military matter rather than a broader political question.

The military's exclusion from participation in important political decisions distinguishes the Spanish transition to democracy from the Portuguese and several recent Latin American transitions examined in this book. In those cases the military had been a dominant actor either within the outgoing authoritarian regime (Argentina, Brazil, Chile, Uruguay, and Peru) or during the transition to democracy (Portugal) and therefore had to feature prominently in the decisions relating to founding a new regime. Only the regime of General Franco could be properly regarded as a civilian authoritarian system, thus making possible the exclusion of the military from key decision-making processes. But even in the case of Spain, one might argue that the exclusion of the military had some negative consequences. Although this course of action was consistent with the military's political neutrality and subordination to civilian control that the founders of the new regime clearly wished to institutionalize, it also led to a dominant military attitude that, at best, could be described as semiloyal.

The events of February 23, 1981, clearly reveal the risks inherent in this strategy. Reactionary critics of democracy in the Valencia military district, some segments of the paramilitary Civil Guard, and the strategically located armored division at Brunete rose in revolt against what they regarded as a breakdown of authority under the rapidly collapsing leadership of Adolfo Suárez and the UCD. There is considerable evidence that a significant number of other regional military commanders were also part of a conspiracy against the new regime. They were not dissuaded from supporting the uprising out of loyalty to the new regime or any deep-seated democratic values, which were largely absent at the upper and middle levels of the officer corps. Instead, only loyalty to the king and the absence of support from civilian politicians convinced the other regional commanders to keep their troops in their barracks and, over the long term, to reconcile themselves to the new democracy.

In this regard, important procedural features of the Spanish "model" of democratic transition proved to be crucial. Institutional continuity in the chain of command was guaranteed by the selection by none other than Francisco Franco of Juan Carlos as king, head of state, and commander in chief. Several public statements by Franco (including his last testament, read on television after his death by his friend and prime minister, Arias Navarro) asked his supporters to give Juan Carlos "the same affection and loyalty that you have afforded me, and the same support and collaboration that I have had" (Powell 1991, p. 120). This "backward legitimacy" (Di Palma 1980) was not undermined by the transition process itself. Suárez's strategy unfolded within the institutions and in accord with the rules of the authoritarian regime, and he went to great efforts to secure support for the monarchy from traditionally republican political groups from the very earliest stages of the transition. In the end, the unquestioned legitimacy of the king was essential to putting down the 1981 rebellion, as he personally ordered each of the regional military commanders not to support the coup and to "maintain the constitutional order under the current legal order" (Powell 1991, p. 304).

As argued earlier, the absence of support from any political party – and in particular, the dramatic (if not melodramatic) display of democratic loyalty by Manuel Fraga, unquestioned leader of the Spanish right – was also crucial to thwarting the coup and maintaining regime stability. In this sense, and as hypothesized in Chapter 1, the elite consensual unity among all nationwide parties secured between 1977 and 1979 served to make the new democratic regime resilient and capable of surviving even the most severe challenges. The stabilizing influence of the earlier elite settlement was further strengthened by the expansion of the scope of consensual unity that followed the 1981 coup attempt. In the aftermath of this attempt's failure (which had scored a startling tactical success in its early stages) and in the face of solid regime support from all nationwide parties,[13] support within the military for an authoritarian alternative collapsed. And as the older generation of officers trained in Franco's military academies gives way to newer cohorts of military elites, nostalgia for the authoritarian past can be expected to disappear altogether.

Elite norms and values

Although these procedural aspects of elite settlements are of considerable significance, a proper understanding of successful efforts to achieve elite consensus cannot ignore the basic values, historical memories, and behavioral styles of individual members of the political elite. Even though we must take care to avoid tautological arguments regarding these kinds of variables, we can say in general that negotiations involving pragmatic political leaders, whose historical memories lead them to perceive potential threats to stability and who place great value on achieving stable democracy, are more likely to lead to an elite settlement than will negotiations among dogmatic individuals, who are unaware of the fragility of the system or who have no overriding desire to establish a stable democracy.

There is evidence that the relative pragmatism of individuals selected to participate in the crucial negotiations regarding the constitution of 1978 was explicitly considered. With regard to the *ponencia*, for example, the Socialists and Communists chose as their respective representatives Gregorio Peces-Barba and Jordi Solé Tura, both of whom were regarded as among the most moderate and pragmatic members of their parties; Cataláns were represented by Miguel Roca i Junyent, who subsequently acquired a reputation for close collaboration with the UCD government in Madrid; and having exhibited symptoms of dogmatism, rigidity, and sectarianism, the UCD *ponente* Miguel Rodríguez Herrero de Miñón was removed from the UCD's negotiating team at a critical point in the negotiations (the "night of José Luis") and temporarily replaced by the more pragmatic José Pérez Llorca. It is also noteworthy that the dynamic and strong-willed AP representative, Manuel Fraga Iribarne, was systematically excluded from the nocturnal negotiations of the "politics of consensus" in order to facilitate compromise among the other parties. Finally, one factor that perhaps contributed to the failure of the last-minute negotiations

13 The extent of support for the regime was most apparent in the massive street marches that took place throughout the country on February 27. The symbolism of Manuel Fraga walking arm-in-arm with Marcelino Camacho (leader of the Communist trade union, the Comisiones obreras) in one such demonstration was captured in a now-famous photo published by newspapers throughout Spain.

between the UCD and the PNV in July 1978 was the dogmatism and rigidity of the PNV's representative, Xabier Arzallus.[14]

Historical memories of the suffering caused by the civil war and Franquist authoritarianism were also clearly relevant to the Spanish elite settlement. Virtually all of the constituent elites of 1978 were keenly aware of the origins of the civil war and the role played by the 1931 constituent process per se in bringing it about. In their speeches before the committee and plenary sessions of the Cortes and in their writings and public utterances, the leaders of all four major Spanish parties made innumerable references to that historic conflict and to their awareness of what Santiago Carrillo described as "the dangers that menace our society" (*Informaciones*, December 5, 1978). For example, as Emilio Attard Alonso, president of the constitutional committee of the Congress of Deputies, stated during the first week of his committee's deliberations, "We are fully conscious that the dialectical undertakings of 1931 began in a quarrel and ended in civil war" (*Informaciones*, May 9, 1978). And Adolfo Suárez observed in a 1984 interview that his greatest concern following the death of Franco was the possibility of another civil war.

Historical memories do not, however, invariably produce moderation in political attitudes and behavior. History can be used in efforts to counsel restraint, but it can also be used to reawaken old hatreds, to rekindle old passions; it can be used to justify either appeals for national reconciliation or calls for revenge. How history is recalled and invoked probably depends on the individual in question, particularly the extent to which his or her personal experiences have been unambiguously unpleasant. In this regard, the elites who most vigorously exerted a moderating influence in the democratization process were older Communists, many of whom had been jailed, tortured, or exiled during the Franco regime. Memories of previous, costly conflicts thus seems to have been important in convincing decision-making elites that the creation of a stable democracy was vastly more important than revenge or the narrow pursuit of partisan interests.

A review of the Spanish transition to democracy suggests one final variable that confounds systematic analysis – luck. A different series of events would have transpired if the ultraconservative prime minister (and close friend of Franco) Luis Carrero Blanco had not been assassinated in 1973; if the term of the president of the Cortes and of

14 Similarly, it has been argued that one reason for the failure of the 1931 constituent process was the widespread desire among key elites to preserve ideological purity and to reject political compromise as a betrayal of principle (Payne 1970, pp. 85–91).

the Council of the Realm had not expired at the time of Franco's death (enabling Juan Carlos to appoint to those key posts his former tutor and close collaborator, Torcuato Fernández-Miranda); if Adolfo Suárez had not replaced as prime minister the less flexible Carlos Arias Navarro; if the PSOE had been headed by the maximalist Luis Gómez Llorente rather than the moderate Felipe González; if Silva or Fernández de la Mora (both of whom voted against the constitution) instead of Fraga had been dominant in the AP; if Santiago Carrillo had not led his party away from Stalinism and toward Eurocommunism; if it had been Juan Carlos who had been accidentally shot and killed by his brother, rather than the other way around; or if King Juan Carlos had behaved like his grandfather, Alfonso XIII. Implicit in this analysis is the observation that elite settlements are highly contingent events, requiring the right circumstances and the right people in the right place at the right time. This is to say that settlements are eminently *political* events.

References

Abelson, Robert P., Elliot Aronson, William J. McGuire, Theodore Newcomb, Milton Rosenberg, and Percy Tannenbaum. 1968. *Theories of Cognitive Consistency*. Chicago: Rand McNally.

Agüero, Felipe. 1990. "Democratic Consolidation and the Military in Southern Europe and Latin America." Paper presented at SSRC conference, The Politics of Democratic Consolidation in Southern Europe, Rome, December 14–15.

1991. "The Assertion of Civilian Supremacy in Post-Authoritarian Contexts: Spain in Comparative Perspective." Ph.D. diss., Duke University.

Bordegarai, Kepa, and Robert Pastor. 1979. *Estatuto vasco*. San Sebastián: Ediciones Vascas.

Calvo Sotelo, Leopoldo. 1990. *Memoria viva de la transición*. Barcelona: Plaza & Janes.

Carr, Raymond, and Juan Pablo Fusi. 1979. *Spain: From Dictatorship to Democracy*. London: Allen & Unwin.

Clark, Robert P. 1984. *The Basque Insurgents*. Madison: University of Wisconsin Press.

Di Palma, Giuseppe. 1980. "Founding Coalitions in Southern Europe: Legitimacy and Hegemony." *Government and Opposition* 15: 162–89.

Gillespie, Richard. 1989. *The Spanish Socialist Party: A History of Factionalism*. Oxford: Clarendon Press.

Gilmour, David. 1985. *The Transformation of Spain: From Franco to the Constitutional Monarchy*. London: Quartet Books.

Gil Robles, José María. 1968. *No fue posible la paz*. Barcelona: Ariel.

Gómez Llorente, Luis. 1978. Statement before the constitutional committee. In Cortes españolas, *Diario de sesiones del congreso de los diputados: Comisión de asuntos constitucionales y libertades públicas*, May 11, pp. 2195–7.

Gunther, Richard. 1980. *Public Policy in a No-Party State: Spanish Planning and Budgeting in the Twilight of the Franquist Era*. Berkeley and Los Angeles: University of California Press.

1986a. "The Parties in Opposition." In *The Politics of Democratic Spain*, ed. Stanley G. Payne. Chicago: Chicago Council on Foreign Relations.

1986b. "The Spanish Socialist Party." In *The Politics of Democratic Spain*, ed. Stanley G. Payne. Chicago: Chicago Council on Foreign Relations.

1989. "Electoral Laws, Party Systems and Elites: The Case of Spain." *American Political Science Review* 83: 835–58.

Gunther, Richard, and Roger A. Blough. 1981. "Religious Conflict and Consensus in Spain: A Tale of Two Constitutions." *World Affairs* 143: 366–412.

Gunther, Richard, Giacomo Sani, and Goldie Shabad. 1986. *Spain After Franco: The Making of a Competitive Party System*. Berkeley and Los Angeles: University of California Press.

Hare, A. P. 1952. "A Study of Interaction and Consensus in Different Sized Groups." *American Psychological Review* 17: 261–7.

Huneeus, Carlos. 1985. *La Unión de centro democrático y la transición a la democracia en España*. Madrid: Centro de investigaciones sociológicas.

Indik, B. P. 1961. "Organization Size and Member Participation." Paper presented at the meeting of the American Psychological Association, New York City, September.

Karl, Terry. 1986. "Petroleum and Political Pacts: The Transition to Democracy in Venezuela." In *Transitions from Authoritarian Rule: Latin America*, ed. Guillermo O'Donnell, Philippe C. Schmitter, and Laurence Whitehead. Baltimore: Johns Hopkins University Press.

Letamendía, Francisco. 1978. Speech before constitutional committee. May 8. Published in Cortes españolas, *Diario de sesiones del congreso de los diputados: Comisión de asuntos constitucionales y libertades públicas*, vol. 60.

Linz, Juan J. 1970. "From Falange to Movimiento-Organización: The Spanish Single Party and the Franco Regime." In *Authoritarian Politics in Modern Society: The Dynamics of Established One-Party Systems*, ed. Samuel Huntington and Clement Moore. New York: Basic Books.

1972. "Tradition and Modernity in Spain." Unpublished manuscript.

1986. *Conflicto en Euskadi*. Madrid: Espasa Calpe.

1987. "Innovative Leadership in the Transition to Democracy and a New Democracy: The Case of Spain." Paper presented at the conference, Innovative Leadership and International Politics, Leonard Davis Institute for International Relations, Hebrew University, Jerusalem, June 8–10.

1990a. "La Transición a la democracia en España en perspectiva comparada." Unpublished manuscript.

1990b. "Transition to Democracy: A Comparative Perspective." Unpublished manuscript.

Linz, Juan J., Manuel Gómez-Reino, Francisco Andrés Orizo, and Darío Vila Carro. 1981. *Informe sociológico sobre el cambio político en España, 1975–1981*. Madrid: Editorial Euramérica.

Malefakis, Edward. 1982. "Spain and Its Francoist Heritage." In *From Dictatorship to Democracy*, ed. John Herz. Westport, CT: Greenwood Press.

Maravall, José María. 1981. *La Política de la transición*. Madrid: Taurus.

Marriot, R. 1949. "Size of Working Groups and Output." *Occupational Psychology* 23: 47–57.

de Miguel, Amando. 1975. *Sociología del franquismo*. Barcelona: Editorial Euros.

Mori, Arturo. 1933. *Crónica de las Cortes constituyentes de la segunda república española*. Madrid: M. Aguilar.

Morlino, Leonardo, and José Ramón Montero. 1990. "Confidence and Democracy in Southern Europe." Paper delivered at SSRC conference, Problems of Democratic Consolidation, Instituto Juan March de estudios e investigaciones, Madrid, July 6–8.

Moxon-Browne, Edward. 1989. *Political Change in Spain*. London: Routledge & Kegan Paul.

O'Donnell, Guillermo, Philippe C. Schmitter, and Laurence Whitehead, eds. 1986. *Transitions from Authoritarian Rule*. 4 vols. Baltimore: Johns Hopkins University Press.

Oneto, José. 1985. *Anatomía de un cambio de régimen*. Barcelona: Plaza y Janés.

Orizo, Francisco A., Manuel Gómez-Reino, and Darío Vila Carro. 1985. *Juventud española 1984*. Madrid: Ediciones SM.

Palacio Atard, Vicente. 1989. *Juàn Carlos I y el advenimiento de la democracia*. Madrid: Espasa Calpe.

Payne, Stanley G. 1970. *The Spanish Revolution*. New York: Norton.

1984. *Spanish Catholicism*. Madison: University of Wisconsin Press.

1987. *The Franco Regime: 1936–1975*. Madison: University of Wisconsin Press.

Peces-Barba Martínez, Gregorio. 1988. *La Elaboración de la constitución de 1978*. Madrid: Centro de estudio constitucionales.

Powell, Charles T. 1991. *El Piloto del cambio: El Rey, la Monarquía y la transición a la democracia*. Barcelona: Planeta.

Preston, Paul. 1986. *The Triumph of Democracy in Spain*. London: Methuen.

Rodríguez Díaz, Angel. 1989. *Transición política y consolidación constitucional de los partidos políticos*. Madrid: Centro de estudios constitucionales.

Sartori, Giovanni. 1972. "European Political Parties: The Case of Polarized Pluralism." In *Political Parties and Political Development*, ed. Joseph La Palombara and Myron Weiner. Princeton, NJ: Princeton University Press.

Shabad, Goldie. 1986. "After Autonomy." In *The Politics of Democratic Spain*, ed. Stanley G. Payne. Chicago: Chicago Council on Foreign Relations.

Share, Donald. 1989. *Dilemmas of Social Democracy: The Spanish Socialist Workers Party in the 1980s*. Westport, CT: Greenwood Press.

Sinova, Justino. 1984. *Historia de la transición*. Madrid: Diario 16.

Solé Tura, Jordi. 1978. "La Constitución y la lucha por el socialismo." In *La Izquierda y la constitución*, ed. Gregorio Peces-Barba et al. Barcelona: Ediciones taula de canvi.

Tezanos, José Félix, Ramón Cotarelo, and Andrés de Blas, eds. 1989. *La Transición democrática española*. Madrid: Editorial Sistema.

Whitehead, Laurence. 1986. "International Aspects of Democratization." In *Transitions from Authoritarian Rule: Comparative Perspectives*, ed., Guillermo O'Donnell, Philippe C. Schmitter, and Laurence Whitehead. Baltimore: Johns Hopkins University Press.

3

Elite settlements and democratic consolidation: Colombia, Costa Rica, and Venezuela

JOHN A. PEELER

This chapter considers the concepts of elite settlements and convergences with reference to the consolidation of democratic regimes in the three Latin American countries that have had the most stable democracies during recent decades: Colombia, Costa Rica, and Venezuela. Although all three countries currently possess regimes fitting the definition of democracy used in this book, they nevertheless display considerable diversity. Colombia remains, without doubt, the furthest from the democratic ideal. Its traditional political and economic elites, organized around the clientelistic Liberal and Conservative parties, have continued to dominate the state, at least until the general elections and constituent assembly elections of 1990 showed serious cracks in traditional party dominance. Popular political participation outside clientelist networks is discouraged. Persistent guerrilla movements and corresponding counterinsurgency efforts have led to numerous violations of human rights at the hands of insurgents, security forces, and rightist death squads. The rapid expansion of the cocaine trade, with Colombia at its center, has added an immensely powerful and wealthy illicit sector to the society and the polity, one that can be found collaborating at times with both insurgents and rightist forces and that increasingly penetrates the state and legitimate business. The old system of elite domination through liberal democratic institutions is still in place and working, but the society is moving beyond its control. In effect, the Colombian democratic regime is going through a process of deconsolidation.

Costa Rica not only has the longest-established liberal democratic regime in Latin America, but in many respects it meets the criteria for a consolidated democracy. There has been an unbroken series of honest elections since 1953, normally with alternation between Liberación nacional and the main opposition coalition or party. Violations of human rights are minimal, and civil liberties are almost completely respected.[1] On the other hand, despite legally compulsory voting, turnout levels are only modest (about 80 percent), and other forms of political participation are not widespread or intense. The institutions of the welfare state that were firmly established in the 1940s have been steadily eroded by the prolonged economic crisis of the 1980s, with the result that living standards of the poorer sectors and the middle class have deteriorated and economic inequality has increased. But there is no sign that these problems have in any way endangered the democratic regime's stability.

Until 1989, Venezuela appeared to have a democratic regime as fully consolidated as Costa Rica's. There has been an unbroken series of honest elections since 1958, with frequent alternation in power between the two leading parties, Acción democrática and Comité de organización política electoral independiente (COPEI). Human rights and civil liberties have been widely respected, especially since the defeat of guerrilla insurgents in the mid–1960s. There is a free, vigorous, and high-quality press. Since the regime's establishment, it has been a commonplace among Venezuelan and foreign observers that the country's oil wealth lubricated the political process, enhancing stability by permitting the government to throw money at problems without having to raise taxes or redistribute resources. This perception has been tested in the last decade. After oil prices rose rapidly in 1973–4, they have stagnated or fallen, except for another rise in 1978–9. But government expenditures increased rapidly in the 1970s, and they were not adjusted to the harder times that followed. The result has been massive indebtedness, and the need for progressively harsher programs of economic adjustment and retrenchment. All this came to a head in late February 1989, when newly inaugurated President Carlos Andrés Pérez implemented a severe austerity program with a serious impact on the poorer classes who had already seen their standards of living decline. The result was massive riots in Caracas and other cities, huge property damage, the declaration of a state

1 Freedom of speech and press were amply exercised during 1989 in a controversy over the decision of the Costa Rican Censorship Board to ban the showing of *The Last Temptation of Christ*, as offensive to the Christian sensibilities of the majority of the population. Also during 1989, there was extensive discussion of an alleged torture chamber found in the headquarters of the judicial police. These cases are typical of Costa Rica: Abuses of authority and legal restrictions on rights do occur on occasion and are usually widely discussed in the mass media. There may be investigations and punishment of wrongdoing, and there is always a good deal of agonizing about the implications for Costa Rican democracy.

of siege, hundreds of people killed, and thousands arrested and held without charge. Although it seems clear that the regime will survive, this was the worst crisis in the thirty-year history of Venezuelan democracy, one that left the regime with its legitimacy wounded. On balance, however, it appears that the recent crisis has not resulted in regime deconsolidation.

The key issue for this volume is the influence of elite configurations on processes of regime foundation and survival. In these three countries, were the regimes established as a result of "elite settlements" or "elite convergences" or through other mechanism? We will see that settlements quite clearly occurred in Colombia and Venezuela, but less clearly so in Costa Rica. All three countries also displayed elements of an elite convergence subsequent to the original settlements.

The concepts of elite settlement and elite convergence as set forth in Chapter 1 are drawn from historical cases, primarily European, in which the relevant regimes evolved over long periods from stable limited democracies to consolidated democracies. But applying these concepts to the Latin American setting requires us to think more precisely about democratic consolidation. A key to this is the "consensual unity" of elites, which results from an elite settlement or an elite convergence. But how much elite consensus and unity are required? Agreement among elites on procedural values, or the rules of the game, but not necessarily on policy or ideology, is emphasized. Furthermore, how are elite consensus and unity sustained once they are created? The three Latin American countries considered in this chapter permit an exploration of these issues.

It is also important in a study focused on elites to think systematically about the interface between elite behavior and mass behavior. The processes by which such democratic regimes are founded and consolidated cannot be understood unless we consider how masses and elites interact. Broadly speaking, the experiences of Colombia, Costa Rica, and Venezuela suggest that elite settlements become most likely when mass political mobilization threatens to escape the control of elites. Thus, the effectiveness of elite settlements depends on achieving horizontal inclusiveness and vertical control. Horizontal inclusiveness refers to the range of elites who are party to a settlement: Are excluded elites capable of disrupting political stability? Vertical control refers to the capacity of elites to channel popular participation within bounds not threatening to institutional stability (cf. Huntington 1968): To what extent can the mass population be guided or pushed into forms of political participation that do not endanger regimes?

Prior conditions

The social, economic, and political conditions that preceded the establishment of stable democracies were very diverse in Colombia, Costa Rica, and Venezuela. Unlike my analysis, most historiography regarding these countries emphasizes either individual leaders, such as presidents, or grand structures, such as class, imperialism, or the international economy, when attempting to explain the political changes they have undergone.[2] Here, however, we focus on the intermediate variable of elite configurations.

Nueva Granada (now Colombia) was an important colonial center. During the eighteenth century, Bogotá became the capital of a Spanish viceroyalty that included not only present-day Colombia but also Panama and the outlying provinces of Quito (Ecuador) and Venezuela. The highlands of Nueva Granada were important sources of gold for the Spanish crown, and the great Caribbean port of Cartagena was a main port for Spanish fleets sailing to and from western South America. The vast and diverse territory provided numerous opportunities for prosperous agricultural and mining settlements, as well as commerce. Nueva Granada, in short, was one of the principal centers of the Spanish Empire in America. Accordingly, it developed a very strong, self-conscious, and self-confident creole upper class that was among the earliest collaborators of Simón Bolívar in the struggle for independence.

Venezuela was also an important part of the empire, for Caracas was made the capital of a captaincy general in the eighteenth century. Although theoretically subject to the viceroy in Bogotá, Caracas was effectively autonomous. Venezuela's economic importance derived from its status as the empire's principal supplier of cacao, mostly grown on large, slave-based plantations near Caracas. The planter class, from which sprang Simón Bolívar and most of the other leaders of the Venezuelan independence movement, matched the upper class of Nueva Granada in its self-confidence and assertiveness, and elements of these two classes joined to lead the long and ultimately successful struggle for independence in northern South America. Both Bogotá and Caracas, important as they were, were late-coming rivals to the earliest centers of imperial rule in Lima and Mexico City. The local elites in the latter cities had too much stake in the system and never took the lead in seeking independence. The Bogotá and Caracas

2 On Colombian history, see Dix 1987; Guillén Martínez 1979; Hartlyn 1988. On Costa Rica, see Ameringer 1982; Monge Alfaro 1980. On Venezuela, see Lombardi 1982; Salcedo-Bastardo 1979.

elites, by contrast, were more assertive and confident of their ability to prosper on their own, beyond the protective and restraining shadow of the Spanish bureaucracy.

The independence struggle weakened the Nueva Granada elite, but it destroyed the Venezuelan elite. More than any Latin American countries, save Haiti and Mexico, Venezuela's independence struggle was a class struggle, with the local upper class of planters opposed initially by a powerful army of poor cowboys (*llaneros*) from the Orinoco plains. Only after their first leader, José Tomás Boves, was killed in battle was it possible for a new leader, José Antonio Páez, to win them to the side of independence. In Venezuela, the people who gained power after independence were reduced to pacts with plebeian caudillos from the interior, who used clientelism to forge popular bases and mobilize armies. The caudillos typically became president; the Caracas elites served as ministers and financiers. The most prominent caudillo was José Antonio Páez. In Nueva Granada, by contrast, the people who gained power were predominantly from the old upper class, most notably Francisco de Paula Santander.

The political dynamics of the two countries in the nineteenth century became quite distinct, although political discourse in both was couched in terms of the confrontation between Liberals and Conservatives that was virtually universal in Latin America at the time. Venezuelan politics increasingly became a struggle for hegemony among the caudillos, each with a clientelistic local power base that enabled him to raise an army and with ties to monied interests in Caracas that enabled him to buy arms and maintain his troops. Weaker caudillos would become clients of stronger ones, in the hope that the patron might actually win control of the national government and its opportunities for enrichment. Such a coalition might last for a decade or more until a coalition of rival caudillos could defeat its leader. There would usually ensue a transitional period until one of the new caudillos established hegemony over the others. Thus the basic political cycle in Venezuela was from personal hegemony, to indeterminacy, to a new personal hegemony. Some caudillos were Liberals, and others Conservatives, but party affiliation was not a powerful factor, and it ceased being one at all after the definitive defeat of the Conservatives in the civil wars of the 1860s. Every dictator thereafter was nominally Liberal, but in the absence of an alternative, the label came to have no practical meaning. (For a full analysis of this era in Venezuela, consult Gilmore 1965.)

In Colombia, the Liberal and Conservative parties actually became the central organizing mechanisms of politics. This was perhaps a reflection of the surviving strength of the colonial ruling class: It remained possible for members of the colonial elite to bring together enough resources – using property and clientelistic ties – to control the government, without having to put themselves in the hands of rough caudillos of the type who came to dominate Venezuela. The elite simply divided into Liberal and Conservative factions, cemented by clientelism and ideology. As in Venezuela, the political process became a struggle for hegemony, punctuated by periods of indeterminacy. However, hegemony in Colombian politics had more of a partisan than a personal flavor. And a distinctive continuing feature of Colombian politics emerged from this primitive party system: the practice of forming bipartisan coalitions as a way to end periods of turmoil or to facilitate alternations of the hegemonic party. At the end of the bloody War of a Thousand Days (1900–3), for example, the victorious Conservatives invited key Liberals into the government as a means of healing the wounds of war and preventing the emergence of unbridgeable enmities among sectors of the ruling class. Or again, when Rafael Núñez, a Liberal, came to power in 1886 with the goal of terminating a period of radical and divisive Liberal governments, he brought Conservatives into his government. He gained the adoption of a new constitution favorable to the church (anathema to hard-line Liberals), and he got the Conservatives to accept a basically Liberal, laissez-faire–oriented economic policy.

Costa Rica during colonial times and the nineteenth century presented a radical contrast to Colombia and Venezuela. The most distant, isolated, and poverty-stricken province of the captaincy-general of Guatemala, Costa Rica had virtually no economic assets that warranted the crown's attention. It is a commonplace of Costa Rican historiography that the traditional egalitarianism of the country originated in the "equal distribution of poverty" during colonial times (see, e.g., Monge Alfaro 1980). It is now acknowledged that this thesis was overdrawn and that Costa Rica has always had a clearly defined – if not very wealthy – upper class (Stone 1975). In any case, it is true that Costa Rica had neither large plantations with many slaves nor large numbers of subject Indians for labor and that at the time of independence, the country had yet to find an export commodity that would yield even a modicum of prosperity. It is also true that Costa Rican elites were not called upon to fight for independence; rather, it was thrust upon them by decisions made in Guatemala and Mexico in 1821. Consequently, the elites were not bled by war as were their counterparts in Venezuela and Colombia. Their position at the top of a very small hill remained undisturbed.

Costa Rican politics in the century after independence evolved in a manner distinct from that of either Colombia or Venezuela. As in the other two countries, the political process took shape as a struggle for hegemony punctuated by periods of indeterminacy. The actors were individuals rather than parties; in this, Costa Rica resembled Venezuela more than Colombia. But Costa Rica had nothing resembling the *caudillismo* that dominated Venezuelan politics. Rather, as in Colombia, virtually all the actors were members of the old elite. Many of the conflicts between Liberalism and Conservatism echoed in Costa Rica, but the two currents never formed clearly defined parties or factions. The political discourse of Costa Ricans appears to have had little explicit reference to Liberalism and Conservatism. However, regime changes in Costa Rica can be shown to have paralleled changes in other Central American countries where the two tendencies were more clearly defined, and individual Costa Rican presidents had affinities with one or the other camp.[3]

Elections were a regular part of the political process in all three countries, but it is important to emphasize that they were not the principal means for changing governments; rather, they typically served to legitimate an incumbent government or its chosen successor. Once an individual (in Venezuela or Costa Rica) or a party (in Colombia) established hegemony, often by force of arms, the government apparatus would be utilized to control elections, thus perpetuating himself or itself in power. Opposition groups could normally capture the government either by force of arms or, occasionally, by coalescing with government dissidents to win an election in spite of the powers of incumbency.[4] This pattern may be interpreted as signifying continuing elite disunity and regime instability (see Higley and Burton 1989).

The three countries had parallel economic histories in one respect: They all became committed primarily to coffee export as the basis of their economies. However, the timing, characteristics, and political consequences of this shift to coffee-oriented export economies differed markedly among them. Costa Rica and Venezuela were virtually the first countries to undertake coffee production on a large scale, in the 1840s. Indeed, for much of the nineteenth century, Venezuela was the world's leading producer. Coffee cultivation gave added political

3 Woodward (1985) makes this case strongly, in effect using Guatemalan politics as a template and seeking to show that politics in the rest of the isthmus tended to reflect or parallel developments in Guatemala.

4 The Costa Rican election of 1889 is commonly considered the beginning of democracy in that country because the incumbent government was forced by popular demonstrations to accept an electoral defeat. The Colombian election of 1886 involved a split in the dominant Liberal Party, allowing the dissident Rafael Núñez to inaugurate a coalition that evolved into a Conservative hegemony.

weight to Venezuela's Andean region, and particularly to the far southwestern state of Táchira, but caudillos from other regions continued to control the government until the successful insurrection of 1899 inaugurated an Andean hegemony that remained unbroken until 1945. In the hands of Juan Vicente Gómez (1908–35), the logic of *caudillismo* was developed so fully, according to Gilmore (1965), that Gómez was necessarily the last caudillo, for he systematically destroyed his rivals and used the windfall of petroleum to build the state to the point that *caudillismo* was no longer possible after his death in 1935.

Coffee was the key to the transformation of Costa Rica from a colonial backwater into the wealthiest country of Central America. The prime area for cultivation was the Central Valley, so coffee had the effect of reinforcing the power of the central region and its traditional upper class. There was some tendency toward land concentration as the benefits of coffee cultivation tended to gravitate toward those who started with more land or wealth, but Costa Rica remained a country of smallholding peasants at least until the middle of this century.

The systematic strengthening of the Costa Rican state was begun by President Braulio Carrillo in the late 1830s, in concert with the efforts to encourage coffee cultivation (cf. Vega Carballo 1981, Cerdas Cruz 1985). As coffee came to dominate the economy, planters increasingly controlled the state and used some of the proceeds of the coffee export to further develop state capacities that served the interests of coffee cultivation and export (e.g., provision of road, railroad, and port facilities). Later, in the 1880s, elements of the upper class who owed their prosperity to coffee but who were not principally occupied in its cultivation came to dominate politics, showing a considerable sophistication in promoting Costa Rican development in a manner that would maximize the country's autonomy relative to strong external forces. For example, the government contracted with an American engineer, Minor Keith, to finish a railway from San José to the Caribbean port of Limón, in return for the concession of vast undeveloped acreage on the Atlantic coastal plain. This land was later used by the United Fruit Company for banana plantations. Whereas in other countries (e.g., Honduras), United Fruit was able to corrupt and control the state, and thereby avoid having to fulfill the contracts it signed, in Costa Rica the state remained capable of bargaining with the company.

Another important sign of elite sophistication in Costa Rica was the decision in the 1880s to provide public schooling for the whole population. In most other Latin American countries during this period such a commitment would have been seen as nonsensical if not completely wrongheaded. But the Liberal leaders of the 1880s and their successors in Costa Rica saw that the country would be strengthened by having a literate citizenry. The original aim was certainly not to create democracy: It was assumed that the "better sort" of people would continue to lead the country, and indeed, they have done so through all Costa Rica's vicissitudes during the present century. Curiously, Costa Ricans commonly date the beginning of their democracy from 1889, when the Conservatives, having lost a rigged election, organized Costa Rica's first major popular protests that forced the Liberal government (which had pioneered public education) to yield. On the whole, and even though it was not intended, widespread public education has been part of the basis of democracy in Costa Rica (Stone 1975).

Colombia became a large-scale producer of coffee only in the 1880s. As in Venezuela, the coffee boom served to strengthen a particular region, in this case Antioquia. During this century, profits from coffee provided the foundation for the first major wave of Colombian industrialization, centered in the *antioqueño* capital of Medellín. However, the regional elites who benefited from coffee were, for the most part, already well-established members of the national elite; their relative position was improved, and there was no Colombian counterpart to the advent of the new Andean elite in Venezuela during the nineteenth century.

The needs of the emerging Colombian coffee industry had a great deal to do with a coming together of elites, engineered by Rafael Núñez, after 1886. During the preceding thirty years, the country had suffered a radically Conservative, proclerical regime that provoked a bloody civil war, as well as imposition by the victorious Liberals of a radically decentralized federal system that gave rise to continuing disorders. Neither the central government nor the provinces were able to provide the services necessary for expanding the coffee economy. The constitution of 1886 reflected a consensus among "people of substance" in favor of "order and progress,"[5] by (1) establishing a strong, centralized state that negated extreme Liberalism; (2) entrenching the Catholic church while reaffirming religious liberty so that Catholicism was protected at the same time that doctrinaire Conservatism was avoided; and (3) enshrining the Liberal concepts of enterprise and property essential to promoting economic growth. In

5 This positivist slogan was so widespread in the region at the time that it was enshrined in the flag of the Brazilian Republic established in 1889.

spite of all that has happened in Colombia since 1886, that constitution remains in effect today.

By the second decade of the twentieth century, these three countries displayed remarkable differences politically. Venezuela was in the grip of the Gómez dictatorship that presided over the early stages of petroleum exploitation, which eventually transformed the country. The political order was virtually coterminous with the dictator's clientele. Colombia was being ruled by a succession of elected Conservative governments in a context of restricted suffrage and clientelistically controlled elections. Costa Rica was under the rule of a similar series of elected presidents, vaguely Liberal for the most part (and punctuated by an abortive military regime, 1917–19), with suffrage restricted but elections less completely controlled than in Colombia. The stage was set for years of economic crisis and world war, with the attendant social and political upheaval in each country.

Years of crisis

The economic and political stresses associated with the Great Depression and World War II led to profound and lasting changes in all three countries. The deterioration of economic conditions in the 1930s promoted an expansion of political activity by the working class, and political movements emerged that both promoted and benefited from popular political participation. Communist parties were founded in the early 1930s, and they sought to mobilize workers, organize unions, and establish revolutionary political movements. Noncommunist popular movements also emerged, with eclectic political and economic programs that included universal suffrage, economic nationalism, a guiding state role in a mixed economy, and a welfare state. These movements later became Acción democrática (AD) in Venezuela and the Partido liberación nacional (PLN) in Costa Rica; in Colombia, the populist movement of Jorge Eliécer Gaitán, within the Liberal party, is the principal example. Although their programs appear reformist today, their import at the time was correctly seen as revolutionary in the contexts of the calcified Gómez dictatorship in Venezuela and the elitist republics of gentlemen that ruled Colombia and Costa Rica.[6]

In Venezuela, the death of Juan Vicente Gómez in 1935 opened the way for a political struggle that had already begun in the shadows, between military and civilian elites who were the heirs presumptive of the tyrant, and new mass-based political movements (Communist

6 In addition to Peeler 1985, for this period see Aguilar Bulgarelli 1980; Guzmán Campos et al. 1980; Martz 1966; Oquist 1980; Schifter 1979.

and non-Communist). During the next ten years, Gómez's two successors tried to bring about a controlled liberalization of society. This effort failed in 1945 when Acción democrática (AD) collaborated with mid-ranking army officers to overthrow the government of Elías Medina Angarita. The ensuing reformist government lasted three years (hence its name, the Trienio). The AD sought to bring about a rapid popular transformation of the society, including the full establishment of liberal democracy, a major increase in the state's share of petroleum profits, labor laws favorable to unions, secular educational reform, and important elements of a welfare state. The AD was the only political organization with a popular base at that time, and thus in three elections during the period it overwhelmed its opponents. Accordingly, Venezuelan economic elites, foreign petroleum companies, and rival political party elites all had reasons for wanting the AD's overthrow, and there was widespread celebration in these quarters when the same military faction that had been the AD's ally in 1945 carried out a coup in 1948. But the officer who became dictator, Marcos Pérez Jiménez, proved so corrupt and repressive that most of those who had supported the 1948 coup were working actively for his overthrow by 1957, including a large popular underground led by Communist and AD cadres. Dictatorial practices that had been routine under Gómez were no longer acceptable in a now more modernized society.

In Colombia, the Conservative hegemony that began in 1886 collapsed in 1930, when a split in the party allowed the Liberals to win national elections, in coalition with dissident Conservatives. Four years later, the more partisan Liberal government of Alfonso López Pumarejo initiated the "revolution on the march," a program of modernizing and democratizing reforms that included universal male suffrage, labor law reform, and welfare state measures. The Liberals, like their Conservative predecessors, sought to use the vast powers of the central government to cement their hold on power. Their expansion of the suffrage and innovative legislation promised to give them a virtual lock on power by winning the loyalty of most newly enfranchised voters. This seemed all the more likely given the emergence of a dynamic populist, Jorge Eliécer Gaitán, within the Liberal camp. Gaitán, unlike López, was not part of the established elites, and he called for an end to the elitist political and economic order and for its replacement by a popular regime. Indeed, Gaitán may be considered the first truly popular political leader in Colombian history (Sharpless 1978). The Conservative counterattack was led by Laureano Gómez, who sought to mobilize a mass base for his party, not only by appeals to traditional Catholic values, but also by inflammatory condemnations of Liberals as subversive and even diabolical. Colombian politics in the late 1930s and 1940s was thus increasingly polarized. When the Liberals split between Gaitanistas and regulars in 1946, the Conservatives were able to win the presidential election with a minority in favor of Mariano Ospina Pérez. With Gómez in charge of the party machinery, they attempted to expel the Liberals from all centers of power and to entrench themselves with an extensive use of violence. Liberals increasingly responded in kind. After Gaitán was assassinated on the streets of Bogotá in 1948, massive riots threatened to bring down the government and initiate a popular revolution. In an effort to maintain order, key Liberal leaders joined the Conservative government. But official and Conservative violence against the Liberals continued, leading ultimately to a Liberal boycott of presidential elections in 1949 and thus the election of Laureano Gómez. Thereafter, violence increasingly followed its own dynamic, as local, personal agendas of revenge and plunder made it steadily less possible for party leaders to use violence selectively for their own purposes. By 1953, all factions of both parties, except the backers of the incumbent Gómez, supported a seizure of power by the commander in chief of the army, general Gustavo Rojas Pinilla, with the objective of ending the violence. By 1957, however, Rojas had shown himself bent on retaining power, and he was building his own popularly based political movement in an effort to supplant the traditional parties by taking away their mass support. The response of the traditional elites was to unify in a successful effort to oust him.

The political crisis in Costa Rica began in the 1930s with the organization of the Communist party and its leadership of an important strike of banana workers, an initiative that earned them the lasting loyalty of that sector of the working class. But the crisis did not become acute until after the inauguration of President Rafael Angel Calderón Guardia, in 1940. Calderón had been a classic establishment politician, working his way up by cleverly serving his predecessors and patrons. This included transferring his loyalty from three-time president Ricardo Jiménez to León Cortés Castro in 1936, when the latter, having gained the presidency with the patronage of Jiménez, took over the Republican party machine. Cortés then sponsored the election of Calderón in 1940, though Cortés no doubt intended to exercise overall control from behind the scenes, much as Jiménez had for many years. But Calderón did to Cortés what the latter had done to Jiménez, taking control of the party for himself.

Calderón was then faced with the hostility of many of the political elites to which he had belonged, especially the ultraconservative large coffee growers. Many of these people rallied around Cortés and formed the Democratic party. Searching for a way to consolidate his power over the opposition of his old comrades, Calderón chose a populist strategy, seeking to cultivate working-class support. In this he was strongly influenced by his close friend, Archbishop Víctor Sanabria, and by Catholic social doctrine. To provide workers with tangible benefits that might attract them to his cause, he formed an alliance with the Communist party, whose highly organized membership and cadres provided a ready political apparatus.[7] Using the Republican majority in the Assembly, Calderón pushed through several innovative laws, most notably an advanced social security system and a new labor code favorable to the unions. In classic clientelist style, he then sought to use the new government programs and benefits to cement political support for himself.

Calderón's clear aim of perpetuating himself as political boss, coupled with his Communist alliance, made his Conservative opponents all the more militant and desperate. But opposition also emerged from a different quarter: the moderate left. The Center for the Study of National Problems was a group of socialist intellectuals who had developed a critique of the existing state of Costa Rican society and an alternative model for development. The Social Democratic party was formed out of an alliance between the Center and a left splinter of the Democratic party led by José Figueres. The Social Democrats objected to the political uses of Calderón's reforms, though they supported the reforms in principle. More broadly, they condemned the increasingly open corruption of the Calderonista regime. Finally, they rejected Calderón's alliance with the Communists, with whom the Social Democrats were competing for control of organized labor.

After Calderón secured the election of his successor, Teodoro Picado, in 1944, the line was clearly drawn between the disparate coalitions supporting and opposing the government. Following the midterm elections in 1946, the opposition successfully demanded effective control of the electoral tribunal as a condition for participating in the 1948 presidential election. In that election, Calderón sought to return to the presidency against an opposition unified behind the candidacy of Conservative newspaper publisher Otilio Ulate. When the election results showed that Ulate had won, the Calderonista majority in the Assembly voted to annul the election on grounds of

7 In the context of World War II, it was common for Latin American governments to be allied with Communist parties, which was accepted by the United States because the Soviet Union was an ally after 1941. The Medina government in Venezuela was also allied with the Communists. With the end of the war (and the advent of the cold war), these ties increasingly caused friction with the United States. For a careful study of U.S. policy toward Costa Rica between 1940 and 1948, see Schifter 1986.

fraud. Figueres, meanwhile, had been building an armed force at his farm in southern Costa Rica; he marched on San José demanding the government's resignation and recognition of Ulate as the duly elected president. After a short but bloody civil war, Calderón, Picado, and the Communist leadership negotiated a surrender and were allowed to leave the country. José Figueres and the Army of National Liberation were masters of the scene.

Establishing democratic regimes

The transition to democracy in all three countries involved explicit pact making on the part of competing elites that had the effect of attenuating previously intense conflicts over policy and office, thereby permitting the establishment of competition within an agreed-upon framework of rules. The pacting elites did not explicitly foreswear their conflicting programs, but the pacts signified agreement that it was in the mutual interest of the established elites to prevent conflicts from threatening social stability. The outcomes of these pacts conform to the definition of elite consensus and unity given in Chapter 1.

Colombia provides the clearest instance of an elite settlement, though not one leading to the establishment of a consolidated democracy.[8] Confronting a military government that showed signs of building an independent popular base and perpetuating itself in power, Colombia's warring Conservative and Liberal elites began to come together in 1956, when former presidents Laureano Gómez (Conservative) and Alberto Lleras Camargo (Liberal) met in Gómez's exile in Benidorm, Spain. They agreed on a five-point statement that called for joint Liberal–Conservative action to bring about a swift return to democratic government and that anticipated the need for a coalition government. When the Ospina faction of the Conservatives broke with Rojas in early 1957, its leaders signed a similar pact with the Liberals, though the Gómez faction abstained. After the overthrow of Rojas in May 1957 (itself the outcome of negotiations between party elites and military leaders), another pact was signed in Sitges, Spain, by Gómez and Lleras Camargo; again the Ospina faction was marginalized. The pact of Sitges made the terms of the coalition more precise. Alternation in the presidency was stipulated, with the first president to be a Conservative. The principle of parity between the parties in other public positions was also ratified. But the two Conservative factions could not resolve their conflict, and finally the Pact

8 See Dix 1987; Echeverri Uruburu 1986; Hartlyn 1988 and 1989, chap. 3; Kline 1980; Wilde 1978.

of San Carlos was signed, stipulating that Congress would be elected first (with equality between parties and free competition between factions) and that it would choose the Conservative president. The result of these negotiations and agreements, the National Front, was approved in a plebiscite in December 1957. But the Congress elected in 1958 proved unable to agree on a Conservative president because of continuing factional disagreements among the Conservatives. Further elite negotiations revised the agreement to allow for the first president to be a Liberal and to extend the duration of the National Front from twelve to sixteen years.

As finally implemented through a constitutional amendment, the National Front called for the two traditional parties to alternate in the presidency over four terms of four years each. The two parties would share equally all seats in the Chamber of Deputies, the Senate, and lower-level elective bodies. All appointive posts would also be equally shared. Thus the partisan balance was completely insulated from elections, which mattered only insofar as they determined the fate of individual leaders and factions within the parties. Moreover, other political parties were excluded from participating independently in elections: They could compete only by offering candidates and lists within the Liberal or Conservative party.

The National Front was a direct response by the traditional political elites to a dual threat. On one hand, the competitive mobilization of mass followings had escaped elite control and taken the form of rampant violence. On the other, Rojas Pinilla's military government had tried to displace the parties by stealing their mass support. The party leaders saw the need to cooperate in mass demobilization in order to restore control through tested clientelistic mechanisms. To the extent that this could be achieved, the military would be deprived of another opportunity to intervene. In addition to the obvious demobilizing effects of guaranteed party parity, other aspects of the electoral laws discouraged voting. Most notable in this respect were and are regulations governing voter registration and voting itself that are quite cumbersome and make it virtually impossible for many people to vote (Peeler 1985, pp. 97–8).

This elite arrangement for political demobilization lasted for all of its planned sixteen years, despite serious challenges. During the 1960s, chronic violence in many parts of the countryside gradually cohered in several revolutionary guerrilla movements capable of maintaining themselves in their strongholds against all government counterinsurgency efforts. But although they were often able to embarrass the government, none of the insurgents was able to threaten the regime's survival. There were also two major challenges to the

National Front from within the constitutional system. The Movimiento revolucionario liberal (MRL) of Alfonso López Michelsen (son of the former president) mounted a formidable challenge before the 1966 elections, but López was then absorbed into the Liberal establishment. A more serious challenge was posed by former dictator Gustavo Rojas Pinilla in 1970, when as the nominee of the Alianza nacional popular (ANAPO) he nearly defeated the official presidential candidate, Misael Pastrana (indeed, allegations of electoral fraud were widespread). During the National Front period, voting turnout fell to very low levels (below even those of the United States!), and it has increased only slightly since the resumption of competitive elections in 1974. Other forms of political participation were also at low levels under the Front. In short, the National Front accomplished the objectives of the traditional party elites who negotiated it. Attempts to move toward a more consolidated democratic regime since 1974, however, have encountered numerous difficulties, which will be discussed later.

Venezuela also had a clearly defined elite settlement, one that was at least as complex in its formation as that of Colombia.[9] There were more actors and more diverse actors centrally involved in the Venezuelan process than in Colombia. In the course of his dictatorship, Pérez Jiménez had alienated a steadily broadening circle of Venezuelans, elite and mass. By 1957, there were active consultations and cooperation taking place among the various sectors opposed to the dictator. Many of the younger cadres of Acción democrática were working underground in close alliance with their counterparts in the Communist party, seeking not only to oust the dictator but also to create the conditions for a revolutionary transformation of Venezuela. The existence of this working "revolutionary pact" gave a sense of urgency to more specifically elite consultations and negotiations during 1957–8.

The other major actors included (1) top leaders of the center–left AD, the center–right, the Social–Christian COPEI, the center–left Unión republicana democrática (URD), and the Communist party (PCV); (2) the military elite not allied with Pérez Jiménez; (3) the business elite; and (4) the labor union elite. Despite being bitter rivals during the Trienio, the AD, URD, and PCV collaborated against the Pérez Jiménez government after 1953. By 1956, COPEI, too, had been driven into opposition. Communication and consultation increased, culminating in a meeting of the leaders of all parties except the PCV

9 On the elite settlement in Venezuela, see Arroyo Talavera 1988; Blank 1984; Karl 1987; Levine 1989; López Maya and Gómez Calcaño 1989.

in New York City in December 1957. Also participating in this New York meeting was Eugenio Mendoza, Venezuela's most important industrialist. In addition, party and business leaders were in contact with key leaders of the armed forces, encouraging those who were already inclined to terminate the Pérez Jiménez government. These consultations bore fruit when the dictator was overthrown on January 23, 1958. Two days later a provisional junta was established that included three military officers, Eugenio Mendoza, and one other businessman. This junta had the tacit approval of the party leaders.

During 1958, several pacts laid the foundation for a new democratic order (López Maya and Gómez Calcaño 1989, pp. 68–76, 109–23). The Worker–Employer Pact of Agreement (April 1958) was actively promoted by the party leaders as a means of preventing destabilizing economic conflicts. Commissions were established as a means of reconciling the interests of the parties, and a strong impulse was given to collective bargaining, which had the effect of strengthening the confederations and unions under AD leadership. The Pact of Punto Fijo was signed on October 31, 1958, by the top leadership of the URD, COPEI, and AD, as the campaign for the first election was about to enter its last month. The party leaders agreed to defend constitutional government against any possible coup d'état, agreed to form a Government of National Unity (to guard against any systematic opposition that might weaken the democratic movement), and agreed to formulate a minimum common program, to be enacted regardless of which party won the December elections.

The Pact of Punto Fijo resulted in the Declaration of Principles and the Minimum Program, the latter being adopted by the three principal presidential candidates on December 6, 1958, shortly before the election. The candidates committed themselves to frame a new democratic constitution containing protections for economic and social rights. They recognized the central role of the state in directing the economy, agreed to produce a long-term economic development plan, but also recognized and respected private enterprise and foreign investment. They called for agrarian reform, labor law reform, and revision of relations with the petroleum companies. Finally, they called for modernization of the armed forces, which were to be considered apolitical, obedient, and noninterventionist. This program not only realized the centrist consensus so laboriously negotiated by the parties (with business and labor leaders as silent partners); it also marked the definitive rejection of the commitment to radical transformation that had developed among Communist and AD activists underground. But this rejection of the radical alternative provoked the violent insurrection that shook Venezuela in the early 1960s.

Two Venezuelan scholars, López Maya and Gómez Calcaño (1989, pp. 74–5), point out that the centrist leaders devoted much effort in the early years of the regime to forging an understanding with the armed forces that would lead the latter to accept the apolitical, noninterventionist role assigned to them. The main thrust of these efforts was to improve the socioeconomic conditions of military personnel and assure them of full decision-making autonomy in all strictly military affairs. These scholars also view the concordat with the Vatican (signed in 1964) as an important prelude to the overall settlement of 1958. This pact transformed hostile relations between the church and the AD during the Trienio, and it thus eliminated a potential conflict between the AD and COPEI a dozen years later.

The Communists and left-wing factions within the AD and the URD were largely left out of the complex negotiations that comprised the 1958 settlement. It is difficult to see how the settlement could have successfully included all the major centrist parties, as well as the business, church, and military elites, if an effort had been made to respond to the left's demands for radical social transformation. In reaction and inspired by the recent success of Fidel Castro in Cuba, the Communists and the left wings of the AD and the URD raised the banner of socialist revolution in 1961. A guerrilla insurgency inflicted considerable damage and loss of life over the next several years, trying without success to disrupt the 1963 elections. By the late 1960s, however, the insurgency was defeated, and many of the former guerrillas accepted amnesty from the government of Rafael Caldera (COPEI) and integrated themselves into political life as peaceful political parties of the left, most notably the Movement Toward Socialism (MAS) and the Revolutionary Left Movement (MIR). There is clear evidence that the centrist elites intended to incorporate the left into the political system at this time and that the left intended to accept the legitimacy of the liberal democratic system (see especially López Maya and Gómez Calcaño 1989; Myers 1986). To this extent, Venezuela's democratic consolidation involved an element of an elite convergence.

Elite convergence was even more apparent in the Costa Rican case.[10] The negotiations that led to the establishment of liberal democracy are best seen as beginning in the crisis of 1948, which, as we have seen, marked the complete breakdown of elite unity. As it became clear that Figueres had the upper hand in the civil war, several interests pushed for a settlement. The Calderonistas wanted to avoid the destruction of their reforms and of their political position. The

10 See Aguilar Bulgarelli 1980; Oconotrillo 1982; Rovira Mas 1988.

Communists wanted to retain legal status and their foothold in organized labor. Figueres's conservative and business allies, backers of Ulate, wanted the latter declared president without having to depend on Figueres's bayonets. The Social Democrats wanted the way cleared for creation of the new social democratic order envisioned in their program. But Figueres himself seemed intent on a total military victory that would leave him free to act in whatever manner he chose.

The church and the U.S. embassy worked actively to promote a settlement. Archbishop Sanabria's position was basically that a way must be found to stop the bloodshed. The U.S. position was more complex and profoundly ambivalent (see Schifter 1986). The Americans were increasingly concerned about the Communist presence in the Picado and Calderón governments, but on the other hand, Calderón had been a highly reliable ally in World War II, and he was, furthermore, a close friend of Nicaraguan President Anastasio Somoza, another faithful U.S. ally. But, Somoza was temporarily at odds with the United States over the Nicaraguan presidential succession. The United States also distrusted Figueres's close alliance with President Juan José Arévalo of Guatemala, a reformer already viewed with suspicion in U.S. government circles (compare Schifter 1986 with Schlesinger and Kinzer 1982 on this period). Figueres's strong anti-Communism recommended him, but his advocacy of extensive reforms elicited some uneasiness. He was not well known to U.S. policymakers. Thus the United States was receiving conflicting cues (indeed, the State Department and the ambassador were not always of the same persuasion) in a situation that was not perceived as central to U.S. interests. It is thus not surprising that when the crisis heated up in the late 1940s, the United States did not play an active role. But with the advent of civil war and reduction of the alternatives to Calderón (and the Communists) or Figueres, American policy crystallized in favor of Calderón's negotiated departure. The U.S. ambassador, along with the papal nuncio, was crucial to arranging this departure in the final days of the war, thus averting an assault on San José itself.

On May 1, 1948, having entered the city with his army a week earlier, Figueres signed a pact with Otilio Ulate, stating that the latter would assume office within eighteen months and that the country would be ruled by a provisional junta in the meantime. The junta would be responsible for holding an election for a Constituent Assembly to draft a new constitution and would have the authority to rule by decree during its tenure. Figueres, as president of the junta, thus received extensive provisional powers, which were used, for example, to abolish the army, nationalize banking, and give the state the authority to guide the economy. These and other measures were intended to lay the groundwork for the social democratic program of restructuring society. This plan was frustrated, however, when the Social Democrats' neglect of popular organization led to their defeat in elections for the Constituent Assembly, which yielded a strong majority for Ulate's conservative Unión nacional. The innovative draft constitution proposed by the junta was rejected in favor of minor amendments to the existing document. These changes included ratifying most of the innovations decreed by the junta, but the Social Democrats nevertheless had to give up their hopes of leading a thorough transformation of Costa Rica. When this was clear, Figueres and the junta yielded power to Ulate.

It is not really accurate to say that Figueres and the Social Democrats *had* to give up their hopes, for Figueres and the Army of National Liberation had a monopoly of military force locally, and the United States was not inclined to intervene. An attempt by Calderón to invade from Nicaragua merely rallied support for Figueres. In short, he could have done anything he wanted, including imposing a personal dictatorship. The 1948 pact with Ulate was not strictly necessary. That it was undertaken and honored seems to reflect a commitment by Figueres to the principles of procedural democracy, independent of his commitment to the substantive program of the Social Democrats.

The Figueres–Ulate pact of 1948 was an agreement between allies, who certainly had serious disagreements about public policy but who had nevertheless been able to collaborate fruitfully for years in the struggle against Calderón. Yet, the pact fell short of an elite settlement: It merely regulated competition, within a liberal democratic framework, between the two major parts of the victorious opposition. From 1948 until the mid-1950s, Calderón and his supporters were outside the political process, twice trying to overthrow the government through invasions from Nicaragua. Only with the election of 1958 did Calderón reintegrate himself in the political process, accepting the institutional framework and the party system that had taken shape. He did so by joining the loose conservative coalition that was forming to oppose the National Liberation party, which had been built up by Figueres after the junta left office in 1949 and which led Figueres to victory in the 1953 elections. Only in 1958, then, did the elite transformation that began in 1948 include the principal loser in the civil war. But, there was no explicit agreement or pact defining the terms of Calderón's reintegration. The elite agreements reached in 1948–9 facilitated Calderón's reentry by leaving his key institutional innovations (social security, in particular) intact, though without any

Calderonistas to administer them. This enabled Calderón (as it enables his son today) to claim political credit among the voters for having established social security in Costa Rica. In this way, the decisions of 1948–9 laid the basis for peaceful political competition, by lending legitimacy not only to the victors but also to the most important of the vanquished.

Thus the foundation of Costa Rica's democratic regime does not fit the model of an elite settlement in all respects; the model of an elite convergence is equally relevant. Indeed, Costa Rica may be seen as having undergone a three-step convergence, as the Communists and other left parties, constitutionally outlawed in 1949, were not permitted unrestricted electoral participation until 1970.[11] This absorption of the left into legal political participation was less clear-cut than in Venezuela. For the most part, established elites maneuvered to let it happen without having to take responsibility for it and thus without risking the alienation of their conservative backers. The Communists tried forming a series of fronts, probing for a formula that would trigger the constitutional proscription on Communist parties. José Figueres was the only forthright figure in the episode: He remarked that because he had been the one who first outlawed the party, it was only fitting that he be the one to call for its legalization. The constitutional prohibition was finally officially lifted in 1975 (see Ocontrillo 1982; Salom 1987).

Success in absorbing the left without undermining stability was enhanced in Costa Rica and Venezuela by a combination of a strongly presidential government and a system of proportional representation in congressional elections. As I have argued elsewhere (Peeler 1985, chap. 3), a strong presidency tends to promote centrist, bipolar party systems, while marginalizing parties of the left. At the same time, proportional representation assures leftist elites of an institutional base and a platform for disseminating their views. Thus centrist elites can permit legalization of the left on the assumption that it is unlikely to win a presidential election. Conversely, leftist elites can accept the liberal democratic constitutional order confident that they will not be excluded from public forums. (By contrast, a U.S.-style plurality electoral system would give the left little incentive to seek legalization, as the prospects of winning seats in Congress would be minimal.)

11 Note that Costa Rica never endured a leftist insurgency like that of Venezuela. The proscription of the left was a result of the passions and interests of the victors in 1948–9, reinforced over the years by the international environment of the cold war that made it risky for any Costa Rican government to end the proscription. Note that unlike Calderón, the left received no policy satisfaction: All they got was the privilege of participating.

This same combination would presumably work in Colombia, too, if the government had enough control over security forces and death squads to prevent assassination and other harassment of leftist elites.

Consolidating democratic regimes

Since the establishment of their democratic regimes, all three countries have confronted serious challenges. Venezuela and Costa Rica have done so, if not with complete success, at least in ways that have maintained and consolidated their democratic regimes. Their success reflects the continuation and adaptation of consensual unity among the major political elites, and the adhesion of new elites to this consensus. Colombia's experience has been far more problematic. The consensual unity of the mainstream Liberal and Conservative elites has not decayed, but neither has it evolved in response to changing conditions. Two major counterelites – leaders of the organized leftist guerrilla forces and the drug lords – have been able to threaten the stability of the system, and there has been no new settlement that might incorporate them.

Venezuela[12] has had an unbroken series of honest and competitive elections every five years since 1958. The opposition won the presidency in 1968, 1973, 1978, and 1983. The party system has evolved through a period of extreme fragmentation in the late 1960s, to the present bipolar system dominated by the AD and COPEI, with the left (the MAS and the MIR) as a stable minority presence with about 10 percent of the vote. To all intents and purposes, the left has been successfully absorbed by the democratic political system. Voting turnout has consistently been high, and other forms of political participation have been substantial. There is, for example, an active and diverse organizational life in which interest groups (especially business, labor, and peasant) actively participate in the political process.

The major challenges confronting Venezuela in the 1980s were the social and political consequences of the worldwide stagnation and decline of petroleum prices. Successive governments since that of Gómez in the 1930s have used petroleum revenues to enhance the capabilities of the state to deal with the problems of Venezuelan society. The government's share of oil profits expanded gradually over the years as new contracts were negotiated. Careful management of this resource meant that the Venezuelan government was traditionally

12 On the consolidation of democracy in Venezuela and its current problems, see Arroyo Talavera 1988; Brewer-Carías 1988; Carrera Damas 1988; Cruz 1988; Levine 1989; Martz and Myers 1986.

one of the most solvent in the Third World. When the world oil crisis of 1973–4 sent prices skyrocketing, it was not surprising that newly elected President Carlos Andrés Pérez adopted highly ambitious and costly programs. First iron and steel, and later petroleum itself, were nationalized. Government social programs were rapidly expanded. Rising government expenditures were financed with international loans based on the assumption of continuing increases in oil prices. But when prices leveled off, the government failed to adjust, and the country's external debt began to be a major problem. This was made worse by the inability of the succeeding administration of Luis Herrera Campins to carry out an austerity program. By 1983, Venezuela found itself alongside Mexico and Nigeria as an oil-rich country in deep economic trouble. Little progress was made during the administration of Jaime Lusinchi, so that when Pérez returned to the presidency in early 1989, he saw little alternative but to impose an orthodox austerity program. The resulting riots and repression, noted earlier, profoundly shook the country. As yet, however, there is no indication that the stability of the democratic regime is in danger.

Costa Rica,[13] although lacking the historic cushion of petroleum, has had a political evolution similar to Venezuela's. An unbroken series of honest and competitive elections since 1953 have seen the opposition win the presidency in 1953, 1958, 1962, 1966, 1970, 1978, 1982, and 1990. The party system has become strongly bipolar, though Costa Rica never underwent the extreme fragmentation that characterized Venezuela in the late 1960s. Since 1970, the left has been a regular participant in elections, but as a tiny minority averaging well under 10 percent of the vote. Thus, as in Venezuela, the left has been effectively absorbed into the system. Participation levels and voting turnout are respectable, though somewhat lower than those in Venezuela.

Costa Rica had serious economic problems during the 1980s: Its external debt, on a per-capita basis, is comparable to Venezuela's, even though Costa Rica's per-capita GNP is lower. We have already alluded to the negative effect that this economic crisis has had on standards of living. But even though strikes and protests have increased, there have not been the sort of massive disruptions that occurred in Venezuela.

The other major set of challenges that have confronted Costa Rica have arisen from the revolutionary processes in neighboring Nicaragua and El Salvador and from the United State's response. In 1978–

13 On the consolidation of democracy in Costa Rica and its current problems, see Barahona 1988; Torres Rivas et al. 1987.

9, the Costa Rican government of Rodrigo Carazo gained popularity through its active support of the Sandinista insurgency. But after the Sandinista triumph, relations with Managua soured rapidly when the deeply rooted anti-Communism of most of the Costa Rican elite, and of much of the population, manifested itself in sympathy for anti-Sandinista groups. Still, few Costa Ricans had any enthusiasm for actively combating the Sandinistas. After 1982, the Reagan administration pushed strongly for Costa Rican support of the Nicaraguan *contra* forces. The government of Luis Alberto Monge, vulnerable to pressure because of the country's economic troubles, played a double game, insisting publicly on Costa Rica's neutrality while tacitly allowing *contra* forces to operate discreetly out of northern Costa Rica. His successor, Oscar Arias, took advantage of serious divisions in the United States over its Central American policy to press for a Central American peace plan and, as part of that initiative, to end Costa Rican support for the *contras*.

The interminable frustrations of economic policy have been a drag on a succession of Costa Rican governments, and they have to some extent weakened the legitimacy of the democratic regime. There is no sign, however, that the stability of the regime is in serious danger (cf. Seligson and Gómez 1989). Indeed, Arias's peace initiative noticeably strengthened Costa Rican national pride, especially after Arias was awarded the Nobel Peace Prize.

The role of the United States in Costa Rica has not been particularly extensive or intensive, when one considers U.S. involvement in other Central American and Caribbean countries (e.g., Nicaragua, Guatemala, Panama). Yet we have seen that the U.S. role was important at two critical junctures in the evolution of modern Costa Rican politics: the crisis of 1948 and the regional crisis of the 1980s. This is not to say that the United States has determined the course of events but only that its role is neglected at the cost of serious misunderstanding. By comparison, the United States has generally played a less important, though certainly not negligible, role in Venezuelan and Colombian politics during the past thirty to forty years.

The course of politics in Colombia since the end of the National Front in 1974 cannot be characterized as democratic consolidation. If anything, we are witnessing a process of deconsolidation, of gradual breakdown.[14] The major problems were mentioned earlier: an inability either to defeat or to reach a settlement with several powerful guerrilla groups, the growing power and impact of drug traffickers, and the

14 On the recent evolution of Colombia, see Camacho 1986; Comisión de estudios 1988; Hartlyn 1989; Santamaría and Silva Luján 1986.

spread of violence throughout the country. In the face of these formidable problems, the formal aspects of the political regime have remained remarkably stable. Full electoral competition has been unbroken since 1974, with the opposition winning the presidency in 1982 and 1986. Left parties and coalitions have competed in elections throughout the period, generally receiving under 5 percent of the vote. Voting turnout and other forms of political participation have increased since the end of the National Front, but they remain at rather low levels compared with those of Venezuela and Costa Rica.

Elections held in 1990 may indicate the early stages of fundamental shifts. The first of the guerilla groups, M-19, to reintegrate itself into civil political life, after a poor performance in congressional elections, finished third in the presidential race (12.3 percent, more than the official candidate of the Conservatives won). The Conservative party split, with elder statesman Alvaro Gómez leading his National Salvation Movement to a second-place showing. The Liberal party easily led both congressional and presidential votes, and César Gaviria Trujillo was elected president. The voters also approved a referendum to call a constitutional convention, elections for which were held in December 1990. The meteoric rise of M-19 continued, as it received about 35 percent of the vote, against 26 percent for Gómez's National Salvation Movement. The governing Liberals were in third place; the official Conservatives fourth. The convention, to meet during 1991, will have unrestricted authority to revise the constitution.[15]

It is at less formal levels that the crisis of the regime is more apparent. The effort to deal with the guerilla movements that have been active since the 1960s has been schizophrenic, alternately emphasizing repression and the search for a negotiated political settlement that would permit the integration of these movements into national political life. The repressive impulse reached its apogee during the presidency of Julio César Turbay (Liberal), from 1978 to 1982, when the armed forces were given virtually free rein to use force against guerrillas and suspected guerrilla sympathizers. The predictable result was a considerable increase in violations of human rights. In addition to the direct actions of the military and police, paramilitary violence, directed principally against legal parties of the left, has become increasingly common.

Reacting to human rights violations and to the evident lack of progress in the counterinsurgency program, Turbay's successor, Belisario Betancur (Conservative), president from 1982 to 1986, embarked on a serious effort (called the Apertura democrática) to negotiate an end

15 See Brooke 1990; *Latin American Weekly Report*, June 7, 1990.

to the insurgencies. A cease-fire was declared by the government, but it was not fully honored by the armed forces or the various insurgent groups. Nevertheless, negotiations with some of the groups were begun, and significant numbers of fighters accepted a government amnesty and sought to enter the legal political arena. The fate of Betancur's peace initiative was sealed, though, when in 1985 one of the insurgent groups, M–19, seized the Palace of Justice in Bogotá, demanding a national dialogue that would lead to democratic reforms. The military's response was disproportionate and, it appears, beyond the control of the president. Rejecting any negotiation, a full military assault on the building ensued, without regard for the fate of hundreds of hostages, of whom many died, including several supreme court justices. The repressive impulse was again ascendant.

Under Liberal President Virgilio Barco (1986–90), a more cautious effort at a negotiated settlement was undertaken, in spite of vocal military skepticism and without tangible result. The government's position was that it would be quite willing to negotiate the reintegration of the guerrillas into political life if they were willing to lay down their arms. Because the insurgents did not trust the military and the paramilitary death squads to leave them alone,[16] the government's negotiating position led nowhere.

In 1988, M-19 challenged the government again, this time kidnapping the Conservative party leader and former presidential candidate, Alvaro Gómez (son of the late Laureano). They did not ask for ransom but, rather, called again for a serious dialogue leading to basic institutional changes that would have the effect of democratizing Colombia. This time the military could not do what they had done in 1985, as they did not know where Gómez was being held. But their hard-line stance, along with that of the dominant Turbay faction of the Liberal party, prevented the government from negotiating. Weeks of impasse went by, until elements of the Conservative party, the church, and the business sector initiated contacts on their own and ultimately brought in the government. Eventually, Gómez was released, and negotiations have continued between M-19 and the government. In early 1990, the two sides reached an agreement by which M-19 would give up its arms in return for recognition as a legal political force and a packet of constitutional reforms to be ratified in a national referendum (see Udall 1989). The M-19 presidential candidate, Carlos Pizarro Leongómez, was assassinated shortly before the May 1990 elections. He was replaced by Antonio Navarro Wolf, who then fin-

16 And with good reason: Hundreds of members of legal left parties have been assassinated by death squads in recent years.

ished third, as noted earlier (see *Latin American Weekly Report*, June 7, 1990).

The other most important insurgent group, the Colombian Revolutionary Armed Forces (FARC) has also been negotiating. In March 1990, Bernardo Jaramillo, presidential candidate of the Patriotic Union, the principal leftist political coalition that is frequently linked to the FARC, was assassinated in the Bogotá airport. Those who ordered the killing are not known, but over one thousand Patriotic Union leaders have been killed by right-wing death squads in the last six years (Wells 1990). It is also possible that the drug cartels were behind the murder, but this seems less likely given the previous pattern of rightist violence against the left.

The government has been progressively less able to concentrate its attention on the insurgencies because of the growing size and power of the underground drug economy. Colombia has for may years been a major supplier of marijuana to North America, but in the last ten years it has also become the nerve center of the rapidly growing cocaine industry. The cities of Medellín and Cali are headquarters for massive drug trade enterprises that control a constantly changing flow of cocaine, marijuana, and money to and from all parts of the world. From a Colombian point of view, the positive side of this traffic are the uncounted dollars that it pumps into the country.[17] But this is heavily outweighed by the negative consequences, notably for the Colombian political elite and the political system. The leading drug entrepreneurs are beyond the control of the Colombian state, and they are not part of the elites who have dominated the country for so long. They have no interest in the well-being of Colombians except as it may be conducive to their own profit. If their interest dictates, they will collaborate with revolutionary insurgents, but they are even more likely to bribe or intimidate mainstream politicians and public officials. Thus, it is increasingly common to find drug lords assuming a direct role in the political process by dispensing material benefits far beyond those available to traditional political bosses and by using the resulting clientelistic loyalties to advance their political careers.[18] An obvious implication is that the poor majority who have been the foundation of the established order may now be drawn away, if not by the revolutionary appeals of the guerillas, then by the well-financed clientelism of the drug organizations.

17 There is no apparent reason that Colombia should not have as bad a debt problem as most other Latin American countries do, but in fact it does not, and the reason probably is at least partially hidden drug profits. Consult Castillo 1987.

18 For a good study of the mechanisms of clientelism in Colombia, with cross-national applicability, see Díaz Uribe 1986.

Confronting this dual threat, the established elites and the state have shown themselves remarkably incapable of innovation. Both the major parties and the military have been unreceptive and often hostile to efforts to promote new approaches that would require significant changes in Colombian social structure. Their response has basically been a reaffirmation of two strategies that have worked in the past: repression and negotiation. But because the elite capacity for action is weak and dispersed, the two strategies have frequently canceled each other out, as happened with Betancur's *apertura*. More fundamentally, in twenty-five years of counterinsurgency and in ten years of a drug war, the Colombian state has shown itself incapable of prevailing in either struggle by repressive means, and the strategy of negotiation has not worked because the established elites have been unwilling to make the concessions that a new settlement would require.

The electoral changes of 1990 may be a sign of fundamental and lasting shifts in Colombian politics. The rise of M-19 as an electoral force, the split of the Conservatives, and the eclipse of both traditional parties in the Constituent Assembly elections could mean a definitive break. The convention will have unrestricted power to change the constitution, and it will very likely abolish extradition, thereby pleasing the drug elites. It could implement electoral reforms that would play havoc with the clientelist political base of the traditional parties. It could commit the nation to such social reforms as land redistribution. Citizen rights may be significantly expanded, and state prerogatives restricted. But how much of what could happen will happen? The traditional parties will control political institutions at all levels, and even the Conservative split can be overrated; Alvaro Gómez, after all, is scarcely a fresh face emerging from the popular masses. Moreover, the military retains substantial autonomy and is willing to use it. Even as M-19 was winning its election victory in the Assembly elections, the army was raiding the headquarters of the largest remaining active guerrilla group, the Colombian Revolutionary armed forces (FARC) (Brooke 1990).

Conclusion

Political changes in Colombia, Costa Rica, and Venezuela raise important theoretical issues about elite settlements and elite convergences. All three countries can be viewed as having experienced an elite settlement followed by some amount of elite convergence. Their patterns suggest that elite settlements and elite convergences are not necessarily alternative routes to elite consensus and unity but, rather, are successive stages in its emergence. Regime stability in these countries has, in turn, depended on the persistence of this elite process. Thus, in Colombia and Venezuela, where classic elite settlements among centrist elites took place, the later absorption of excluded leftist elites has had the character of a convergence. In Colombia, this convergence remains incomplete, with important guerrilla forces still outside the political system. Whether the elites who made the original settlement will be able to persuade these groups to accept the existing political–economic order is an open question. Even more perplexing is whether and how the leaders of the flourishing drug trade will be incorporated. One possibility with respect to both outsider elites is a new settlement, possibly with the new Constituent Assembly as midwife.

By contrast, the stability of the Venezuelan regime has been maintained by incorporating left-wing elites that were originally disaffected. This has been accomplished through constant and conscious elite attention to balancing interests, although the amnesty extended by Caldera and accepted by the insurgent elites in 1969 might be seen as a new settlement in which the left agreed to accept and work within the existing political order.

In Costa Rica, the Figueres–Ulate Pact of 1948 permitted the establishment of a democratic regime, but it was narrowly based: It involved only the victorious allies of the civil war. Elite settlements always exclude some sectors, but the Costa Rican settlement was much more exclusive than the Venezuelan settlement. Why were the Costa Ricans successful in expanding this initially restrictive settlement, but the Colombians were not? A key factor may have been the greater control that the Costa Rican state had over its security forces. This permitted not only the Calderonistas but also the left to take their places in the legislature without fear of repression by death squads and the like – precisely the fate that has befallen the legal left in Colombia since the 1970s. The convergences marked by Calderón's acceptance of the new regime in 1958, and the regime's definitive acceptance of a legal left in 1970, did not involve additional pacts, although it can be demonstrated that both elites and masses in Costa Rica are very conscious of the value of democratic institutions and that they seek to avoid actions that might undermine them (cf. Peeler 1985, chap. 3; Seligson and Gómez 1989).

The Colombian case points up very clearly that an elite settlement is no more permanent than any other historical phenomenon. The rise of new, unincorporated elites and mass social forces has posed grave challenges for the established political elites. Either the Colombian elites will be able to forge a new, broader settlement, or the country will slide further into the abyss.

Finally, we return to the role of mass behavior in shaping the behavior of elites. It is a key argument of this volume that elites make the decisions that vitally affect the character of political regimes. But it is clear from the three cases examined here that it was mass political action, sometimes mobilized by elites but often generated by the population itself, that impelled elites to negotiate among themselves, to change their behaviors, and to reshape a regime by expanding the horizontal inclusiveness of settlements and by restoring vertical control of elites over masses. As much as a game among elites, then, politics is a dialectic between the ruled, who demand more control over their destiny, and the elites, who try with imperfect and uncertain tools to rule them.

References

Aguilar Bulgarelli, Oscar. 1980. *Costa Rica y sus hechos políticos de 1948*. 2nd ed. San José: EDUCA.

Ameringer, Charles. 1982. *Democracy in Costa Rica*. New York: Praeger.

Arroyo Talavera, Eduardo. 1988. *Elecciones y negociaciones: Los Límites de la democracia en Venezuela*. Caracas: Fondo editorial CONICIT.

Barahona, Francisco, coord. 1988. *Costa Rica hacia el 2000*. Caracas: Nueva sociedad.

Blank, David Eugene. 1984. *Venezuela: Politics in a Petroleum Republic*. New York: Praeger.

Brewer-Carías, Allen R. 1988. *Problemas del estado de partidos*. Caracas: Ed. jurídica venezolana.

Brooke, James. 1990. "Former Rebels in First Place in Colombian Election." *New York Times*, December 10, p. A10.

Camacho G., Alvaro. 1986. *La Colombia de hoy*. Bogotá: Fondo editorial CEREC.

Carrera Damas, Germán. 1988. *La Necesaria Reforma democrática del estado*. Caracas: Grijalbo.

Castillo, Fabio. 1987. *Los Jinetes de la cocaina*. Bogotá: Editorial documentos periodísticos.

Cerdas Cruz, Rodolfo. 1985. *Formación del estado en Costa Rica (1821–1842)*. San José: Ed. Universidad de Costa Rica.

Comisión de estudios sobre la violencia. 1988. *Colombia: Violencia y democracia* Bogotá: Universidad nacional de Colombia.

Cruz, Rafael de la. 1988. *Venezuela en busca de un nuevo pacto social*. Caracas: Alfadil.

Díaz Uribe, Eduardo. 1986. *El Clientelismo en Colombia*. Bogotá: El Ancora editores.

Dix, Robert H. 1980. "Consociational Democracy: The Case of Colombia." *Comparative Politics* 12: 303–21.

1987. *The Politics of Colombia*. New York: Praeger.

Echeverri Uruburu, Alvaro. 1986. *Elites y proceso político en Colombia, 1950–1978*. Bogotá: Fundación universitaria autónoma de Colombia.

Gilmore, Robert. 1965. *Caudillism and Militarism in Venezuela, 1830–1910*. Athens: Ohio University Press.

Guillén Martínez, Fernando. 1979. *El Poder político en Colombia*. Bogotá: Punta de Lanza.

Guzmán Campos, German, Orlando Fals Bonda, and Eduardo Umaña Luna. 1980. *La Violencia en Colombia*. 2 vols. 9th ed. Bogotá: Carlos Valencia.

Hartlyn, Jonathan. 1988. *The Politics of Coalition Rule in Colombia*. Cambridge: Cambridge University Press.

1989. "Colombia: The Politics of Violence and Accommodation." In *Democracy in Developing Countries: Latin America*, ed. Larry Diamond, Juan Linz, and Seymour Martin Lipset. Boulder, Co: Lynne Rienner.

Held, David. 1987. *Models of Democracy*. Stanford, CA: Stanford University Press.

Higley, John, and Michael G. Burton. 1989. "The Elite Variable in Democratic Transitions and Breakdowns." *American Sociological Review* 54:17–32.

Huntington, Samuel P. 1968. *Political Order in Changing Societies*. New Haven, CT: Yale University Press.

Karl, Terry. 1987. "Petroleum and Political Pacts: The Transition to Democracy in Venezuela." *Latin American Research Review* 22:63–94.

Kline, Harvey F. 1980. "The National Front: Historical Perspective and Overview." In *Politics of Compromise: Coalition Government in Colombia*, ed. R. Albert Berry et al. New Brunswick, NJ: Transaction.

Latin American Weekly Report. 1990. June 7, pp.1–2.

Levine, Daniel H. 1989. "Venezuela: The Nature, Sources, and Future Prospects of Democracy." In *Democracy in Developing Countries: Latin America*, ed. Larry Diamond, Juan Linz, and Seymour Martin Lipset. Boulder, CO: Lynne Rienner.

Lombardi, John V. 1982. *Venezuela: The Search for Order, the Dream of Progress*. New York: Oxford University Press.

López Maya, Margarita, and Luis Gómez Calcaño. 1989. "Desarrollo y hegemonía en la sociedad venezolana: 1958 a 1985." In *De Punto fijo al pacto social*, ed. Maragarita López Maya et al. Caracas: Fondo editorial acta científica venezolana.

Martz, John D. 1966. *Acción Democrática: Evolution of a Modern Political Party in Venezuela*. Princeton, NJ: Princeton University Press.

Martz, John D., and David J. Myers, eds. 1986. *Venezuela: The Democratic Experience*. New York: Praeger.

Monge Alfaro, Carlos. 1980. *Historia de Costa Rica*. 16th ed. San José: Libería trejos.

Myers, David J. 1986. "The Venezuelan Party System: Regime Maintenance Under Stress." In *Venezuela: The Democratic Experience*, ed. John D. Martz and David J. Myers, Princeton, NJ: Princeton University Press.

Oconotrillo, Eduardo. 1982. *Un siglo de política costarricense*. San José: Ed. Universidad estatal a distancia.

Oquist, Paul. 1980. *Violence, Conflict, and Politics in Colombia*. New York: Academic Press.

Peeler, John A. 1985. *Latin American Democracies: Colombia, Costa Rica, Venezuela*. Chapel Hill: University of North Carolina Press.

Roijira Mas, Jorge. 1988. *Estado y política económica en Costa Rica*. 3rd ed. San José: Ed. Porvenir.

Salcedo-Bastardo, J. L. 1979. *Historia fundamental de Venezuela*. Caracas: Universidad central.

Salom, Roberto. 1987. *La Crisis de la izquierda en Costa Rica*. San José: Ed. Porvenir.

Santamaría S., Ricardo, and Gabriel Silva Luján. 1986. *Proceso político en Colombia: Del Frente nacional a la apertura democrática*. Bogotá: Fondo editorial CEREC.

Schifter, Jacobo. 1979. *La Fase oculta de la guerra civil en Costa Rica*. San José: EDUCA.

1986. *Las Alianzas conflictivas*. San José: Libro libre.

Schlesinger, Stephen, and Stephen Kinzer. 1982. *Bitter Fruit: The Untold Story of the American Coup in Guatemala*. Garden City, NY: Anchor Books.

Seligson, Mitchell A., and Miguel Gómez B. 1989. "Ordinary Elections in Extraordinary Times: The Political Economy of Voting in Costa Rica." In *Elections and Democracy in Central America*, ed. John A. Booth and Mitchell A. Seligson. Chapel Hill: University of North Carolina Press.

Sharpless, Richard E. 1978. *Gaitán of Colombia: A Political Biography*. Pittsburgh: University of Pittsburgh Press.

Stone, Samuel. 1975. *La Dinastía de los conquistadores*. San José: EDUCA.

Torres Rivas, Edelberto, et al. 1987. *Costa Rica: Crisis y desafíos*. San José: DEI.

Udall, Caroline. 1989. "M–19 on Verge of Demobilizing." *The Times of the Americas*, December 27, p. 1.

Vega Carballo, José Luis. 1981. *Orden y progreso: La Formación del estado nacional en Costa Rica*. San José: Instituto centroamericano de administración pública.

Wells, Tom. 1990. "Colombian Candidate Assassinated." *Philadelphia Inquirer*, March 23, p. 11A.

Wilde, Alexander. 1978. "Conversations Among Gentlemen: Oligarchical Democracy in Colombia." In *The Breakdown of Democratic Regimes: Latin America*, ed. Juan Linz and Alfred Stepan. Baltimore: Johns Hopkins University Press.

Woodward, Ralph L. 1985. *Central America: A Nation Divided*. 2nd ed. New York: Oxford University Press.

4

Mexico's elite settlement: conjuncture and consequences

ALAN KNIGHT

Elite settlements are rare but decisive events, triggered by recent experiences of costly but inconclusive conflict (or, less dramatically, of prolonged, debilitating factionalism) and, perhaps, by a major crisis. They are accomplished swiftly, even though subsequent consolidation of the settlement may take years; they involve "face-to-face, partially secret, negotiations among the paramount leaders of the major elite factions," who enjoy "considerable autonomy from mass followings and pressures," the participation of "experienced political leaders," and, possibly, formal written agreements and "eminently public documents"; they demand mutual conciliation, which in turn is premised on a perception of shared elite interests and, very likely, "elite fears of levelling sentiments as a prod to quick action"; their most "fundamental and lasting consequence" is a "common elite acceptance of a new code of political conduct" involving continued mutual tolerance and conciliation; and this legacy may, over time, prove conducive to the development of a democratic form of rule, which, in a sense, extends to society at large the principles of mutual tolerance (the "rules of the game") that the elites have pioneered (Burton and Higley 1987, pp. 11–25). As a result, elite settlements may afford the basis for a consolidated democracy.

This, of course, is the ideal type: The utility of the concept does not require that every item be present in every putative elite settlement. However, it is worth adding that the utility of the concept may vary from person to person, discipline to discipline. Political scientists in a nomothetic quest for broad generalizations look for recurrent patterns, perhaps possessing predictive power. For them, the elite settlement concept offers a potentially useful item in the construction of such generalizations, and the heuristic payoff comes with the plotting of meaningful patterns over broad comparative areas. Historians engaged in the idiographic analysis of discrete cases are more likely to judge the utility of the concept in narrower terms, according to its "fit" in a particular historical context. My chief concern in this chapter is to consider the appropriateness of the elite settlement concept in regard to Mexico, tackling, first, the putative settlement of 1928–9, second, that settlement's longer term political consequences, and, finally (and most tentatively), the broader utility and appropriateness of the concept and its theoretical implications in a wider historical context, albeit from the perspective of a historian rather than a political scientist.

The making of the Mexican settlement

On the afternoon of July 17, 1928, Alvaro Obregón, president-elect of Mexico, attended a political luncheon at La Bombilla restaurant in the southern suburbs of Mexico City, a popular watering hole for the Mexican political class. Concerned about Obregón's security (he had recently escaped two assassination attempts),[1] his entourage had urged him not to go and had even concocted a plausible and compelling alternative engagement (Dulles 1972, pp. 366–7). But Obregón demurred and decided to attend. As they were about to leave, he asked one of his companions, in his typical bluff, wisecracking style, "Aren't you afraid to go with us? Someone might set off a bomb." At the luncheon – a typically long, lavish, Mexican occasion, complete with orchestra, floral decorations, and a large clutch of prominent *políticos* – Obregón was approached by a young man with a sketch pad. He was José León de Toral, an art teacher and Catholic activist, who was drawing portraits of the guests. Urged on by his guardian angel (he later said), Toral approached the president-elect and shot him repeatedly in the back.[2]

Obregón was far from being the first or only victim of political assassination (indeed, the old definition of czarism – autocracy tempered by assassination – fits revolutionary Mexico tolerably well). Madero had been gunned down in 1913, Zapata in 1919, Carranza in 1920, and Villa in 1923. And these were just the more celebrated victims. But Obregón's death was, in national political terms, the most significant and critical. Along with his fellow-Sonoran, Plutarco Elías

1 For details of previous assassination attempts, see the report by Colonel Alex J. McNab, U.S. Military Attaché, Mexico City, to Secretary of State, August 30, 1928, in State Department Archives, Internal Affairs of Mexico 1910–29 (henceforth abbreviated as SD), 812.00/29302.

2 Lengthy versions of the assassination story, its protagonists, and aftermath are given by McNab (note 1); *El Universal* and *Excelsior*, August 20, 1928; and Dulles 1972, chaps. 41, 42, 45.

Calles, he had been the chief architect of the postrevolutionary state of the 1920s. Together, they had formed an effective dyarchy, the twin pillars of the Sonoran dynasty (1920–34). Obregón had served as president between 1920 and 1924, weathering military rebellion, economic recession, and pressure from the United States. Calles had succeeded him in 1924 until 1928, embarking on (and then later backing away from) more radical policies of land distribution, labor reform, economic nationalism, and, above all, anticlericalism. In the election of July 1, 1928, Obregón had been comfortably reelected, following a constitutional amendment allowing such a reelection to take place (Dulles 1972, p. 351). His assassination barely two weeks later thus created a major political crisis. Until November 30, Calles remained the incumbent president. But, with dyarchy converted de facto to monarchy, no obvious successor, no providential caudillo, could be found: "No one has as yet been able to find the man" who might succeed Calles (*Excelsior*, August 22, 1928).

Several alternatives beckoned: a prolongation of Calles's presidency, an interim presidency and a fresh election, or civil war and renewed political chaos (Meyer 1981, p. 22). As it was, Calles spurned those who advised prolonging his presidency and instead took steps to defuse tensions, to unite the various factions of the revolutionary family, and to engineer the election by Congress of a provisional president. In addition, he took advantage of the crisis to appeal for the end of *caudillismo* and the inauguration of the rule of institutions. This presaged the creation of the first omnibus revolutionary party, the Partido nacional revolucionario (PNR), in March 1929. Taken together, these events would seem to meet the criteria of an elite settlement; certainly, from the historian's perspective, the elite settlement concept is a useful and relevant one for an analysis of the 1928–9 crisis and its outcome. But in some respects, the Mexican case diverges from the ideal type (which is hardly surprising), and it may be possible to use this example of an elite settlement à la Mexicana in order to refine or qualify the general category.

The perception of crisis was palpable: "In the early days the situation was one of such perplexity that no one had any idea of how we would get out of the mess."[3] Newspapers sold as never before (Dulles 1972, p. 371). Dire predictions and sober warnings were bandied about: If Calles were to step down, it would mean the "total ruin of the country"; it would generate a crisis in Congress and a

3 Marte R. Gómez to Ramón P. De Negri, September 13, 1928, in Marte R. Gómez, *Vida política contemporánea: Cartas de Marte R. Gómez* (1978), Mexico, Fondo de cultura económica (FCE), vol. 1, p. 205.

renewal of civil war in Mexico.[4] But at the same time, crisis generated a mood of conciliation and forbearance that extended beyond the "revolutionary family." It was not surprising that Calles should enjoin the army to "keep perfect unity," that the powerful Obregonista political faction should appeal for "serenity and unity," or that its de facto leader, Aarón Sáenz, should urge "unity and harmony within the party" (Dulles 1972, pp. 382, 389; *El Universal*, August 23, 1928). But opposition groups, such as the Partido antireeleccionista, also joined the chorus, calling for the "various factions, separated until now, generously [to] renounce all passions, ambitions, and quarrels and, with goodwill, [to] lend their aid in the great work of revolutionary unification."[5] Implicit – and often explicit – in this rhetoric of union was a call for political institutionalization. The successor to President Calles, declared the Callista Puig Casauranc, would be the law, a refrain that was taken up by the press, with appeals for a "more stable and legal system" and an end to the fratricidal carnage that threatened to turn the revolution into "a cradle of anarchy" (*Excelsior*, August 21, 1928; *El Universal*, August 22, 1928). Not surprisingly, the same theme was reiterated in the months to come, as the revolutionary elites set about creating a new official party, the Partido nacional revolucionario (PNR) which, in the words of its first president, would constitute a "single national front" (*frente único nacional*) and which, in the words of another prominent Callista, would enable the revolutionaries to forget old rancors and to unite in order to "guide the country along its new democratic path" (Nava Nava 1984, pp. 46–7).

Such was the political rhetoric. Meanwhile, the practical political response was rapid. In the wake of the assassination, Calles began to take soundings with the major revolutionary leaders: the military, state governors, members of congress. "Generals and politicians poured into Mexico City from all parts of the country;" the Hotel Régis, a favorite hostlery, "daily took on more and more the appearance of a political convention" (Dulles 1972, pp. 382–3). "There is ample evidence," reported U.S. Ambassador Dwight Morrow, "of the existence of intense political activity."[6] The timetable was pressing: Obregón died in July; the revolutionaries caucused in August; and Congress was due to meet at the beginning of September, when it expected to hear Calles's decision concerning the new presidential term, which would begin on December 1.

4 Attorney General to Secretary of State, enclosing report by special agent Gus T. Jones, August 1, 1928, SD 812.00/29287; *El Universal*, August 27, 1928.

5 H. F. A. Schoenfeld, Mexico City, to Secretary of State, August 17, 1928, S.D. 812.00/29285.

6 Ambassador Morrow to Secretary of State, August 30, 1928, S.D. 812.00/29304.

Calles's address to Congress was a key event, "the most significant political pronouncement made in Mexico for many years."[7] Its content is well known: The president made a powerful appeal for calm, order, unity, and a deliberate shift toward political institutionalization. He would not prolong his presidency. It was time, he declared, to relinquish the rule of the caudillo and to create a "nation of institutions and laws." He flattered the "noble and disinterested" army but insisted that the provisional president who succeeded him should be a civilian. And he held out the prospect of a true political pluralism, promising "the definitive entry of Mexico into the realm of institutions and laws and, with a view to regulating our political life, the establishment of genuine organic national parties" (Dulles 1972, pp. 384–7; *Excelsior*, September 2, 1928). Although this statesman-like performance – which was well received throughout the country, even by some of Calles's critics – helped avert an immediate crisis, the political agenda was still packed and the political future was precarious. In particular, Calles and his collaborators faced the initial tricky task of arranging the presidential succession and, subsequently, the Herculean labor of creating a more viable institutional politics.

The timetable remained busy. On September 5, Calles received the leading generals of the revolution at the National Palace and won their assent to a civilian presidential succession. On the same day a caucus of prominent *políticos* met in order to head off the Obregonista *enragés*, led by the Topete clan. And later in the month, Calles conferred with a congressional delegation, securing its support for the middle-of-the-road Obregonista Emilio Portes Gil as provisional president (Dulles 1972, pp. 388–92; Garrido 1986, pp. 86–7).

With Portes Gil safely installed at the beginning of December, preparations for the first PNR convention got under way. The new organizing committee issued a manifesto, called for recruits and affiliates, devised a (somewhat bland) program, drew up party statutes, and, finally, convened the inaugural party convention for March 1–4, 1929 (Garrido 1986, pp. 92–102, 110–17). The relative rapidity of events was sustained at the convention itself, not least because it coincided with a major military insurrection. By the time the convention had approved the credentials of some 950 delegates, had heard the rhetorical exordia of the principal orators, and had voted on the main business – the choice of a party presidential candidate – there was little time for serious debate about policy or party organization; hence the "scant discussion and hurried automatic (*maquinal*) way in which the basic documents of the PNR were approved" (Nava Nava

7 Ambassador Morrow to Secretary of State, September 3, 1928, S.D. 812.00/29309.

1984, p. 46). The sheer speed of the operation indicated the sense of crisis and the political momentum that had been built up since the late summer of 1928. But it reflected, too, the fact that the project of a united revolutionary party was not a new one. It had been floated and even attempted several times since the revolution: with the Obregón presidential candidacy in 1919; with the abortive Confederación nacional revolucionaria of 1922; with the electoral front that had backed Calles in 1924; with the quasi-official PLM and its rival, the Alianza de partidos socialistas, in the mid–1920s; with Calles's repeatedly unsuccessful attempts to create a solid revolutionary bloc in Congress; and with the Alianza de partidos Obregonistas in 1928 (Garrido 1986, pp. 54, 58, 61–2, 64, 66, 69–70, 73). Furthermore, Mexico's revolutionaries were well aware of and influenced by contemporary party organizations elsewhere in the world: the French Radicals, the German Socialists, the British Labor party, the Peruvian APRA, the Chinese KMT, the Italian Fascists (Garrido 1986, pp. 64, 90–1). As leaders such as Calles and Marte R. Gómez put it, the Mexican Revolution had succeeded in the "economic–social" field but had failed politically. It was a "more or less defined" social program contrasted with a "retrograde political program," evidenced in revolutionary dissent and praetorianism. The time thus was now ripe to "take a leap forward that will balance our social and political advance."[8]

Although the elite settlement of 1928–9 was rapid, unpredictable, and capable of derailment (it was, we might say, "underdetermined"), it did not come like a bolt from the blue. Rather, it was responding to the deep-seated aims and interests of many of the revolutionary leaders who in the past had tried, but failed, to achieve a stable institutionalization of revolutionary politics. The crisis of 1928 made possible a successful process of settlement, in which elite decisions and conflicts were played out in a situation of flux and uncertainty, but such a settlement was, we might say, latent in the revolutionary legacy (as it was in the case of late seventeenth-century England, too). It was not inevitable; hence the events of 1928–9 are of crucial importance in determining the final outcome. But it is clear that the creation of a successful official party was both a distinct possibility and a goal to which certain groups were positively committed and that this possibility derived from the victorious revolution of 1910–15. Without that prior experience (which is not at issue here), no elite settlement along the lines of 1928–9 would have been conceivable.

8 Dulles 1972, p. 457; Marte R. Gómez to Ramón P. De Negri, September 13, 1928, in Gómez, *Vida política comtemporánea*, p. 207.

So, too, with 1688. These postrevolutionary elite settlements rode on the back of preceding social revolutions. Whether horse is more important than jockey is an old racing conundrum, to which most experts would reply that although jockeys can certainly lose races (i.e., elites can squander postrevolutionary opportunities), it is horses, not jockeys, that win races (this is a roundabout way of questioning the proposition that "in many ways, elite settlements are as consequential as social revolutions" (Burton and Higley 1987, p. 3).

Leaving this broad and contentious question and focusing squarely on the events of 1928–9, it is clear that the process of crisis management and party formation was one in which elites took the lead and collaborated on the basis of reciprocal concessions. But which elites? And with what degree of autonomy?

Elites and masses

First, we should stress that the Mexican elite settlement was highly exclusionary as well as inclusionary. Exclusion took two forms. First, the elites that met, negotiated, and came together to constitute the new party were the revolutionary elites, the legatees of the armed revolution of 1910–20. They by no means enjoyed a monopoly of power. To put it another way and to revert to the working definition being used, there existed rival elites who "by virtue of their strategic positions in powerful organizations [were able] to affect national political outcomes regularly and substantially" (Burton and Higley 1987, p. 11). The most obvious example was the Catholic church, which had been at odds with the revolutionary regime at least since 1914 and which, at the time of Obregón's death at the hands of a Catholic assassin, was involved in a prolonged military confrontation with the regime, especially in the west–central region of Mexico (Meyer 1973–4). Neither church nor state, it is true, was a monolith; there were important individuals within each that favored détente rather than further confrontation and bloodshed (ironically, Obregón was one of them; Toral later admitted, albeit after severe torture, that "he had misjudged Obregón and should not have killed him" (Dulles 1972, p. 376). Calles, originally a dogmatic *comecuras* (priest-baiter), had by 1928 softened his extreme anticlericalism. In his September 1 address to Congress, he urged the creation of a revolutionary party that would, in turn, encourage the formation of an organized – but peaceful, electoral – conservative counterpart, an appeal that was echoed by the organizing committee of the new PNR (Dulles 1972, p. 410). And in mid–1929 a rough modus vivendi with the church was concluded, and so the bloody Cristero rebellion drew to a close.

None of this, however, implied the participation of clerical forces in the elite settlement. Not only did they not participate (confessional parties were constitutionally banned); they also were explicitly excluded from the pacting process, and the fierce repression of dissident Catholics – "isolated groups of fanatics," as General Joaquín Amaro contemptuously dismissed them – continued throughout the 1928–9 period of the settlement (*El Universal*, August 30, 1928). Indeed, the settlement and its institutional embodiment, the PNR, were seen as a dike against clericalism. Marte R. Gómez hoped that by unifying the revolutionaries "in idea and action," the new PNR would "set a barrier (*poner un hasta aquí*) to the clerical reactionary party that has caused so much and great damage to our country."[9] When proclaiming that the new provisional president, Portes Gil, represented public opinion, Manuel Pérez Treviño qualified his point by stipulating his "revolutionary and Obregonista" opinion, for "it is of no concern at all to us whether other opinion, which we call the reaction, is satisfied or not" (Dulles 1972, p. 393). Portes Gil himself agreed. The PNR, he explained, was a government party devised to defend the principles of the revolution: "It is necessary that [the privileged classes] submit to the revolutionary program of the government. If so, they are welcome, but I say that fundamentally they must recognize as indisputable the realization of the program of the revolution" (*Excelsior*, May 28, 1930). In other words, the new party was a vehicle of the revolution, "*la revolución hecha gobierno*," and it would welcome clerical and conservative converts only if they repented and fully converted (Garrido 1986, p. 152). Similar exclusionist rhetoric characterized President Ortiz Rubio and the party newspaper, *El Nacional Revolucionario* (Garrido 1986, pp. 135, 138). There was not much evidence here of "warring national elite factions . . . reorganizing their relations by negotiating compromises on their most basic disagreements" (Burton and Higley 1987, p. 2). Subsequent events showed – and were the necessary proof – that this exclusionary and belligerent attitude was much more typical than Calles's rhetorical olive branch.

Also excluded, though less explicitly, was the private sector. True, it was not yet organized in powerful corporate lobbies (although the process had begun), and so politically active entrepreneurs chose to colonize and coopt the revolutionary leadership rather than to oppose it directly. Relations between the private sector and the regime tended to be informal, pragmatic, and variable over time and place. What is clear, however, is that business leaders did not directly participate in

9 Marte R. Gómez to Felipe Santibáñez, November 16, 1928, in Gómez, *Vida política contemporánea*, pp. 217–18.

the pacting of 1928–9, except that several important revolutionary leaders were businessmen. But they did owe their access to the pacting process to their political rather than their entrepreneurial standing. The biggest bastion of independent entrepreneurship, the Monterrey Group, entertained high hopes that the PNR would choose the governor of Nuevo León, the Obregonista *político* and businessman Aarón Saénz, as its presidential candidate for the 1929 election. Instead (as we shall see), Saénz was brushed aside – in part precisely because of his conservative inclinations and connections – and Calles's protégé, Pascual Ortiz Rubio, was railroaded through the convention. Meanwhile, the interim president, Portes Gil, initiated the codification of Article 123 (the "Magna Carta of Mexican labor"), which represented a further challenge to the *regiomontanos* (Saragoza 1988, pp. 151–67). Far from uniting state, party, and private enterprise, the events of 1928–9 pried them apart. The Monterrey Group, alienated from the PNR, set about organizing a powerful employers' confederation quite distinct from and critical of the state–party apparatus (Garrido 1986, p. 139). By 1936 the two sides were in open confrontation (Saragoza 1988, chap. 8).

Though excluding to a greater or lesser extent the major elites that lacked any revolutionary credentials, the pacting *políticos* of 1928–9 also froze out some of their supposed comrades. In other words, the settlement was not wholly inclusionary, even from the standpoint of the "revolutionary family."[10] Again, this is not surprising, nor (I think) does it invalidate the notion of an elite settlement. But it does require that the latter allow for some divisions and discrimination within the dominant political elite. In the Mexican case, the revolutionary family had, throughout the 1910s and 1920s, proved to be a quarrelsome and fractious fraternity. Even after the bloody civil wars between 1910 and 1920 had subsided, the major factional divisions remained, which generated significant military rebellions in 1923, 1927 (almost), and 1929 (as we will see). In addition, the country suffered from a constant undercurrent of violence, quite apart from the more overt and deadly church–state conflict: Rival political factions feuded in the provinces; municipal politics were infected with *pistolerismo*; trade unions fought (literally) for local supremacy; and even the Chamber of Deputies had

10 The "revolutionary family" is a term that Mexicanists habitually use with more abandon than precision: It denotes the group that took power during the armed revolution of 1910–20 and whose descendants, political and biological, have ruled to this day. It represents, therefore, series of generational political elites. The term (which enjoyed currency at least as early as the 1920s) neatly captures the combination of bonding and rivalry, comradeship and competition, that characterized the revolutionary elite(s).

its occasional shoot-outs. This was the necessary backdrop to the settlement of 1928–9, which was designed by its makers to staunch the tide of violence – which in the immediate crisis threatened to reach new heights – and to enforce the rule of central government institutions. Whereas the Colombian elites came together in 1957 to end the violence, the Mexican elites – participants in the great hecatomb of 1910–20 – came together in 1928–9 to avert potential violence. But in doing so, they had to sacrifice several of their own. The chief victims were the leadership of the dominant labor confederation, the Confederación regional obrera mexicana, (CROM), and a section of the Obregonista military, groups that, incidentally, were bitter mutual enemies.

Under the patronage of President Calles and the corrupt, swaggering leadership of Luis Napoleón Morones, the CROM had established itself by the mid-1920s as the dominant labor confederation in Mexico. It brazenly claimed two million members; it fielded a political party, the Partido laborista, which was the closest to a genuine national party that the country possessed in the 1920s; it supplied a clutch of state governors and congressmen, as well as two cabinet ministers, including Morones himself; it warred with the church, with the oil companies, and with rival trade unions of the independent left and the Catholic right; it toppled governors whom it disliked; it flirted with the creation of a workers' militia; and it backed Morones's challenge for the presidency. This challenge was thwarted by Obregón's reelection, which threatened an erosion of the CROM's power, and when Obregón was assassinated, the CROM's many enemies saw their opportunity to turn on the faltering confederation. Morones, they alleged, had entered into unholy alliance with the clerical killers of the president-elect. The charge was groundless, but it carried weight.[11] Calles, never one to base his politics on personal affection, had to throw Morones and his CROM *compadres* to the Obregonista wolves. Morones lost his cabinet position; CROMistas were removed from statehouses and Congress; rival trade unions stepped up their attacks on CROMista rivals; and before long, the CROM itself began to disintegrate. The creature to a considerable extent of government favor, it could not survive when that favor was withdrawn. The CROM did not die (it still lives, a shadow of its former self), but it lost its access to power, its quasi-monopoly status. In consequence, it played no real part in the pact making of 1928–9. Morones was not

11 Consul Franklin, Saltillo, August 6, 1928, S.D. 812.00/29280; Marte R. Gómez to Ramón P. De Negri, September 13, 1928, in Gómez, *Vida político comtemporánea*, p. 205.

party to the caucusing in Mexico City. And as the new PNR began to gather to its broad bosom the multifarious political parties of Mexico, the Partido laborista, the political arm of the CROM, was excluded (Córdova 1981, chaps. 1, 2; Dulles 1972, pp. 381, 411; Garrido 1986, p. 95). Before long, Morones was marshaling other excluded groups, including the significant Partido nacional agrarista, in a joint front (the Alianza revolucionaria nacional) that was pledged to quixotic opposition to the new PNR (Garrido 1986, pp. 147, 154–5).

The chief critics and opponents of the CROM were the Obregonista military. Products, like Obregón himself, of the armed revolution, they were leery of organized labor and of the political institutionalization that Calles sought to implement through his alliance with the CROM. Talk of workers' militias hardly endeared them to the CROM, either. Having successfully headed off a presidential bid by Morones in 1928, they reacted to the death of their hero and mentor by turning on the CROM and rending its leadership. Briefly, in the fall of 1928, the Obregonista leaders seemed to be in the saddle. But they were soon dismounted by Calles, and in spring 1929, a large Obregonista faction rose in open rebellion. These events (which we need not rehearse here in detail) shed light on both Calles's motivation and the manufacture of the Mexican elite settlement. In the wake of the assassination Calles was prepared to go a long way to assuage the Obregonistas' indignation and ambition. He coolly sacrificed his old CROMista allies and nobly proclaimed that he would not prolong his own presidency, which many of his partisans, like Tejeda and Montes de Oca, advocated (Dulles 1972, p. 383). With CROMismo down and out and Callismo in apparent retreat, Obregonismo, albeit deprived of its eponymous caudillo, seemed unstoppable. When it came to canvassing the names of provisional and constitutional presidential candidates, Obregonista names (Topete, Portes Gil, Sáenz, Escobar) filled the hat. Sure enough, the choice for provisional president – made by Congress at Calles's instigation – fell to Emilio Portes Gil, a known Obregonista, a bitter enemy of the CROM, but a civilian rather than a general.

Calles's call for institutional politics was not mere disinterested statesmanship. The repudiation of caudillo politics, the appeal to the rule of law, implied a civilian succession. The Obregonista military, confident that their chosen civilian candidate (the northern governor and entrepreneur Aarón Sáenz) was a shoe-in, did not complain. But as the preparations for the first PNR convention progressed, Calles and his collaborators outmaneuvered Sáenz. A political nonentity, Pascual Ortiz Rubio, was plucked from the Mexican embassy in Brazil and prodded into the political arena. As the party convention neared, it became clear that the Sáenz candidacy was faltering, and at the convention itself Sáenz, seeing defeat snatched from the jaws of victory, stormed from the assembly, calling it a farce and taking with him a bunch of his partisans (Meyer 1981, pp. 59–61). Almost immediately, an Obregonista military revolt (which had been gestating for some weeks) came to term. It was led by General José Escobar who, the previous September, had proclaimed that "barrack uprisings have passed into history" (Dulles 1972, p. 390). Perhaps a quarter of the military rose in arms, challenging the central government in Coahuila, Veracruz, Sonora, Sinaloa, and Oaxaca; mutual vituperation between "in" and "out" revolutionaries ran the whole gamut of rhetorical abuse (Dulles 1972, p. 438; Nava Nava 1984, p. 45). As in 1923 and 1927, therefore, the presidential succession triggered a preemptive revolt by those who knew that they had lost. As in 1923 and 1927, too, the government crushed the rebels. Calles assumed control of the War Ministry; the United States backed the government; armed agraristas successfully combated the rebels, notably in Veracruz; and rebel overtures to the insurgent Cristeros proved fruitless (Fowler Salamini 1978, p. 63; Meyer 1981, pp. 64–84). By April the revolt had been put down, and the customary executions and exiles further culled the ranks of the dissident military. The last serious military revolt of the long revolutionary cycle was over.[12]

On the one hand, the government of the elite settlement had shown its mettle (in 1923 over half the army had defected, and the war had been imminent; six years later the Obregonista revolt was much more easily contained). But the fact of the revolt confirmed that the settlement itself had been far from all-inclusive and had clearly failed to incorporate or satisfy all elite groups, including those like the Obregonista military, close to the center of power who had played a significant part in the initial settlement. This suggests, first, that elite settlements are pacts both between and against certain elite groups and that, second, even during the rapid process of negotiation and realignment (we are talking about eight months at most) the balance of forces shifted and resulted in the expulsion and defeat of an important faction. Indeed, exclusion soon went further and embraced both the (broadly) middle-class Vasconcelista liberals and the Mexican Communist party, who were fiercely repressed in the course of 1929. One historian talks of a "reign of terror" (Garrido 1986, pp. 143, 146–7; Romero 1987, p. 26; Skirius 1978, pp. 140–3, 182, 186). Yet this did

12 Saturnino Cedillo's 1938 revolt, which is traditionally referred to as Mexico's last military uprising, was a personalist, highly localized, insurrection that caused the government few problems.

not signify the failure of the settlement; on the contrary, it showed that those who contested its outcome did so in vain and at their own peril. The settlement stuck and was further reinforced by the defeat, dispersal, and discomfiture of its opponents.

Where were the masses during this hectic and crucial period of political realignment? The elite settlement theory requires a considerable degree of elite autonomy: first, because elite negotiations must be rapid, concerted, and face to face (thus elites cannot be constantly conferring with and reporting back to their mass constituencies); and, second, because these constituencies are presumed to be more principled and intransigent, less subtle and accommodating, than their elite masters. The first assumption appears valid, certainly in the Mexican case, but the second appears, to me, to be arbitrary and unproven. However, I shall suggest that the question of the relationship between elite and mass is not resolved simply by reviewing the events of the settlement and noting (as I shall note) that the masses figured more as an audience (sometimes a rather bored audience) than as active participants. Underlying the settlement was a certain structural relationship between elites and masses that deserves attention and that critically affected the settlement process – its rationale, assumptions, and objectives. The basic, and hardly startling, point that emerges is that for all their autonomy, elites had to reckon with a mass presence in politics; therefore, in theoretical terms, it is as inadvisable to adopt an excessively narrow focus only on elites as it is to reduce elite politics to crude class reflexes. Elite and class interpretations are not mutually incompatible, certainly not for the theoretically eclectic historian, who may read both Mosca and Marx with profit.[13]

The process of the elite settlement in Mexico was determined by elites acting in relative autonomy. True, the assassination of Obregón shook the country: Newspaper sales shot up, as Toral's trial, execution, and burial excited extensive morbid interest. But it did not produce any spontaneous popular reaction as did the Colombian

13 For contemporary analogues, see Paul Cammack, "A Critical Assessment of the New Elite Paradigm," and the response by John Higley, Michael G. Burton, and G. Lowell Field, "In Defense of Elite Theory," *American Sociological Review* 55 (1990): 415–26. From a somewhat simple point of view, in fact, elite theory and Marxism have something in common (which distances both from certain other social science paradigms). Elite theorists may favor the analysis of elites, Marxists of the masses, but both agree that society is stratified and that the allocation of property and power is highly skewed (even though they use different terms to describe this enduring inequality). C. Wright Mills might stand as an example of this loose compatibility, which has been noted by expert analysts, too: See T. B. Bottomore, *Elites and Society* (Harmondsworth: Penguin Books, 1966), pp. 32 and 56.

Bogotazo of 1949, triggered by the assassination of Gaitán. The prevailing mood seems to have been one of cautious *attentisme*, a mood encouraged, no doubt, by the war weariness pervading west–central Mexico and the economic doldrums that affected the country as a whole (Nava Nava 1984, pp. 78–87). In the business-like north, especially, it was felt that "anything would be preferable to another revolution."[14] To that extent, Calles's cautious statesmanship caught the country's mood, and we may contrast the outcome with that of, say, 1914–15, when a broad desire for peace and revolutionary harmony was thwarted by the head-on collision of Villa and Carranza (an example of elite ambition and aggression outrunning popular pacifism that, I suspect, is far from unique and that must cast doubt on the assumption that elite moderation invariably, or usually, contrasts with popular extremism (Knight 1986, vol. 2, pp. 274–5). In 1914–15 the rival elites went to war, and the rank and file followed. Fourteen years later, when the elites opted for conciliation, they had little difficulty in carrying the people with them. Furthermore, the settlement process incurred relatively little popular participation. Incumbent elites caucused and jockeyed, especially in Mexico City; demonstrations and rallies were few; and the election of delegates to the PNR convention was (like the election of delegates to the celebrated constitutional congress of 1916–17) a desultory affair (Garrido 1986, pp. 97, 102, 107, 111–12). Subsequently, the deliberations of the Querétaro party convention appear to have attracted little popular interest.

It would be rash to conclude, however, that the elite's autonomy was absolute or that popular pressure was irrelevant. Popular mobilization remained limited because, to a degree, the settlement process mirrored popular hopes and expectations, and when the Escobar revolt threatened to overturn it, popular forces, such as the *agraristas* of Veracruz, rallied to the regime in significant numbers (Fowler Salamini 1978, pp. 61–3). This reflected an aspect of postrevolutionary Mexico that no political elite could overlook: Since the revolution – indeed, because of the revolution – Mexico had become a society in which mass organizations were important and popular participation in politics could not be ignored. That, of course, did not mean that Mexico was a functioning liberal democracy. Its mass organizations were built on clientelism, bossism, and violence; popular participation was manifested in street rallies and brawls, guerrilla activity, the unionization of workers, and the mobilization of *campesinos*. All these phenomena were political facts of life that the pacting elites had to take into consideration. Overt appeals, such as Calles's celebrated

14 Consul Franklin, Saltillo, August 6, 1928, S.D. 812.00/29280.

September 1 speech, were pitched to a mass public outside the Congress as well as to the congregated elites within. The speech was broadcast nationally by radio, and radio was again used to launch the new PNR (Dulles 1972, p. 384; Garrido 1986, pp. 97, 153). Public opinion took an interest (it was reckoned) in the congressional debates over the provisional presidency (Dulles 1972, p. 394). In their private deliberations, too, the elites recognized the mass dimension of politics. Sáenz was passed over as the PNR candidate, in part because the pundits doubted his appeal, especially to "those in the workshops and in the fields." If chosen, he would incur the opposition of the *agrarista* lobby (Dulles 1972, p. 429). And when the elites gathered around the table in smoke-filled rooms, the chips they played with were, in part, the mass constituencies that they could command, and command only conditionally. In addition, as we have seen, the Escobarista revolt of March 1929 elicited a strong popular response, the product of successful government mobilization, the perceived conservatism of the rebels, and the popular desire for stability and reform over war and reaction. And the new PNR was launched with an eye to the masses, a commitment to a "vast social mission" (*una vasta labor social*), and a range of ancillary social and educational activities that derived in part from European party models (Garrido 1986, pp. 142, 152–3). PNR presidential candidate Ortiz Rubio undertook an extensive *gira electoral* (the first since Francisco Madero's in 1909–10), and party campaigning during 1930 involved mass demonstrations designed to display the unity of the revolution (Garrido 1986, pp. 137, 155–6; Meyer 1981, p. 85). The politics of the elite settlement were, it is true, national, centralized, and incestuous, but in order to make the settlement stick its authors needed popular support, manifested in a myriad of local conflicts and skirmishes. High politics (as I have commented elsewhere) depended on low politics, national decision making meshed with local decision making (Knight 1986, vol. 2, pp. x–xi). The revolution of 1910–20 had ended the extreme autonomy of the elites of the old regime; thus any postrevolutionary elite settlement had to be conducted according to the terms of a fluid, often violent, "massified" politics.[15]

Indeed, the settlement was in part provoked by the latent fear of mass mobilization that underlay the entire postrevolutionary period.

15 The "extreme autonomy of the elites of the old regime" implies autonomy vis-à-vis the masses (or "popular classes"), not just autonomy. Arguably, the Porfirian political elites were tightly linked to – and faithfully represented – the landed oligarchy. The revolution ruptured that link and established a regime whose class attachments and identifications were relatively variable over time and space (at least down to the 1940s).

Between 1910 and 1920 much of northern and central Mexico had thrown over the political traces, and the country had become a patchwork of semiautonomous revolutionary fiefs, many captained by rough-and-ready popular caudillos who enjoyed a fair measure of popular support and esteem (Brading 1980). So great was the dislocation and decentralization of power that the very concept of elite looks out of place in such an unusual political universe. Who are the elites when the world is turned upside down? This period was short-lived, however, and as the world was gradually righted, new elites emerged and consolidated themselves. But through the 1920s and 1930s Mexican elites remained variegated and fractious, especially if the vital provincial, as against national, perspective is adopted. In parts of the south the plantocracy still ruled, albeit under pressure; the northern bourgeoisie prospered (at least until the later 1920s); and the new revolutionary elite – generals, above all – acquired property to match their power. But there were also elites, some of popular extraction, who depended on continued popular support for their advancement: new-style caciques like Portes Gil (Tamaulipas), Zuno (Jalisco), Garrillo Puerto (Yucatán), and Tejeda (Veracruz); agrarian rabble-rousers like Manuel Montes of Puebla or Primo Tapia of Michoacan. Their threat to the central government was twofold: First, they marshaled popular forces that, in some cases, advocated more radical policies than the middle-of-the-road Sonorans favored, and second, they represented fissiparous forces within the sprawling Mexican federation. In response, the Sonoran central government sought to curtail both political radicalism and regional separatism, in order to advance capitalist development and state building.[16] Of course, the radicals were not the only threat: The church, the United States, and the dissident military added to the Sonorans' headaches.

In light of this political panorama, the elite settlement of 1928–9 must be seen as a key element in the central government's battle to assert its power over divergent political and regional interests. The institutionalization that Calles proclaimed implied a further attenuation of independent political movements (of both right and left) in the provinces. The elite settlement thus reflected a clear perception – by Calles and his collaborators – that power had to be centralized, to the advantage of the regime and to the detriment of both popular and regional forces. The implication was that regional bosses – like

16 The reification and schematization evident in this sentence would make a good historian of postrevolutionary Mexico cringe. Each element of the sentence really demands pages of further qualification and explanation.

Margarito Ramírez, *jefe nato* (leader by birth) of the Partido revolucionario de Jalisco – would have to acknowledge the supremacy of the "center" of Mexico City, the federal government, and the new national party (Garrido 1986, pp. 73, 122–3; Romero 1987, pp. 23, 45–6, 48). The center, in turn, would curb the local squabbles that bred endemic political instability (Garrido 1986, p. 123). As party president Pérez Treviño proclaimed: "The revolution is also organization, it is above all organization" (Meyer 1981, pp. 88–9). Smart provincial elites (like the Figueroas of Guerrero) realized which way the wind was blowing and discarded old-style autonomist *caudillismo* in favor of new-style collaboration with (which meant subordination to) the national government and party (Jacobs 1980, pp. 90–1). The rationale, as well as the mechanism, of the Mexican elite settlement thus cannot be understood without due appreciation of the role the masses played, even if they were often offstage actors. Equally, as I have already suggested, the settlement must be located within the trajectory of postrevolutionary state building and must be seen as embracing not only a class dimension (which Marxist critics readily advocate) but also a regional dimension. When national elites pacted in Mexico, they pacted to the advantage of the elites as against the masses and also to the advantage of the center as against the provinces. The settlement therefore heralded both stability of government and centralization of power.

Conjunctural consequences

I turn now to the outcome. Here, two primary questions arise. First, what kind of elite emerged from the elite settlement of 1928–9? Second, was the outcome conducive to subsequent democratization?

The typology and terminology favored by this volume involve three forms of elite: disunified, consensually unified, and ideologically unified (see Chapter 1). Like many organizing concepts that are encountered in the social sciences, these are relatively straightforward in their application to polar examples but rather harder when it comes to the (many) intermediate cases. We all may agree that Lebanon offers an example of a disunified elite, Switzerland of a consensually unified elite, and Albania (at least until 1990) of an ideologically unified elite. But the Lebanons, Switzerlands, and Albanias of the political world are untypical. True, the list of consensually unified elites can be extended to include the major, stable, Western democracies, but they, too, when viewed over a long perspective, contain their pockets of elite dissent. The stability of the regimes they operate cannot, in all cases, be taken for granted, and above all, they remain a small minority within the global sample of national elites.[17] The category of disunified elites is presumably populated by a host of quite disparate Third World countries, ranging from Angola to Argentina, whereas the category of ideologically unified elites, which once neatly encapsulated the Second World, is now looking distinctly underpopulated, save for the Chinese and the North Koreans (and, until recently, the Albanians).

A further problem arises with this typology, at least in the case of Mexico (but also, I suspect, in other cases, too). I have already suggested that the Mexican elite settlement involved exclusion as well as inclusion and that elite pacts are struck to exclude certain elites and to admit, accommodate, and conciliate others. The notion of an all-embracing elite settlement is probably a myth. But this suggestion, if valid, carries important implications for the analysis of ensuing regime types. If all elites are involved in a settlement leading to a stable regime, then it is probably feasible to distinguish the ensuing regime in terms of either consensual or ideological elite unity. But if, as in the Mexican case, the settlement is partial and exclusionary, how can the ensuing regime be neatly distinguished in these terms? Rather, a distinction must be made between the included, politically privileged elites and their excluded, politically marginalized rivals. Let us call them the "in" elites and the "out" elites, and in order to switch from generalization to example, let us trace the process of elite settlement and regime stabilization in Mexico during and after the 1920s.

During the 1920s, Mexico's elites, viewed in their totality, were disunified: Church and state were at loggerheads; landlords and (to a lesser extent) entrepreneurs were leery of the revolutionary regime; and the country presented a patchwork image of conflicting class and regional interests (Benjamin and Wasserman, 1990). In many respects this political panorama, the legacy of the armed revolution, extended into the 1930s and was not substantially modified until after 1940. Meanwhile, the revolutionary elite itself was also divided, albeit less by profound ideological or class differences than according to principles of Darwinian struggle for survival and preeminence. Obregón's ouster of Carranza in 1920, De la Huerta's near ouster of Obregón in 1923–4, the potential revolt and actual repression of 1927, and the

17 When I refer to "elite dissent," I mean, of course, fundamental dissent over basic principles, not the run-of-the-mill dissent that is inseparable from elite politics. My main query concerns the time period: If France's Third Republic (c. 1875–1940) is labeled an "unconsolidated democracy" (see Chapter 1), then the criteria for democratic consolidation are very stringent in terms of both stability and longevity. It may be premature or invidious to admit cases such as Venezuela, Colombia, or even Spain, if Third Republic France is to be excluded.

Escobarista challenge to Calles in 1929 all are examples of a Darwinian (or Hobbesian) competition within the revolution itself. Its protagonists might agree on their common enmity toward the church, the foreign oil companies, or the sinister stage ghost of "reaction," but they could not agree among themselves concerning the division of the political spoils. Because they broadly agreed on values and ends, they were ideologically unified, but such unity by no means guaranteed accommodation and concerted political action.[18] Such a situation is hardly unusual. The barons who battled in the interminable Wars of the Roses scarcely possessed the imagination to float rival ideological visions, but that did not prevent them from butchering one another, and their retainers in a Hobbesian struggle for power. Arguably, the contest between Liberals and Conservatives in many Latin American societies in the nineteenth and early twentieth centuries owed less to overt ideological differences than to conflicting clientelist, familial, and regional factions. One way of emphasizing the point is to ask what difference the outcome made. A Yorkist or Lancastrian victory would not have made much difference to the structure or ideology of late medieval England. Liberals and Conservatives could rule nineteenth-century Colombia or Guatemala without fundamentally changing those countries' broad patterns of development. So, too, in Mexico in the 1920s. Carranza, Obregón, De la Huerta, Gómez, Serrano, and Escobar all were members of the victorious revolutionary coalition, brothers in the revolutionary family; they were ideological kin, divided chiefly by their fratricidal lust for power.

The 1929 elite settlement served as a powerful bromide. It calmed political passions, concentrated power in the hands of the pacted elites, and, with the new party, created an instrument whereby the center could further accelerate the centralization and institutionalization of that power. The abortive rebellion of March 1929 – a much weaker challenge to the government than the De la Huerta uprising of 1923–4 – confirmed the dangers of dissent and the advantages of loyalty. So, too, did the decline of Morones and the discomfiture of Vasconcelos. Several indicators (neglected by most commentators) illustrate the changing climate of intra-elite politics. When Sáenz was

18 This raises an important comparative point: Ideologically unified elites are often capable of savage domestic infighting. Burton and Higley (1987) seem to allow for this, referring to "the outward appearance of nearly complete unity" among such elite. Examples are the Chinese Communist leadership since 1949 and the Nazi elite, whose chaotic and competitive internal politicking has been termed "institutional social Darwinism." See David Schoenbaum, *Hitler's Social Revolution* (New York: Norton, 1980).

finessed out of the presidential candidacy that he believed was his, he did not flirt with rebellion; rather, he returned to sulk in his tent in Nuevo León, spurning the Escobarista rebels. When Vasconcelos was (by his own account) defrauded of the presidency in the fixed election of November 1929, he cried foul and sought to emulate Madero's 1910 call to revolution ("With Madero yesterday! With Vasconcelos today!" was the cry). But the cry went largely unheard, and shrewd but sympathetic observers like Gómez Morín warned Vasconcelos that, in effect, 1929 was not 1910 and that any challenge to the new PNR required preparation, organization, and sustained mobilization, not a spontaneous uprising of an indignant people, as in 1910 (Krauze 1976, pp. 273–8). To this end, ten years later, Gómez Morín founded the Partido de acción nacional (PAN).

Vasconcelos and Gómez Morín were erstwhile members of the revolutionary elite, now disillusioned with their old comrades. But many of the latter, too, shared this recognition that politics had changed and that armed rebellions – the crude praetorian plebiscites of the 1910s and 1920s – were no longer realistic avenues to power. Intra-elite conflicts remained acute: Congress was riven with conflict between the Rojos and the Blancos from 1929 to 1932, and the states of the federation were similarly troubled. But these conflicts did not spill over onto the battlefield, nor did they jeopardize the stability of the central government which, in fact, acquired greater control and stability during these years. Ideological and factional differences (Mexican analogues of the Whig and Tory division of post–1688 England) did not disappear, but the "in" elites increasingly shared assumptions concerning their competition for power: that it should be pacific rather than praetorian, that it should occur within rather than against the party, and that it should involve the impersonal institutions of central government rather than the personalist authority of provincial caudillos.

Thus Cárdenas made his run for the presidency from within the PNR (he was twice party president). Adalberto Tejeda, who nurtured no less ambition, tried to build a regional base in Veracruz and was thwarted (indeed, Cárdenas, as minister of war, was responsible for disarming Tejeda's *agraristas* in 1933) (Fowler Salamini 1978, pp. 115–17). Two years later, when Cárdenas successfully threw off the oppressive tutelage of Calles, his erstwhile mentor and *jefe máximo* of the revolution, Calles went quietly, along with a clutch of his old collaborators. The story bears retelling: Calles was rousted out of bed at 10 P.M., wearing his blue and white pajamas and, allegedly, reading a copy of *Mein Kampf* (this last touch seems almost too good to be true and about on a par with the conveniently incriminating possessions of General Manuel Noriega, unearthed by the American forces who invaded Panama in 1989). "I consider myself your prisoner," Calles told the soldiers, "you may put me before the firing squad." But this was pessimism (or bravado). Calles was not stood up against a wall, as so many of his revolutionary predecessors had been but, rather, was told to pack his bags; and by dawn, he had been bundled aboard a plane for the United States (Ambassador Josephus Daniels obligingly arranged a visa by phone).

The incident suggests a distinct mitigation of the Hobbesian struggle for power: In 1927 Calles had had some dissident generals summarily executed, whereas nine years later he suffered only the ignominy of exile. Nor was this an isolated case. Although low-level political violence remained endemic in Mexico through the 1930s, intra-elite carnage declined, in part because of Cárdenas's more equable character, perhaps, but rather more because the successful process of institutionalization, triggered by the elite settlement of 1928–9, made such carnage less necessary and less attractive. As a hostile observer admitted, "Sordid killing, as a way of enforcing the official will, has well-nigh disappeared" (Kluckhohn 1939, p. 3). When Amaro challenged for the presidency in somewhat praetorian fashion in 1938–9, his candidacy shriveled. When Almazán lost the election (unfairly) in 1940, his call for revolution proved even more feeble than Vasconcelos's had been in 1929. And the winner, Avila Camacho, "the unknown soldier," triumphed on the basis of electoral fixing, a bland campaign (ideologically indistinguishable from Almazán's), and a watery appeal to consensus. In 1942, when participation in the war gave an additional fillip to official patriotism and consensus, seven Mexican presidents were able to stand shoulder to shoulder on the balcony of the presidential palace, reviewing the troops. They included Ortiz Rubio, who had been made and unmade by Calles, Calles, who had been ousted by Cárdenas, and Cárdenas, whose political legacy was currently being dissipated by Avila Camacho (Torres Ramírez 1979, p. 130). Thereafter, as the Cardenista reforms and coalition were progressively destroyed, Cárdenas, the sphinx of Jiquilpan, remained tactfully mute. The lessons of the 1930s were that political advancement required an inside track in the PNR; that hard work and loyalty counted for more than rhetoric and belligerence; that the center now dominated the provinces; that military force had receded to something resembling an *ultima ratio* and was no longer the first resort of the offended caudillo; and that the revolution, now possessed of a powerful prescriptive right, demanded of its disciples a self-abnegating political discipline.

This did not mean, of course, that intra-elite, intraparty competition for power and promotion had abated but simply that the rules of the competition had changed. Advancement now depended on accepting the new rules, playing by them, and accepting victories with magnanimity, defeats with stoicism. The struggle for political survival went on, but elites were no longer red in tooth and claw. And elite loyalty to the system thus became one of its key resources, a major source of stability down to the present. Presidential candidates passed over by the *dedazo* still bite their tongues and, however grudgingly, endorse the winner. Conversely, those few who do break ranks (as Cuauhtémoc Cárdenas and Porfirio Muñoz Ledo did in 1987) are tarred with the brush of political treason, of lèse-PRI.

It seems valid to conclude that the elite settlement of 1928–9 contributed significantly to the establishment of these political guidelines, which have in turn underpinned Mexican political stability for sixty years. In terms of the model, the settlement fostered a consensual unity among the revolutionary elite such that elite divisions were fudged, accommodated, and conciliated, and the temptation to resort to force, confrontation, and extraparty rabble-rousing was much reduced. This is the reason that the PRI schism and the Cardenista breakaway of 1987–8 were so novel and striking.

This process of consensus building concerned only the official elite, gathered in the PNR, PRM, and PRI. I earlier pointed out that powerful rival elites existed in Mexico (church, landlords, and business being the most obvious examples). Their place in the process was different and requires a separate analysis. Inasmuch as the settlement of 1928–9 was designed to benefit and consolidate the revolutionary elites at the expense of their non- or antirevolutionary rivals, the latter could hardly bask in the sun of consensus. For them, the new official party was a corrupt engine of oppression. Indeed, they would have agreed with Lord Halifax (a participant in the 1688 elite settlement) that "the best Party is but a kind of conspiracy against the rest of the nation" (Halifax 1969, p. 209). Furthermore, the 1930s saw increased polarization between "in" (revolutionary) and "out" (non- or antirevolutionary) elites. The Cárdenas regime expropriated a swathe of haciendas, took over the oil companies and railroads (turning over the latter to the workers to run), instituted a form of "socialist" education, and pursued a progressive foreign policy, notably with its support for the Republican cause in the Spanish civil war. The right, both clerical and secular, was outraged. Cárdenas was a Bolshevik, a subversive, and a traitor to Mexico and (many aging "revolutionaries" argued) to the revolution. Fascist Gold Shirts fought with Communists in the Zócalo; Catholics continued to feud with anticlericals; and the quasi-Falangist Unión nacional sinarquista marshaled thousands of peasants and petty-bourgeois malcontents in the Bajío. It is impossible to avoid the conclusion that the 1928–9 elite settlement, though fostering consensual unity within the revolutionary elite, encouraged – or at the very least permitted – a deepening of divisions within the country as a whole, pitting revolutionary elites against their non- or antirevolutionary rivals. This enhanced rivalry, of course, tended to encourage the internal unity of the PNR and the PRM, so the combination of internal consensual union and external ideological intransigence was entirely logical.

This combination makes any simple application to 1930s Mexico of the threefold typology of elites (disunified, consensually unified, ideologically unified) difficult or impossible. From an all-embracing national perspective, Mexican elites remained disunified, as they had been in the 1910s and the 1920s. But this wide-angle perspective misses the crucial establishment of consensual unity within the governing revolutionary elite, which was the product of the 1928–9 settlement. Meanwhile, the comportment of the "in" revolutionary elite toward its "out" rivals implied a distinct ideological unity, premised on the mission of the revolution: anticlericalism, "socialism," and hostility to *latifundismo* and big business. The three typological options can thus be usefully deployed, but it would be crude and misleading to apply any one label to Mexican politics in the 1930s. Because the initial elite settlement was exclusionary as well as inclusionary, it was inevitable that it would excite external ideological opposition and conflict as well as internal accommodation and consensus. I shall, in conclusion, suggest that this pattern is not confined to Mexico, is not random or contingent, and, in fact, has a certain inherent logic.

Structural consequences

Finally, with regard to Mexico, I turn to the longer-term outcome and the relationship of elite settlement to democratization. Mexico has enjoyed over sixty years of relative political stability (*sesenta años de paz social*, as PRIísta political slogans proclaimed throughout Mexico in the summer of 1989). No military coup has succeeded or remotely looked like succeeding; presidents have come and gone fairly smoothly; and opposition parties, although permitted and, since the 1970s, cautiously encouraged, have failed to mount a challenge to the PRI's national monopoly of power, at least until the late 1980s. Even now, it is (in my view) premature to say that Mexico is clearly heading for a consolidated democracy or that the official party's monopoly of power, dating back to the elite settlement of 1929, is clearly coming to an end. This leaves wide open the question of the relationship between elite settlement and consolidated democracy. Certainly, the evidence for linear advance from settlement through stability to democracy is weak and offset by plenty of contradictory evidence, which suggests that the stability born of elite settlement has served to maintain entrenched elite interests and to head off genuine democratization.

Recurrent demands for – and occasional official efforts toward – democratization have come to little. The PRM was reformed in the 1940s (when it assumed its current title, the PRI), but reform bolstered central control rather than diluting it. A bolt from the party in 1952 (which closely paralleled the Cardenista bolt in 1987) failed to provoke reform. Carlos Madrazo attempted an internal democratization of the PRI in the 1960s but did not succeed. Years of one-party monopoly and rising electoral abstentionism finally induced the political reform of the 1970s, which encouraged the opposition. But by the same token, it converted antisystem protest to mobilization within the system, and at least in the eyes of its initiators, it legitimized more than it undermined PRIísta control. Finally, the 1980s – years of mounting political opposition and severe economic problems – taxed the PRI's powers of control and cooption but did not appear to exhaust them. President Miguel De la Madrid flirted with free elections in the north in 1982–3 but soon backed off (or was forced back). His successor, President Carlos Salinas, elected in highly contentious circumstances on the basis of a sharply diminished PRI vote, conceded a governorship (Baja California) to the PAN in 1989 (the first such concession in the party's history) but stole – or condoned the stealing of – elections elsewhere, notably in the Cardenista stronghold of Michoacan. While economic liberalization, a project dear to the heart of technocrats like De la Madrid and Salinas, forges ahead, political liberalization limps behind. The functional relationship of these twin processes (assumed by some North American observers) remains unclear. To the extent that economic liberalization strains the already-strained social compact between rulers and ruled, it may encourage authoritarian rather than liberal politics, that is, the politics of Michoacan rather than the politics of Baja California.

Meanwhile, no PRIísta president wants to be accused of "losing the revolution," of sacrificing the labor of generations who built the party, the state, and the enviable stability of the revolutionary regime. If political reform reinforces this precious inheritance, political reform will follow. But if reform jeopardizes the monopoly of the party and threatens a genuine pluralist system, with all of its attendant uncertainties and imponderables, reform will likely be spurned. That, at least, is a fair reading of the track record of the PNR, the PRM, and the PRI over the last sixty years. Even if a quixotic president opts for reform, the vested interests adamant for drift – the caciques, party bosses, labor leaders – have shown that they can exercise a certain veto power. Democratization from above is unlikely to occur, rhetoric notwithstanding. It may occur, as it did in Victorian England, as a result of demands from below, which entrenched elites dare not resist for fear of worse alternatives. That was the key to the PRI's unprecedented, though still unique, concession of the Baja California governorship. Blatant denial would have caused more trouble than prudent concession would. The elite settlement and the stability it facilitated have not, therefore, fostered democratization but, if anything, a cautious adherence to the status quo, which has its attractions as Central America bleeds to death and the major countries of South America lurch from military oppression to democratic dissension and economic chaos.

This does not mean that Mexico's political record since the 1930s has been one of glacial immobility. At the risk of cliché, we may apply Lampedusa's aphorism: Mexico has had to change in order to stay the same. In other words, the maintenance of de facto one-party rule has required constant renegotiation, accommodation, and cooption (and, of course, repression). Mexican society has changed drastically in the years since 1929, and the official party has had to react to these changes, as an urban society replaced a rural one, as manufacturing supplanted the old enclave industries, as conflict with the United States gave way to détente, as the mass media knitted together a previously disparate, parochial population. In response to these changes the ruling party has not, as I said, democratized either itself or the broader political system. But it has favored selective political inclusion and cooption; hence a pertinent label for the regime, that of "inclusionary authoritarianism" (Stevens 1974).

This process may be interpreted in terms of the elite model, taking into account the qualifications raised previously. In simple terms, the consensual unity of the "in" elite has been doggedly maintained. Meanwhile, the ideological unity of that elite vis-à-vis the "out" elites has been moderated, though never wholly abandoned. The chronology of this process can be dated with some precision. During and after 1938 the radicalism of the Cárdenas administration declined, and in the face of growing economic difficulties and mounting conservative opposition (Sinarquismo, the PAN, newly organized entrepreneurial groups), the administration tacked toward the center and softened its ideological stance. The oil expropriation of March 1938, though it represented the high point of Cardenista economic nationalism, also afforded a platform for a new national realignment, which embraced many of the regime's old enemies, notably the Catholic church. Prelates and conservative *políticos* were shrewd enough to realize that the tide was turning and that they had a golden opportunity both directly to oppose and indirectly to colonize the regime (Knight 1988). Confronted by a more vocal and confident conservative opposition yet tempted, at the same time, by signs of conservative conciliation and (we might say) "entryism," the administration responded positively: Over the protests of diehard radicals (the Cardenistas' *de hueso colorado*), the regime mitigated its reform policies, throttling back agrarian distribution, curbing labor dissent, and cutting the federal budget deficit. The choice of the moderate, middle-of-the road Manuel Avila Camacho over the radical Francisco Múgica as the PRM's presidential candidate in 1940 confirmed this trend and ensured that it would accelerate during the 1940s. Avila Camacho proceeded to denounce radicalism (ironically, the Mexican Communist party proved a faithful ally throughout most of his *sexenio*) and to placate the conservatives. "I am a believer," he forthrightly proclaimed in September 1940, a statement that no president would have dared utter during the heyday of revolutionary anticlericalism and ideological unity in the 1920s and 1930s.

This flight to the political center acquired yet greater momentum during World War II, which encouraged patriotic unity at home and détente with the United States, abroad. It also spurred Mexican industrialization, generating handsome profits for entrepreneurs (and their political allies) while severely depressing real wages. Although business interests were never formally admitted to the PRI, they increasingly cooperated with the regime, enjoyed the benefits of the post–1940 economic miracle, and came to exercise considerable political influence, whether through bribes, informal contacts, or the useful veto power of capital flight (Maxfield and Anzaldúa 1987). Some postwar presidents briefly challenged private enterprise: Luis Echeverría in 1970–6, José López Portillo in 1982. But such contentious episodes were more than offset by the unofficial state–business compact that increasingly underwrote Mexican economic development and political stability. It was precisely because incidents like the bank nationalization of 1982 seemed to breach this compact that they provoked such virulent, and in many respects successful, entrepreneurial reactions.

The regime thus placated the church, which in turn reciprocated by disavowing the more outspoken antisystem Catholic activists. Business groups, though avoiding a close embrace with the PRI and retaining a certain affiliation with the opposition PAN, generally supported a regime that protected their fundamental interests. The middle classes, enemies of Cardenismo, became the bulwark of the Confederación nacional de organizaciones populares (CNOP) (the PRI's so-called popular sector) and the beneficiaries of *desarrollo estabilizador* during the 1950s and 1960s. As a result of this process, initiated in around 1938 to 1940 and sustained, with certain inevitable vicissitudes, until the present, the initial ideological unity of the "revolutionary" elite has been blurred and compromised. We now witness a regime that, in the name of revolutionary flexibility, is dismantling much of the socioeconomic apparatus of the original institutional revolution: protectionism, union power, *agrarismo*, and public enterprises.

This, I repeat, does not constitute or even herald a consolidated democracy. It implies an inclusionary authoritarianism, whereby once-excluded elements are conciliated, coopted, and given some informal access to power. Politics becomes less polarized, especially at the national level. Old enemies are placated, even if they are not admitted to the inner sanctum of state power (they may not seek admission, as a certain political distancing may suit the economic elites). As long as state and party broadly respect these powerful extraparty interests, which they generally do, these interests will in turn respect the rules of the political game. Challenges, like the 1982 bank nationalization, provoke a counterchallenge: a warning that the unofficial pact must not be broken. It seems fair to describe this process as one of growing consensus, premised not on equal, plural access to political power and still less on a functioning liberal democracy but, rather, on a tacit bargain between incumbent political elites, whose conduct, we have noted, is premised on the consensual rules of intraparty competition, dating back to the settlement of 1928–9, and "out" elites whose renunciation of direct political power is compensated by unofficial contacts, regular assurances, and a proven veto power. Of course, this overt separation of power between political and economic elites is a hallmark of many capitalist societies, not just the Mexican. What makes the Mexican case unusual is the absence of either genuine party competition or outright (exclusionary) authoritarianism. Business, the church, and the middle class have not had to rely for the protection of their fundamental interests on a powerful conservative or Christian Democratic party or on a politically interventionist military.

This outcome reinforces the argument advanced earlier concerning the (possibly negative) relationship between elite settlement and democratic consolidation. The very success of the elite settlement encouraged "out" elites to come to terms with it; the PAN, which began as a quasi-fascist, antisystem movement, soon transmuted into a moderate, Christian Democratic, and loyal opposition.[19] On the other hand, the dominant revolutionary elites, increasingly firmly ensconced in power and purged of the suicidal tendencies that afflicted them in the 1920s, softened their ideological exclusiveness and began to widen the boundaries of consensus. They would not abdicate their political monopoly, but they would go some way to accommodate and conciliate the "out" elites. They did so partly because it was good politics (it bought off some formidable enemies) and partly because the dynamics of both Mexican and global development impelled them away from Cardenista collectivism and toward free enterprise, capital accumulation, and cold-war international alignments. In other words, the decline of "ideological unity" and its replacement by the form of dual consensual unity just described cannot be inferred from the logic of elite bargaining alone but must be related to the dynamics of Mexican and world history in the period since World War II. Just as the dynamics of the 1930s tended to reinforce ideological unity and revolutionary exclusion, so those of the 1940s and after favored consensual overtures and "revolutionary" inclusion, at least in regard to business, the church, the middle class, and the multinationals. To the extent that these interests were conciliated, furthermore, rival interests (organized labor above all) had to be penalized: with sharply declining real wages, purges, and coercive subordination to the state, by means of the celebrated *charrazos* of the 1940s. Again, consensus building had its victims as well as its beneficiaries; the ensuing consensus, though broad enough to be stable and effective, was not all-embracing.

Conclusions

This chapter has concentrated on a particular case, arguing that the elite settlement concept is apt and useful but that the implications that flow from it require certain qualifications. In particular, I have contended that the original settlement in Mexico was exclusionary as well as inclusionary and that although it certainly constrained the Hobbesian war of all against all among the incumbent elites, pointing them in the direction of internal consensual unity, it also resulted in sharp ideological polarization between the newly pacted elites and their nonrevolutionary rivals. After 1938–40 this polarization weak-

19 More recently, the PAN has been divided into different camps and ideological currents, one of which ("neo-Panismo") has favored a more intransigent stance, both ideologically and tactically. On the other hand, many Panistas now advocate and practice collaboration with the PRI.

ened, for reasons that are not necessarily intrinsic to the model but that derived from the broad political and economic dynamics of the period. The boundaries of consensus spread, or more accurately, they now embraced erstwhile enemies, such as the church and business, while expelling erstwhile allies, such as the independent labor unions.[20] The result was a highly stable constellation of forces, with the original revolutionary elites still enjoying a monopoly of national power while deferring to the broad interests of their newfound allies. The latter did not enter the party or staff the state, and so the ensuing consensus was politically unbalanced (which misled some myopic observers into discerning socialism in Mexico!). But it worked. It imparted the political stability that underwrote the "miracle" of the 1950s and 1960s and, to date, even the painful restructuring of the 1980s. But it did not promote a consolidated democracy; if anything, it stood in the way of full democratization. The incumbent elites, the cadres of the PRI, showed no intention of relinquishing power unless forced, and the extrapolitical elites, business in particular, espoused "democracy" chiefly as a means to chastise the PRI in the wake of the bank nationalization. It may therefore be questioned how far the PANista right would encourage, or even tolerate, a genuine democratization of Mexican politics. For many of them, as for many U.S. policymakers in the world at large, democracy can be a tactic as much as an ideal.

This is not to deny the strength of grass-roots democratic demands, which have a long history in Mexico, especially at the local and regional level. By dint of hard work and at the price of hard knocks they have made gains: in major *sindicatos*, like the Sindicato nacional de trabajadores de la educación (SNTE); in municipalities, like Juchitan; even in states like Baja California (Craig and Foweraker 1990). The PRI has been obliged to make limited concessions, but only in the face of dogged opposition. Consensus building among certain key elites by no means opens the floodgates of democratic reform; indeed, it may serve to reinforce them. Conversely, these limited democratic concessions require substantial popular mobilization. In nineteenth-century England, democratic reform was not conceded from on high but won from below, long after the elite settlement of 1688 was concluded. "Without the stimulus of a popular movement that was strong enough to shift bourgeois notables to the left," Eley generalizes for Europe as a whole, "the constitutionalist movements of the last cen-

20 More reification and schematization. The relationship of the government and PRI to the labor movement has been complex and shifting. What is clear, though, is that labor enjoyed much greater access to power in the 1930s than it has done since.

tury were unlikely to embrace a significant element of democracy" (Blackbourn and Eley 1984, pp. 19, 80). Elites had to be made to realize that reform was the least of several evils. Political stability, premised on a previously successful elite settlement, by no means guaranteed democratization. It merely meant that elites who cherished an inherited political stability were reluctant to forfeit it and thus looked to ways in which popular demands might be met without impairing political stability. Sometimes that calculation encouraged conciliation, as in England in 1832 or Baja California in 1989. Other times it spurred repression, as in England in 1819 (Peterloo) or Mexico in 1968 (Tlatelolco). Stability, born of elite settlement, certainly conditioned the circumstances in which demands for democratization were voiced and evaluated. But the evidence of these cases does not suggest a clear and positive causal connection. In England, 144 years elapsed between the elite settlement of 1688 and the Act of 1832, which marked the first major concession to parliamentary reform; 179 years passed before the second reform bill (1867), which roughly established universal manhood suffrage; and 240 years went by before universal suffrage was instituted in 1928. A mechanical comparison with Mexico would suggest a transition to genuine mass democracy somewhere between 2073 and 2169. Of course, historians are the last people to indulge in such mechanical comparisons. But the point is valid: The sheer elapse of time between settlement and democratic consolidation must call into question the close positive relationship between the two and raise the possibility that they may be randomly or even negatively related. Latin American countries that have never experienced elite settlements enjoy a fuller and freer democracy than does Mexico, even though their democracy is frequently fragile and vulnerable. The Mexican regime, like the "Venetian oligarchy" of eighteenth-century England, is relatively stable, but it is hardly democratic.

This prompts a final comparative observation. Both the Mexican and English cases display apparent elite settlements that established stable, successful regimes, the envy of their continental counterparts. The result was neither democratic nor fully inclusionary. The Mexican settlement cut out several important elites, as did the English; Catholic elites were victims in both cases (we may fancifully equate the Jacobites with Cristeros and Sinarquistas, protagonists of a confessional regime). Also excluded were radical groups that challenged the elite settlement on the basis of class antagonism and that evoked fearful memories of the recent revolution (another striking common factor). The respective settlements also encouraged a certain consensual unity among the incumbent elites – the PNR in Mexico, the Whigs and (prosystem) Tories in England. Accepting the rules of the game for their own peaceful intra-elite competition, the elites tightened ranks against their class and confessional enemies. After 1688 the majority of the English propertied class enjoyed considerable power, freedom, and, we may say, "consensual unity." The position of Mexico's revolutionary elites after 1928–9 was broadly comparable. Toward outsiders, who had not bought into the providential pact, both regimes were implacable. Consensual unity within was matched by ideological unity in the face of external challenges; that is, both regimes established a canon of revolutionary rectitude that excluded important elites, Catholics and radicals in particular. By the mid-eighteenth century, "for all practical purposes England was a one-party state" (Hill 1969, p. 218; Porter 1990, p. 112). Over time, however, the stability and self-confidence bred of a successful elite settlement spread the boundaries of consensus, which is not to say that democracy resulted. Rather, the keen edge of ideological unity was dulled, and excluded elites were gradually tolerated, even admitted to power. In England the Test and Corporation acts were repealed, and the Catholics were emancipated; in Mexico Avila Camacho declared himself a believer, and Salinas de Gortari welcomed the pope at Mexico City's airport. Pacted elites were prepared to reconciliate with "out" elites as long as they accepted the rules of the pact. As President Lyndon Johnson eloquently put it, it was better to have someone inside the tent pissing out than outside the tent pissing in. This did not mean that the tent was particularly capacious or open to all comers. Lowering ideological barriers and broadening the boundaries of elite consensus were pragmatic responses to changing circumstances (their explanation would require a further analysis of these circumstances). But they did not imply the establishment of a consolidated democracy. That required sustained popular pressure, which incumbent elites resisted as long as they dared. It may be that a long experience of political stability and progressive elite conciliation (England since 1688, Mexico since 1928) provides a useful school for subsequent, incremental democratization. But the wait is so long, and the increments so grudging, that the causal link remains tenuous. We could just as well argue that a long experience of political stability and progressive intra-elite conciliation fends off crisis, minimizes popular mobilization, and preserves elite cohesion in the face of demands from below. In this respect and in the interest of objectivity, we should perhaps look for elite settlements (or their functional analogues) not only in societies that have already achieved democracy but also in those that (like Mexico) have not or those that (like Meiji Japan or Bismarckian Germany) remained resolutely authoritarian for generations. For in these cases, too, elites rebounded from crises and struck deals that implied a certain mutual conciliation and enjoyed a certain permanence (the Meiji Restoration, the "marriage of steel and rye"). But these pacts, embodied in Barrington Moore's "revolutions from above," represented barriers to, not advances toward, consolidated democracies (Blackbourn and Eley 1984, p. 84).

The elite settlement concept thus possesses (for the historian) a distinct analytical utility. It fits the Mexican case snugly. It helps explain the genesis of political stability in Mexico and probably elsewhere, too. But it tells us rather less about the genesis of democracy, which, in many cases, including the Mexican, has been a long time aborning.

References

Benjamin, Thomas, and Mark Wasserman. 1990. *Revolution in the Provinces*. Albuquerque: University of New Mexico Press.

Blackbourn, David, and Geoff Eley. 1984. *The Peculiarities of German History, Bourgeois Society and Politics in Nineteenth-Century Germany*. Oxford: Oxford University Press.

Brading, D. A., ed. 1980. *Caudillo and Peasant in the Mexican Revolution*. Cambridge: Cambridge University Press.

Burton, Michael G., and John Higley. 1987. "Elite Settlements." *American Sociological Review* 52, 295–307.

Córdova, Arnaldo. 1981. *La Clase obrera en la historia de México: En una epoca de crisis*. Mexico City: Siglo Veintiuno.

Craig, Anne, and Joseph Foweraker, eds. 1990. *New Sòcial Movements and Political Change in Mexico*. Boulder, CO: Lynn Reiner.

Dulles, John W. F. 1972. *Yesterday in Mexico: A Chronicle of the Revolution, 1919–1936*. Austin: University of Texas Press.

Fowler Salamini, Heather. 1978. *Agrarian Radicalism in Veracruz, 1920–1938*. Lincoln: University of Nebraska Press.

Garrido, Luis Javier. 1986. *El Partido de la revolución institucionalizada*. Mexico City: SEP.

Halifax, Lord. 1969. *Complete Works*. Harmondsworth: Penguin Books.

Hill, Christopher. 1969. *From Reformation to Industrial Revolution*. Harmondsworth: Penguin Books.

Jacobs, Ian. 1980. "Rancheros of Guerrero: The Figueroa Brothers and the Revolution." In *Caudillo and Peasant in the Mexican Revolution*, ed. D. A. Brading. Cambridge: Cambridge University Press.

Kluckhohn, Frank C. 1939. *The Mexican Challenge*. New York: Doubleday.

Knight, Alan. 1986. *The Mexican Revolution*. 2 vols. Cambridge: Cambridge University Press.

1988. "The Politics of the Expropriation." Paper given at the February 1988 conference on the Mexican petroleum industry, University of Texas at Austin.

Krauze, Enrique. 1976. *Caudillos culturales en la revolución mexicana*. Mexico City: Siglo Veintiuno.

Maxfield, Sylvia, and Ricardo Anzaldúa. 1987. *Government and Private Sector in Contemporary Mexico*. La Jolla: Center for U.S.–Mexican Studies, University of California at San Diego.

Meyer, Jean. 1973–4. *La Cristiada.* 3 vols. Mexico City: Siglo Veintiuno.

Meyer, Lorenzo. 1981. *Historia de la revolución mexicana: Periodo 1928–34, los inicios de la institucionalización.* Mexico City: El Colegio de México.

Nava Nava, Carmen. 1984. *Ideología del partido de la revolución mexicana.* Jiquilpan: Centro de estudios de la revolución mexicana "Lázaro Cárdenas," A.C.

Porter, Roy. 1990. *English Society in the Eighteenth Century.* Harmondsworth: Penguin Books.

Romero, Laura Patricia, coord. 1987. *Jalisco desde la revolución.* Vol. 3: *La Consolidación del estado y los conflictos políticos.* Guadalajara: Universidad de Guadalajara.

Saragoza, Alex M. 1988. *The Monterrey Elite and the Mexican State.* Austin: University of Texas Press.

Skirius, John. 1978. *Vasconcelos y la cruzada de 1929.* Mexico City: Siglo Veintiuno.

Stevens, Evelyn P. 1974. *Protest and Response in Mexico.* Cambridge, MA: MIT Press.

Torres Ramírez, Blanca. 1979. *Historia de la revolución mexicana: México en la segunda guerra mundial.* Mexico City: El Colegio de México.

5

Elite unification and democratic consolidation in Italy: a historical overview

MAURIZIO COTTA

Italian political history provides a rich opportunity for investigating the relationship between elites and democracy. For most of its 130 years as a nation-state, Italy has been beset with elite and mass conflicts, with a marked absence of a consolidated democratic regime. It has frequently been attributed to continuing elite disunity, not only by historians and political scientists, but also by contemporary actors. There have been repeated efforts to unify Italian elites, and the persistence of these efforts testifies to the difficulty of achieving (and preserving) a consensually unified national elite (Burton and Higley 1987) and a consolidated democracy. The Italian case thus is a chance to discuss specific requirements for elite unification and democratic consolidation. The questions that we shall ask are What attempts at elite unification took place over this long period? Why were those attempts unsuccessful, at least until fairly recently? Why has the creation of a consensually unified national elite in Italy been such a difficult and lengthy process? And finally, how valid is an overall interpretation of Italian political history that stresses elite disunity as the main source of regime instability?

Before attempting to answer these questions, or at least suggesting the direction in which answers may be found, some general observations are necessary. One is that although we can state now that the problem of elite disunity was never really solved until our own time, this does not mean that disunity was uniformly extreme throughout Italy's first century as a nation-state. In fact, there were several points at which elite unity seemed to have been achieved or

This chapter has been written with the generous support of the Italian Consiglio nazionale delle ricerche. The author wishes also to thank the Department of Government of the University of Texas at Austin for its generous hospitality, and John Higley, Richard Gunther, Alan Knight, and Kenneth Maxwell for their valuable commentaries.

at least very nearly achieved. The four most important times were (1) the *trasformismo* period after the government shift from the right to the left in 1876; (2) the high point of socialist moderation and willingness to accept parliamentary government just before World War I, combined with the Liberal–Catholic electoral alliance of that period; (3) the anti-Fascist alliance of virtually all elites at the end of World War II; and perhaps (4) the early 1960s when the center–left alliance was expected to resolve the "Communist question" by marginalizing the Communist party.

Assessing the nature of these putative elite unifications is difficult. Were they simply failed attempts, or were they successful unifications that subsequently broke down? Merely noting that each was followed rather quickly by a serious political crisis involving renewed political instability (and even a democratic breakdown after 1922) does not answer the question, because the reasoning becomes circular: Elite unity was not achieved, thus causing subsequent crises and instability, which demonstrated that elite unity was not achieved! In order to avoid running in such circles, it is necessary to examine the internal characteristics of each apparent unification, as well as the circumstances in which it occurred, and then to compare them with the theses regarding elite settlements and elite convergence set forth in Chapter 1.

There is a further methodological problem. It concerns the extent to which we should rely on our own "objective" assessments based on post facto observations of these processes, rather than on the contemporary perceptions and evaluations of the elites that took part in them. At first glance, our assessments appear to be less prejudiced than those of the actors who were involved because we have no stakes in the political games they played and because we know what happened as a result of those games. We are therefore better placed to judge whether an elite transformation from disunity to unity, via a settlement, a convergence, or some other process (see Chapter 1 of this book, and Burton and Higley 1987), actually occurred. But are our later assessments so superior? Do we not risk mistaking temporal sequences for causal ones? Interpreting a given period or process from the point of view of what happened afterwards may distort what actually took place. Thus the recurrence of elite disunity and conflict after an apparent elite unification might have resulted from new factors that were independent of the unification, but making it no less real simply because it did not last.

Taking into account the perceptions and judgments of contemporary actors about the occurrence or nonoccurrence of elite unifications recognizes that their assessments affected the elites' actions in important ways, perhaps along the lines of self-fulfilling prophecies. On the other hand, contemporary actors are often strongly influenced by their experiences and thus may be blind to emerging trends. Because of bitter memories of past conflicts, for example, they may exaggerate the extent to which an elite group remains untrustworthy or disallegiant, and they may likewise underestimate the dangers that an emerging elite poses.

No entirely satisfactory solutions to these dilemmas are possible. It therefore is best to adopt a balanced strategy, trying to combine the perceptions of contemporary actors with our various "objective" post facto ideas of what took place. I will chart in the following pages the long and troubled path from elite disunity to elite unity in Italy. I will focus on the four historical moments in which elite unifications may have occurred, looking for their peculiarities, assessing their effects on political regimes, and explaining why this unity was so elusive.

Trasformismo: a unification of liberal elites?

The first important change in Italian inter-elite relations occurred in the years following 1876 when previously conflicting elites joined to create a dominant new political force. The question is whether this amounted to an elite unification based on a strong consensus about the rules of the game and established institutions, thus laying the basis for democratic consolidation.

From a political point of view, 1876 was indeed an extraordinary year. The only full alternation of governmental majorities in Italian parliamentary history took place when the government of the "right" was defeated in a parliamentary vote and was replaced by a cabinet dominated by leaders of the "left."[1] The right had led the process of national unification, and it dominated political life after the nation-state was created in 1861. But in 1876, it gave way peacefully to the opposition. It is important to note that this alternation (a "revolution," as many contemporaries were quick to call it) unfolded strictly within the parliamentary and executive arena. Only later was it sanctioned by an election in which the left won a popular majority – or more

1 In this historical context the words *right* (*destra*) and *left* (*sinistra*) are used to translate the names commonly given at that time to the two major parliamentary groups during the period of limited suffrage. None of them was really an organized party but, rather, a loose coalition of parliamentarians. Within each group there were rather independent subgroups based on regional background, ideological proximity, and the like (Capone 1981). With the passage of time a new group, the *extreme* (*estrema*) or *extreme left*, made up of Radicals, Republicans, and Socialists, gained importance.

precisely, a majority among the 8.5 percent of adult males who alone had voting rights at the time (Ballini 1988, p. 79). The alternation of 1876 was therefore very much an elite affair, and it was made possible by the building of a parliamentary coalition between the left opposition and some splinter groups in the right. What is interesting from our point of view, however, are the political developments that followed.

With the so-called *trasformismo* that took place between 1883 and 1886, elites of the right and left joined to produce what came to be called the "constitutional party" (Capone 1981). This "party" dominated parliamentary life for the next quarter of a century. It was, of course, not a party in the sense that we use the word today, but rather, it was a relatively unitary parliamentary elite whose factions and members shared a basic consensus on the existing institutional order. Many different groups persisted within this party, but their boundaries were blurred and fluid.

If we look at these events from the point of view of the role played by the political elites who operated what amounted to a stable limited democracy after 1876, we can easily find some of the elements in this book's theoretical framework. We find, first, a peaceful, accepted alternation in executive power among competing elites, the right, and the left. This has often been considered an important measure of democratic stability though some would question whether it is also a necessary one (see Di Palma 1990, p. 36), particularly when the elites involved have previously been seriously divided over both procedural aspects of the regime and substantive issues.

In both respects, elite divisions had indeed been prominent features of Italian politics before 1876. First, the elites of right and left disagreed over the way in which national unification was achieved under the leadership of Camillo Cavour and the Piedmontese monarchy. This had involved a gradual incorporation "from above" of the many small Italian states by the kingdom of Piedmont and the extension to them of the latter's constitutional order, whereas leaders of the left thought that the process should have included much more "popular" mobilization, by which they meant a mobilization of the educated middle classes and intellectuals, not the working class and peasantry. Second, after 1861, the two elite camps continued to disagree about the role of the monarch in the constitutional order, with the right maintaining a strong allegiance to the idea of monarchy (albeit a parliamentary one) and most of the leaders of the left harboring republican ideals. Third, the right espoused a liberalism bordering on conservatism, whereas the left's liberalism had a strong democratic, sometimes even Jacobin, thrust. These procedural and substantive conflicts between right and left also had a sociological basis. A significant part of the right's elites came from aristocratic and high bourgeois families, whereas members of the left came predominantly from less-elevated bourgeois backgrounds and were often lawyers, academics, journalists, and sometimes businessmen (Farneti 1971).

The differences between the two elite camps had been especially pronounced during the process of national unification, when the right inveighed against the left's alleged "revolutionary" program to prevent it from playing a role in government. But this division gradually lost its intensity after the nation-state was born and after Rome was conquered in 1870. Because of the important role played by the monarchy in promoting national unification, the left became less militant in its republicanism, and over time many of its prominent leaders became supporters of the monarchy. Similarly, the left also moderated its democratic orientation to the extent that though extensions of the suffrage continued to be urged, many of its members were disinclined to push for universal suffrage because they feared that "clericals" and "reactionaries" might profit from the support of the uneducated masses. In view of these developments, the government alternation of 1876, far from constituting an unexpected "revolution," can be seen as the culmination of a gradual convergence among the two elite camps that took place in the parliamentary arena during the preceding ten years (Aquarone 1972).

The alternation of 1876 and the subsequent fusion of elites during the *trasformismo* period thus led to a situation in which dissensions and divisions among the elites moved from the system level to the level of negotiable policy differences. The result was not only a wider elite consensus on the desirability of the regime but also a greater integration of elites from markedly different social-class origins and geographic regions. The old entrenched elites of the right were partly displaced by relatively new elites of the left, but to the extent that they survived they became part of the new elite formation.

An important aspect of this process of elite circulation and reintegration after 1876 was that it was led by the previously dissident and challenging elites of the left. The modus operandi can be seen either as a gradual evolution in elite composition and functioning or, perhaps more precisely, as a progressive deradicalization of dissident elites. The process thus had several earmarks of an elite convergence rather than an elite settlement. First, during the years immediately following national unification, there was an elite formation, the right, that commanded a sufficient majority in Parliament to maintain the upper hand, defending and consolidating the new constitutional monarchy against the left's threats of a more radical regime change (and also against a possible authoritarian backlash).[2] Second, the dissident elites gradually moderated their positions in order to avoid permanent exclusion from executive power. Finally, the process led to the 1876 electoral victory of the previously dissident elites, whereafter they governed in accordance with established institutions and procedures. Although one can also identify a number of explicit agreements of the sort that suggest an elite settlement, none was sufficiently comprehensive to qualify as a settlement. Instead, it was mainly the day-to-day interaction of elites in and around Parliament that eventuated in the *trasformismo* of the 1880s.

Given these indications of an elite convergence, two questions are immediately raised: First, did the process really produce a consensually unified national elite? Second, did it lay the basis for a consolidated democratic regime?

At first glance the process of elite unification appears to have been successful. If we look at political–parliamentary elites in the 1880s, the great left–right divisions of the earlier period seem to have been overcome. In fact, many contemporary observers actually lamented the disappearance of "great, ideal" differences between the elite camps. In Parliament, conflicts now centered more on regional and personalistic issues and the defense of special interests linked to the developing industrialization than on serious ideological questions. Governments were generally based on large majorities that encompassed both left and right. Only a small group on the extreme left (the so-called Estrema made up of Republicans, Radicals, and Socialists) remained at the margins of this substantial elite consensus.

Within another decade, however, the government was confronting serious popular discontent and disorders (in Sicily in 1893–4 and in Milan in 1898). In reacting to these events, strong differences of opinion emerged among the liberal political elites, with one side ready to embark on a severe repression of popular protests and the other side wishing to safeguard civil and political liberties. The Di Rudiní and Pelloux governments opted for repressive measures, and in Milan, there were large-scale arrests of Socialist (but also Catholic) political and union leaders, and numerous dissident organizations were disbanded. The political tensions originating from this cycle of mass mobilizations and repression were soon reflected in a parliamentary crisis, whose high point came in 1899 when strenuous filibustering

2 A more radical constitutional transformation as asked by the left would have been theoretically more democratic but would probably have produced a direct confrontation (fateful at that time for representative institutions) between republicanism and an authoritarian defense of the monarchy.

by the extreme left opposition blocked the latest repressive measures that had been introduced by the government of the day. Uneasy about the turn of events, moderate elements of the left soon deserted the government and brought about its fall (see Seton-Watson 1967, pp. 183–95). Conflicting interpretations of the constitutional order were again at the center of elite debates, and the relative unity of the parliamentary elite appeared to be dissolving.

How should this sequence of events be interpreted? The first observation must be that the elite consensus and unity achieved in the 1870s and 1880s did not result in an increased elite ability to control and channel the popular mobilization of peasants and industrial workers, which proceeded apace during the 1880s and 1890s. A second observation is that the lack of any elite response to these mass mobilizations other than repression was bound to test severely the elite's still fragile consensus and unity. But it is worth asking whether the political turbulence that Italy experienced during the 1890s originated at the elite level (and had to do with insufficient elite unity) or whether it was primarily a problem of incorporating an awakening mass population into the political system. Throughout Europe in this period, the relationship between elites and masses was undergoing great change, and the question is which of the two levels of the political system played the role of independent variable as far as political outcomes were concerned.

Answering this question is difficult. Undoubtedly, mass mobilization had its own somewhat autonomous dynamics. The changing social and economic conditions linked with industrialization were bound to produce increased popular activism that challenged a still oligarchical social and political system, in Italy as elsewhere. In this sense, mass mobilization can be seen as the independent variable. A closer analysis of elite relations during and after the *trasformismo* period, however, reveals that the elite unity that developed during those years was always very limited, and to this extent continuing elite disunity can be viewed also as an independent variable.

Within the parliamentary arena, as already noted, only relatively small elite groups located at the extreme left and the extreme right had remained outside the great amalgamation of right and left elites during the 1870s and 1880s. But in view of what happened during the 1890s, it can be said ex post facto that the elite consensus that underlay this amalgamation was always rather superficial. As soon as serious problems arose, the agreement on the rules of the game was seen to be very shaky. We should also add that after the *trasformismo* period no significant progress was made in the direction of a stronger organizational interconnectedness among the parliamentary elites. To some extent the ideological amalgamation of the 1880s even weakened existing linkages because the disappearance of the older distinct "parties" probably left Parliament more fragmented and volatile than earlier, and this made elite consensus and unity all the more fragile.

The limited nature of the elite unity achieved in the *trasformismo* years becomes even more apparent when we look beyond Parliament to the larger political arena. There we find a number of old and new elites that played little or no part in the parliamentary game and that had not been part of the convergence process we have discussed. What is more, the unity achieved among parliamentary elites was often perceived both by themselves and by elites outside Parliament as a barrier that had been raised "against" these other elites to prevent them from playing a significant role in the political system. For example, in passing the electoral reform act of 1882, which provided for a limited extension of the suffrage based on literacy qualifications, both the more democratic and the more conservative components of the parliamentary elite feared that further lowering the threshold for voting might open the way to the Socialists and clericals (Romanelli 1988, pp. 151, 171).

It must be also stressed – and this brings us back to the theme of elite–mass relations – that the two most important excluded elites were those that were in the best position, at a time of increasing mass mobilization, to play a role in leading and channeling popular demands. On one side was the Catholic elite (with its lay and clerical components), and on the other was the still small but rapidly emerging Socialist elite. Although for different reasons, both had little place in the parliamentary arena – the Socialists because of the still-limited size of the organized working class and because of suffrage restrictions and the Catholics because of the order not to participate in electoral political life (the so-called *non expedit*) issued by the pope after the Italian conquest of Rome. But because of the increasingly successful mass organizations (unions, cooperatives, cultural and political associations, etc.) that both elites were creating toward the end of the century, they possessed at least a significant negative power, that of preventing the liberal elites themselves from gaining larger popular followings.

One might finally ask whether the timing of the convergence among liberal elites did not significantly limit its importance for the consolidation of a democratic regime. The liberal elites were probably amalgamated "too late," in the sense that this came at a historical point at which, in view of the industrializing and other modernizing processes going on in the society at large, it meant only the resolution of "old" issues (like the problem of the role of the monarchy) but was inadequate to facing new challenges, particularly that of finding ways to incorporate the masses into democratic politics.

To summarize, we can say that the *trasformismo* amounted to something like an elite convergence among parliamentary elites. In regard to the effects of this convergence, interpretations differ. A benign interpretation would point to the regime's ability to overcome the crisis of the 1890s without a permanent breach of the liberal constitution. A less benign interpretation would emphasize how the strong, but far from overwhelming, wave of popular discontent triggered a serious crisis within the established elite that brought the regime very near to breakdown. A balanced view would at least question whether the limited elite unification under *trasformismo* was ever sufficient to lay the basis for the broadening and consolidating democracy. The most serious weakness of the Italian political system at the turn of the century was the continuing exclusion of emerging elites, coupled with the inability of the liberal elites to find consensual ways of incorporating those elites and the increasingly mobilized mass population into the established political game. Elite and mass variables thus end up as tightly intertwined.

The attempt to incorporate outsiders: 1900–1913

After the political and constitutional crisis at the end of the nineteenth century, new processes of elite unification got under way and continued until the years preceding World War I. These processes directly involved the two most important elite groups, the Socialists and the Catholics, that had previously been largely outside parliamentary politics. Compared with the *trasformismo* period in which a limited elite convergence meant an alternation in government power followed by a broad amalgamation of liberal elites, after 1900, elite unification meant attempts by the established liberal elites, led by Giovanni Giolitti, to coopt the Socialist and Catholic elites.[3] Cooptation of the Socialists took place mainly within the parliamentary arena, and it resembled a further process of convergence; cooptation of the Catholics unfolded primarily in the electoral arena, and it entailed a more explicit elite pact that resembled an elite settlement.

Parliamentary politics during the first decade of this century was

3 The Piedmontese politician Giovanni Giolitti was by far the dominant political figure from the beginning of the century to World War I. Either leading the government personally (1903–5, 1906–9, 1911–13) or exercising his influence from behind the scenes, he established what his enemies often called a "parliamentary dictatorship."

marked by ongoing policy agreements between Liberal governments and Socialist parliamentary leaders. This process, which had its ups and downs, also involved leaders of the Socialist trade unions and cooperative associations that in those years were gaining wider mass support. Liberal governments derived needed parliamentary support or, at least, benevolent abstentions on crucial votes from the Socialists, and this was useful because the Liberal majorities in parliament lacked much cohesion.[4] For the Socialist leaders, the main benefit of these agreements was the Liberals' acceptance of some of their policy proposals, which enabled them to deliver concrete results to their working-class followers.

In the autumn of 1903, Giovanni Giolitti made the unprecedented offer of a cabinet post to one of the most prominent Socialist leaders, Filippo Turati (Bonomi 1944, p. 155). Although Turati rejected Giolitti's offer, it was a basis for improved relations between the Liberals and the Socialists. The failure of moderate Socialist leaders to control a national strike in 1904 was a setback in these relations, but two years later, in 1906, Socialist MPs supported the Sonnino cabinet (which was a strange coalition of conservative Liberals and the extreme left). In a few months, however, they withdrew their support and stormed out of Parliament to protest a bloody clash that had occurred between strikers and the police. Despite these vicissitudes, attempts to coopt the Socialist elite continued. The high point in the process was reached between 1908 and 1911. The Socialist party was at that time led by its reformist wing, made up of MPs who had progressively abandoned their belief in a future revolution and had come to accept parliamentary institutions and even (though less openly) the monarchy.[5] Links within Parliament between Liberal and Socialist MPs steadily strengthened, and in 1909 Andrea Costa, who had earlier been a flamboyant Socialist revolutionary but had since become a respected moderate, was elected, with Liberal support, to the position of deputy speaker in the Chamber of Deputies. Costa's election appeared to set the seal on the successful incorporation of the Socialist opposition into the parliamentary game.

In 1911, Giolitti again asked Socialist leaders in Parliament to enter his cabinet as ministers, and a Socialist leader, Leonida Bissolati, even

4 The Socialist party had won fifteen seats (or 3 percent of the lower chamber) in 1897, doubled its representation to thirty-three seats (or 6 percent) in 1900, and reached fifty-two seats in 1913 (10 percent) (see Ballini 1988, pp. 127–77).

5 The best historical discussion of these events is that by Vigezzi (1976). But very insightful contributions to the understanding of the Liberal–Socialist relationship can be gained from the writings of the leaders of the two sides: Giolitti (1923) for the Liberal side and Turati and Kuliscioff (1977) for the Socialist side.

paid a visit to the king during the consultations that ensued. The question of the monarchy remained an extremely sensitive issue with the Socialists, one charged with much symbolism. To stress this, Bissolati deliberately refused to wear the top hat required by etiquette when visiting the king. In the end, the Socialist leaders remained outside the cabinet, but it was nevertheless clear that they had become accepted political partners.

The crucial conditions that made possible this rapprochement were the deradicalization of dominant Socialist ideology – "Marx was being sent to the attic," as Giolitti could say – and at the same time the greater readiness by the Liberal elite to view working-class demands as legitimate. And as happened in the *trasformismo* period between leaders of the right and the left, numerous interactions between Liberal and Socialist MPs in the parliamentary setting did much to pacify their relations.

What is striking, however, is how quickly this process was reversed. In 1912 the moderate and reformist leadership lost control of the Socialist party and was replaced by a more intransigent and (at least verbally) revolutionary wing. In that year, when some Socialist parliamentarians joined other MPs in paying a visit to the king, who was recovering from wounds incurred during an assassination attempt, this tribute to the symbol of the established order was used by the leaders of the majority in the Socialist party to justify expelling some of the most prominent moderate leaders. In fact, the moderate leaders did not remain united: Although some remained as a minority within the party, others left and, after creating a new socialist party that had little success in mobilizing mass support, became entirely integrated into the established elite. Moderate Socialist leaders thus split into two groups, and as a result they were never able to regain control of the main Socialist party (at least until the advent of Fascism). For their part, the new and more radical Socialist leadership shifted the party's focus from parliamentary politics to mass mobilization, actively fomenting major demonstrations against the regime in 1912. They vehemently condemned cooperation with other political forces as treason against the proletariat, and they invoked the specter of a revolutionary overthrow of the existing social and political order. As is well known, one of the principal figures in this radical Socialist leadership was Benito Mussolini, who, at the beginning of World War I, left the party and spectacularly converted to a right-wing, ultranationalist position, founding the Fascist party in 1919 (see De Felice 1973).

A crucial event that contributed to this change in the Socialist camp was undoubtedly the colonial war launched by the Liberal government against Libya in 1912. For the traditionally pacifist Socialists, the war came as a shock, and it enabled their more militant wing to accuse the party's moderate leaders of having been duped by their bourgeois colleagues. But the suddenness with which the Liberal–Socialist rapprochement was reversed also suggests that integration of the two elite groups in the parliamentary arena had created a gap between the Socialists' top elites and their cadres. Instead of the Socialist party as a whole being integrated into the existing political system, many of its leaders had been coopted as individuals. But the price of this elite convergence was the moderate Socialist elite's loss of its base of support in the party.

The attempt to incorporate Catholic elites took a quite different path. At the root of the problem was the church–state conflict that had developed in many European societies during the eighteenth and nineteenth centuries (Rokkan 1970). In Italy, this conflict had a special twist because of the state's annexation of territories that belonged to the pope. Thus, the conquest of Rome in 1870 led to a papal order forbidding Catholics from participating in electoral politics as either candidates or voters. The political consequences of this order (the *non expedit*), and more generally of the conflict between Liberal and Catholic elites, became increasingly salient with subsequent extensions of the franchise. Given the church's strong following among large sections of the rural population (but also among the middle and upper classes), Liberal elites were prevented from mobilizing mass support that would offset growing popular support for the Socialists.

With the passage of time, however, a thaw in relations between the Catholic church and the Liberal-dominated state began. Among the reasons for this warm-up was the shared fear of revolutionary socialism, the longing of many Catholics to be seen as patriotic citizens, and the willingness of many Liberal politicians to abandon some of their anticlerical attitudes (see De Rosa 1966; Molony 1977). In the national elections of 1904 and 1909, thanks to a reinterpretation of the *non expedit*, common candidacies were negotiated in a few constituencies between Catholics and moderate Liberals. But the breakthrough came in 1913, just before the first elections with universal male suffrage were called and just after the moderate Socialist leadership had been eclipsed by the party's more doctrinaire wing. The papal ban against Catholic participation was lifted for all practical purposes, and this, plus the activism of some lay leaders of the Catholic movement, enabled Liberal and Catholic elites to reach an agreement of national scope, the so-called Gentiloni Pact. Under this agreement, Liberal–Catholic electoral alliances were formed in a large number of constituencies, and more than two hundred deputies were elected with the support of Catholic voters, thus providing the Liberal government with a large parliamentary majority. But when the pact's existence was revealed after the election, the Liberals suffered political embarrassment, and the "real" terms of the agreement became the subject of wide speculation. Accused by the anticlerical left of having sold out to clerical interests, the Liberals tried to deny any *do ut des* ("give to get"), as well as any compromising of their deputies' independence. Meanwhile, Catholic leaders, eager to use their new political clout, insisted that the pact meant that the deputies elected with Catholic votes would have to support certain policies, especially religious education in the schools and no change in the law governing marriage that forbade divorce (Dalla Torre 1962).

Ambiguities and unresolved issues in the pact were soon evident. The Liberal elite believed that political leadership was to remain in its hands, but the Catholic elite saw the alliance that the pact sanctioned as an instrument for achieving its policy goals. Nonetheless, the overall result was that some Catholic leaders now played their first role in Italy's national politics. During World War I, a Catholic parliamentarian, Filippo Meda, served as a cabinet minister. But to conclude that strong consensus and stable unity were achieved between Liberal and Catholic elites would be unwarranted. Indeed, no further agreement building on the Gentiloni Pact was attempted in the next years, and a fate not unlike that of the moderate Socialist leaders in 1912 befell the Catholic leaders who negotiated the 1913 pact. Only six years later, new Catholic leaders who had played little or no role in negotiating it and who argued that the pact entailed subordination of Catholic voters to Liberal hegemony, created the Italian Popular party (PPI). This new party competed openly and often bitterly with the Liberals, and it emerged from its first electoral outing, in November 1919, as the second largest party in the country (behind the Socialists). Although the Liberals taken together remained the largest force in Parliament, they were split into many conflicting factions and lost control of the political game they had enjoyed before the war (Farneti 1978).

It is plausible to see the Gentiloni Pact of 1913 as the first step in a convergence between Catholic and Liberal elites that, had it continued, would have created a dominant center–right electoral coalition in Italian politics. But the sticking point was the Liberals' insistence that the Catholics be incorporated in a subordinate position. The moderate Catholic leaders who negotiated the pact were probably ready to accept this subordination once they had gained Liberal concessions on the policies most important to them. But other important factions in the Catholic elite were unwilling to participate in such an alliance over the longer run because they saw in it the risk of losing many potential working-class supporters to the Socialists. In addition, the fact that the Liberals had not yet developed a modern party organization and still played by the old rules of personalistic parliamentary politics hampered the formation of an effective coalition. The failure of the Gentiloni Pact to create a durable mechanism for Catholic–Liberal cooperation meant that a more conflictual relationship between the two elites was likely in the difficult post–World War I years. As we know now, this difficult relationship and the obstacles it contained for stable governments were important reasons for the breakdown of Italian democracy in the 1920s (Farneti 1978).

Looking back at these twin efforts by the entrenched Liberal elite to incorporate the emerging Socialist and Catholic elites (and their mass followings), it is not hard to find a common thread: Both were undertaken for the purpose of ensuring Liberal hegemony. The Liberals sought to trade important policy concessions to Socialists and Catholics in return for parliamentary or electoral support. But the exchanges were not conducive to a balanced elite relationship: The Liberals intended to maintain their traditional grip on the government process and their overall control of the political system. They wanted only to coopt the new elites in subordinate positions, not to share power with them in any significant way.

More dramatically with the Socialists, but also to some extent with the Catholics, this attempted Liberal cooptation backfired. Moderate leaders disposed toward compromise were overthrown in the Socialist camp and outflanked in the Catholic camp. Power and mass support were garnered by more militant leaders in both camps. Moreover, to the extent that it exploited the mutual antagonisms and fears between Socialists and Catholics, the Liberal strategy of cooptation had an intrinsic potential for inflaming these deep divisions in Italian society.

In any event, the international and domestic upheavals of World War I dealt the Liberal strategy a death blow, for the war destroyed the very basis of the strategy: Liberal dominance. It divided the Liberal elite deeply between intransigent nationalists and less bellicose internationalists, and it triggered processes of mass mobilization that were entirely foreign to the Liberals' old elitist ways of conducting politics. Consequently, after the war, there was neither space nor opportunity for resuming the prewar efforts at incorporating emerging elites. A clear indication of these changed circumstances was the utter inability of the Liberals' most prominent leader, Giolitti, to play a role after the war anything like the one he had played before it.

The failure of elite incorporation via subordinate cooptation meant that after 1919 the three elite camps (Liberals, Catholics, and Socialists) had to find more equitable patterns of inter-elite cooperation. Not only did they have to surmount their traditional policy differences made sharper in the postwar conditions of social and economic crisis, but they also had to build a common consensus on the fundamental values, institutions, and rules of the democratic process strong enough to weather the challenges of the new situation of mass democracy. This would have required defusing the mutual elite suspicions and distrust that had reached dangerous proportions by the time of World War I, while at the same time reasserting moderate control and checking the centrifugal tendencies in all three camps. With the upsurge of new and avowedly antidemocratic elites and movements after the war – Nationalists and Fascists on the right, Communists on the left – these tasks were even more difficult, probably impossible. As we know, despite some attempts, Liberal, Socialist, and Catholic elites were not able to surmount their policy differences and mutual suspicions in time to build a political coalition capable of blocking the rise of the strongest new antidemocratic movement, Fascism. Once it was clear that no such coalition could be built, the Liberals, supported by the monarchy and a part of the Catholic elite, tried their old strategy of elite cooptation one last time. But the coopted elite – Mussolini and his associates – proved to be stronger than the coopting elite(s), and the unconsolidated democratic regime soon collapsed. Ironically, for a while the Fascist regime that followed succeeded in producing a broader elite unity than had existed at any time since national unification. But it was a unity built around submissiveness to Mussolini's project of an authoritarian state, rather than around a voluntary consensus on democratic institutions and values.

From temporary unity to confrontation: the anti-Fascist grand coalition of 1943–1947

A crucial reason that the early attempts at elite unification failed in Italy was their lack of inclusiveness. On each occasion, one or more important elite groups remained outside the unification process. But in the year after the fall of Mussolini and the Fascist regime in July 1943, an unprecedentedly broad agreement among elites was achieved. As we will see, this too proved to be temporary. But the ways in which it approximated an elite settlement and the importance of its legacy for Italian politics in succeeding decades require discussion.

A grand coalition of anti-Fascist forces was built during 1943 and 1944 (Morlino 1981). The first step was an agreement among all the parties that had been reconstituted by the time of Mussolini's fall to form a Committee for National Liberation (CLN) that would coordinate their actions during the last phase of World War II and the transition to a new democratic regime. Only the small Republican party (PRI) refused to participate. From left to right, the committee contained leaders of the Communist party (PCI), the Socialist party (at that time the PSIUP), the Action party (PdA, a Liberal–Socialist group made up essentially of intellectuals), the Christian Democracy party (DC), the Labor Democracy party (DdL), and the Liberal party (PLI) (see Bonomi 1947). This was the first time that leaders of the "new" mass parties (PCI, PSIUP, DC) had entered into a national agreement on other than a bilateral basis and in other than a subordinate position vis-à-vis the entrenched elites. The CLN functioned according to collegial and paritarian principles. Each party had a vote, although most decisions were based on unanimity. From the start, however, it was clear that leaders of the three largest mass parties – the PCI, PSIUP, and DC – would play the dominant roles.

The CLN was formed under the pressure of the continuing German occupation of northern and central Italy and of the reconstitution of a Fascist regime in that area. By agreeing to participate in it, all the parties renounced any actions that might undercut one another. This required putting aside strong ideological and programmatic differences, as well as overlooking the long history of interparty conflict and distrust. That these unprecedented steps could be taken at all can be traced to the common opposition that the Fascist regime and the occupying German forces inspired and to the pressing need to subordinate narrow partisan interests to the goal of freeing the country. Another factor that favored the parties' coming together was the monarchy's efforts in the first months after Mussolini's fall to relegate the parties to the sidelines and control the transition process with the support of the state apparatus (Gambino 1978, p. 6). A unified front was needed if the parties were to retain their centrality.

Partisan calculations were part of it too, of course. For example, if the moderate parties had excluded the Communists, they would have been in a weaker position in the armed struggle against German occupation, because the PCI had developed an extensive clandestine organizational network and a strong military force. Conversely, if the Communists had taken a more intransigent position vis-à-vis the moderate parties, which indeed some of its leaders in northern and central Italy advocated, they would have risked isolating their party in southern Italy, which was under Allied (British and American) occupation (Ellwood 1985). More generally, all parts of the resistance movement needed the support of the Allies for weapons and supplies. The Communists' strong connections with one of the Allied powers, the Soviet

Union, was another reason for not excluding them, and those connections further disposed the Communists to cooperate. Once the PCI's leader, Palmiro Togliatti, returned to Italy from the Soviet Union in the spring of 1944 and convinced his party to put aside its antimonarchical stance, at least for the time being, the basis for Communist participation was thus set (see Pasquino 1986, pp. 52–4). It can be said therefore that both internal and external factors facilitated the anti-Fascist elite alliance.

A central point of the CLN agreement was the decision to elect, after the war's end, a constituent assembly that would write a new constitution to replace the old pre-Fascist one (the Statuto Albertino that had not been abolished by the Fascist regime and so theoretically was still in force). Apart from symbolizing a deliberate break with the Fascist state as well as with the pre-Fascist democratic regime that so obviously had failed to work, this decision was important because it showed the intention of all anti-Fascist parties to take control of the regime transition themselves and to prevent the monarchy and its state bureaucratic allies from leading the process.

A crucial step in cementing the anti-Fascist coalition was the agreement reached in the spring of 1944 between the parties and the monarchy to postpone until after the war any decision on the "institutional issue" of whether Italy should be a monarchy or a republic and to join forces despite the monarchy's past collusion with Fascism and despite the strong republican desires of some of the parties. An external factor also helped facilitate this agreement: Although most of the parties (or at least their leaders) favored a republic, one of the occupying powers, Britain, strongly supported the monarchy and made it clear that it would not readily accept a unilateral decision by the party leaders on this question.

The 1944 agreement to cooperate with the monarchy led directly to governments in which all anti-Fascist forces participated.[6] But the effects of this pact lasted only until June 1946 when a popular referendum settled the institutional issue in favor of a republic. It is interesting to note that after a long debate in the CLN, the parties agreed to decide this issue through a referendum, rather than to have the Constituent Assembly try to resolve it. The party elites thereby skirted a divisive issue on which no unanimity would have been possible, and in particular, leaders of the centrist parties, especially

6 The second Badoglio cabinet (April–June 1944) was still led by a nonpolitician and an agent of the king, but it included representatives of the parties. The next government, the Bonomi cabinet, had as prime minister one of the party leaders.

the Christian Democrats, avoided having to take a position that would only alienate one or another segment of their supporters.

With minor exceptions, cooperation in forming governmental coalitions, in drafting the new constitution and electoral laws, and in taking some of the critical decisions regarding economic matters persisted among the party elites until 1947.[7] To complete the picture, we should add the June 1944 agreement reached among labor union leaders with different political allegiances (mainly Communists, Socialists, and Catholics) that sought to overcome past hostilities between them and to create a united labor organization. This agreement among trade union elites was followed in November 1945 by a compromise between leaders of the new union federation (CGIL) and leaders of the employers' federation (Confindustria) that enabled solutions to some of the dramatic problems of the postwar economy.

The long and sometimes confused process of drafting the constitution and other important laws, such as the electoral law, that unfolded between the elections of June 1946 and December 1947 also manifested significant elite unity. Agreements could not, of course, be reached on all disputed points by all the significant groups, and the writing of the new constitution involved shifting and unexpected alliances among the Communists, Socialists, Christian Democrats, and other parties on the left and the right (Cotta 1990). For instance, a crucial decision to uphold the historic Lateran Pacts of 1929 between church and state was reached thanks to an agreement between the Communists and the Christian Democrats, but against the opposition of the Socialists and some Liberals. But the overall result of this sometimes-byzantine process was that no elite could claim full victory, but none could claim that it systematically lost, either. Not surprisingly, the new constitution was almost unanimously accepted in the Constituent Assembly, by a vote of 453 to 63. It is worth recalling that in France in the same period, the first draft of the constitution for the Fourth Republic was resoundingly defeated in a popular referendum, whereas the second draft was approved by a bare majority. In Italy, however, no major political force, even during the tense polarization that began in 1948, publicly rejected the constitutional text, and the largest opposition party, the PCI, has consistently proclaimed its allegiance to the constitution ever since. Indeed, in a paradoxical but

7 The cooperation among parties was not always easy. During the second Bonomi cabinet (December 1944–June 1945), the Socialists and the Action party refused to take part in the government, and later in 1946, the Liberal party did not enter the second De Gasperi cabinet (Piscitelli 1975).

understandable reversal of positions, the PCI, once confined to permanent exclusion from government, became the most determined supporter of the constitutional text, even of some aspects it had originally opposed. On the other hand, some of the governing parties preferred to delay the implementation of some parts of the constitution (e.g., on regional autonomy and on a constitutional court) that they originally favored once they perceived that implementing the provisions would strengthen the opposition and weaken the government. Finally, although the referendum majority that chose a republican rather than a monarchical form of government was not overwhelming in its size, no large-scale rejection of the new republic's institutions ensued (a small monarchist party existed until the 1970s, but it was never a serious political factor).

If we look back at the inter-elite processes that unfolded between 1943 and 1947, their fit with the concept of an elite settlement is significant though not perfect. It is true that the processes were not always controlled by a few top leaders. And although some of the agreements were reached in secret, others were negotiated in more public settings. But a consensus among all major political and social elites concerning the institutional features of the new democratic regime and its fundamental rules of the game was in fact achieved. As well, compromises were hammered out on some important substantive matters. The question is, then, whether there was actually a transformation into a consensually unified national elite through what amounted to an elite settlement. And if there was, why did it not last? The pattern of elite cooperation and consensus did not persist much beyond 1947 when the two largest parties of the left, the PCI and the PSI (the new label for the Socialists), were ousted from the government. With the elections of 1948, a climate of harsh left–right confrontation was created. The major consequence was the long-term disqualification of the Communists, the largest opposition party, and the shorter-term disqualification of the Socialists as acceptable and trustworthy governing partners. What is worse, this breakdown of cooperation among the parties in governing quickly became a conflict over the very nature of the political and social order itself.

The international and domestic reasons for this breakdown have been frequently discussed. The cleavage between East and West that rapidly crystallized after the end of World War II was mirrored in Italian politics by the two largest parties, the DC and the PCI, aligning themselves internationally (each with smaller allied parties) with the opposing cold-war camps. Because the two camps were not only organized into opposed international alliances but also stood for radically conflicting visions of the political and social order – the West for pluralist democracy and a market economy, the East for one-party totalitarianism and a centralized economy – the polar commitments of the Italian elites made consensus among them impossible.

But one should not overlook the fact that various internal dynamics also fueled elite conflicts. Among them needs to be mentioned the way in which the end of the peculiar wartime climate of cooperation interacted with the beginning of competitive politics in a dense sequence of elections: spring 1946 (elections for the Constituent Assembly), spring and fall 1946 (local elections), and spring 1948 (elections for the first regular Parliament). As already noted, the special needs of the war years induced the parties to play down their ideological and policy differences and to reach compromises that more often than not amounted to postponing rather than solving divisive questions. However, with the end of the war, the moment to make many decisions on which deep disagreements were likely had come. The original interparty agreements had taken place in a situation of noncompetitive politics in which the parties were not yet fighting for votes, mass mobilization was extremely low, and in which each party had an equal vote in the CLN's deliberations. But with the start of an intense electoral season in 1946, incentives to emphasize party differences were strong. This was particularly so because there was now electoral competition not only among the parties that had been part of the CLN but also between them and new parties that were growing outside the anti-Fascist alliance. Especially troublesome was the emergence of two right-wing parties (Uomo qualunque and the Monarchists) that seemed able to bid for significant popular followings as well as for the support of some economic and religious elites. Their challenge was highly salient to the one party of the anti-Fascist alliance that, because of its political position between center and right, stood to lose most from their success – the Christian Democrats. In the local elections of autumn 1946, when the new right-wing parties made sizable inroads into the DC's electorate and gained endorsement by sections of the Catholic church through attacks on the DC–PCI alliance, important Christian Democratic leaders began to demand, in self-defense, that the party distance itself from the left.

The 1947 breakdown of governmental cooperation between the DC and PCI (together with the PSI) was a response to the international situation and also to this electoral struggle and to increasing difficulties in agreeing on economic policies. The new alignment of the parties and the highly polarized electoral campaign of 1948 effectively stifled the rise of right-wing parties whose democratic loyalty was at best dubious, and the Christian Democrats emerged as the dominant party for the next forty years. On the other side, the Communists became the "permanent" opposition party, a situation from which they have still not entirely recovered.

Whether under more favorable conditions a continuation of governmental cooperation among the three large anti-Fascist parties (DC, PCI, and PSI) or, more likely, a less traumatic shift from grand coalition to majority governments could have transformed the elite cooperation dictated by wartime needs and the transition to a postwar regime into a less comprehensive, but nonetheless durable, elite consensus on institutions and rules of the game is open to speculation. A crucial question would have been, in any case, the direction in which the party most ideologically remote from the tradition of pluralist democracy, the PCI, would have evolved. What is certain is that in the international and domestic circumstances that in fact occurred, a continuation of the anti-Fascist alliance increasingly came to be perceived by leaders of the centrist and moderate left and right parties as a serious threat to their political prospects, as well as a danger for the democratic regime itself. During those years, one had only to notice the demise of Eastern European democratic regimes, in which similar broad alliances with Communist parties had been tried, to make the latter view credible.

Two lessons can be learned from this episode: First, the passage from a situation of limited elite competition and mass mobilization to one of full competition and intensive mobilization constitutes an acid test for the persistence of an elite settlement. Second, international conditions and forces that are beyond the control of the elites who fashion a settlement can dramatically reduce the prospects that it will last.

Elite convergence after 1948: a long-term process and its stages

The confrontation between governmental parties and the leftist opposition that developed after 1947 has deeply colored Italian politics. It has produced distinctive patterns of nonalternation in government (because of the disqualification of the largest opposition party, the Communists) and of "stable instability" (unstable cabinets but within a political setting firmly defined by a large centrist party, the Christian Democrats, able to build the alliances necessary for parliamentary majorities).[8] The image of the largest opposition party's being a threat

8 The keystone of this complex equilibrium, the Christian Democracy party, was until the 1970s very clearly the largest party, but it never by itself achieved the majority required in the two chambers of Parliament to form a government. Only in 1948 did the DC win a majority in the lower chamber, but even then it did not have it in the Senate. Coalition or minority cabinets have therefore been the rule (Cotta 1988).

to pluralist democracy, should it ever control government executive power, has been held for a long time (and mutually reinforced) by a majority of elites and a majority of the mass public. Thus Christian Democratic leaders have regularly and successfully invoked the Communist threat in election campaigns, but they have also been constrained by the mass perceptions of this threat that they have deliberately fostered in their electorate. Indeed, when left-leaning DC leaders tried to promote a rapprochement (or "historic compromise") with the Communists in the mid-1970s, they faced significant resistance by an important section of DC voters which in the 1976 election used the preference vote allowed by the Italian electoral system to support the more anti-Communist candidates on the Christian Democratic slates.

These distinctive patterns have had somewhat contradictory political effects. On the one hand, the Italian democratic regime existed – probably until some point in the 1970s – under a widely perceived risk of collapse and under the constraints deriving from this situation. Although by as early as the end of 1948 it had become sufficiently clear that a revolutionary insurrection was not an option for the Communist party and although the party itself repudiated that option, its strong links with a nondemocratic regime, the Soviet Union, and its regular claims about the superiority of Soviet-type regimes to bourgeois democracies regularly fueled suspicions about the PCI's "real" intentions among its opponents. It was not until the 1970s that these suspicions began to abate in any serious way. At the same time, it must be said that fear of the Communists has helped stabilize support for the moderate democratic parties, insulating them to a great extent from performance-related judgments, and it has thus contributed to the survival of the democratic regime. As a result, the post-Fascist regime has been very different from the pre-Fascist one. In the pre-Fascist regime, prodemocratic elites were extremely fragmented and lacked strong organizational ties to the masses, which made them easy prey for antidemocratic elites on the right and left. But in the post-Fascist regime, since 1948, the democratic parties, especially the DC, have constituted a very powerful political force – with strong links to both crucial social elites and the mass level – able to dominate electoral politics and thus to ensure the country's governability. Even though it is true that the DC leadership has always been highly factionalized, the fact that there never has been a significant party split suggests that the unity of DC leaders is greater than is sometimes thought.

If polarization and the lack of a democratic consensus at the elite and mass levels were constitutive, highly visible features of Italian politics (especially in the electoral arena) from 1947 until well into the 1970s (Sartori 1976, 1984), Italian politics had another face that should not be overlooked. This was an ongoing process of integrating left-wing elites and parties into the political mainstream, a process that was partial and uncertain at first but, with the passage of time, a process that became more significant. As we will see, the visibility, forms, and successes of this integrative process have varied. We should add that there also has been a parallel process of integrating extremist right-wing elites and parties into the mainstream, but because right-wing groups have been smaller and less important, this second process will not be discussed here.

The process of integrating the left can be said to have originated in the failure of the governing parties to reap the benefits of the electoral reform that they pushed through Parliament before the 1953 election. This reform would have given a large parliamentary majority to the party or coalition that received 50 percent of the votes. In the 1953 election, however, the center–right coalition led by the Christian Democrats failed to reach that threshold, and the reform therefore had no effect. It was later rescinded. It should be remembered that the electoral system was not defined by the constitution of 1947 but only by parliamentary legislation. However, a proportional representation system had been part of the original agreement of the anti-Fascist coalition, and in this political sense it has been an unquestioned, quasi-constitutional rule of the Italian political game ever since. In any event, after the 1953 attempt to alter the electoral processes and the workings of the institutional system in a more "majoritarian" direction (Lijphart 1984) – an attempt that coincided with the most critical moment in postwar parliamentary politics because of the fierce battle waged by the opposition to block the electoral law's passage – a purely exclusionary strategy vis-à-vis the opposition was not tried again by the dominant elites. Instead, a more complicated game involving both integration and exclusion developed. To some extent, this game was a conscious elite strategy, but in part it grew in a less controlled and more spontaneous way according to changing political and institutional constraints and opportunities.

The first important episode was an attempt to divide the leftist opposition by opening the "governmental area" to the more moderate but relatively weak Socialist party. Here it should be remembered that after 1946 the Socialists were closely allied with the Communists, fighting the 1948 elections under the same Popular Front label and siding clearly with the Soviet Union in the emerging cold war. Because of these positions, the Socialists were expelled from the International Organization of Socialist Parties.

Starting in 1963, Socialist leaders became pivotal partners in the game of forming government coalitions. But from the standpoint of integrating the opposition into the mainstream, this "opening to the left" was only a half-success. First, it soon brought about a split in the Socialist elite, in which part of the leadership broke with the party and formed a new Partito socialista italiano di unitá proletaria (PSIUP) in 1964 which closely allied itself to the PCI. Second, it did not produce an expected weakening in voter support for the parts of the left that remained excluded. On the contrary, the PCI gained a larger electoral following at the expense of the Socialists, increasing its vote from 22 percent (1958) before the "opening to the left" to 28 percent (1972) after its high point, whereas the Socialist vote declined from 14.5 percent to 11 percent during the same period. Moreover, after an initial period of fairly stable governments (by Italian standards) the center–left alliance became increasingly fractious, and the average life of governments decreased from fifteen months between 1963 and 1968 to eight to nine months between 1968 and 1976. Once again it was demonstrated that incorporating (or coopting) a previously excluded elite can seriously weaken that elite and strengthen those left outside.

After the failure of this attempt to solve the problems of a highly polarized political system by coopting the more moderate Socialists while continuing to exclude the more extreme Communists, a still more intricate process entailing the Communists began. Initially, this took place mainly in the parliamentary arena and was hardly apparent to the public outside. In the public electoral arena, government and opposition forces continued to attack each other frontally. It was not until the 1983 election that the Christian Democrats abandoned their "risk of Communism" campaign theme. But inside the walls of Parliament, some measure of cooperation between the two camps gradually developed.

Thanks to a combination of institutional and political incentives, the legislative process was the most important locus for this development (see Di Palma 1978). First, the parliamentary setting provided numerous opportunities for an opposition, particularly for a large and cohesive party like the PCI, to make its weight felt in the cumbersome legislative process. Second, the political heterogeneity of the DC and its various coalition partners on many issues often made it imperative that they gain some degree of tolerance from the opposition in order to get their initiatives approved. Third, the factions within the governing coalition could find opposition support to defeat initiatives with which they were unhappy. The opposition could thus participate in the parliamentary process, even though it was widely depicted in the more visible electoral arena as a menace to democracy.

Other important occasions for interaction between the two elite camps arose from Parliament's responsibility for electing (often requiring very large majorities) candidates to fill a number of important public offices. These offices include the speakers and deputy speakers of the two parliamentary chambers, the president of the republic, and the judges of the constitutional court. Over time, leaders of the PCI played increasingly important roles in negotiating the candidates and parliamentary votes for these positions (Cotta 1990).

The extent of cooperation between the two camps was apparent by 1971 when Parliament's standing orders were reformed with the support of all the major parties. An important aspect of the new standing orders was that they rejected the privileged position of the government and of its majority in the legislative process, putting all parliamentary groups on the same footing in drawing up the parliamentary agenda. The new rules thus sanctioned and further stimulated the interactions that had developed between the governing and opposition elites.

In one sense, the culmination of this parliamentary integration of the opposition elite was the agreement in 1976 that included the Communist party in the parliamentary majority (but not in the cabinet) supporting the Christian Democratic government of the time. Covering the Communists, Socialists, Social Democrats, Republicans, Christian Democrats, and Liberals, this agreement excluded only the minor parties of the extreme right and left. Its consequence was the assignment to the Communists of a number of parliamentary offices from which they had previously been excluded (e.g., speaker of the chamber of deputies and the presidencies of some legislative committees). The agreement also meant an elaborate exchange of policy concessions in economic and foreign affairs, a particularly important concession being the PCI's acceptance of Italy's membership in NATO.

It would be wrong to see this 1976 agreement as just another step in the integrative process at the parliamentary level that we have been describing. For the first time, executive power came under the direct (though not sole) influence of the PCI, and in this respect the agreement embodied a much more visible and dramatic mutual elite acceptance. Effectively, the major anti-Communist elites acknowledged the democratic reliability of the largest opposition party. In more abstract terms, the 1976 agreement amounted to a shift from gradual and limited elite convergence to a broad settlement of most longstanding suspicions and hostilities between the major elite camps.

Why did this dramatic change occur at that point? An answer requires us to take into account a complex balance of factors that, to some extent, can support two different interpretations. One of these is a more deterministic interpretation that stresses the "inevitability" of elite convergence as a result of the incremental integration of elites "condemned" to coexistence by conditions then prevailing in Italy. The other is an interpretation that places more weight on contingent crises that occurred in the mid-1970s and that, although not devoid of risks for the stability of democracy, proved in the end propitious for elite unification.

There are indeed some signs that suggest that elite convergence had reached an advanced stage by the 1970s. We have already mentioned the increasingly close relations among parliamentary elites that undoubtedly accustomed them to bargaining rather than hurling brickbats at one another. There was also a gradual process of change in the PCI's ideological positions, especially its prudent but steady distancing from the Soviet Union as a political model, with the PCI's condemnation of the Soviet invasion of Czechoslovakia in 1968 being a turning point. More generally, the PCI increasingly turned to a less dogmatic version of Marxism.

It must be said, however, that the idea of a linear process of political depolarization and elite convergence is not entirely convincing. At some levels, in fact, Italian society appeared to be more acutely polarized during the 1970s than in the 1960s. After 1968, for example, the ideologization of cultural and political life dramatically intensified, and industrial relations (in Italy, closely connected with partisan politics) became more, not less, conflictual and strike prone. This new climate was a fertile breeding ground for terrorists, who launched an onslaught against the established order in the late 1970s. The greater polarization seems, with other factors, responsible for weakening the governmental parties, which lost votes under the impact of successful competition by the opposition and thus became less able to find common ground.

The final years of the Fifth Parliament (1972–6) and the elections of 1976 were the culmination of these difficulties.[9] The coalition of political elites that had been dominant for nearly thirty years appeared to be breaking down. Indeed, the dissolution of the Fifth Parliament showed the increased difficulty of creating a coalition with a majority

9 Looking at electoral results, we see the extreme left (PCI and other smaller leftist parties) increase its share of votes from 25 to 36 percent between 1963 and 1976, while the so-called governmental area (i.e. Socialists, Christian Democrats, plus smaller centrist parties) shrinks from 67 to 56 percent (Farneti 1985).

from among the traditional governing parties. In particular, the Socialists would no longer agree to support a government that excluded the PCI. Thus, the 1976 election was held under widespread expectations that the PCI would replace the DC as the biggest party (the so-called *sorpasso*) and that the left as a whole would gain a majority in parliament (Parisi and Pasquino 1977, p. 15).

How things would have evolved if this had come to pass is difficult to say. Since 1973, when they were shocked by the violent overthrow of Salvador Allende's socialist regime in Chile, the PCI leadership had adhered to the "historical compromise" line, asking not for a government of the left alone but for a broad coalition including the "Catholic world" and the DC. However, there were strong forces in the left, particularly among intellectuals and middle-level elites, that opposed an alliance with the DC and pushed instead for breaking the Christian Democratic hegemony. A clear victory by the left would probably have increased their influence. It is difficult to say whether this could have produced a development along the lines of Chile's Unidad popular. But the chances are that Italian politics would have followed a path different from the one it actually took (see Sartori 1978 for an exercise in scenario building). In any case, the result of the 1976 elections, contrary to most expectations, produced a tie instead of a clear victory for either side. The PCI, indeed, had a resounding success, but the Christian Democrats held their ground and retained the psychologically important advantage of being the largest party. Moreover, the left as a whole failed to win a majority in Parliament. The upshot was a balance, with the old elites being unable to govern alone and the Communist elite no longer excluded, but with the DC core of the elites showing unexpected resilience. These conditions were probably the most favorable for pushing in the direction of an agreement between the two camps, as for each of them any other course would have been more risky.

Going back to the explanations of how long-term elite disunity can be overcome, we are confronted with a choice between an interpretation that attributes greater importance to the gradual development of value consensus and organizational interconnectedness among elites in the form of a convergence, and an interpretation that emphasizes the importance of crises or other (sometimes external) contingent conditions that dispose elites toward sudden settlements (Burton and Higley 1987; Rustow 1970). The two interpretations should not be seen as entirely incompatible, and evidence for both is available in the Italian case. If we hypothesize that cooperative elite behavior may be induced by a crisis only when a certain level of consensus has already been reached or, alternatively, that a slow and gradual convergence can sometimes be accelerated by a crisis, then we can reconcile the two interpretations.

To this review of elite unification during the 1960s and 1970s must be added the observation that unification occurred principally at the parliamentary level of party politics but did not extend fully to the governmental level. Full PCI participation in cabinets, which the Communists eventually began to demand after more than a year of giving external support to Christian Democratic minority cabinets, did not materialize. This final step, which from a symbolic point of view would powerfully mark the achievement of full elite consensus and unity, was not taken then and it has yet to be taken. Why, after three years of intense cooperation at the elite level (that among other things made possible a common front for successfully combating the spread of terrorism), the DC–PCI coalition broke apart and sent the Communists back to what has again seemed like a permanent opposition status is a matter of dispute. There is some reason to believe that a major factor behind the increasing intransigence of the two largest coalition partners (DC and PCI) over such policy issues as acceptance of the European Monetary Agreement, which provided the occasion for terminating the coalition, was the fear by both partners that they would lose ground to competitors (both electoral and nonelectoral) on their respective flanks.

From our point of view, however, the fact that the grand coalition experiment of the late 1970s has not yet opened the way to an alternation in government (analogous to those that occurred in the Austrian and German cases) may not be so relevant. In fact, the legacies of that coalition for a deeper consolidation of the democratic regime have been significant. Thus, the depolarization of the political system at both the elite and the mass level has advanced greatly. The acceptance of all political actors as legitimate competitors has become more widespread, suggesting that even when policy positions differ, an elite consensus on institutions and procedural rules has been reached. And there also are signs of a much greater structural integration among elites. Just to mention one sign – small but symbolically significant – it has become common for representatives of all the major parties to be invited to one another's national conventions and even to deliver speeches at those conventions. Similarly, various institutional positions inside and outside Parliament are routinely distributed among all the major parties, with a Communist continuing to hold the speaker's position in the Chamber of Deputies.

The conclusion may therefore be that the breakup of the DC–PCI coalition at the government level has not meant a setback for elite unification. Unlike all earlier experiences in Italian history, the failure of this specific inter-elite agreement has not resulted in a significant increase in elite radicalization and disunity. In fact, the end of the coalition experiment coincided also with the end of the PCI's electoral growth and with the onset of a steady decline in its support, as well as with the renewed ability of leaders of the traditional governing parties to reach the agreements required for sustaining governments. These changes have, in turn, become strong reasons for the Communist elite to push even harder for its own transformation, to the point that changing the very name of the PCI in order to symbolize a break with its own past as clearly as possible is now a central item on the party agenda. Finally, no significant political force has appeared at the extreme left to capitalize on the PCI's increasing moderation. In short, the consolidation of Italian democracy has, on balance, proceeded apace during the ten years since the end of the DC–PCI coalition.

Less than a conclusion

After this rather schematic discussion of a series of historical episodes regarding the changing relationships among Italian elites, a full-fledged conclusion with a satisfactory explanation of the conditions responsible for these changes and their consequences (whether they were failures or successes) is perhaps not possible. There is space, however, for some less than systematic remarks that may offer suggestions for further research and discussion.

A first consideration is that both historical successes and failures can provide useful insights for building a theory that explains how elite transformations from disunity to consensual unity take place, the conditions that favor them, and how these transformations are related to democratic consolidation. It should not be forgotten that failed elite transformations are unquestionably more numerous than successful transformations, and they therefore constitute rich empirical grounds for testing relevant hypotheses. The Italian case alone shows that out of four or five attempted transformations (depending on how one counts the "opening to the left" in the early 1960s), only one succeeded.

In regard to the forms of these transformations from elite disunity to elite consensus and unity, Italian history provides diverse examples. Some of the attempted transformations approximated the form of an elite settlement, and others more closely resembled an elite convergence. Italian history suggests, moreover, that there can be some amount of contamination between these two kinds of elite transformation. Indeed, elite pacts (which are most directly related to the processes of elite settlements) sometimes punctuate elite convergence. And elite settlements may be preceded (and made possible) by a process of elite convergence. The Italian experience also teaches that a crucial factor that shapes the kind of transformation that elites go through is their reciprocal power positions at any given point. If their positions are far from paritarian, it is likely that only a "cooptive" transformation will occur, whereas if their positions are more balanced, then a settlement or more gradual convergence will be possible.

The Italian experiences also suggest that elite unifications do not necessarily develop in a linear fashion. Although past attempts at unification can have some legacies for future developments in the direction of unity, the process is seldom or never simply a sequence of steps in which each new step amounts to a clear increase in elite unity. This was certainly the case in Italy's crisis of the 1920s after a long trend that, despite occasional setbacks, seemed to be moving toward steadily greater unity.

A major question that emerges from our review of the Italian episodes concerns the duration and effects of elite transformations over time. In a nutshell, why do short-term successes (or that at least appear as such) become longer-term failures? In the search for answers, an obvious candidate would seem to be the ability of the elites involved to extend the reach of the unification process to all relevant groups and to incorporate new elites that subsequently emerge. In some of the episodes that we have examined, longer-term failure appears to have been rather clearly linked to the continuing exclusion of some relevant elites. It may indeed be the case that elite unifications are deliberately exclusionary in the first instance. Past enmities between some elites are overcome in order to exclude other groups that are perceived as more dangerous. But this may also happen less deliberately, as under certain conditions the process of unification itself produces divisions between compromise-oriented and intransigent elite members, with the latter becoming alienated and hostile. Especially fateful for the achievement of elite consensus and unity is a situation in which the intransigent group commands a larger mass following than the compromisers do, thus leaving the latter without much power.

In some cases, failure also seems related to the nature of the organizational instruments adopted when attempting an elite transformation. If these instruments do not establish and sustain sufficiently institutionalized inter-elite linkages, the chances that elite unity will last are poor. This suggests that the nature and working of different integrative institutions, and also the context they create for elite interactions, are important subjects for further investigation.

The Italian experience also contains much evidence about the importance of mass behavior for the success or failure of elite transformations. The ability of the elites to control and incorporate their mass followings into newly cooperative patterns seems essential to the longer-term success of elite agreements. How elite–mass linkages are structured (and this refers very much to parties and also to other forms of organization) is therefore a vital area for further research.

Finally, although some of the factors mentioned are to a certain extent within the control of elites, we must also remember that others, for instance, international conditions, may be much less so. Whether such contingent conditions are favorable or unfavorable may do much to explain why partial and tentative transformations blossom into full successes or unravel into complete failures.

References

Aquarone, Alberto. 1972. *Alla ricerca del'Italia liberale*. Naples: Guida.

Ballini, Pier Luigi. 1988. *Le Elezioni nella storia d'Italia dall'unitá al fascismo*. Bologna: Il Mulino.

Bonomi, Ivanoe. 1944. *La Politica italiana da porta pia a vittorio veneto*. Turin: Einaudi.

1947. *Diario di un anno: 2 Giugno 1943–10 Giugno 1944*. Milan: Garzanti.

Burton, Michael, and John Higley. 1987. "Elite Settlements." *American Sociological Review* 52: 295–307.

Capone, Alfredo. 1981. *Destra e sinistra da Cavour a Crispi*. Turin: UTET.

Cotta, Maurizio. 1988. "Italy." In *Cabinets in Western Europe*, ed. Jean Blondel and Ferdinand Mueller-Rommel. London: Macmillan.

1990. "The Role of Parliament in a Weak Consolidation of the Democratic Regime: The Italian Case." In *Parliament and Democratic Consolidation in Southern Europe*, ed. Ulrike Liebert and Maurizio Cotta. London: Pinter.

Dalla Torre, Giuseppe. 1962. *I Cattolici e la vita pubblica italiana*. Rome: Cinque lune.

De Felice, Renzo. 1973. *Mussolini il rivoluzionario: 1883–1920*. Turin: Einaudi.

De Rosa, Gabriele. 1966. *Storia del movimento cattolico in Italia*. Bari: Laterza.

Di Palma, Giuseppe. 1978. *Surviving Without Governing*. Berkeley and Los Angeles: University of California Press.

1990 "Parliaments, Consolidation, Institutionalization: A Minimalist View." In *Parliament and Democratic Consolidation in Southern Europe*, ed. Ulrike Liebert and Maurizio Cotta. London: Pinter.

Ellwood, David W. 1985. *Italy 1943–45*. Leicester: Leicester University Press.

Farneti, Paolo. 1971. *Sistema politico e società civile*. Turin: Giappichelli.

1978. "Social Conflict, Parliamentary Fragmentation, Institutional Shift and the Rise of Fascism: Italy." In *The Breakdown of Democratic Regimes*, ed. Juan J. Linz and Alfred Stepan. Baltimore: Johns Hopkins University Press.

1985. *The Italian Party System*. New York: St. Martin's Press.

Gambino, Antonio. 1978. *Storia del dopoguerra*. Bari: Laterza.

Giolitti, Giovanni. 1923. *Memoirs of My Life*. London: Chapman and Dodd.

Lijphart, Arendt. 1984. *Democracies*. New Haven, CT: Yale University Press.

Molony, John Neylon. 1977. *The Emergence of Political Catholicism in Italy*. London: Croom Helm.

Morlino, Leonardo. 1981. "Del Fascismo a una democracia débil: El Cambio de régimen en Italia (1939–1948)." In *Transición a la democracia en el sur de Europa y América Latina*, ed. Julián Santamaría. Madrid: Centro de investigaciones sociológicas.

Parisi, Arturo, and Gianfranco Pasquino. 1977. "20 giugno: Struttura politica e comportamento elettorale." In *Continuitá e mutamento elettorale*, ed. Arturo Parisi and Gianfrano Pasquino. Bologna: Il Mulino.

Pasquino, Gianfranco. 1986. "The Demise of the First Fascist Regime and Italy's Transition to Democracy: 1943–48." In *Transitions from Authoritarian Rule: Southern Europe*, ed. Guillermo O'Donnell, Philippe C. Schmitter, and Laurence Whitehead. Baltimore: Johns Hopkins University Press.

Piscitelli, Enzo. 1975. *Da Parri a de Gasperi*. Milan: Feltrinelli.

Rokkan, Stein. 1970. "Nation-building, Cleavage Formation and the Structuring of Mass Politics." In *Citizens, Elections, Parties*, ed. Stein Rokkan. Oslo: Universitetsforlaget.

Romanelli, Raffaele. 1988. *Il Comando impossibile: Stato y societá nell'Italia liberale*. Bologna: Il Mulino.

Rustow, Dankwart A. 1970. "Transitions to Democracy: Toward a Dynamic Model." *Comparative Politics* 2: 337–63.

Sartori, Giovanni. 1976. *Parties and Party Systems*. Cambridge: Cambridge University Press.

1978. "Calculating the Risk." In *Eurocommunism: The Italian Case*, ed. Austin Ranney and Giovanni Sartori. Washington, DC: American Enterprise Institute.

1984. *Teoria dei partiti e caso italiano*. Milan: SugarCo.

Scoppola, Pietro. 1977. *La Proposta politica di De Gasperi*. Bologna: Il Mulino.

Seton-Watson, Christopher. 1967. *Italy from Liberalism to Fascism: 1870–1925*. London: Methuen.

Turati, Filippo, and Anna Kuliscioff. 1977. *Carteggio*. Turin: G. Einaudi.

Vigezzi, Brunello. 1976. *Giolitti e Turati: Un incontro mancato*. Milan: Ricciardi.

6

The role of civil–military pacts in elite settlements and elite convergence: democratic consolidation in Uruguay

CHARLES GUY GILLESPIE

During the 1980s, one Latin American military regime after another underwent a transition to democracy, although with widely varying results in terms of the restoration of civilian control over governments. This chapter focuses on one country in which a uniquely explicit effort was made to negotiate a military withdrawal to the barracks. Uruguay's Naval Club Accord of August 1984 represented the successful culmination of a series of such efforts. It did not represent a full-scale elite settlement so much as a shift in the key elites disposed to cooperate in democratic politics. The pact came at the expense of one of the major elites in the country (the leaders of the Blanco party), who were excluded. Thus the process by which democracy has been subsequently (re-) consolidated involved the reincorporation of the Blanco elite by a process of convergence.

Democracy emerged in Uruguay in the first quarter of this century as a result of a slow elite convergence between two established party elites, the Blancos and the Colorados (Gillespie and González 1989). By the 1970s, however, the two traditional party elites no longer were the only important elites in the country's politics. Military commanders had risen to a position of autonomy and influence that made them crucial actors. Likewise, the growth of parties on the left made their leaders influential. What was required for democracy to be reequilibrated was thus either a comprehensive elite settlement or a new process of convergence that would bring all four elites into fundamental consensus regarding democratic institutions and the rules of the game. The crisis of Uruguayan democracy after 1968 can be seen as a series of failures to achieve either of these changes (Gillespie 1983, 1984). Uruguay had the rare historical experience of making the transition from a consolidated democracy to an unconsolidated one, and eventually twelve years of military rule were inaugurated in 1973.[1]

The rise and fall of Uruguayan democracy

During this century Uruguay has experienced fifty years of democracy. Using the same definitions as throughout this book, a consolidated democracy was inaugurated in 1918 with the compromise on a new constitution between the Colorados and the Blancos. For fifteen years there was mass inclusion and elite consensus on the rules of the game. Partly under the impact of the Great Depression, in 1933 an elected president illegally rewrote the constitution after a pact with the most important opposition leader, thereby ushering in a period of pseudo-democracy. Full freedoms were restored in 1942, and for the next twenty-five years Uruguay may be considered to have been a consolidated democracy once more. But the rise of new antisystem elites between 1968 and 1973 meant the breakdown of elite consensus and the emergence of an unconsolidated democracy. From 1973 until 1985 Uruguay was ruled by the military.

A necessary starting point for an analysis of Uruguayan political development is an emphasis on the inapplicability of pessimistic cultural determinism to Latin America's most homogeneous, European, urban, and educated nation. Its traditional political parties, the Colorados and the Blancos (officially known as the National party), are almost a century and a half old, and the values and practices of competitive democratic politics are deeply embedded in the society. The contrast with neighboring Argentina's militarist, elitist, and antidemocratic and clerical traditions is widely recognized.

The transition from a stable limited democracy dominated by elites to something approximating a consolidated democracy occurred gradually in the last quarter of the nineteenth century and the first quarter of the twentieth century. This calls to mind Dahl's hypothesis that the historical sequence of regime liberalization before mass participation is more favorable than the reverse or than their simultaneous occurrence (Dahl 1971). By the time of the first elections held on the basis of universal adult male suffrage in 1918, political elites and parliamentary practices had competed for four decades. Unlike Chile, Uruguay's progress toward mass democracy was early, and unlike Argentina it was built on a competitive parliamentary tradition rather

1 Indeed, using reasonable definitions of consolidation, Robert Dahl has concluded that Uruguay may be the only consolidated democracy to have ever collapsed (see Dahl 1985, pp. 38–44).

than representing a discontinuous leap. Nor did it lead to the electoral annihilation of the conservative opposition, as occurred in Argentina about the same time.

Between 1865 and 1958, Colorados of one kind or another were able to maintain a constant hold over the national government (though in the nineteenth century this frequently required military dictatorships). The National party (or the Blancos) survived as a party of protest, defending the periphery against the center (Montevideo) and tending to side with ranching interests against the increasing pressure of the urban-commercial sector that grew under state protection. The Blancos rebelled in 1875, 1897, and 1904, in the boom period that began with a sharp rise in wool exports. Their ultimate defeat signified both the triumph of Montevideo over the caudillos of the interior oligarchy and the victory for the rural enclosures over their displaced victims. In marked contrast with Argentina, and indeed the rest of Latin America, the "oligarchy" was irrevocably weakened and forced to share the ship of state with the sizable rural "middle class" and the urban bourgeoisie.

Despite the dominance of the Colorado party and the conflict among socioeconomic elites, Uruguay's democratic regime resulted from the competitive balance among rival forces that was more visible in its political society than in its class structure. But what were the forces molding that political society?

After a great civil war came to an end in 1852, Uruguay made a fitful attempt at parliamentary coexistence between the two parties until the new phenomenon of a militarist dictatorship by Lorenzo Latorre (1876–80). The export-led boom of the last quarter of the nineteenth century, associated particularly with the greatly expanded consumption of wool, was a period of rapid economic progress and repressive political centralization. The price of civilian restoration in the 1880s paid by the Colorados anxious to tame the military was a truce with the various Blanco caudillos of the rural hinterland, who had to be given positions of leadership in the periphery.

The first stage of democratization was thus based on a parceling out of power between the two elite camps. It lasted only about a generation because in 1903–4 the two sides again fought a bloody civil war. After this, rapid urbanization brought as much as one half of the population to the capital and surrounding agricultural region. This enabled the Colorados to transform what had been a patrician party into a powerful mass political machine, and it was on this basis that the Colorados' hegemony was reconstructed. Moreover, the advent of the Colorados' greatest president, liberal reformer Don José Batlle y Ordóñez, in 1903 led to a successful coupling of capitalism and state formation that achieved something very rare in Latin America: a profound and continuous democratization of politics and society.

Power-sharing practices and factionalism in both traditional parties prevented an overconcentration of state power, which in theory increased rapidly under Batlle's reforms, with the creation of government agencies, state banks, and public enterprises. Thus, concern that overcentralized economies and polities might not be propitious for competitive democracy was not a problem in Uruguay. Although defeated in the 1903–4 civil war, the Blancos were not destroyed: They adapted more or less successfully to the role of loyal opposition. In fact, each rebellion before the last had brought them some sort of payoff that in some respects might be called *consociational*. In 1917 the Blancos were able to deflect Batlle's plans to revise the constitution by forcing him to concede the principle of "coparticipation": minority representation in the collegial executive that he was determined that Uruguay should have. Batlle was further forced to compromise by agreeing to the popular election of a president alongside the Colegiado (a nine-member executive). Thereafter, almost every one of the frequent constitutional changes that were to occur would be carried out under a pact between the majority factions of the two parties. These pacts did not, however, produce elite unity because substantial minorities in both parties always opposed the changes.

In comparative terms Uruguay was notable for its political stability. An interesting long-term product of this stability was the generation of a strong esprit de corps among politicians, who formed a recognizable political class. They normally practiced liberal professions, above all law, and were therefore often educated together. (There was only one university in Uruguay until the military permitted the creation of an embryonic Catholic rival in 1984.)

Particularly significant was the 1931 "Pork-Barrel Pact" that extended the principle of coparticipation to the selection of boards of directors for public enterprises, thereby formalizing the process of party factions' colonizing the state bureaucracy that Batlle had been unable to stamp out. Henceforth both parties were guaranteed access to the patronage resources that came to constitute their key electoral appeal. The semiauthoritarian coup by President Gabriel Terra in 1933 had the backing of the reactionary wings of both traditional parties, ushering in a period of pseudo-democracy and elite disunity.

This discussion brings us to the problem of conflict management discussed by Lijphart (1969, 1977) and Nordlinger (1972). Many institutional practices in Uruguay have been specifically seen as designed to lessen conflict among elites, including

1. Guaranteed Blanco rule of certain interior "departments" or counties (at various times in the late nineteenth century).
2. Periods of collegial executive with minority participation (1918–33 and 1951–66).
3. Proportional division of "spoils" in terms of multiparty distribution of patronage and administrative posts in the many state agencies and public enterprises (from 1931).
4. The creation of a Senate permanently divided equally between the Colorados and the Blancos (1934–42).
5. Frequent resort to interparty pacts, especially before constitutional changes.

During the 1950s and 1960s, just as Uruguay was entering a prolonged economic crisis, political competition between the Blancos and the Colorados became increasingly intense. In 1958 the Blancos won legislative and executive elections for the first time in this century and attempted to introduce orthodox IMF (International Monetary Fund) stabilization policies. Because these were electorally suicidal, they were soon abandoned. In 1967 the Colorados came back to power, this time under a toughened "Gaullist" single-person presidency. Over the next six years the crisis of democracy gathered pace. The deterioration of the economy as measured in rapid inflation and declining real wages led to massive labor unrest, to which the government responded harshly. The radicalization of the student movement fed the growth of an urban guerrilla movement, the Tupamaros, whose avowed aim was the destruction of Uruguay's traditional institutions. By this point Uruguay was clearly no longer a consolidated democracy, as the elite consensus evaporated and the popular political forces began to be repressed (Boeker 1990, pp. 78–9, 89–90).

Close cooperation between the leaders of the Colorado and Blanco parties might have saved the democratic regime. This was not to be, however. Accusations of fraud were made in the 1971 elections, which were extremely close, and the new Colorado president, Juan María Bordaberry, failed in his bid to reach a postelection accord with the leader of the Blanco majority, Wilson Ferreira. Instead of standing together, the politicians began to court the military, wrongly believing that they could use it for their own purposes.

The stalemate of military rule

In 1973 a collegial military dictatorship replaced Uruguay's deconsolidated democracy. The breakdown of democracy occurred in two stages: A military mutiny subdued the president in February, and a coup closed the legislature in June, in advance of mass arrests, purges, censorship, and repression. Although the right-wing President Bordaberry was permitted to remain as a civilian figurehead, power passed into the hands of various collegial institutions designed by the colonels and generals. These included the joint chiefs of staff, or Estado mayor conjunto (ESMACO), created to coordinate the successful liquidation of the Tupamaros, and the National Security Council (COSENA), which included the commanders in chief of the army, navy, and air force, as well as various ministers, to supervise the president. A new top legislative organ, the Junta de oficiales generales, was made up of the country's twenty-six ranking generals.

Whereas power quickly accumulated in the hands of one man (Pinochet) in Chile, Uruguay's generals were anxious to construct a rigorously collegial regime. Thus the early years of the regime were fraught with various purges, the first losers being those at one time identified with demands for progressive reforms, often (probably inaccurately) described as Peruvianists (Kaufman 1978). Unfortunately (both for political scientists and opposition politicians), the armed forces were extremely adept at concealing their internal power struggles from outside view.

In O'Donnell's terminology, the level of "threat" to the survival of capitalism and its existing elites and institutions was far lower than in Chile. The combined forces of Uruguay's left had obtained just 18 percent of the vote in the 1971 elections, a historic advance, but not one that represented the destruction of the dominant two-party system. Although Uruguay's Frente Amplio included the Christian Democrats, it was barely able to win half the Unidad popular's share of the votes in Chile's 1970 elections. Likewise, it was soon clear that Uruguay's military *proceso*, as it was euphemistically called, rested on a far narrower base of support than did the Pinochet regime, despite the very large size of Uruguay's middle class and its comparatively small industrial proletariat.

The Uruguayan military were very successful at wiping out "subversion." Having penetrated and destroyed the Tupamaros in 1972, they completely dismantled both the centralized trade union confederation (CNT) after the unsuccessful general strike against the coup (1973), and all leftist parties (1974–6). Although the Uruguayan Communist party was one of the larger Communist parties in South America relative to population, it was totally deactivated in successive waves of arrests between 1973 and 1976. After 1973 there was a decade without strikes or terrorist activities of any importance. The activities of the so-called traditional parties – the Colorados and the Blancos – were merely "suspended," and their former leaders were banned from politics by an Institutional Act (1976).

The military regime was able to suppress all opposition, owing to the relatively small size of the country's overall population, and it raised the costs of opposition to intolerable levels by McCarthyite purges of employees, particularly in the very large public sector. The regime did not banish or exile opponents (emigration for political and economic reasons was, in any case, massive), but it imprisoned them, giving the country one of the highest per-capita prison populations in the world, according to Amnesty International data. Despite the eery quiet, the greatest difficulty for the military was the lack of what Garretón (1979) has termed a "foundational project" akin to that of Chile's military regime which undertook a radical restructuring of Chile's state and society. By contrast, Uruguay's military insisted that they had taken power merely to defend democracy from subversion, to clean up corruption, and to strengthen tottering institutions. The broad outlines of economic policy were in fact inherited from the previous civilian government.

What then was the future of Uruguay's authoritarian situation?[2] Following convulsions in 1976 that led to the installation of a new president (with no apparent impact on decision making), an Institutional Act designed to remove the old leadership of the traditional parties as a prelude to the parties' eventual controlled restoration was decreed. In the same year, Jimmy Carter was elected president of the United States, and he belatedly reversed America's support for the regime, pressuring it to improve human rights and return to elections. The military thereupon announced a "timetable" for reinstitutionalization,[3] which had the (nonelected) Council of the Nation write a new constitution to be submitted to a plebiscite in 1980.

A grim array of restrictions on democratic rights and freedoms was present in the constitution by the time it was published. The military propaganda campaign that saturated the media before the November 1980 referendum attempted to portray the desired yes vote as a vote for a return to democracy. But few voters seem to have been taken in by this maneuver. The constitution, though holding out hope of earlier elections than stated in the document that was approved by referendum in Chile the same year, would clearly not have led to the full restoration of democracy or the return of the military to their barracks. The military were clearly anxious to construct a regime in which they would have a supervisory role.

What set Uruguay apart from neighboring military regimes at the

2 Following Linz, the word *situation* is used deliberately here, as military rule did not constitute a consolidated regime. But for convenience I shall often refer to the *regime*, even though authoritarianism was not stable.

3 Because the timetable did not envisage a full restoration of democracy, one cannot refer to it as a blueprint for redemocratization.

beginning of the 1980s was the still enormously high level of political fear among its people and the very limited vocal opposition to the government. At this stage, the media were monolithically "officialist" as a result of self-censorship, even though a couple of television debates were held on the new constitution, and the Colorado newspaper *El Día* published some criticism of its provisions. Intellectual life was stultifying, the country's only university purged beyond recognition. In short, with as yet no social movements, no unions, little church activity (in a traditionally secular nation), and even interest groups as innocuous as the Rural Federation of Ranchers subject to harassment, Uruguayan civil society seemed to be quite lifeless. It was with this level of control and mass quiescence that the military sought to restore limited elections.

Much to the opposition's surprise, however, the new constitution was rejected by the voters, and the military admitted its own defeat. This admission at least reflected a residual commitment to democratic practices.

Missed opportunities

After a new power struggle, retired General Gregorio Alvarez was inaugurated as president in 1981, and he announced that in 1982 the traditional parties would be allowed to choose new leaders by means of primaries. These new leaders would then sit down with members of the Armed Forces Political Affairs Commission (COMASPO) to make another attempt at designing a constitution that would incorporate the military's favored national security doctrines. As it turned out, open primaries merely confirmed the further erosion of the military's support and the increasing strength of the intransigent elements in the traditional parties bolstered, to be sure, by the votes of many leftists who had no parties of their own to vote for. Left-wing voters had the choice of abstaining, casting blank ballots, or boosting the most oppositionist factions in each major party, but most of them seem to have done the last (Gillespie 1986).

The clear winner of the primaries was in fact the exiled Blanco senator Wilson Ferreira, whose testimony before the U.S. Congress had been instrumental in blocking military aid to protest human rights violations. Ferreira's goal was outright capitulation of the military regime, and the transformation of the Blanco party from a conservative antistate intervention, rather rural party of notables into a mass movement of loyal followers with populist, libertarian, nationalist, and even democratic socialist strands. He was determined to get back into politics, despite being banned, in exile, and wanted for arrest on various charges by the military courts. He therefore made every effort to prevent the new Blanco leaders (many of them his close associates) from attending the talks with the military at the Parque Hotel in 1983, but he failed to stop them.

Again the military overplayed their hand by insisting on too long a list of constitutional changes at the 1983 talks. The traditional parties might have accepted the permanent abolition of the left (which had not been allowed to take part in the primaries), but they wanted their own leaders back and a real civilianization of the regime.

The civilian opposition thus faced the Parque Hotel talks internally divided. Those attending were willing to do business; however, exasperated by the lack of flexibility on the part of the military, they walked out after a few weeks and then united in radical opposition. The talks were too public, making both sides extremely cautious in their statements and in any offers they made. In short, by holding out for a harsh and restricted democracy, little different from the one that the voters had rejected in 1980, the military were not offering terms that could be presented to the voters in a favorable light. This was the overriding consideration for politicians who had to face elections and who feared accusations of "sellout," especially from the left. So it was that the military threw away a golden opportunity to achieve their aims by means of a reform pact. In doing so, they played into the hands of their most radical opponents – Wilson Ferreira and the Marxist left, who had formed an alliance in exile known as the Convergencia democrática. Although the exiled Convergencia group was widely denounced by Colorados inside Uruguay, domestically both of the traditional parties soon decided to forge a tactical alliance with the still-illegal left and with Uruguay's burgeoning social movements, known as the Intersectorial. This led to the largest demonstration in the country's history on the last Sunday in November 1983 (traditionally election day) at Montevideo's Obelisk.

The decisions of the military regime showed increasing signs of incoherence during the latter part of 1983. Yet, unmistakable indications of a belated liberalization could be seen. All remaining Blanco and Colorado politicians, with the exception of Wilson Ferreira, had their political rights restored. In January 1984, the reborn trade union federation (Plenario intersindical de los trabajadores, PIT), which was a member of the Intersectorial, staged a successful general strike that paralyzed activity in the capital. There were clearly pressures within the military for a harsh reaction to the politicians' radicalization, a plan notably favored by President Alvarez. However, the hard-liners came up against the problem that the government had deliberately created "valid interlocutors" in the traditional parties by means of the

Table 6.1. *Politicians' beliefs regarding the determinants of democratization: answers to the question "Which is more important to democratic transition and consolidation?" (in percentages)*

	Left	Blancos	Colorados	All[a]
1. The capacities of party leaders to act with some consensus in the transition and to create institutions and govern while respecting minorities and the opposition.	35.3	52.2	65.2	55.9
2. Acceptance of the democratic process by different sectoral interests and organizations: unions, businessmen, armed forces, foreign interests, etc.	64.7	30.4	21.7	33.8
3. Both are equally important.	0.0	17.4	13.0	10.3
	100.0	100.0	99.9	100.0
	(n = 17)	(n = 23)	(n = 23)	(n = 67)

[a]Includes one Patriotic Union, three Civic Union leaders, and a nonparty high-ranking military officer.

primary elections, and their legitimacy was conspicuously superior to that of the government. Although there was a situation of stalemate, it could hardly last.

Politician's attitudes toward transition strategies

There are two fundamentally different outlooks regarding democratic transitions. One emphasizes the role of mass organizations and social movements in civil society, and the other stresses elite consensus, particularly among politicians. A crucial choice facing political leaders is whether to emphasize mass protest and resistance to authoritarian rule or to engage in elite bargaining and negotiation. In 1984 and early 1985, I interviewed over seventy leading politicians in Uruguay regarding what they saw as the best tactics for bringing military rule to an end and restoring democracy (Gillespie 1991). As Table 6.1 shows, a clear majority of them believed that it was the capacity of party elites rather than social groups to act together that would determine the success of the attempted transition to democracy.

The role of popular movements in the transition became one of close subordination to the left by the time of the "civic stoppage" on June 27, 1984. The latter was really a general strike, but at the Colorados' urging, the parties chose not to call it one. Mass mobilization was used largely to demonstrate potential power, for example, in such symbolic one-day strikes, rather than to create disorder that might have provoked a military reaction. Uruguay had a more limited history of mass social protests than did many Latin American nations, and this continued to be the case as its military rule weakened. The main factor was the perception of leftist elites that resistance alone might be counterproductive and that negotiations with the military were therefore the only solution. A fully united and militant opposition almost certainly would not have toppled the regime.

In February, Colorado leader Julio María Sanguinetti had proposed reorganizing the existing Intersectorial into two halves. One half would consist of just the parties, with the participation of the union federation as the most important social movement, and would be named the Multipartidaria. The other half would group the various smaller social movements under the banner Intersocial (*Jaque*, February 24, 1983, p. 3). The Blancos immediately opposed the idea and stepped up the caliber of their delegation to the forum. Nonetheless, the two representatives of the PIT labor federation, who were close to the parties of the Broad Front, agreed with Sanguinetti's proposal, and so it was adopted. This was a revealing early sign of many Blancos' desire to mobilize social movements against the military regime. With their limited links to social movements, however, they were unable to force the military to capitulate.

Signs of convergence among military soft-liners, Colorados, and the left

The armed forces were committed to handing over power to elected civilians according to the promised timetable, and they were sorely conscious of their lack of legitimacy. Yet they insisted on certain guarantees, and they remained remarkably united and in control of the situation. The commitment to elections was broadly held among all generals, but there was far less agreement on the terms they should extract from the politicians and on which politicians they should allow to run. Given their desire to hand over power to responsible leaders, the military were determined not simply to abdicate.

The complex outcome of the struggle inside the armed forces was a waning of President Gregorio Alvarez's authority and the triumph of those who, though not always "soft-liners" in their hearts, were committed to preserving the unity of their institution. On June 7 Hugo Medina took over from Aranco as army commander, the former being required to resign for reasons of age under the Organic Military Law. That retirements and promotions continued in this regularized fashion even at moments of important political divisions testified to the relative unity of the armed forces and their maintenance of professionalism. Medina's inaugural speech was clear in its intention: The military must again become "apolitical"; chaos had been "left behind"; and they would defend the freedoms of the "same people" from which they themselves were drawn (*El Día*, June 8, 1984, p. 5).

When his appointment as army commander was confirmed, Medina told reporters to their amazement: "It is my responsibility to figure out how the Army is going to get out of this situation, and this is worrying me hugely (*El Día* May 29, 1984, p. 1)." Medina subsequently emphasized to me that being the commander of the army, and thus chosen by a secret ballot of the current army junta, his powers and responsibilities as custodian of the *proceso* were far superior to those of the president (personal interview, Columbia SC, March 27, 1987). Nevertheless, President Alvarez was much more committed to preserving the military's original aims than were the active-service generals. From this point on, the commander of the army systematically opposed the obstacles that President Alvarez attempted to place in the way of the transition, and he pressed for an agreement with the politicians.

Two notable events occurred during March 1984. General Liber Seregni, the left's leader, was released after eight years in prison. He immediately made a speech calling for the legalization of the left while implicitly accepting his own continued proscription, thereby striking a significant note of moderation. Almost simultaneously, the Colorados accused the exiled Blanco leader, Wilson Ferreira, of attempting to reach a secret deal with President Alvarez, by which he would be allowed back into politics. Much was made of the Blancos' having broken ranks.

Seeking to limit the damage from his exile, Wilson Ferreira remained publicly adamant that there was nothing to negotiate. Elections would simply have to be held in November with the 1967 constitution in full force and all candidates and parties permitted to take part. Any remaining predictions that the left might back the Blancos' radical position were dispelled, however, when the plenum of the Broad Front voted, with Seregni's strong backing, that all supporters must cease their activities in the Convergencia democrática. When I asked General Seregni if it had always been inevitable that there would be no continuation of the left alliance with Wilson Ferreira, he replied, "No, it was not inevitable. . . . There were some talks, but they could not get anywhere. The National party has different economic interests" (personal interview, Montevideo, April 30, 1984). By contrast, when the news came that Seregni would be freed, Colorado leader Julio

María Sanguinetti immediately granted an interview to a friendly magazine, in which he predicted that Seregni would be "a very important factor in the pacification of the country," and he praised Seregni's intelligence and democratic convictions (*Jaque*, March 9, 1984, p. 3). It is highly unlikely that Sanguinetti would have done this without foreknowledge of the moderate political line that Seregni planned to adopt.

The end of opposition unity: the split over negotiations

Wilson Ferreira apparently had difficulties in assessing the political situation from his vantage point in exile. The fragile unity of the opposition was seriously damaged, and now other politicians' qualms about eventually sacrificing Wilson were weakening. In fact, the Blanco party suffered from internal divisions that prevented it from making up its mind, and it issued the most contradictory statements regarding its willingness to negotiate. A retired general told me in exasperation that the military were utterly disgusted by the Blancos' shifting tactics. When Wilson argued in a speech in Argentina that the military had become so isolated from Uruguayan society as its "jailers" that they were "no longer a part of it," he effectively rendered negotiation nigh impossible. By contrast, the advantages of having released Seregni were becoming clear to the military. His leadership of the left was a major factor in stabilizing the tense political climate.

With Seregni free, Wilson faced the growing danger of becoming marginalized by the fast-moving events inside Uruguay. He therefore returned to Montevideo on June 16, 1984, in a specially chartered ferry crammed with politicians and foreign press correspondents. As soon as he set foot on Uruguayan soil, however, he was arrested and flown by helicopter to a military prison in the interior. Wilson's gamble had doubly failed: The government had not fallen, and he had been taken prisoner. As it turned out, his return to the country and detention only worsened the Blancos' problems, by making it impossible for them to enter negotiations and by creating bitter internal wrangling. In retrospect, it is easy to fault Wilson's decision to return at that juncture. But he was in a no-win situation: To remain in exile was to risk marginalization, and to return was to risk incarceration.

As one of Wilson's closest associates later told me: "The National party argues that a frontal no can achieve a complete military withdrawal . . . the Colorados' attitude allows the armed forces to feel more confident in their demands and go further (personal interview, Montevideo, July 11, 1984). The fundamental difficulty of the Blancos' position was, however, that with the left favoring negotiation under

Seregni's leadership, their "frontal no" would remain a vain gesture. The dynamics of the situation, as the deadline for registering election candidates approached, was such that all politicians were anxious for some agreement. A close associate of Seregni's in the secretariat of the Broad Front reiterated privately what he saw as Seregni's crucial divergence with Wilson Ferreira:

> The military project had failed, but they still had arms and foreign allies . . . the National party was too maximalist. . . . It is not that we rejected an alliance with the National party – we invented the Multipartidaria and the Concertación – but the opposition front could not lead to the eradication of the differences between parties.

There could be no clearer statement of the Broad Front's differences of outlook compared with those of the National party. Not only did it feel that the Blancos, and Ferreira in particular, had misjudged the strength of the military, but there was an undercurrent of resentment at the Blancos' hubris and a refusal to grant them favored status compared with that of the Colorado party.

What factors determined the politicians' calculations in choosing between a negotiated way out and a "frontal no"? In my interviews with party leaders during the middle months of 1984, I offered them a range of tactics that I asked them to evaluate. The first tactic was phrased: "The only way to force those in power to give way to democracy is to maintain and intensify popular pressure and not to enter negotiations." Their responses are reported in Table 6.2. Whereas the Colorados disagreed strongly with such an assertion, almost two thirds of the Blancos agreed "a lot" or "rather a lot." It was painfully obvious that a chasm was opening up between the Colorados' willingness to accept some kind of negotiated reform of the regime and the Blancos' insistence that there must be a complete break.[4] For all the interviews carried out with leaders of the left, a pattern of responses closer to that of the Colorados than the Blancos was detected, but with a greater spread.

A second tactic that might have been thought to contradict the previous one evaluated by the respondents was phrased: "Though popular pressure must not cease, it must be kept under control, and the time must come . . . to negotiate." The Colorados tended to agree with this statement far more than did those on the left. Oddly enough, given their previously avowed antagonism to negotiations, the Blancos' average fell in between those of the other two parties. Presumably the reason that the left was less enthusiastic about this statement lay

4 If we count only those interviews undertaken before the Naval Club Accord, the Blancos showed even greater militancy.

Table 6.2. *Summary of responses regarding negotiating tactics (in percentages)*

	Frente	Blancos	Colorados
1. "The only way to force those in power to give way to democracy is to intensify popular pressure and not to enter negotiations."	20	63	0
2. "Though popular pressure should not cease, it must be controlled, and the time must come when the leaders of the largest parties negotiate the transition's rules of the game with those in power."	80	79	95
3. "It is going to be impossible or very hard to get broad sections of the opposition to agree to negotiate the transition process with the established powers."	20	45	15
	$(n = 10)$	$(n = 17)$	$(n = 18)$

Note: Percentages reported are those agreeing "a lot" or "rather a lot."

in its belief that controlled mobilization and negotiation were complementary rather than incompatible.

When the politicians were asked whether they agreed that "it is going to be impossible, or very hard, to get broad sectors of the opposition to agree to negotiate the transition process with the established powers," the Colorados were particularly inclined to disagree. Examination of the early interviews alone shows that the Blancos began to differ significantly from the Colorados and the Frentistas in their responses to this question only after the Naval Club Accord had been enacted. There were no prior signs that the Blancos originally had been less optimistic that a consensus could be reached on the terms for military extrication, even though we already saw that they were far more inclined toward maintaining pressure on the regime and opposed to negotiations. In other words, though the Blancos were becoming isolated politically, they seem to have been unaware of it.

In sum, the attitudes expressed by the Colorado leaders were consistently the most cautious and moderate. When directly questioned, the Blancos were the most inclined to reject negotiations, and yet they were more willing, than were leaders of the left, to restrain mass mobilization and to ally with regime soft-liners in order to help them isolate hard-liners. This suggests that there were greater cross-pressures in the strategic outlook of both the Blancos and the left,

Table 6.3. *Should governments rule by consensus? "There are two ways in which parties – ideally – should take part in political decisions. Which do you prefer?" (in percentages)*

	Left	Blancos	Colorados	All[a]
1. Decisions should be reached by the majority parties and should reflect the will of the governing coalition.	12	46	28	29
2. Important decisions should be reached by majorities going beyond the government and reflecting the interests of major opposition groups.	88	54	72	71
	100	100	100	100
	(*n* = 17)	(*n* = 24)	(*n* = 25)	(*n* = 70)

[a]Includes one Patriotic Union and three Civic Union leaders.

with neither necessarily very much at ease with their eventual courses of action.

Granted that the vast majority of politicians favored a pact among the parties for the duration of the transition,[5] a question that revealed greater disagreement asked whether in general (i.e., not just during the transition), governments should rule by seeking consensus. The important finding listed in Table 6.3 is that a majority of politicians in all parties favored a consensual form of politics. The Blancos were the most likely to favor majoritarianism (but they were deeply split on the issue). One may wonder whether this tendency reflected their expectations of imminent access to power once the military withdrew, and a reluctance to share it. This would explain the party's high-stakes strategy. The left's rejection of majoritarianism presumably reflected its traditional marginality and the difficulties it had in influencing policy and also its fear that it would be left out of the transition and remain illegal.

In short, the conditions for maintaining unity among all parties until the military had returned to the barracks had dissolved. New elites were to be included in a partial settlement at the Naval Club Accord, but a major sector of the traditional elite was to feel excluded and usurped.

Just ten days after Blanco leader Wilson returned to Uruguay and

5 Nine out of the ten Colorado and Broad Front politicians whom I interviewed agreed that there should be a pact among the parties akin to those of the Colombian and Venezuelan transitions to democracy. Eight out of the ten Blancos concurred.

was imprisoned, and on the eve of a second general strike, the Multipartidaria announced that it would seek an audience with the military. The timing was calculated to take the sting out of the strike. The Colorados, Broad Front, and small Civic Union were by now determined to negotiate with the military. The Blancos therefore immediately withdrew from the Multipartidaria, accusing their rivals of a heinous betrayal. When the PIT labor federation, ASCEEP students' association, and FUCVAM cooperative housing movement proposed another day of popular protests, the prodialogue parties of the Multipartidaria rejected the idea as inopportune. The significant thing was that the political leaders of the Broad Front already had regained enough control to block this idea, which might have upset the delicate state of talks.

The Naval Club Accord: an elite settlement?

The military were now forced to face reality and admit that they would have to accept legalization of the left. Otherwise, all the left's votes would merely go to Wilson, ensuring his victory over the Colorados, as had essentially happened for his supporters in the 1982 primaries.

In actual fact, the conversations with the commanders in chief reached the brink of collapse over the question of rehabilitating the Broad Front, which the Multipartidaria insisted come before, and the commanders after, the final agreement.[6] On July 27, according to a participant in the secret talks, Sanguinetti's insistence on the immediate legalization of the Broad Front finally caused the commanders in chief to give in and announce Institutional Act no. 18. Under its terms, about 6,500 leftist politicians had their democratic rights restored, though about 3,000 remained banned. A verbal commitment was made to release 411 prisoners who had served more than half their sentences, but the act also restored the vote to the military, adding 70,000 (probably conservative) voters to the electoral rolls.[7] Finally on August 1, a formula was agreed upon for suspending civil rights in times of emergency.

The military were, of course, adamantly opposed to any "revenge trials," but Sanguinetti had promised to oppose these in his nomination speech. Meanwhile, Medina justified the lack of a specific clause granting the military immunity by saying that it would have been tantamount to admitting guilt, and it would in any case have

6 Personal interview with a delegate of the Multipartidaria to the talks, Montevideo, March 27, 1985. The negotiations were secret, and no written record of them was kept, nor was any document signed at their conclusion.

7 From the point of view of increasing the inclusionary dimension of the elite settlement, giving the military the vote may have been no bad thing.

stymied the talks (Boeker 1990, p. 80). The Blancos charged that a secret deal was made that there would be no human rights trials, but it is not clear why such a deal would have been more useful to the military than would Sanguinetti's word before the Colorado convention. One of the things that probably made the Naval Club Accord possible was precisely such instances of ambiguity. Ambiguity can be functional when debating highly charged issues.

The major thing that had been decided was not articulated: Elections would go ahead without all candidates – and specifically without Ferreira – permitted to take part. The Broad Front, however, would be rehabilitated, giving rise to the possibility of splitting the antimilitary vote and thereby allowing the Colorados to win. Finally, a number of substantive compromises were reached regarding military prerogatives. Otherwise, the provisions for various possible constitutional changes and the continuation of institutional acts were more of a device to tie up loose ends – and permit the commanders to avoid too much loss of face in the eyes of subordinates – than guideposts to the future form of democratic institutions. Sanguinetti made it clear that if he won the election, from the day he took office, there would be no more banned parties.

The plenum of the Broad Front voted in favor of the terms, thirty-one to fourteen, with six abstentions – only the extreme Left refused to endorse the agreement. Of the fifteen members of the Blanco executive, only two voted in favor. The Colorados' support for the accord was unanimous.

Technically, the continuation of political imprisonment, the banning of certain candidates and parties, as well as the retention of various institutional acts until they might be abolished by plebiscite, amounted to a transitional form of restricted democracy. But it was not one that was likely to last very long. Indeed, the Blancos insisted that if they won in November, they would immediately call new fully free elections and not feel bound by any clauses of what they called the "pact." In any event, they lost the elections. Nevertheless, the very first acts of the new Colorado president and Parliament were the liberation of all political prisoners, the legalization of all parties, and the abolition of almost all institutional acts, so that after March 1, 1985, Uruguay was almost back to its full 1967 constitution.

Elite settlements in perspective: explaining the emergence of consensus

The path of the Uruguayan transition came as close as any other in Latin America did to a *reforma pactada* (negotiated reform), to use Juan Linz's (1982) term. The military's hopes for tough guarantees were frustrated, as were the Blancos' hopes for a *ruptura* (complete break). In Guillermo O'Donnell's model of negotiated military extrication, the opposition soft-liners are required to reach a deal with the regime moderates, and both thereby isolate their respective hard-liners. Opportunists must be outmaneuvered among the opposition as well, in order to ensure that a real transition, rather than a process of cooptation, takes place (O'Donnell 1979). The Uruguayan case follows the O'Donnell model closely, with the peculiar twist that the left joined with the moderate and conservative Colorados to forge the pact, whereas the radicalized Blancos denounced the proceedings. Thus the partial settlement was not based on a new elite consensus, but it did entail agreement among a majority of the political elite. It thus glaringly contradicted the consociational model of a reform pact for transition (Lijphart 1969, 1977). From the proaccord point of view, the Blancos were demagogic "free riders," whereas from the Blancos' own point of view, the other parties were opportunistically serving their own interests – the left by achieving its legalization, the Colorados by greatly increasing their chances of electoral victory (which were also not hurt by Wilson's jailing).

From a less partisan point of view, we may suggest that the discordant strategies had a number of overall advantages for the transition to democracy. On the one hand, the Blancos' intransigence enabled the other parties to extract the best possible terms from the military at the Naval Club, and it also enabled all the major parties to take part in the first elections. On the other hand, the left pursued a highly stabilizing and confidence-building role designed to soothe the military and win centrist votes in the elections. Thus, although it was often called a pact, the Naval Club Accord was not a short-term maneuver but a foundational moment of historic significance qualifying for the stronger label of a *settlement*, albeit partial.

Overall, the Colorados repeatedly expressed the most concern that there might be a crackdown by hard-liners in the armed forces. Their concern was particularly marked following the result of the plebiscite in 1980, again in 1983 when the Parque Hotel talks collapsed, and at the end of the year when the president made a forceful speech against the traditional parties' alliance with the left in the Intersectorial. The level of fear on the left was intermediate, though the Frentistas' mean assessment of the risk of involution in 1980 was significantly higher than that of the Blancos.

The most striking thing that I learned in my interviews with Uruguayan elites was the consistently lower estimate of the danger of authoritarian regression by the Blanco respondents. The issue was not whether the Blancos were sincere in their confidence – given the performance of the Wilsonistas in the primaries, they almost certainly were – but why? One might hypothesize that their outlook was both a function of an inadequate understanding of the military institution and a rationalization of the strategy of pushing for a complete democratic rupture that they had adopted under Wilson's leadership.

The intransigent line of the Blancos vis-à-vis the military was further evident when politicians were asked whether they would agree to take part in elections while the other parties remained banned. Half the Blancos said they would not, but only one third of the Frentistas and an eighth of the Colorados interviewed were equally intransigent. When questioned about the conditions under which they would take part in elections if the military decreed changes in the constitution without the consent of the parties, again the Blancos were the most intransigent and the Colorados the least.

A crucial factor in the Colorados' decision to negotiate, and to some extent the left's decision to accompany them, was the climate of public opinion. Polls strongly confirmed the perception that the mass of Uruguayans thought that the parties should negotiate with the military, and a majority was willing, if necessary, to settle for less than fully free elections (Gillespie 1991). Perhaps the most revealing data showed that a great majority of Blanco supporters believed that elections would go ahead: 75 percent. This was less than the number of Colorados (86 percent) but more than the proportion of Frentistas. In other words, a fatalistic attitude was developing among Blanco supporters. The steady growth of the proportion of citizens in favor of elections, even without all candidates, was an important indicator of the country's mood.

Despite their original threat to cast blank ballots or abstain if Wilson were not allowed to run, the Blancos were eventually forced to give in and nominate a proxy candidate for president – Alberto Zumarán. Pressure from local politicians who relied on the spoils of office was simply too great to countenance a boycott. The charges that the terms of the deal amounted to a disguised continuation of military rule through manipulated elections lacked plausibility, given that even the Communists and the extreme left were allowed to run lists within the Frente. When the Communists' leader, Rodney Arismendi, returned from exile in Moscow, he was greeted by a vast rally, a motorcade from the airport, and a platform from which to speak – an ironic contrast with Wilson's reception.

One of the most fundamentally contentious issues of Uruguay's transition was the question of what to do with the imprisoned guerrillas. Regarding an amnesty, which the military had strongly rejected, the Blancos and Frente leaders that I interviewed agreed on a relatively radical stance. But a majority of my Colorado interviewees actually opposed any amnesty for those who had been convicted of "crimes of blood." This must have been a major point in their favor as far as the military were concerned, although the Colorados did speak vaguely of pardoning those prisoners who had completed half their sentence. What was interesting in the personal statements of politicians who had favored negotiations when it came to the question of an amnesty was their apparent desire to reach agreement with other sectors. One close aide to Seregni in the Broad Front observed: "The National party insisted on a general and unrestricted amnesty, but we know that this was impossible. It is not a problem of their [the Blancos'] being extreme, but being inflexible" (personal interview, Montevideo, December 12, 1984).

The danger that they might be subject to trial for violations of human rights, as was happening just across the River Plate in Argentina, was of even greater concern to the military. Surprisingly, the Blancos were the least tough on this issue when interviewed individually. Though all parties were circumspect in admitting that it might be necessary on pragmatic grounds to bolt shut the Pandora's box of human rights, it was clear that the left had the strongest feelings on the subject. Wilson (who had narrowly escaped assassination in 1976) had also adopted a tough line in his speeches, yet other Blancos were apparently anxious to appear reasonable. Above all, what the data show is that the left did not have any deep-seated agreement with the Colorados, just as the Blancos did not have any particularly divergent attitudes toward the political substance of the restored democracy. The proaccord parties were simply responding to incentives as the military had laid them out. The military, in turn, had successfully divided the potentially dangerous multiparty coalition that they had faced at the beginning of 1984. The real determinants of party strategies were the incentives of power. Excluded to all intents and purposes from winning "first prize" (i.e., the presidency), in large part as a result of a deliberate stratagem by the military, the Blancos chose to denounce the rules but still take part. By contrast, incorporation of the left into the transition represented a major bonus for its future commitment to peaceful and democratic politics. Similarly, the incorporation of the armed forces tied them to the success of the new democracy.

The Naval Club Accord thus approximated an elite settlement, despite the Blancos' absence. But it might best be termed a "partially inclusive" settlement. In fact, a case can be made that the Blancos' exclusion was essential to the form of agreement reached at the Naval

Club. In Uruguay the civilian elites at the negotiating table benefited enormously from their ability to point out that the alternative to a deal with them would be to play straight into the hands of Wilson Ferreira. Their negotiating position was therefore even stronger than it would have been had the process been truly inclusive.

Conclusion: from partial settlement to convergence[8]

One week after the November 1984 election, Wilson Ferreira was finally released from jail by the military. In an important speech to his followers outside Montevideo's City Hall, he made it clear that he accepted the results of the elections and the defeat of his strategy for an unconditional break with authoritarian rule. In the following months the Colorados and the Blancos slowly began to mend their fences and cooperate in passing legislation. By a process of convergence, therefore, the remaining sector of Uruguay's elite that had been excluded from the Naval Club Accord retroactively joined the democratic consensus.

In the face of dire obstacles, attempts were made to promote democratic *convivencia*, or peaceful coexistence among the country's three main elites: the military, labor leaders, and politicians. Progress toward elite convergence was by no means smooth or easy, however. The major bones of contention were the question of amnesty for members of the security forces accused of past human rights abuses, the labor unions' demands for higher wages, and the problem of interparty relations.

Many generals and most colonels were far from happy with the Naval Club Accord and subsequent developments such as the March 1985 amnesty for political prisoners (including guerrillas). Yet despite military apprehensions, the new government of Julio María Sanguinetti moved cautiously (Boeker 1990, p. 93). Above all, it decided to retain the same commanders that it inherited from the last phase of the dictatorship. Politicians had to be wary of actions that might bring discredit on those sectors of the military that had originally agreed to the extrication – a consideration of particular importance because Medina had been attacked for allowing the name of the armed forces to be tarnished.

For its part, the opposition generally acted with discretion when dealing with military affairs. Ferreira even agreed to meet in secret with the high command to clear up their differences. Opinion polls

8 This section draws heavily on unpublished notes by Miguel Arregui, for which I am particularly grateful.

showed that an overwhelming majority of Montevideo voters in all parties favored punishing members of the security forces guilty of human rights violations. But only a slender minority believed that they would in fact ever be punished. Throughout 1985, denunciations of human rights violations under the previous military government increased. The government attempted to buy time. President Sanguinetti ruled out mass trials of armed forces officers in the Argentine manner, declaring: "The best thing that can happen to the past is to leave it to the historians." In an interview with a French newspaper he stated: "Listen. Some of our military perhaps have certain responsibilities, but so do the terrorists, and weighty they are. Now, we gave them an amnesty. It is natural to have given an amnesty to the military, too" (*Le Monde*, November 3–4, 1984). Meanwhile, military sources expressed confidence that penalties for crimes committed during the repression would not be imposed.[9] On the other hand, the government reduced the military's bloated budget, and it froze recruitment (Boeker 1990, p. 82).

In June 1986 the government introduced a bill to grant to members of the armed forces immunity from prosecution for past violations of human rights, although this was defeated by the combined opposition of the Blancos and the Broad Front. Finally, after a long hiatus during which the military began to threaten that they would boycott any civil trials that were attempted, the majority of the Blancos introduced a new bill that granted immunity as a form of "statute of limitations," and this became law. As it happened, however, the issue was very far from settled. The parties of the left and the minority wing of the Blancos immediately called on citizens to collect signatures to force a plebiscite to have the law repealed. Civil–military relations thus became increasingly tense during the next two years.

The Colorado government and the Wilsonista Blancos campaigned for retention of the law, arguing that repeal would lead to chaos and instability. That argument is what seems to have ultimately swayed the voters in the plebiscite on April 16, 1989. Although the defenders of the law only won 42.5 percent of the votes in Montevideo, in the interior they took 67.3 percent, giving a national proportion of 55.4 percent (*Búsqueda* no. 481, April 20–26, 1989, p. 4). With the retention of the "law of limitations" a milestone was passed in the convergence of civil and military elites. Army Commander General Medina went out of his way to thank the government publicly. For those who wished to close the book on the military's actions once and for all, the verdict of the people was encouraging evidence that bygones

9 Unattributed remarks made to Arregui in interviews with the military.

could be bygones. Perhaps the most impressive evidence that the human rights issue had lost its explosive capacity to polarize the military and the nation was the successful holding of an academic seminar on problems of human rights and democracy attended by four active-duty generals, a broad spectrum of politicians, and many leaders from the human rights community (*Búsqueda* no. 492, July 6–12, 1989, p. 48).

Progress toward incorporation of the labor union elites was far less evident. Many of Uruguay's labor organizations inherited a strategic conception of unions as a revolutionary weapon of resistance to the state and employers, as well as a tool for the defense of economic interests. Almost at once the PIT–CNT union federation campaigned directly against the Colorados' economic policies. Like the other Southern Cone countries, Uruguay's economy was devastated by the military's free-market experiments that had produced the most savage compression of real wages in the region. Treating 1970 as 100, the index of real wages in Uruguay fell to 55.3 by 1983, compared with 90.8 in Argentina and 86.8 in Chile, where wages had begun to recover by the late 1970s (Ramos 1986, p. 60). There are no data on deteriorating working conditions, but it may be surmised that they had been equally neglected under the military government.

A major issue, given the sudden restoration of full freedom to organize and strike for higher wages and better conditions, was whether the unions could exercise restraint in the interests of stabilizing democracy. Grass-roots labor militants were opposed to such restraint, and from late 1984 there was an escalating wave of strikes and factory occupations. After the return to democracy, strikes spread to the public sector, repeatedly paralyzing state services such as the courts, posts, and customs, in which wages had fallen furthest under the military regime. The first general strike took place six months into the Sanguinetti administration. Many stoppages were beyond the control of union leaders, who found themselves completely overtaken by the militancy of middle- and lower-level activists where the political balance was hard to measure, or in mass assemblies of workers and employees where it was often irrelevant. In destroying union cadres the military had upset a delicate balance of power that had been painstakingly created over decades. Old cadres, many of them Communists who had been in exile or in prison, found it hard to win the backing of new "grass-roots" militants. Other changes came with the advent of white-collar radicalism and the expansion of the PIT–CNT to include all unions, including those previously independent. A powerful union that fell into both categories was the Civil Servants' Union, COFE.

Hopes for a "neocorporatist" solution to Uruguay's distributive struggle foundered repeatedly on the internal political turbulence of the unions and their distance from the Blanco and Colorado parties. During 1984 the concept of concerted action had become a buzzword on the lips of every politician. With all-party support, the unions took part in the 1984 "Concertación" talks about negotiating joint policies before the Colorados took office. They also participated in the abortive discussions of a social pact in mid-1985. These were suspended, however, when the government claimed that the unions' attitudes were proving dangerous and "antidemocratic." Talks in 1986 on a "National Accord" did not include labor, but only the political parties. The accord was thus consociational rather than corporatist.

By 1987, the defeat of various unions after prolonged strikes, the strengthened position of the Communists, and the consolidation of leaders had contributed to the reestablishment of control from above and thus to greater industrial peace. When the PIT–CNT held an extraordinary congress in May, the Communists already constituted a sizable majority. The government considered it preferable, or at least the lesser of two evils, that the Communist party control the trade union apparatus, given that it was much more amenable to negotiations than were the other militant groups. At the same time, the party acted as an efficient brake on potentially violent or "adventurist" temptations among marginal groups on the left. This situation led to a decline in strike activity during 1987 and 1988 and to a greater degree of economism in labor demands.

In sum, even though talks regarding a social pact failed, the left and labor union elites found themselves committed to restraining labor's demands. Expectations were never raised that democracy would immediately solve economic deprivation. Although labor leaders remained very dissatisfied with government policies, there was a noticeable convergence between them and the politicians, compared with the disastrous confrontations of the late 1960s and early 1970s.

If the challenges to politics posed by the military and the unions were at least dampened, what signs were there of the party system's more healthy functioning? Democratic consolidation often raises the dilemma of government by majority versus government by consensus. This in turn involves the problem of the proper role of a loyal opposition in a democratic system. Given Uruguay's multiparty system, polls suggest that a clear majority of Uruguayans believed that governments should seek compromise with opposition parties rather than attempting to rule on their own (*Búsqueda* no. 491, June 29–July 5, 1989, p. 40). However, this was precisely what the Colorados had not done during the democracy's crisis from 1968 to 1973.

The outcome of the Naval Club Accord might have been a permanent polarization between the Blancos and the other parties, but the 1984 election result induced the Blancos to compete for the center ground once more, and it confirmed the moderation of both the Colorados and the left. Hardly had he been released from jail than Wilson Ferreira introduced the term *governability* to Uruguay, hinting that he would ensure Sanguinetti a "grace" period of two or three years. During that time the National party would refrain from systematic opposition and ease the legislative passage of government policies.

Once the new Parliament met, the Colorado–Broad Front alliance forged at the Naval Club quickly broke down, and the two parties instead occupied opposite poles in the Congress, with the Blancos tending to oscillate between them as arbiters. Despite his willingness to resort to the veto and to threaten early elections on crucial issues such as the budget or human rights, Sanguinetti sought consensus when he encountered steadfast opposition and when he sensed the nation was deeply divided. In practice, this meant giving a great deal of influence to Wilson Ferreira.

Sanguinetti responded with toughness to those crises that threatened the stability of his cabinet. Although the Colorados had only just over two fifths of the seats in Parliament, which exposed their ministers to censure, they had enough to prevent the legislature from overriding an executive veto. By this finely balanced arithmetic, pressure for compromise was thus built into the structure of political competition. In January 1986, following a summit meeting with Wilson Ferreira, Sanguinetti proposed a National Accord on specific policies, and he again called for opposition participation in his government.

This drawing together of the Blancos and Colorados – the first step toward elite convergence – put the left in danger of being eliminated from political decision making, but it attempted to avoid this by also appealing to the center ground of politics. Indeed, one of the most important symptoms of competition for the center among parties was the strategy of the left. Seregni insisted on the need to convert the Broad Front into a "real alternative for power," abandoning its traditionally "contestatory" role. For example, agreements with the other parties in 1985 meant that the left was for the first time allotted seats on the boards of directors of some state enterprises, and it later signed the National Accord.[10]

Overall, the behavior of all major parties was a healthy contrast

10 A broad range of legislation was envisaged in the National Accord, but its main significance lay in its symbolism of unity rather than in its practical implementation.

with their egoism and polarization before the 1973 military intervention. By late 1986 the majority of Blanco leaders favored political compromise, and the wheel had come full circle. The Blancos' new strategy of moving toward the center and supporting the government complemented the attempt to rebuild the party's appeal among right-wing voters. The centripetal dynamic of electoral competition was the major factor in promoting the abrupt return to a search for partisan consensus. Leadership strategies and public opinion (as revealed in regular polls) interacted in ways that were politically stabilizing.

Democratic consolidation usually benefits from the emergence of strong parties, but what is even more indispensable is a strong party system. The minimum requirements for the foundation of a party system able to promote democratic consolidation would seem to be democratization of the left and right, centripetal electoral competition, and a degree of cooperation among parties based on "loyal opposition" and "tolerant government" (Gillespie 1986). In this sense, Uruguay's party system is extremely strong by Latin American standards. One of the key features of party systems that nurture democratic survival is that they provide guaranteed "space" for losers (Morlino 1986). Before 1973, Uruguay's historic ability to provide such a space for conservatives contrasted with the electoral frustration of the left (which therefore turned to revolutionary strategies, even under democracy). What is encouraging is that since 1984, Uruguay has also been more successful at coopting a loyal left into the electoral game.

A major aspect of party strengthening concerns the linkages between parties and organized systems of interest representation. The great challenge to Uruguay's new democracy (even more than the military) was the successful handling of labor demands. Nonetheless, despite attempts by the Colorados in the 1950s, and the Blancos in the 1980s, to develop links with labor, the union movement remains strongly allied with the left. The forging of links between parties and interest groups favors the consolidation of a political arena based on representation and bargaining rather than praetorianism. In practice this was achieved by means of the odd tactical convergence between the Colorados and the Communists, although it is not clear whether this arrangement will survive the advent of a more neoconservative Blanco government in 1990.

A serious potential obstacle to democratic consolidation is, of course, the survival of an undemocratic right. One of the few blessings of the recent Latin American authoritarian regimes was that none of them was ultimately very effective at solving economic problems, even as they themselves defined them, let alone at meeting the social demands of their citizens. In Uruguay the antidemocratic right certainly went into retreat in both traditional parties. The Pachequista wing of the Colorado party lost its controlling position in 1984, compared with that of 1971. Nevertheless, it retained a certain leverage over the government: Without it, centrist and progressive Colorados could have no hope of winning an election. The alienation of their right was precisely the main reason for the Blancos' major electoral defeat in 1984. Mindful of the electoral imperative, they then returned to the defense of their traditionally conservative supporters. The interests of capital are thus well represented in both the Colorado and the Blanco parties, thereby making the benefits of participating in the democratic game greater than the costs (to borrow Dahl's terminology). Indeed, in the 1989 elections – the second since the transition – conservative candidates came out ahead in both the Colorado and the Blanco parties.

A third danger to democracy comes from the antidemocratic left. Given the Broad Front's role in Uruguay's transition, the signs are that the experience of authoritarianism led to a revalorization of democracy by almost all of the left. Furthermore, the dynamic of electoral competition in 1984 rewarded those sectors of the Broad Front that moved closest to the center. This centripetal pattern of electoral competition is very stabilizing for liberal democracy, other things being equal. In the end, however, it also fueled left-wing divisions, culminating in the departure of the center–left from the Broad Front in 1989. This paved the way for the Tupamaros to join the alliance for the first time; so on balance, the progressive incorporation of the far left into democratic politics seems to be continuing.

In comparative terms, Uruguay's civilian and military elites made the most explicit attempt anywhere in the 1980s to reach a mutually beneficial settlement that would put an end to their "civil war" once and for all. Yet the persistence of bitter conflicts among the parties over the terms of the Naval Club Accord threatened to compromise the stability of the new democratic regime right from the start. Nevertheless, the final proof of the National party's willingness to compromise came in late 1986, when it at last agreed to introduce the bill closing the book on past violations of human rights. Nothing obliged the Blancos to accept the terms of the transition or the Colorados' electoral victory, however convincing the latter may have been. Nothing obliged them to stand by the terms of the Naval Club Accord or to introduce the bill for a military amnesty. However, as the Wilsonistas argued, a certain route to democracy had been taken, and the price was a statute of limitations. The important thing for all concerned was that the past was the past, not only for the military, but for the Blancos as well.

The Naval Club Accord had incorporated the military elite and the left-labor elite into a settlement that made them loyal to the restored democratic system. By the route of elite convergence, thereafter, this partial elite settlement was expanded to reincorporate the Blancos, so that all major Uruguayan elites finally had a stake in the success of the new democracy. Here then was a good example of the flexibility and dynamic consensus that must accompany stability in processes of democratic consolidation. Whether consolidation is complete in any given nation may be a misleading question, in the sense that democracies are in a constant process of adapting to new challenges. Compared with its neighbors in South America, however, Uruguay's democracy already looked remarkably consolidated only five years after the end of military rule.

References

Boeker, Paul. 1990. *Lost Illusions*. New York: Marcus Wiener.

Dahl, Robert. 1971. *Polyarchy: Participation and Opposition*. New Haven, CT: Yale University Press.

1985. *A Preface to Economic Democracy*. Berkeley and Los Angeles: University of California Press.

Garretón, Manuel. 1979. "En torno a la discusión de los nuevos regímenes autoritarios en América Latina." Wilson Center Latin American Program Working Paper no. 52.

Gillespie, Charles. 1983. "The Breakdown of Democracy in Uruguay: Alternative Political Models." Wilson Center Latin American Program Working Paper no. 143.

1984. "Desentrañando la crisis de la democracia uruguaya." In *Uruguay y la democracia*, vol. 1, ed. Charles Gillespie, Louis Goodman, Juan Rial, and Peter Winn. Montevideo: Banda oriental.

1986. "Activists and the Floating Voter: The Unheeded Lessons of Uruguay's 1982 Primaries." In *Elections and Democratization in Latin America: 1980–85*, ed. Paul Drake and Eduardo Silva. San Diego: Center for Iberian and Latin American Studies.

1991. *Negotiating Democracy: Politicians and Generals in Uruguay*. Cambridge: Cambridge University Press.

Gillespie, Charles, and Luis González. 1989. "Uruguay: The Survival of Old and Autonomous Institutions." In *Democracy in Developing Countries: Latin America*, ed. Larry Diamond, Juan Linz, and Seymour Martin Lipset. Boulder, CO: Lynne Rienner.

Jaque. 1984. "Se está negociando." February 24, p. 3.

1984. "Seregni será un pilar de la salida democrática." March 9, p. 3.

Kaufman, Edy. 1978. *Uruguay in Transition*. New Brunswick, NJ: Transaction.

Lijphart, Arend. 1969. "Consociational Democracy." *World Politics* 21:2.

1977. *Democracy in Plural Societies*. New Haven, CT: Yale University Press.

Linz, Juan. 1982. "The Transition from Authoritarian Political Regimes to Democratic Political Systems and the Problems of the Consolidation of Political Democracy." Paper presented to the Tokyo Roundtable of the International Political Science Association, March 29–April 1.

Le Monde. 1984. "Un entretien avec le Président Sanguinetti." November 3–4.

Morlino, Leonardo. 1986. "Consolidamento democratico: Alcune ipotesi esplicative." *Rivista italiana de scienza politica* 13:3.

Nordlinger, Eric. 1972. *Conflict Regulation in Divided Societies*. Occasional Paper no. 29. Cambridge, MA: Harvard Center for International Affairs.

O'Donnell, Guillermo. 1979. "Notas para el estudio de los procesos de democratización a partir del estado burocrático–autoritario." *Estudios CEDES* 2:5.

Ramos, Joseph. 1986. *Neoconservative Economics in the Southern Cone of Latin America, 1973–1983*. Baltimore: Johns Hopkins University Press.

7

Patterns of elite negotiation and confrontation in Argentina and Chile

MARCELO CAVAROZZI

The three countries of Latin America's Southern Cone – Chile, Argentina, and Uruguay – followed quite distinct political paths during the twentieth century. These paths, however, have converged during the last two decades. First, the three countries experienced successful military coups during the 1970s; later, during the 1980s, all three military regimes were replaced by constitutional democracies. This chapter focuses on the cases of Chile and Argentina. In Chile, the military regime was installed in 1973, when the armed forces violently deposed the socialist government of Salvador Allende; in Argentina, the military regime was initiated in 1976 when a military junta put an end to the chaotic populist regime led by Isabel Perón. I shall examine two related issues: (1) the legacies of the two countries' preauthoritarian pasts and the way that those legacies have contributed to shape each country's transition to democracy and (2) the patterns of elite behavior during the transitions and the likelihood that political democracy will be consolidated.

The successful Chilean transition to democracy (which unfolded between 1988 and 1990) and the prospects for its consolidation were greatly facilitated by what appears to have been an elite settlement with two distinct phases. This process involved, on the one hand, an agreement between the Christian Democrats and a segment of the socialist left that led to the formation of what I shall call the antiauthoritarian Grand Coalition and, on the other hand, a relatively comprehensive settlement between this Grand Coalition and a portion of the elites that had supported the authoritarian regime of General Augusto Pinochet. Conversely, the more abrupt Argentine transition was unleashed by the political and military collapse of that country's military regime. Therefore, as the authoritarian coalition completely unraveled, no broad elite agreement was required to pave the way for the transition. Furthermore, the tone of the transition was one of confrontation rather than compromise between the two main forces opposing the military regime, Radicalism and Peronism. These two parties fought a brief but bitter electoral campaign that left them as uncompromising political enemies.

In this chapter I shall explore the hypothesis that an elite settlement was possible in Chile because of propensities toward compromise that began in the 1930s and because of a political deadlock in the late 1980s that could be overcome only through negotiation among previously warring sectors of the elite. In Argentina, by contrast, the political trends prevailing during the last half-century and the pattern of the 1982–3 transition to democracy conspired against the possibility of achieving elite unity. Accordingly, the prospects for democratic consolidation are good in Chile and poor in Argentina.

The three Southern Cone countries shared a feature unique in Latin America at the turn of the century: Each had established an effective political order in which pluralism existed to a certain, limited, extent.[1] Political stability and constitutional rule were achieved before World War I, with formal and informal norms of intra-elite competition being an attribute of all three oligarchic regimes.[2]

The late 1920s were, however, a period of political turmoil in both Argentina and Chile. The dictatorship of Colonel Carlos Ibáñez in Chile and the 1930 military coup in Argentina put an end to the two most successful examples of stable limited democracy in Latin America at that time. A process of democratization and expansion of political participation contributed to these breakdowns. This process had advanced much further in the Argentine case, where three presidents had been elected – in 1916, 1922, and 1928 – by an expanded franchise that included the vast majority of Argentine-born adult males.[3] In Chile, the 1920 presidential election culminated in the victory of a member of one of the oligarchy's two traditional parties, the Liberal Arturo Alessandri.[4] For the first time in Chile's political history, Ales-

1 The two other stable regimes of the period, Mexico and Brazil, were much less pluralistic than Argentina, Chile, and Uruguay.

2 In fact, Chile's unique record of political stability had started in the 1830s with the autocratic República portaliana. The only interruption was the brief 1891 civil war which led to the establishment of a parliamentary republic that survived until 1924. In Argentina, ordered presidential successions began in 1862. But only after the conflict between Buenos Aires and the rest of the country was settled in 1880 (with the defeat of the former) did the oligarchic republic become stable.

3 Immigrants were not enfranchised. This was quite important in Argentina, where a high proportion of the adult population was foreign born. In 1914, more than half of the adult men living in Buenos Aires were foreigners.

4 Like most of its Latin American counterparts in the late nineteenth and early twentieth centuries, the Chilean Liberal party was not politically progressive. Its only

sandri appealed to the populace in order to beat his opponent, a more traditional Conservative party politician. The main point is that in both cases, military interventions occurred at the precise time that political participation was expanding. The breakdown of constitutional rule thus resulted in the simultaneous and parallel demise of the oligarchic political model and of the democratic reformers who were challenging the oligarchies from within. This simultaneous occlusion of the precepts of nineteenth-century liberalism and democratic reform was associated with a brief and hectic period when Fascist and corporatist ideologies became fashionable.

The political routes that the two countries followed began to diverge in the 1930s. In Chile, Alessandri's successful comeback in 1932, and especially the Popular Front's victory in the 1938 election, resulted in political reequilibration and the inauguration of a second period of political stability that lasted until the overthrow of the Socialist president Salvador Allende in 1973. In Argentina, however, the next fifty years witnessed a succession of political formulas – authoritarian inclusionary populism, weak semidemocratic civilian regimes, and military dictatorships – all of which failed to achieve political stability and produced increasing levels of confrontation.

As previously noted, the political paths of the two countries seemed once again to resemble each other more closely during the 1970s. The beginning of General Pinochet's dictatorship in Chile was soon followed by the collapse of the second Peronist government and the decision of the Argentine military to attempt yet again to found an authoritarian regime. The two military regimes differed both in their duration and in the extent to which their attempts at economic and political reform were successful. During the 1980s, however, neither regime could avoid a transition to democratically elected civilian governments. The Argentine military regime collapsed suddenly in 1982–3 as a result of the total failure of its economic programs as well as its defeat in the war against Britain. Subsequently, the Radical politician Raúl Alfonsín assumed the presidency after a surprising defeat of the Peronist candidate in the October 1983 elections. In Chile, Pinochet's bid to remain in power until 1998 was rejected by the electorate in a 1988 plebescite. According to the 1980 constitution he drafted, Pinochet was thus forced to call for general elections in 1989, in which the Christian Democrat Patricio Aylwin was elected president as the candidate of a unified opposition.

difference from the Conservative party was its opposition to the influence exerted by the Catholic church on educational and cultural matters.

The Chilean Popular Front and Peronism: contrasting patterns in the emergence of mass-based political systems

Neither in Chile nor in Argentina did the original transition from oligarchic political systems avoid institutional breakdowns. The political turbulence of the late 1920s and early 1930s resulted not only in the delegitimation of nineteenth-century liberalism but also in the emergence of an alternative antiliberal discourse. This discourse condemned political democracy as either ineffective or dangerous, seeking to replace it with corporatist institutions, and justified massive state intervention in the economy.

In both countries, the corporatist attempt ultimately failed to generate a stable political system, though the circumstances of the respective failures were quite different. In Chile, during the presidency of the military strongman Carlos Ibáñez (1927–31), Parliament was closed and political party activities were severely curtailed. During the half-dozen years of Ibáñez's dominance, however, no explicit corporatist ideology was articulated, and in due course he was discredited by the downturn in Chile's economic fortunes associated with the 1929–31 world crisis. Widespread popular discontent with the Ibáñez regime led the military to conclude that their open political involvement was counterproductive for their own cohesion and long-term existence. Consequently, the military leaders decided to refrain from further political intervention. Thus, when fully articulated antidemocratic projects were advanced by quasi-fascistic ideologues, they failed to attract the support of the military elite.[5]

In Argentina, the corporatist creed was espoused by military and civilian associates of the 1930 coup leader, General José F. Uriburu. Nevertheless, his openly fascist proposals were rejected by the bulk of the officer corps, which aligned itself with General Agustín Justo. Hence, Uriburu could not implement his project to eradicate political parties and parliamentary institutions, and he was forced to step down from the presidency in 1932. In turn, Justo, with the support of the more traditional conservatives, became president in a particularly fraudulent election.

After the turmoil of the late 1920s and the early 1930s and the abortive attempts at corporatism, the possibilities for political re-

5 The corporatist proposals of the 1930s were made by the "Party of the Producers," and the vernacular *nacistas* led by Jorge González von Marees. The latter's political career culminated with a strange twist: In 1938, Alessandri's conservative government ordered a bloody repression of the *nacistas*. González von Marees decided to support the Popular Front presidential candidate, thus providing the votes that the Radical Aguirre Cerda needed to defeat his Conservative opponent.

equilibration and a gradual return to liberal democracy thus were real in Chile and Argentina. At this point, however, the two countries began to move in quite different political directions.

Beginning in the 1930s, the Chilean political system underwent a significant change as a party system that included all segments of the political–ideological spectrum emerged. This meant that the traditional triumvirate of Liberals, Conservatives, and Radicals – the first two representing different factions of the dominant landowning class and the latter the new middle classes – was expanded into a multiparty system incorporating the Communist and the Socialist parties, which had been created in 1921 and 1933, respectively.

One of the distinct features of Chile's left-wing landscape was that the mainstream of the Socialist party was often to the left of the Communists. Beginning in 1935, with the Seventh Congress of the Comintern, the Chilean Communists followed a moderate political course designed to consolidate the political fronts, including the "bourgeois" parties. Between 1935 and 1973, the Communist party remained a highly cohesive force both refraining from and actively condemning armed insurrection and the use of political violence. Even during the long decade when the party was outlawed (1947–57) and hundreds of its members were sent to concentration camps, it continued to eschew violence and to act within the framework of bourgeois democracy. Conversely, the Socialist party was divided into several factions that often formed splinter parties. Some of these factions developed much more ambiguous positions vis-à-vis political democracy. During the 1940s, for example, one right-wing faction became violently anti-Communist and supported the repression of its rivals. During the 1960s and early 1970s, the most important sectors of the Socialist party, including those controlling the party organization, actively endorsed the Cuban revolution while proclaiming that parliamentary democracy was merely the facade of bourgeois domination, which the party intended to destroy.

In any case, the effect of the transformation of the 1930s was twofold: It provided the newly organized sectors of the middle and working classes with a niche in the representational system, but it also gave the Radicals a strategic position within the system. Although the Radicals never gained more than 25 percent of the vote in congressional elections, the new configuration enabled them to win three successive presidential elections. Beginning with the formation of the Popular Front in the late 1930s, the Radical party thus became the linchpin of the political system. Even though the Popular Front broke up as early as 1940, the Radicals remained as an irreplaceable political broker, with the party alternatively swinging from the left to the right, by switching alliances. Sometimes it joined with the parties of the left – thus reenacting the Popular Front coalition – and at other times it allied with the Conservatives and the Liberals. There was a distinct pattern in these shifts: The support of the left-wing parties allowed Radical candidates to win presidential elections in 1938, 1942, and 1946, but after each election, the governing party then moved to the right to secure the congressional support of either a Conservative or a Liberal faction. In short, Radical politicians regularly "betrayed" their electoral partners once they achieved a favorable result.

What were the reasons for the reequilibration of the Chilean political system and the parallel consolidation of a multiparty system (the only one in Latin America during the first half of this century)? To begin with, political and business elites achieved a relative degree of consensus on the basis of a deal whereby, on the one hand, conservative forces tolerated ideological pluralism, Communist supremacy within the unions of the urban workers, and an expansion of the state's regulatory powers in economic affairs. On the other hand, left-wing parties agreed to participate in electoral politics without challenging two implicit strictures: (1) that the franchise remain frozen at a relatively low level – only 10 percent of the total population was registered and participated in elections – and (2) that they abstain from attempting to organize the rural population of Chile's Central Valley.[6] By and large, the peasantry remained the captured political clientele of the large landowners and their political representatives.[7]

The elite understandings reached in Chile during the 1940s did not amount to an elite settlement. In fact, adherence to these understandings by the most powerful elites was always precarious, and it was subject to the workings of two institutional safeguards. First, right-wing politicians – the Liberals and the Conservatives – retained the power to block controversial initiatives by Radical presidents in Congress, in part because the electoral strength of both parties was enhanced by an inequitable apportionment of representatives from rural districts. Second, the Radical presidents' appointments of top governmental officials avoided antagonizing Chilean business elites. This was especially true in the cases of strategic state agencies and enterprises dealing with the promotion of industrial development. Nearly all of the appointees were nonpartisan technicians who were com-

6 In the two other Southern Cone countries, Argentina and Uruguay, the franchise included over a quarter of the total population.

7 With the exception of a few capitalistic pockets, the Chilean agrarian system combined a class of latifundia owners and a subsistence-oriented peasantry. Production lagged during the first half of the twentieth century, and the country became a net importer of foodstuffs.

mitted to a free-enterprise ideology and sharp restrictions on the decision-making power of elected officials.

The consensus that Chilean elites reached during the 1930s and the 1940s was thus quite tenuous. It depended not only on the continued adherence of conservative segments of the elite – which was, in turn, dependent on the maintenance of the two aforementioned safeguards – but also on the commitment of the two left-wing parties, especially certain Socialist factions, to real limits on the extent of democracy, and this commitment was ambivalent at best. Until the early 1950s, this ambivalence did not have much relevance because neither of the two major leftist parties managed to gain more than 10 or 12 percent of the votes. In addition, the Communists and Socialists rejected the formation of a left-wing political alliance, thus precluding any possibility that they would become real contenders in presidential elections.

The fragility of the Chilean political consensus became progressively more obvious beginning in the early 1950s, however. This was due in part to the fact that the political system did not absorb with ease the enfranchisement of women and the rural poor resulting from changes in both the legislation and the registration mechanisms. The franchise expanded tenfold in less than two decades. But there was another cause of political instability: The coalitional strategies that had prevailed in the party system during almost two decades lost their appeal to the elites that pursued them. Each of the major political forces attempted to capture the top prize in the electoral game, the presidency, without resorting to alliances with other forces.

The Radical party lost the presidential election of 1952. In fact, its candidate ran a poor third in a three-cornered race. Beginning with 1952, each subsequent presidential election was won by a different party or party coalition: In 1952, a populist front led by the former military leader, General Carlos Ibáñez; in 1958, a Liberal–Conservative right-wing front; in 1964, Christian Democracy; and in 1970, the left-wing Unidad popular.[8] The sequence of political events followed a rather repetitive pattern. Every president tried to gain majoritarian social support, but all failed; the failure, in turn, brought about the permanent or temporary eclipse of the president's party. No party in power was capable of even being a real contender for the presidency

8 Unidad popular included several parties, although the Communists and the Socialists were its two major components. These two historical parties of the left had shifted from antagonism to cooperation beginning in 1957 when they created the FRAP (Popular Action front).

at the next election.[9] This pattern gradually weakened the party system, undermining its capacity to channel and contain social conflicts.

The gradual weakening of the Chilean party system during the 1950s and the 1960s was not irreversible, as we shall see. Most of the parties survived under Pinochet, and key factions of the Christian Democrats and the Socialists, and of the right wing as well, eventually redefined their strategies to engage once again in coalitional behavior.

The Argentine response to the political vacuum resulting from the abortive attempt to consolidate a corporatist regime was quite different from the Chilean one. The Conservative restoration inaugurated in 1932 had as its main goal turning back Argentina's political clock by twenty years. General Justo and the anti-fascist Conservative politicians who backed him sought to recreate the conditions for the "success" of the initial project associated with the promulgation of the 1912 Sáenz Peña Law. Their goal was gradually to reopen the political arena by coopting the middle-class Radical party, by allowing it a share of power short of capturing the presidency.[10] However, Justo and his allies failed just as their predecessors had failed two decades earlier. Their failure led to another military coup, in 1943, this time staged against the reactionary Conservative president, Ramón Castillo. This second Conservative frustration was related to two successive phenomena, developing in the late 1930s and the early 1940s.

The first complication for the Conservatives was that the Radicals were not willing to play the role of a tame second fiddle. As a consequence, the much more moderate Radical politician who had become the leader of the party after Hipólito Yrigoyen's death, Marcelo T. de Alvear, refused Justo's invitation to join the Concordancia. This was a loose confederation of Conservative factions and right-wing Radicals, and it was conceived as a mechanism for redemocratizing the Argentine political system in stages. The planned sequence was that a Conservative president would be followed by a moderate Radical selected by the two parties and legitimized by less than open

9 The Ibañista coalition was dissolved before 1958 and did not participate in that year's election; the right-wing front withdrew its candidate in 1964 when it decided to support the Christian Democrat Eduardo Frei; and in 1970, the Christian Democrat candidate came out third behind Salvador Allende and the right-wing former president, Jorge Alessandri.

10 The gradualist scheme of the conservative reformer of the 1910s, Sáenz Peña, was thwarted by the victory of the Radicals in the 1916 presidential election. Obviously, they were supposed to lose the first free election in Argentine political history.

elections, which would finally lead to the implementation of a free democratic vote.

A paradoxical contrast could be made with Chile. The much weaker Chilean Radical party felt it was necessary to negotiate with other parties in order to gain power, whereas their Argentine counterparts, who were electorally stronger, chose to follow an intransigent strategy. This strategy succeeded in that it blocked the gradual democratization envisioned by the moderate Conservatives, but it also prevented the Radicals from regaining power. The failure to negotiate an agreement in the mid-1930s was further compounded a few years later by the untimely deaths in 1941 of both Alvear and Justo's successor, Roberto Ortiz. The latter, himself a former Radical politician closely associated with Alvear, had been selected by Justo in order to fulfill the second stage of the democratizing sequence. He was close to achieving a deal when both men died of natural causes. Ortiz was replaced by a staunch Conservative, Vice-President Castillo, who was strongly opposed to any deal with his antagonists.

The opportunity for a deal between Conservatives and Radicals did not reappear in the 1940s, as both of the traditional parties were engulfed by the arrival of a new force in Argentine politics, Peronism. In fact, Peronism, which was originally inspired by Italian Fascism and later turned into a peculiar populist party of the workers and the people of the poor provinces, transformed Argentina in many deep and irreversible ways.[11] As a result, the divisions that had split Argentine elites for forty years were superseded by a new cleavage, Peronism–anti-Peronism, which remained the root cause of Argentine political instability until the 1970s.

Peronism retained one of the more potent elements of the antidemocratic political ideologies of the 1930s: the aspiration to achieve ideological unification of the country's elites. In turn, this aspiration was one of the main reasons that the emergence of Peronism reinforced Argentina's political instability. A paradoxical aspect of Peronism was that though it failed to achieve elite unity, it successfully incorporated the masses into the political system. Juan Perón's original goal was to seduce the country's most powerful elites – that is, the military, business, and the Catholic church – and to fuse them into a "national movement." Although significant parts of these elites

11 The electoral success of Peronism from the 1940s to the 1980s was related to the combination of two parties in one. In the metropolitan centers of the country, the party resembled a labor party not unlike European labor parties. In the impoverished provinces of the northeast and the northwest, however, Peronism tended to express the orientations of backward oligarchies and the poor.

were joined in the movement's initial coalition in 1945–6, the first Peronist government progressively alienated all those groups. At the same time, however, Peronism was creating a new elite of trade union leaders while fully incorporating workers and women into politics. On the one hand, workers and women became citizens; on the other, the social distance between the elites and the masses was considerably reduced.

There were other contradictory aspects of Peronism. It became an unbeatable electoral force, and one year before its demise in 1955, it obtained the support of almost two thirds of the electorate. This electoral success contributed to Peronism's political downfall, however, because it reinforced the disloyalty toward the political system among all rival parties, from Communists to Radicals and Conservatives. These parties were understandably outraged by Perón's tactics of gerrymandering, media manipulation, and bending legislative procedural norms, all of which was seen as rejecting the very idea of political competition. Perón claimed, after all, that his party was the only natural representative of the people. In addition, the traditional elites resented their loss of influence over policymaking, as well as the increasing social egalitarianism.

Predictably, most of the social and political elites joined in 1955 to overthrow Perón, and they did so in the name of democracy. It was not surprising, however, that the 1955 coup brought about neither democracy nor reconciliation. During the next eighteen years, Argentines were not allowed to vote for Peronist candidates, a circumstance that nurtured political alienation and that condemned civilian governments to illegitimacy and futility. Throughout this period, moreover, the unity of the anti-Peronist front was little more than a mirage: Disagreements over what to do about Peronism and how much political freedom should be allowed appeared as early as 1956. These disagreements led to successive coups and to the downfalls of civilian and military regimes alike.

These conflicts increased until they culminated in the full militarization of politics during the 1970s. But while the conflicts intensified, the main dividing lines became more confusing. Several political groups, especially within the Radical party and the left, sought to ally themselves with Peronism. They did this to undermine or exert pressure on civilian and military regimes and to use Peronism as a vehicle for gaining access to power. Meanwhile, segments of the business elite resented attempts at economic liberalization, and they accordingly mellowed in their opposition to basic tenets of Perón's economic doctrines. In a word, Argentine politics was "Peronized" during the eighteen years that Peronism was outlawed (1955–73). The political game became more complex, but at the same time, more opaque, as most conflicts and issues were subsumed under *la cuestión peronista*.

In turn (and this was not surprising) Peronism itself internalized conflicts and cleavages that were previously external to it. As a result, and despite all the changes Peronism went through over the preceding twenty years, its return to power in 1973 reenacted, albeit in a more explosive way, the political cul-de-sac of the 1950s. As both a political movement and an electoral contender, Peronism was again a formidable force, and it was apparent that no one could govern Argentina without it. With reluctance, the military had no alternative but to relinquish power to Perón's appointed candidate, Héctor Cámpora. But events rapidly proved that Peronism was not capable of governing the country: It transferred its internal conflicts and unsolved dilemmas to state institutions, and its government was quickly destroyed from within. The tenuous equilibrium of the 1960s, during which the country had avoided the extremes of political violence and economic crisis, was broken.

Despite the contrasting political routes followed by Chile and Argentina between 1930 and 1970, their economic trends were similar. The growth of a manufacturing sector producing for the domestic market (i.e., the pattern of import-substitution industrialization) generated considerable economic dynamism during those decades. In both countries (as was also the case in countries like Brazil and Mexico), the expansion of the state's intervention in the economy became a key feature of the import-substitution model. The roles of the state included (1) the creation of agencies dealing with monetary and foreign exchange controls, (2) the replacement of international capital markets by the political regulation of capital flows, (3) the state regulation of wages and prices, and (4) the creation of public enterprises that were engaged in both productive ventures and public utilities.

Unlike Brazil and Mexico, where the rates of economic growth associated with import substitution and state interventionism were quite high, Argentina's economy after the late 1940s followed a course similar to that of Chile: slow growth and high inflation. But it is important to note that Argentina lacked the mechanisms for politically mediating the socioeconomic conflicts that surfaced in Chile after 1938. The fact that these mechanisms were generated in Chile and that they survived for several decades in the midst of economic stagnation and sometimes severe social conflict testifies to the political resourcefulness of Chile's elites.

The conclusion to be drawn here is that the parallel breakdowns that Chile and Argentina experienced in the 1970s should not obscure the different legacies of their respective preauthoritarian political histories. These different legacies may prove to be an important factor in shaping the final outcomes of the current processes of regime consolidation.

Redemocratization in the 1980s: military regimes, transitions, and prospects for consolidation

The situation preceding the coups of the 1970s in Argentina and Chile had several common features, as well as a contrasting element that was related to prevailing trends in the political classes of both countries during the early years of that decade.

1. *The voiding of political institutions.* During the year and a half before the coups, parliamentary entities, including political parties and individual political leaders, became less and less able to mediate and regulate social and economic conflict. The 1972–3 period in Chile and the years between 1974 and 1976 in Argentina witnessed a significant increase in the level of confrontation. With the death of Perón in 1974, Argentina lost the last chance to avoid a complete institutional breakdown. When the ailing general returned to Argentina in 1972, he had changed most of his old antidemocratic beliefs and had become the cornerstone of an attempt to institutionalize political democracy. But, the Peronist movement was a battleground on which left-wing guerrillas, fascist paramilitary squads, and union cliques confronted one another violently. These partisan conflicts led to explosive disputes over the control of state institutions and the political system as a whole. Likewise in Chile, beginning in mid-1972 the business associations representing large and small firms resorted to adversarial tactics aimed at destabilizing the Unidad popular regime. Lockouts and transportation strikes brought havoc to the country's economy which, in any case, was near collapse as a result of the failure to control inflation and black markets. President Allende made a last attempt to restore the political balance by incorporating active-duty military officers into his cabinet. This move proved successful only for a while; in mid-1973 the army's generals forced their commander in chief, the prodemocratic General Carlos Prats, to resign. His successor, General Pinochet, took over and immediately began to organize the military rebellion that culminated in the September 1973 coup.

2. *The militarization of politics.* An additional aspect of the precoup situation in both countries was the increasing level of political violence. In the case of Chile, violence remained largely rhetorical, with

socialists calling for completion of the revolution and capitalists demanding military intervention. In Argentina, beginning in 1974, the various factions within Peronism resorted to terrorist tactics and illegal methods of state repression in their attempts to eliminate their antagonists. In both countries, the military concluded that they were fighting a war against an internal enemy and that the extermination of subversion required that the armed forces apply the same unconventional methods that were being used by the left-wing guerrillas, that is, torture, kidnappings, and assassinations. Furthermore, the armed forces believed that the struggle against Communist subversion required the suspension, at least temporarily, of constitutional rules and guarantees.

3. *The exhaustion of the economic model of import substitution and state interventionism.* The import-substitution model lost its dynamism in the 1970s when domestic markets were all but saturated. This happened earlier in the Southern Cone countries than in Brazil and Mexico. In the former, domestic markets were comparatively small, and no significant segments of the population remained outside them. This, in turn, meant fiscal collapse for the state and severe erosion of the welfare functions that it performed for the middle and working classes. Marginalization and social inequality increased with the slowing of the manufacturing sector and the deterioration of state services. Consequently, conflicts over income distribution increased both in number and intensity, which were reflected in renewed inflationary pressures and in the overburdening of the state's mediation capacities[12]

4. *Political classes in the early 1970s: competing hegemonic projects in Chile and reconciliation in Argentina.* The two decades between 1953 and 1973 in Chile witnessed the gradual unraveling of the political model based on elite compromise. Manuel Antonio Garretón has convincingly argued that this process was largely a result of two factors: (1) the replacement of the Radical party by Christian Democracy as the dominant center party in Chilean politics and (2) the emergence of parallel aspirations among forces on the extremes of the political spectrum to achieve undisputed political supremacy.[13] Hence, polit-

12 During the 1950s and 1960s, annual inflation rates had averaged 40 to 50 percent a year, but in the early 1970s, quarterly inflation rates reached those same levels.

13 Manuel Antonio Garretón, in *The Chilean Political Process* (Boston: Unwin Hyman, 1989), argues that the emergence of the Christian Democrats as the major center party during the 1960s, together with the corresponding decline of the Radicals, left the Chilean political system with no party playing a linchpin role. This coincided with the fact that beginning with the 1958 elections, the left had achieved the

ical polarization was not a consequence of the presence of strong ideologically defined parties but, rather, the result of a combination of circumstances that eroded the overall propensity toward compromise. This was clearly visible in the 1970 presidential election, in which each of the three forces – the victorious left-wing Unidad popular, the right-wing Partido nacional, and the Christian Democrats – received the support of about one third of the electorate.

A catastrophic standoff took place in 1973, when the combined opposition of Nacionales and Christian Democrats won the congressional elections but fell short of the two-thirds majority required to impeach President Allende. A final attempt to avoid a coup collapsed. The Communist party and the moderate Socialists, on the one hand, and the institutionalist sectors of the Christian Democrats, on the other, failed to reach a last-minute compromise designed to prevent military intervention. The intransigence of the Socialist leadership was matched by that of two key Christian Democrats, the former president Eduardo Frei and the party's president Patricio Aylwin. Frei's intransigence was in part nurtured by his hope to become the heir of a brief, merely corrective, military regime, and so he did nothing to prevent the military takeover in September 1973.

By contrast, political trends in Argentina seemed more promising when the 1970s began. After a quarter-century of permanent and deep antagonism, the two major parties, the Peronists and the Radicals, signed La Hora del pueblo. This document reflected the decision of the two party leaders, Perón and Balbín, to create a party system based on the majority's – presumably the Peronists' – respect for other parties, and the opposition's agreement to play a loyal role. La Hora del pueblo represented a major step forward in Argentine politics, and it facilitated the 1973 transition to democracy. The accord had two serious flaws, however. On the one hand, most Peronist factions gave only lip service to the agreement: Despite their ideological differences, left-wing guerrillas, union leaders, and the fascistic nationalists shared a common hostility toward the establishment of a party-dominated political system. On the other hand, by making an explicit commitment to abide by constitutional rules, the Radical leadership implicitly accepted the inevitability of a Peronist victory.

This left the Radicals in the position of being unable to portray itself as a credible institutional alternative, a weakness that proved to be crucial when the Peronist government collapsed as a result of internecine struggles and the ineptitude of Isabel Perón, who replaced her

possibility of winning the presidency, and the right had successfully transformed itself into a mass-based force with both urban and rural appeal.

husband as president when the ailing general died in July 1974. Thus, in 1976, the Radicals – the main opposition party – were vigorously opposed to the military coup, but they were not perceived by a large majority of Argentines as capable of filling the void left by Peronism.

To summarize, the irreconcilable antagonisms between the two main political camps in Chile made the 1973 coup inevitable. Cleavages in Chilean society were quite sharply defined in the early 1970s, and issues dividing the opposing sides could not be compromised. This helps account for the breakdown of what had been one of the most stable political regimes in Latin America. In the long run, however, those same divisions and deadlocks increased the likelihood of an elite settlement. That is, once each political camp abandoned its goal of eliminating its adversaries, the need to settle became compelling.

In Argentina, conversely, the 1976 military coup was virtually unopposed; the generals had only to walk into the Casa Rosada (the presidential palace) to regain political power. The whole universe of political parties had become an undifferentiated mass incapable of providing institutional alternatives. The return to democracy in 1983 required efforts by the Peronists and the Radicals to project distinct political profiles once again. This in turn helped transform Argentina into a competitive political system, reversing the trends of the previous seventy years. But, as I shall argue, it also diminished the likelihood of an elite settlement after the military regime collapsed in 1982.

The military regimes and the transitions of the 1980s

During their initial stages, the Chilean and the Argentine military regimes shared several major features. Both were extraordinarily repressive and succeeded in virtually paralyzing their respective opponents. The two regimes implemented orthodox economic policies explicitly designed not only to eliminate most mechanisms of state interventionism but also to create the preconditions for a new model based on an open economy and the reestablishment of capital markets.

Pinochet was much more successful than his Argentine counterparts. When confronted with obstacles, the Argentine generals seemingly blindly pushed ahead anyway, and in 1982 they launched the disastrous military adventure in the South Atlantic. Their failure precipitated the sudden collapse of the regime and thus led to a new democratic transition in 1983. Unlike the Argentines, the Chilean military was able to correct the mistakes of its initial economic programs, thereby averting the financial and economic collapse to which the policies inspired by the "Chicago Boys" were leading. Beginning in 1982, the Chilean military regime successfully promoted the growth of a new export-oriented sector in agriculture and agroindustry. Meanwhile, Pinochet effectively fought back the social protests in 1983–4 and the opposition's demands that he resign.

In 1980 Pinochet agreed to approve a new constitution. Although this constitution was largely designed to ensure the continuity of the authoritarian regime and of Pinochet's rule, at least until 1998, it also called for holding a plebiscite in 1988. In this plebiscite, citizens would be given the opportunity to accept or reject Pinochet's proposals. In implementing the plebiscite, the military president made a crucial mistake by giving various opposition groups the opportunity to agree on a common objective, the defeat of the military dictatorship. When the plebiscite was finally held in September 1988, the united opposition front received 56 percent of the votes, against 43 percent supporting a new nine-year presidential term for Pinochet. This clear defeat forced the dictator to call for open presidential elections, as was in fact required by his own constitution. The result was a transfer of power to the Grand Coalition candidate, the Christian Democrat Patricio Aylwin, who emerged as the victor in the December 1989 elections with almost exactly the same proportion of votes that the opposition had received one year earlier in the plebiscite.

Actually, the fact that a democratic Chilean government came to power only in March 1990 suggests that it may still be too early to compare the two transition processes. But there are already many signs pointing to new difficulties in Argentina, whereas the course to be followed by the emerging Chilean democracy can only be a matter for speculation.

Chile

During the mid-1980s two opposing maximalist projects were proposed in Chile. The first was inspired by the country's ruler, General Pinochet, and, following O'Donnell and Schmitter, can be defined as the *dictablanda* model. Accordingly, an extended process of political liberalization would be controlled from above for at least another fifteen years, thus allowing the authoritarian government to complete the structural reform of the Chilean economy and society initiated in the 1970s. This project gradually gained support among the upper and middle classes during the 1980s when economic growth averaged 5 to 6 percent of Chile's GNP. The opposing maximalist proposal emerged in the aftermath of the massive social protests of 1982–3 and was expressed in the opposition's demands for the dictator's immediate resignation and the formation of a provisional government.

During the following six years, neither of these maximalist proposals met with success, and the outcome was instead the defeat of Pinochet in the 1988 plebiscite and the election of an opposition politician as president within the framework of the 1980 authoritarian constitution.

I believe that this outcome was the result of two partial but essentially simultaneous elite settlements. The first partial settlement was among most of the opposition elites – the Christian Democrats, the moderate faction of the Socialists, and various smaller groupings on the Christian left – and a considerable segment of the leadership of the authoritarian coalition supporting Pinochet. In a process of successive negotiations, these opposing camps agreed to turn the 1988 plebiscite into an open and fair election and to abide by its result. This meant that the opposition dropped its demands for Pinochet's resignation and that the politicians and businessmen who coalesced around the newly founded Renovación nacional agreed not to support Pinochet's attempt to stay in power in any case. Moreover, the agreement implied that the contending factions would support a set of common rules of the game. Although they obviously favored different electoral outcomes – continuity versus the defeat of Pinochet – each elite camp was willing to risk being defeated in fair elections, thus giving legitimacy to a government controlled by its former enemies.

The second partial settlement was as decisive as the first. It involved the Christian Democrats and a new faction that formed within the Socialist party during the mid-1980s. This faction was informally known as the "Núñez Socialists," after the name of its general secretary. By making an unambiguous commitment to democracy, the Núñez Socialists abandoned their past support for revolutionary violence. Equally important, they also concluded that the institutional breakdown of 1973 had largely been a consequence of the joint failure of the left and Christian Democracy to defend political democracy by reaching a political compromise.

The Núñez Socialists favored a pact with the Christian Democratic party, and as a result, the latter and the Partido por la democracia (which became the electoral front controlled by the Núñez Socialists) agreed to maintain the unity of the opposition beyond the 1988 plebiscite and to present a joint candidate if presidential elections were held in 1989. This implied not only that they were uniting as an opposition front with the purpose of defeating Pinochet's attempt to remain in power until 1998 but also that they envisioned the formation of a joint governmental coalition. This accord had short-term as well as long-term consequences. It immediately created a powerful countervailing force within the left, in which the Communist party had all but abandoned the moderate stance it had maintained since the 1930s. Beginning with the social protests of the early 1980s, the Communists expressed support, albeit ambiguously, for insurrectionary tactics, and they thus replaced the Socialists at the extreme left of the ideological spectrum. However, with the formation of the Grand Coalition, the Communists had little choice but to support the coalition's candidate, the Christian Democrat Patricio Aylwin, opposing Pinochet's nominee, former Treasury Minister Hernán Buchi.

Over the longer run, the convergence of the Christian Democrats and the Socialists meant that the center party, as well as the parliamentary segment of the left, abandoned the isolationist positions they had embraced between 1958 and 1973. As I have argued, the gradual transformation of Chile's political system during the 1960s into a "triangle with no sides," and the uncompromising goals of its three camps, led to the destruction of constitutional democracy.

In fact, the two partial elite settlements that appear to have been made in the late 1980s suggest that Chile is evolving toward a multiparty quadrangle. Crucial and novel linkages among the following groups have been established in this new four-cornered organization: (1) the government coalition made up of Christian Democrats and democratic Socialists; (2) a Socialist formation linking the governing Socialists with the rest of the party, which has remained within the extreme left camp led by the Communist party; (3) a conservative confederation, which includes the Renovación nacional as well as the more authoritarian sectors represented by the UDI (Democratic Independent union); and (4) a tacit formation consisting of the governing coalition and Renovación nacional based on support for democratic rules of the game.

In the 1989 elections, the Renovación nacional emerged as the largest party of the right, running a close second to Christian Democracy in the total number of congressional seats. The final election results are presented in Table 7.1:

Table 7.1. *Final results of 1989 election in Chile*

Party	Deputies	Senators
Christian Democracy	39	13
Renovación nacional	34	11
Partido por la democracia	17	6
UDI (Democratic independent union)	13	2

Table 7.1 (*cont.*)

Party	Deputies	Senators
Socialist party	6	1
Radical party	5	1
Christian left	2	—
Centro democrático libre	1	—
Social democracy	1	—
Humanist party	1	1
Independents	1	3
Appointed (by Pinochet)	—	9
Total	120	47

The Renovación nacional has become a stabilizing force on the right, and its political significance increased throughout 1990. The only relevant actors who were not part of the elite settlement of 1988 – Pinochet, the army, and, to some extent, the UDI leaders – saw their influence partially eroded. Pinochet remains as a potential threat because in accordance with the 1980 constitution, he did not have to resign as commander in chief of the army. It became clear during 1990, however, that the three other branches of the military, especially the air force and the *carabineros* (military police), were distancing themselves from the former dictator. Furthermore, the revelation of a clandestine organization, the so-called Cutufa, and of blatant corruption involving Pinochet's son undermined his image even within the army and among his more ardent supporters. In fact, it was rumored that Pinochet would agree to resign in exchange for an amnesty for himself and his family covering all financial misdeeds. In the summer of 1990–1 it was clear the Pinochet's only hope for maintaining some influence was linked to the possibility that the report on human rights commissioned by President Aylwin could generate some turmoil within the army.

The political system created as a result of these two partial elite settlements in Chile nevertheless still faces four challenges:

1. It must find ways to avoid a repetition of situations in which minority governments confront insurmountable tasks. In this respect, the double-round system for presidential elections is probably an advance over past arrangements in which two of the last three presidents, Alessandri and Allende, were elected with the support of just one third of the electorate.
2. During the first presidential term, the risk (and the temptation) of splitting the political elite between a party-of-government and a party-of-protest must be avoided. Such polarization into two camps could pose a threat to the fragile new regime.

3. The party system must reintegrate the Communist party into the institutional framework, thus avoiding the danger that the Communists, who commanded the support of around 15 percent of the electorate before 1973, may become an antisystem force.
4. Pinochet must be neutralized, and the army's commitment to political stability must be secured. It seems unlikely that the Chilean military will participate in a formal partial settlement like the one concluded in Uruguay in 1984. Nevertheless, Chile's democratic consolidation depends on the return of the armed forces to the pattern of political neutrality that existed between 1932 and 1969.

Argentina

The transition to democracy in Argentina during the early 1980s contrasted paradoxically with the previous political cycle in that country. The outgoing military regime was still able to exercise some leverage in the early 1970s, thus forcing the two main political parties to join in demanding the end of all political proscriptions and the establishment of fair electoral rules. As I suggested, the formation of La Hora del pueblo helped heal a major rift within what had been a disjointed party system. The emerging democratic regime paid a price, however: the inability to offer a political alternative if the first government proved unsuccessful, as it did.

In the early 1980s, conversely, the military had to abandon political power without conditions. Indeed, the armed forces failed even to extract an agreement from civilian politicians concerning an amnesty for human rights violations committed between 1976 and 1982. In contrast with that in 1973, the 1983 election was a close contest with an uncertain result, so uncertain, indeed, that the underdog, Raúl Alfonsín, emerged as the winner when all the votes had been counted. Unlike 1973, moreover, the Peronists and the Radicals were not faced with the need to reach an agreement to force the military to yield power.

On the positive side, in 1983 the Argentine electorate was offered a real choice between two distinct political parties. Furthermore, despite their unexpected defeat, the Peronists received 40 percent of the vote and won a majority in the Senate, thus remaining a powerful political force. Less positively, the hotly contested 1983 elections created a climate of confrontation and animosity between the two major parties. As a result, the political mosaic of the mid-1980s combined some elements of the past and some new elements, in a pattern that was not strongly conducive to the consolidation of a competitive, nonpolarized party system. On one hand, the Peronists underwent a kind of retrenchment, choosing to play the role of an opposition that was only marginally concerned with competitive politics. On the other hand, Alfonsín's Radical party pursued the goal of becoming the dominant party.

Thus in the mid-1980s the two major party elites (and cadres) resuscitated a tradition that had permeated their political experiences and careers: the tendency of each to conceive of itself as the single and central mechanism of any system based on the concept of popular sovereignty. Peronism, on the one hand, tended to present itself as the "natural" representative of the people, whereas Radicalism perceived itself as the necessary and inevitable cornerstone of the democratization of Argentine politics.

During the interregnum that began with the 1983 elections, each of the two major political forces tried to become the exclusive mediator and policymaker. This became a serious problem in the most decisive area of public policy – the economy. The new constitutional government was faced with the most serious economic crisis in Argentine history. In addition to a $43 billion foreign debt, the failure of the military's economic policies left the fledgling democracy with an altogether bankrupt state and an exhausted economic model. The military had succeeded in destroying whatever dynamism was left in the previous model, while at the same time failing to remove some of the more costly prerogatives and entitlements in that model, especially those that benefited the most powerful segments of the business class.

Ineffective economic policies during Alfonsín's first year in power further undermined the situation. Beginning in 1985, it was apparent that inflation rates were rapidly accelerating, and by May of that year the monthly index had already reached 30 percent. The ghosts of hyperinflation and chaos and images of the 1976 precoup context came back to haunt Argentines. Alfonsín's answer was to define the situation as one of a "war economy" and to launch the Austral Plan, a package of measures designed mostly by nonpartisan economists. The Austral Plan was a daring attempt to implement austerity measures in an election year – congressional elections were be held in late 1985. The plan was designed to reduce inflation sharply by eliminating the inertial factors related to expectations. It cut the fiscal deficit, froze prices and wages, and changed the national currency.

During its first year and a half, the Austral Plan was largely successful. It not only achieved its antiinflationary goals, but it also managed to reactivate industrial growth. The freeze on prices and wages received considerable support, despite persistent criticism by some business sectors and most of the Peronist unions. In fact, Alfonsín's Radical party managed to score an impressive victory in the 1985 elections, by beating Peronism in both the advanced metropolitan centers (as it had done in 1983) and most of the backward provinces of the north.

During late 1986 and early 1987, however, Alfonsín and his associates – the so-called operators – made the bad mistake of assuming that the economic battle had been won and that the time was ripe for an ambitious political *tour de force,* the cooptation of a segment of the Peronist union leadership. This operation was conceived as the central element of a project designed to transform Radicalism from a strong party with 40 percent support into a dominant force that could easily achieve an absolute majority in the electorate. From this perspective, Peronism would become a largely ineffectual opposition, reduced to the support of about one third of the electorate, as happened in 1985. The weakening of Peronism was to result from cooptation and from the fact that many of its traditional supporters were alienated by the authoritarian conservative populists led by Herminio Iglesias, who had captured the party's top positions between 1983 and 1985.

The central ingredient of this "hegemonic" project was the appointment of a controversial Peronist union leader, known for his previous support of the military regime, as minister of labor. But the project ended in complete disaster when the Peronist minister caused major disruptions in economic policymaking. In late 1986, economic policies were already under strong pressures from business leaders and from the public in general, all of whom were demanding their relaxation. By mid-1987 all the signs of crisis had reappeared: high inflation, a decline in real wages, and an increase in the fiscal deficit. The Austral Plan lost its consistency, and it rapidly became an uncoordinated set of mechanisms designed to cope with daily emergencies. Furthermore, the military dramatically reappeared on the political stage in Easter of 1987 by staging the first of a series of *planteos* (regime-destabilization attempts or threats) that exposed the weakness of civilian institutions and undermined the president's authority in one of the key areas of democratic consolidation.

The Radical party thus suffered a serious defeat in the 1987 elections, when in addition to all congressional seats, most provincial governorships were at stake. As a consequence, Alfonsín lost almost all credibility, and during its last two years his government was reduced to administering its own demise and to witnessing the full return to "traditional" Argentina, that is, an economy of high inflation (actual hyperinflation during March–July 1989), savage distributive struggles, and the effective blocking of government action by business and other economic operatives.

Several opportunities were thus lost in 1986–7. First, the government failed to capitalize on the initial success of the Austral Plan. Alfonsín, and his minister of economy, Juan Sourrouille, repeatedly announced that success in reducing inflationary expectations would be used as the basis for structural reforms, including modernization of the economy, reform of the state, and elimination of subsidies to business. However, these structural reforms remained rhetorical goals that were not even launched. Second, the Radicals lost a unique chance to promote some sort of settlement with the democratic Peronist faction, the Renovación. The latter had managed to defeat its internal authoritarian opponents by about 1985, and they were largely perceived as victorious in the 1987 general elections. But Alfonsín chose to confront Renovación and, in doing so, nurtured a symmetrical response from the democratic Peronists: They rededicated themselves to taking up oppositional positions at any cost, and they used Congress to block most of the executive branch's initiatives. Furthermore, the two processes, structural adjustment and a Radical–Peronist pact, were necessarily linked. Alfonsín's government needed the tacit or explicit support of the major opposition party to withstand the pressures and protests of those who fought his proposed economic reforms.

Paradoxically, the initial successes of the Peronist Renovación proved incapable of surviving the irreversible decline of the Radical government. Alfonsín's and the Radical party's loss of popularity and credibility affected all politicians, including the Renovadores. Consequently, Alfonsín's wing of the Radical party, as well as the Renovadores, were unsuccessful in imposing their candidates in the 1989 presidential elections. This was especially serious in the case of Peronism, because it resulted in the candidacy of Carlos Menem.

The principal factor that allowed Menem to prevail in the Peronist primaries – the first time in Peronist history that the party had selected its candidate in a democratic fashion – and later to win the presidential elections was Menem's ability to express a visible shift in public opinion regarding politics. As a result of the collapse of the Alfonsín government's economic policies and the consequent deterioration of the economic situation, the population's negative evaluation applied not only to the government but also to the whole political leadership. Argentines began to doubt that politicians and democratic institutions were capable of dealing with an economic crisis that was becoming more serious by the day. In this context, which was exacerbated by the hyperinflationary explosion of February 1989, Menem's tactic of presenting himself as a figure who was outside politics was extremely successful.

Menem's victory also represented the defeat of Peronism's emerging party organization, aborting its consolidation and returning the party to a situation of total dependence on a Peronist president.

In mid-1989 Argentina was plunged into a political whirlpool, bringing about further political fragmentation and economic decline. The window opened in 1983–5 was closed; the failure to articulate a political system capable of regulating economic interactions became apparent. This was not by chance associated with the state's virtual bankruptcy and default on its foreign debt payments. The usual defenses against inflation were useless: Indexation, the shortening of contracts, and periodic wage bargaining were shown to be ineffective in the face of inflationary rates of 100 percent a month.

The collapse of the first democratic government after the 1983 transition demonstrates the corrosive effects of high inflation on political coherence, as well as the extraordinarily negative effects of lost opportunities in fragile democracies. Perhaps the only positive legacy of the Alfonsín years is that the extreme disorganization of the economy and the state has not resulted in institutional breakdown.

I have argued that 1986–7 turned out to be a missed opportunity. The economic adjustment measures of the Austral Plan were initially successful in reducing both the rate of inflation and the public deficit. Hoping to capitalize on this initial success, Alfonsín chose in early 1987 to confront the Peronist party, but he failed. However, the Radicals' defeat in the 1987 elections opened another opportunity, the likelihood that the victorious democratic Peronists, led by Antonio Cafiero, would favor political reconciliation. Instead, in late 1987 Cafiero chose not to pursue this reconciliation with his Radical adversaries, and the Peronist Renovación tried to gain the upper hand by reasserting its bitter and uncompromising opposition to Alfonsín's economic policies. In the end, both camps lost: The two party organizations were eclipsed, and Menem ascended to power.

As president, Menem pursued a different and daring strategy. He has tried to consign the two large parties, including his own, to political limbo. At the same time, he has attempted to mend the historic rift separating Peronism from two of the country's principal elite sectors, business and military leaders. It is still too early to evaluate how successful this strategy has been. Extremely harsh economic policies were implemented in 1990, with the struggle against inflation relying on controlling the money supply and reducing the public deficit. The latter entailed privatizations, suspension of public works, drastic reductions in the salaries and wages of public employees, and a dismantling of the social security system. During the final quarter of 1990, inflation rates began to recede, and the business sector praised Menem for his determination and his adoption of laissez-faire policies.

The cost, however, was the most severe recession in Argentina's history. Investment rates fell to less than 10 percent of the nation's GNP, and unemployment reached unprecedented levels.

The new president's approach to military problems also has been quite innovative. He granted a presidential pardon to all members of the former juntas who had been condemned for the human rights violations between 1976 and 1982. This allowed him to secure the enthusiastic support of the "institutionalist" sector of the army, which easily put down an attempted coup by the *carapintadas* in early December 1990. The *carapintadas*, who were initially hopeful that Menem would side with them in the power struggle within the army, represented a nationalist and fundamentalist reaction favoring the establishment of a regime based on strong-arm tactics and the return of statism.

Will Menem be able to refound Peronism under his charismatic leadership, while securing the support of business and the military for a political model based on economic and social conservatism in the state and other institutions? This question is still open, and the way it is answered in the next few years will determine whether the country's elites have a new chance to consolidate democracy in Argentina.

At a deeper level, the prospects for democratic consolidation depend on reversing the trends of the last eight decades. Before 1983, the political landscape of Argentine society resembled a swamp. In this swamp, it was impossible to draw lines, that is to define precise boundaries between social sectors and between different segments of the elite. It seems apparent that the likelihood of democratic consolidation in Argentina rests on building a political terra firma. The Argentine elites need to define more clearly their respective interests and orientations. This is probably a prerequisite for any elite settlement. In doing so, however, they must simultaneously avoid moving too far in the direction of direct confrontation. The specter of Chile in the early 1970s reminds us of how such confrontations prevent elite accommodation and lead to regime breakdown.

Conclusions

The 1970s witnessed the inauguration of military regimes in Chile and Argentina. Pinochet, as well as the Argentine generals, concluded that the profound changes they favored could not be implemented simply by suppressing parliamentary institutions and civil liberties. The capitalist revolution they envisioned required a radical transformation of the economic and social structures of their countries. These two military regimes, as well as the regime established in 1973 in Uruguay, thus shared the goal of founding a new society based on the restoration of order and the rule of the market. In both countries, moreover, this goal was pursued in a distinct political landscape, that of fully mobilized societies in which the majority of the population had been urbanized and integrated into the market for several decades.

Neither regime succeeded in the long run, because each failed to create and impose a stable political formula. During the 1980s, both had to yield power to democratically elected regimes. The Argentine and the Chilean transitions were substantially different, however. In Chile the transition was the result of a process of negotiation that involved two partial elite settlements. In Argentina the transition was unleashed by a collapse of the military regime that made political bargaining unnecessary. Previously warring segments of the Argentine elite jointly condemned the armed forces, blaming the country's ills on the brutality, political ineffectiveness, economic mistakes, and professional incompetence of the military. There thus was the appearance of a positive and broad Argentine elite consensus that even included former allies of the military. This consensus seemed to center on the unprecedented acceptance of political democracy. In fact, however, the consensus was mainly negative; that is, it was based on a rejection of the military, which became the favorite scapegoats for Argentina's problems. Thus, the underlying causes of elite disunity were not made explicit, much less removed.

I have argued that one of the reasons for the absence of an elite settlement in Argentina was the "ease" of the transition process. In Chile, conversely, once it became apparent that the maximalist proposals of the two sides were unfeasible, they were forced to bargain. Given the lack of agreement on substantive issues – for example, an economic model, standards of social justice – the partial settlement between the opposition's Grand Coalition and the moderate segment of Pinochet's allies was focused on procedural matters. The opposition and the former Pinochetistas agreed about modifying the rules of the 1988 plebiscite and its institutional effects, as well as accepting whatever result it produced.

Within the Chilean opposition, a second partial settlement was achieved between the Christian Democrats and the Socialists. Both parties, whose final confrontation had decisively contributed to the breakdown of democracy in the 1970s, saw that the formation of a majoritarian governmental coalition was needed in order to avoid a repetition of those events. The substance of this settlement was explicitly designed to deal with the challenges that the democratic government installed in 1990 would face: (1) the need to govern in the context of economic adjustments and proliferating social demands and (2) the establishment of stable civilian supremacy over a military that still enjoyed significant prerogatives.

But in addition to these issues, these partial settlements reflected Chile's political past. First, it reflected a process of political learning in which some of the parties explicitly acknowledged the negative effects that their anticoalitional strategies had had on political stability between 1953 and 1973. Also, the 1988 settlements entailed a revaluation of, and a return to, the style of political bargaining developed during the three Radical presidencies (1938–52).

This reference to political trends in Chile before the advent of mass-based political democracy leads to a final conceptual point. The political resources needed to achieve elite settlements, as well as the obstacles that render them improbable, are related to the historical route followed by any given society before the beginning of the state of enlarged political participation associated with universal suffrage. The likelihood of positive elite transformations leading to the consolidation of democracy is in part determined by the characteristics of the predemocratic political system. More specifically, the prospects for democratic consolidation can be affected by patterns of elite bargaining and conflict that develop before the transition to mass political participation. This observation leads me to propose a slight modification in the theoretical framework set forth in Chaper 1 of this book: Burton, Gunther, and Higley argue that "in independent states with long records of political instability and authoritarian rule, distinctive *elite transformations*, carried out by the elites themselves, constitute the main and possibly the only route to democratic consolidation." I agree with the core of the authors' argument, but I think that in the analysis of contemporary political systems, they tend to regard the juncture of the elite settlement (or even the more extended process of elite convergence) as a boundary that separates two historical stages too sharply. Elite settlements, like the English and the Swedish ones, which took place centuries before the advent of mass democracy, paved the way for democratic consolidation in the twentieth century. This does not imply that past political developments that do not result in elite settlements are irrelevant to democratic consolidation at a later stage. More specifically, the examples of Chile and Uruguay suggest that a tradition of intermittent political stability, albeit not associated with full mass democracy, might be an asset for the consolidation of democracy at a later time.

Between independence and the stage of full political mobilization (i.e., during the century that followed the 1820s), Latin American societies moved along three distinct political routes. The first was that of constitutional oligarchic rule, involving attempts to induce political modernization and to control from above the expansion of participation. Argentina, Chile, Uruguay, and, at a later stage, Costa Rica followed this route. In it, sources of elite disunity were related to patterns of middle- and lower-class incorporation into the political system. The second route was that of unchallenged elite supremacy. This was taken by the three countries in which political and economic power was most decentralized on a regional basis: Colombia, Mexico (until 1911), and Brazil. In those countries, elite disunity centered on conflicts among regional elites, as well as on the relationship between the central government and the provincial powers. In the third variant, military *caudillismo* and political instability were the dominant features. Peru, Bolivia, Ecuador, Central America (with the exception of Costa Rica), Venezuela, and Mexico between 1911 and 1929 fall into this category, in which elites faced the task of creating political mechanisms (constitutional or otherwise) to replace the use of military force for managing disputes. On the one hand, elites often tended to agree on freezing the traditional agrarian order, but on the other hand, they were largely incapable of establishing rules for controlling scarce governmental resources.

In each of the three routes, the patterns of elite disunity were different, and so were the problems that had to be solved through an eventual elite settlement or elite convergence. In both Argentina and Chile, the causes of elite disunity were mostly related to the incorporation of the lower and middle classes into the political system. As a result, the two countries experienced serious institutional breakdowns in the 1920s and again in the 1970s. Nevertheless, Chile was able to return to the road to stable democracy, though not without serious convulsions. The partial elite settlements reached in 1988–9 were decisive steps in eliminating the underlying and protracted causes of both potential and real instability. The combined legacies of oligarchic parliamentarism (1891–1924) and party reconciliation (1938–52) also made for relatively resilient patterns of elite bargaining. These patterns, in turn, were not fully eroded during the authoritarian regime of General Pinochet (1973–90). Ultimately, the elites' bargaining predispositions became a political resource that helped bring about the successful settlements of the late 1980s.

Argentina, conversely, provides an example of what can happen in the absence of a tradition of political bargaining among elites. Between 1916 and 1955, Radicals, Conservatives, and Peronists each attempted to achieve political dominance. Consequently, they did not favor negotiation with their political adversaries. The Conservatives sought dominance through electoral fraud (1930–43). The other two parties, which have remained Argentina's largest electoral forces, aspired to build "national movements" capable of both representing the majority of the Argentine population and imposing elite unity. Their unsuccessful attempts to achieve dominance also impaired their capabilities of successfully representing sectoral interests and orientations. In sum, the parties' failure to unite the "whole" paralleled their inability to represent the "parts," that is, the different sectors of Argentine society. At a later stage in the parties' period of preeminence (1955–83), the military reproduced the failures of the civilian elites.

In both countries, the analysis of the predemocratic era helps us comprehend the likelihood of democratic consolidation. Neither of the countries achieved "early" settlements in the fashion of England and Sweden. It would be a mistake, however, to ignore the legacies of their distinct historical processes of partial and even fitful democratization that were superseded by instability and/or authoritarianism at a later stage. In England and Sweden, early elite settlements inaugurated a path toward political democracy that was completed centuries later. In Latin America, Chile and Uruguay are examples of early processes of elite bargaining that culminated only much later in the elite settlements or partial settlements that are inextricably associated with the establishment of consolidated democracies.

8

Elites in an unconsolidated democracy: Peru during the 1980s

HENRY DIETZ

Instability has been a chief feature of political regimes in Peru since the country's independence in the 1820s. Civilian governments have been the exception; military coups have been frequent; and various reformist and leftist parties have usually been repressed, harassed, and otherwise prevented from participating freely in the political system. During the 1980s, however, there were indications that this pattern has been interrupted, if not broken. Three presidential elections and four municipal elections occurred during this decade. The elections conformed to constitutional prescriptions, and they resulted in two peaceful transfers of government executive power – in 1985 and again in 1990 – to opponents of the sitting government, something that had happened only once during the preceding sixty years, in 1945. Thus the pattern of Peruvian politics during the past decade suggested an important shift to procedural democracy. It would be rash, however, to infer from these developments that Peru has undergone a process of democratic consolidation. The regime continues to be attacked by a powerful insurgent force – the Sendero luminoso or "Shining Path" movement – the economy is in tatters; social and economic inequalities are extreme; and the fragmentation of political alignments is pronounced, as evidenced by the overnight emergence and victory of the previously unknown Alberto Fujimori in the 1990 presidential election.

Peru during the 1980s is thus best thought of as an unconsolidated democracy: The regime was functioning according to democratic procedures, with freely contested elections based on universal suffrage, relatively unrestricted mass media, and serious attempts to protect civil liberties, but there were many indications that it lacked stability. In line with the scheme advanced in Chapter 1, one of the major political problems that Peru faces is elite disunity. But in addition, the country faces enormous substantive problems as well. Peru has been in a state of sustained economic and social deterioration since the late 1970s, and its dismal levels of poverty, socioeconomic inequality, demographic change, and political violence are probably the greatest in South America. Indeed, one of the most remarkable aspects of Peru during the 1980s was the coexistence of democratic politics with this more general deterioration in the social fabric.

The democratic transition that Peru underwent in the late 1970s involved an important coming together of previously warring elite factions, specifically the leaders of the APRA (the Popular American Revolutionary alliance) and of the military regime that had been in power since 1968. Through a series of negotiations and understandings, these deeply opposed elites agreed to put their long-standing animosities behind them and to cooperate in returning Peru to democratic politics. But this agreement between two key elite factions did not extend to other important elites. In the language of this volume, Peru's democratic transition did not involve an elite transformation from disunity to consensual unity, although it is important not to minimize the significance of the APRA–military accord that did take place.

What are the chances that Peru's democratic regime might yet undergo consolidation? From our theoretical standpoint, the question is whether some more comprehensive elite settlement may be fashioned or, perhaps more pertinently, whether a gradual elite convergence may get under way. After first examining the role that elites played in Peru's transition to an unconsolidated democracy in the late 1970s and early 1980s, I shall analyze patterns of elite politics during the past ten years in order to assess the prospects for democratic consolidation in the 1990s.

Elite disunity and regime instability after 1968

Peru is one of the most complex and heterogeneous countries of Latin America. Its geographic division into a coastal plain, Andean highlands, and eastern rain forest, together with the domination of Lima, which is eight to ten times larger than Peru's second city, have been the bases of profound ethnic and cultural cleavages throughout the country's modern history. A privileged white urban population situated on the coastal plain is clearly distinct from an impoverished rural Indian peasantry located mainly in the highlands and the rain forest, and both population segments are overlaid by a large mestizo population whose sheer weight of numbers has made it an increasingly important social force since World War II. Moreover, the gap between wealthy and poor people resulting from a maldistribution of economic and political power in Peru has always been extreme, even by Latin American standards.

Until the end of World War I, the government was largely controlled by Lima's small elite in close alliance with a landed oligarchy, the military, and the church (Bourricaud 1970; Malpica 1970; Stephens 1971). Whenever the rule of these elites was threatened, the military would as a matter of course either assume control directly or eliminate the threat through repressive means. But in the late 1920s, such predictable and restricted interactions among elites were disrupted. The emergence of organized labor, successful reform movements for a minimum wage, and an eight-hour working day, as well as urbanization and a modern communications and transportation infrastructure, led to increasing, if often poorly articulated, demands for political participation and change. Out of this ferment came the first mass-based political parties, most especially APRA, which was created by Victor Raúl Haya de la Torre in 1924. APRA derived much of its intellectual and ideological radicalism from José Carlos Mariátegui, the founder of Peru's Communist party. Yet the basis of APRA's mass support came from an alliance of middle-class elements and organized labor. The party was until the 1950s the main radical party in Peru, and from its formation it was perceived by the entrenched elites as a fundamental threat. The 1931 presidential election was the first occasion for open competition among mass-based parties, and in that campaign APRA fought against another populist movement organized by Luis Sánchez Cerro. In a bitterly disputed election, APRA lost, but less than a year later Sánchez was assassinated by an Aprista, and an abortive APRA uprising in the coastal city of Trujillo (Haya de la Torre's birthplace) created a deep enmity between APRA and the military that lasted through the 1960s.

APRA was never able to win a presidential election while Haya de la Torre was alive (he died in 1979), but the possibility that it could win or that it might exercise power through control of Congress or through an alliance with other parties was reason enough for the military to intervene against it a number of times. The party's militancy, violence, and occasionally insurrectionary tactics provided the military with all the motivation it needed to be implacably anti-APRA. In 1945, for example, José Luis Bustamante was elected as a civilian president with APRA support, and he named several Apristas to his cabinet. But in 1948 the military overthrew Bustamante; Haya de la Torre was forced to take political asylum in the Colombian embassy in Lima for the next five years; and the coup leader, General Manuel Odría, pursued and persecuted Apristas until he stepped down in 1956. In that year's elections, APRA bided its time and supported the conservative candidacy of Manuel Prado. By then, Haya de la Torre was searching for a way to shed his party's obstructive and violent image, and he moderated APRA's old radicalism, changing its ideological emphasis to become more anti-Communist. But these moves did not attract significantly more voter support; instead, they caused a party split that culminated in an ill-fated guerrilla insurrection during 1965. In 1962, Haya ran as the APRA candidate, and he came very close to winning the one third of the popular vote required by the constitution for outright victory. Again, however, the military intervened with a coup that put an end to any chance that APRA might have had to cobble together a dominant coalition in Congress. In 1963, new elections were won by Fernando Belaúnde Terry, the candidate of Acción popular (AP), after which Haya, desperate to prove his willingness to compromise, formed a pact with Odría, his old enemy, in an effort to win the presidency at the next scheduled elections in 1969.

In 1968, however, the military intervened yet again with a coup. Historically, as already noted, the military regularly took control of government when civilians demonstrated their incompetence, when some sort of constitutional stalemate occurred, or when civil strife reached an intolerable level. By 1968, Belaúnde's administration was encountering severe economic difficulties, and it showed clear signs of floundering. Moreover, the prospect that APRA might win the following year's election was growing. Thus the coup in 1968 occasioned little surprise. What followed it was much more surprising, however. The military elite, led by General Juan Velasco Alvarado, quickly made it clear that it no longer had confidence in civilian politicians, parties, and electoral politics in general and that it was going to govern Peru indefinitely in order to carry out basic social and economic changes. Styling itself the "revolutionary government of the armed forces," the Velasco regime (1968–75) undertook wide-ranging, but ultimately overambitious, programs of agrarian reform, social mobilization, and state penetration of the economy (Lowenthal 1975; McClintock and Lowenthal 1983). Despite exhortations that "the Revolution is for you!" popular support was not forthcoming. The agrarian reform was unevenly implemented, and most of the poorest peasants were unaffected. Low-income groups were unwilling to support the military's "revolution" without immediate material rewards, and efforts to create large-scale agricultural cooperatives failed. Moreover, macro-economic conditions deteriorated, with world commodity prices slumping, foreign and domestic investments declining, and double- and then triple-digit inflation producing massive currency devaluations and lost purchasing power.

In 1975, a countercoup in the military overthrew General Velasco and his reformist comrades (the so-called *radicales*), replacing him with the more conservative General Francisco Morales Bermúdez, who belonged to the military's *institucionales* faction that was mainly concerned, as its label suggested, with ensuring the military's survival as an institution. Reflecting on this shift in the military, Morales Bermúdez later stated: "The armed forces as an institution could not stay indefinitely in power because it would compromise its existence as an institution and because the doors had to be opened to civilians and national majorities in search of their own destiny" (Morales Bermúdez 1989, p. 179). In an effort to appease the economic elites, Morales Bermúdez scaled back many of his predecessor's reformist schemes, and to appease the political elites, he began to seek a way to restore democratic government. But despite his desire to return the government to civilian hands, there was little reason to think that the long-standing elite disunity and regime instability could be terminated. As the 1970s neared their end, accordingly, there were few reasons for expecting that Peru was about to enter what, by its standards, would prove to be a prolonged period of democratic politics.

Peru's democratic transition

Political parties had not been outlawed by the military regime, and they were the obvious vehicles for a transfer of power. Nor had labor unions been banned, although the military regime had tried to coopt and change them through a variety of largely unsuccessful tactics. Once Morales Bermúdez began to adopt more conservative economic policies, including a number of austerity measures, in an attempt to convince the economic elites that the military's reformist impulse had been stilled, unions and popular groups more generally reacted angrily and sometimes violently with strikes and protests, including a general strike in July 1977. The first such action of its kind since 1919, this strike was supported by the largest union confederation, by all leftist and centrist parties including APRA, and by peasant organizations.

The 1977 strike carried the unmistakable message that attempts by the military to slow or avoid a transfer of power to civilians would result only in greater turmoil that would further undermine the military's already weak credibility. Even before the strike, however, Morales Bermúdez had signaled that he would be willing to discuss a return to popularly elected government. Speaking in Trujillo, the bastion of APRA support, in 1976, he referred to the decades-long feud between APRA and the military and argued: "It is time to forget the struggles between brothers," a sentiment that immensely pleased Haya de la Torre (Sanchez 1989, p. 129). In early 1977, the military government drafted its Plan Tupac Amaru, which proposed turning power over to civilians after electing a Constituent Assembly in 1978 that would draft a new constitution. The plan stated that "if we do not achieve an active consensus and an historical commitment between the armed forces and civilians, the viability of Peru as a democratic society will be in doubt" (Handelman and Sanders 1981, p. 96). This was a statement remarkable not only for its conciliatory nature but also for its premise that democracy was preferred by both civilians and the military.

Through a careful examination of relevant documents as well as a series of personal interviews with surviving elites, Sanchez (1989, pp. 130–1) determined that the military government undertook a series of private discussions with various political and social leaders to determine a political timetable for planning elections and transferring power. On October 4, 1977, the military adopted its Plan Tupac Amaru, which contained just such a detailed schedule. This stipulated that although the military had decided to turn power over to civilians, the democratic transition would have to guarantee that the structural changes in the society made by the military regime would remain intact. A newspaper interview with General Morales Bermúdez on October 16, 1977, made the point clear: "If reforms are not ratified, then the de facto government, that is, the government, annuls the [Constituent] Assembly and the story is over. [But]. . . . the military government, with me or another person, will continue" (Abugattas 1987, p. 133).

The discussions that the military initiated were private, face-to-face meetings between Morales Bermúdez and leaders of all the major political parties: Acción popular, the Partido demócrata cristiano, the Partido popular cristiano, and the Partido comunista peruano. Some of the newer and more radical leftist groups were excluded, however. Morales Bermúdez was open to a variety of suggestions throughout these discussions, but he remained adamant that the new constitution and the transfer of power would have to guarantee that the major changes the military had implemented would not be rolled back. After the ratification of the Plan Tupac Amaru, the military leaders continued their dialogue with the major parties, and in June 1978 a Constituent Assembly election was held to select one hundred delegates who would be charged with producing a new constitution within a year. Twelve parties representing the entire political spectrum won enough votes to be seated in the Assembly. A conspicuous absentee was Belaúnde's AP party, which refused to participate on the grounds that a new constitution was unnecessary and that presidential and legislative elections should instead be held immediately.

The Constituent Assembly elections on June 18, 1978, took place in difficult and threatening circumstances. Many leftist parties and unions were mobilizing supporters to protest the military's economic policies, which suggested that the left was more interested in fomenting strikes and unrest than in electoral processes (CIED 1980). Strike activity and associated violence triggered considerable government repression, and many doubts were expressed that the Assembly elections could or would be held. A strike by 100,000 teachers was eventually supported by all three of Peru's largest labor unions, and a general strike in late May 1978, though not as widely supported as the 1977 general strike, was enormously costly in lost production (Pease and Filomeno 1980a, p. 3077).

These actions were vigorously resisted by the military, which detained or deported large numbers of labor union and leftist political leaders, some of whom were campaigning for election to the Constituent Assembly. It also shut down some newspapers and other publications. Before the election, the military announced that all parties, regardless of their ideological persuasion, would be given free television time. But this move simply allowed the more radical and intransigent parties to mobilize more easily and to repudiate the military government more extensively. Gradually, however, the several sides in the struggle began to realize that the whole attempt to restore civilian government might collapse. The generals realized that public hostility toward their rule was genuinely widespread and not just left wing in nature. For their part, the political leaders realized that the military meant what its leaders said: Too much violence would lead to terminating the transition. Political elites thus had to decide whether the continued mass mobilization and its accompanying violence were worth the risk, and the military elite had to contemplate the enormous upheaval that would result if it canceled the Constituent Assembly election. More and more, the political leaders decided to concentrate on making sure that the right of all parties to be heard during the election campaign would be respected. And the military government replaced General Luis Cisneros, its hard-line minister of the interior, with General Pedro Richter Prada, a more low-key, conciliatory figure who allowed the newspapers and magazines to reopen and who reinstated most political rights under the existing constitution.

Considerable doubt about whether the election would be held continued right up to polling day, but in the event, Peruvians went to the polls and chose the one hundred Assembly delegates from among twelve competing parties. APRA won a plurality of the votes and hence of the delegates (35.3 percent and thirty-seven delegates), followed closely by the various leftist parties (some of which had formed electoral alliances, others of which campaigned independently) with about 33 percent of the vote and thirty-four delegates. The PPC, representing the right, took 23.8 percent of the vote and twenty-five delegates, and two smaller right-wing parties won two seats each. As noted, the AP did not participate. The overall result was that APRA and PPC together could control a working majority of sixty-two delegates, and Haya de la Torre was duly elected president of the Assembly.

This result was important in several respects. First, it showed that APRA was still a major political force throughout the country and that, at least in the absence of Belaúnde's AP, it could command a plurality of votes. Second, it showed that the left was also a major electoral force, despite its manifest tendencies to splinter and its inability to form a united front. Third, the relatively even distribution of the vote among right, left, and center made the election acceptable to most political groups, giving all three elite camps a voice in the constitution-writing process and a stake in its outcome as well. The election was also important because it extended the suffrage to all those eighteen years and older. In short, "the Assembly thus became an accepted and legitimate political forum for the military government, the traditional right [PPC], the traditional populists [APRA], and the left" (Sanchez 1989, p. 147).

Political fragmentation nevertheless remained the order of the day. Leftist parties fought one another over numerous ideological and personal issues, and the APRA–PPC alliance in the Assembly was clearly a fragile expedient. Moreover, although economic decline was producing disruptive strikes and much popular mobilization, there was no single event or clear crisis that might galvanize political leaders to cooperate with much effectiveness. Thus, there were ample grounds for doubting that the Constituent Assembly could produce a new constitution, let alone usher in a successful democratic transition. As if to bear out such doubts, the Assembly opened with an acrimonious debate over whether its principal task was to write a constitution or to act as the legitimate government. Both the left and the center–left demanded that the Assembly become the sovereign ruling body, that it repudiate the military government, and that it assume legislative powers forthwith (Pease and Filomeno 1980a, p. 3172). These demands were, of course, adamantly opposed by the military. As something of a compromise, the Assembly arrogated to itself the right to debate issues of national importance (e.g., human rights violations, economic measures), but by the end of August, the left and the center–left had dropped their original demands, and the Assembly began to take on what might be described as two faces.

The first was its public face, featuring theatrics, histrionics, walkouts by the left, and other symbolic actions in plenary sessions that were open to the public (Sanchez 1989, pp. 149–53). Avidly followed by the media, these sessions began late in the afternoon and frequently ran until early the following morning. The delegates themselves agreed that the plenary sessions were primarily theatrical because of their open nature and the extensive media coverage. The left routinely disagreed with the APRA–PPC majority on most questions, not only for ideological reasons but also because at the time many leftist delegates were actively involved in strikes and other protest activities. The military tried to discredit these leaders by portraying them as disruptive radicals and arresting the most active of them. Upon their arrest, however, these individuals were turned over to the Assembly, which immediately released them (Sanchez 1989, p. 151).

Behind this circus-like atmosphere was the Assembly's other face, and it was a more consensual one. Shortly after the Assembly convened, the principal commission of the constitution, consisting of twenty-five members appointed on the basis of proportional representation, began to meet steadily in sessions that were described by one participant as "arduous but cordial" (Sanchez 1989, p. 154). On the basis of his interviews with surviving elites, Sanchez observed:

> The members of the principal commission, away from the galleries of the Assembly and the news media, conducted themselves "differently" – the speeches and diatribes were replaced by "civilized" discussions concerning the nature of the new [constitution]. One member of the principal commission, not particularly fond of the left, admitted, "We all became great friends." (Sanchez 1989, p. 155)

The principal commission began its work in September 1978, and it finished a draft of the constitution in late March 1979, though it continued to function until the constitution stood ready for signature in July of that year. Meeting for four hours a day, five days a week, it became a forum for substantial inter-elite consultations. Commission members asked for and received much external advice from sources such as former presidents (especially the absent Belaúnde), the church (which urged the separation of church and state), university rectors, various union leaders, and military leaders. This last group was especially important, of course, and by October 1978 there was a weekly meeting between the military government's prime minister, General Oscar Molina, and political leaders. Weekly meetings were also held between APRA and PPC leaders. Less frequent contacts between the military and various leftist party leaders took place as early as August 2, 1978, when General Molina met with Genaro Ledesma, a leading leftist assemblyman (Pease and Filomeno 1980a, p. 3164).

Various subcommissions also exhibited a serious and sober approach to their tasks. The Economic and Financial Regime subcommission brought in a variety of academic experts to help formulate relevant parts of the constitution, and the Agrarian Regime subcommission did the same. However, some subcommissions had trouble because of the conflicting activities of leftist Assembly members who were involved in ongoing strikes and other protests. In the Labor and Union Rights subcommission, in which the left should have had considerable input and influence, only one leftist member out of four participated regularly in its deliberations. The left's inability to speak with a unified voice on matters with which it was particularly concerned also undercut its influence (Sanchez 1989, p. 156).

Military leaders did not simply sit back and let the Constituent Assembly process take its course. In a mid-October 1978 press conference, Morales Bermúdez let it be known that he had authorized the prime minister, General Molina, along with other cabinet members, to begin a series of weekly meetings with political leaders. Such meetings were in fact held regularly between the military and the leaders of APRA and the PPC, though less regularly between the military leaders of left-wing parties (Sanchez 1989, p. 159). The closest contacts were between the military and APRA. Morales Bermúdez and Haya de la Torre met personally at least three times, and numerous close observers agree that by early 1979 the two old enemies had reached some sort of modus vivendi (Sanchez 1989, pp. 159–60). Luis Alberto Sánchez, APRA's second in command, commented that it was "possible to talk even with the devil," and he said that the long-standing animosity between the two leaders had become a thing of the past (Pease and Filomeno 1980b, pp. 3396, 3431). Finally, APRA and the PPC met frequently from the start in order to coordinate their majority in the Assembly.

Three months of plenary sessions were held between the completion of the constitution's draft in April 1979 and the deadline that the military had given the Assembly to do its work. During these final sessions, there was serious debate between the left and APRA and/or the PPC, and at times between the PPC and APRA, over crucial points such as the method for selecting a president, whereas from the outside, the military voiced deep concern about other issues, such as transitional decrees that would constrict its ability to rule until elections were held. At base, military leaders insisted that the 1933 constitution remain the law of the land until the new constitution could be promulgated in 1980. Virtually all parties quietly accepted this view "in order not to antagonize the regime and jeopardize the transfer of power" (Abugattas 1987, p. 137). The Assembly was dissolved in mid-1979, and presidential and legislative elections were scheduled for the following year. Elites from parties of every ideological hue had participated in the transition, as had the military elite, and the goal of moving to a democratic regime overshadowed the fundamental differences that still separated them.

It is clear that the democratic transition could not have occurred without the interactions between APRA and the military leadership, first and foremost, and between these two key elites and the leaders of other parties and institutions, more secondarily. In addition, the processes of electing the Constituent Assembly and of writing the constitution gave all significant elite groups access to decision making about basic matters. This access created many short-term crises, but in the longer run all elites were able to register their concerns. No elite could claim to have been excluded and thus argue that the process was fundamentally illegitimate. In these respects, the Constituent Assembly embodied features of an elite settlement, but it did not lead to a consolidated democracy. One reason was, paradoxically, the openness of the process. Having all elites (and many subelites) involved meant that the resulting constitution was at least minimally acceptable to all, but it also meant that the constitution would not be a focused, strong mechanism that could bolster order and stability. In this sense, the Peruvian experiment in constitution making anticipated the similar process that unfolded in Brazil during the mid-1980s (see Chapter 9).

Peru in the 1980s

The presidential and legislative elections of 1980 were a watershed in several respects. First, they signified Peru's return to democratic government and thus the culmination of the process that began with the 1978 Constituent Assembly election. Second, they were manifestly free and fair contests in which parties from all points of the compass participated. Third, they were the first elections in Peruvian history in which illiterates were allowed to vote. In an ironic twist, the voters returned Belaúnde Terry to the presidency, enabling him to vindicate his 1968 overthrow and exile with a resounding personal victory (about 45 percent of the popular vote). Belaúnde's return to power was sweeping because his AP won absolute majorities in both houses of the legislature. For the moment at least, many voters were prepared to forget the economic chaos that had been evident in 1968 and that had given the military one of its primary justifications for seizing power.

APRA, on the other hand, was in disarray. Haya de la Torre died shortly after signing the constitution in 1979, and his party was engaged in a bitter succession struggle. Whether it would prove to be more than a movement dependent on the lingering presence and charisma of Haya de la Torre was an open question. After a conservative faction split off, the mainstream APRA leaders pulled together behind Armando Villaneuva, a longtime party loyalist, but the APRA finished a poor second in the election, with 27 percent of the vote.

In late 1979, before the election, Belaúnde Terry tried to put together a dominant center–right coalition by calling for a Peruvian version of the Pact of Punto Fijo that had been so crucial to Venezuela's democratic transition in 1958 (see Chapter 3). On 20 November 1979, Belaúnde, Luis Bedoya Reyes of the PPC, and Villanueva from the APRA met to discuss the possibilities of reaching such an accord, but it never came about, principally because of APRA's reluctance to align itself with the right, despite its alliance with the PPC to control the Constituent Assembly. The PPC then named Bedoya as its candidate, but the party came in third with just under 10 percent of the vote. This showing contrasted sharply with the PPC's strength in the 1978 Constituent Assembly election (about 24 percent). Clearly, the presence of Belaúnde and the AP in the 1980 election cut deeply into the PPC's support.

Despite its strong showing in the Constituent Assembly election, the left could not survive political prosperity, and it splintered fatally in 1980. Any complete account of the splits, fractures, and agonized attempts to patch together a more powerful leftist coalition is a study in itself (see CIED 1980; Pease and Filomeno 1980b, 1982). Suffice it to say that several leftist parties began negotiations to form electoral coalitions in October 1979, and by January 1980 a group called the Leftist Revolutionary alliance (ARI) emerged from a partnership of Maoist and Trotskyite parties. Another leftist front composed of the more traditional leftist parties also came together about the same time. But as the election approached, ideological and programmatic differences, personal rivalries, and an inability to agree on the distribution of congressional seats caused one party after another to abandon these and other coalitions. Javier Díez Canseco, a prominent leader of one leftist party, literally wept while reading telegrams from provincial organizations that begged the national parties to stay together (*Car-*

etas, March 3, 1980, p. 13). In the end, the five left-wing presidential candidates together garnered only 16 percent of the popular vote.

Following his victory, Belaúnde made efforts at conciliation. He created a commission to establish a government based on a broad front of parties, and he offered two ministerial positions each to the PPC and APRA. Though APRA rejected the offer (the PPC accepted it), Villanueva visited Belaúnde and promised that his party would act as a constructive opposition. The AP leaders continued their dialogue with other parties, and before inauguration day they had met with virtually all political groups. In addition, Belaúnde met with the military leadership during May and June 1980, receiving a promise from General Morales Bermúdez that the military government would not make any important policy decisions without first consulting Belaúnde, who promised in return that he would not interfere with the military command structure (Pease and Filomeno 1982, p. 4004).

Belaúnde thus entered office in 1980 with popular support and with many indications of the willingness of opposing elites to cooperate in preventing a recurrence of old conflicts and enmities. The party system was well developed, with vigorous spokesmen for a wide range of ideological positions, and the military had come down strongly on the side of civilian rule after achieving a truce with APRA, its oldest and most bitter enemy. But these favorable political circumstances were offset by a variety of problems, especially a much-expanded electorate that was suffering under a deepening economic crisis, fairly high levels of mass mobilization after the electoral campaigns, strikes and other popular actions of the previous two years, and the Shining Path insurgency that was about to begin its unprecedented violence.

In November 1980, six months after Belaúnde's triumph, the AP won the Lima mayoral election and various provincial city elections, although by margins that were somewhat less than those in the presidential and legislative elections. The left, which had finally coalesced into a fragile aggregation called the United Left (IU), ran on a platform that favored Lima's low-income groups but that also showed a commitment to electoral politics and the democratic process. The IU thus demonstrated some grass-roots strength, whereas APRA continued to be in disarray after Villanueva's defeat, and it finished badly in the voting outside its traditional northern strongholds.

By the time of the November 1983 local elections, Belaúnde's policies had proved ineffective in combating the economic crisis. APRA had in the meantime smoothed over its internal differences, and the IU was still intact. The AP fared badly in these local races, finishing fourth (of four major parties) in Lima, whereas the APRA and IU showed considerable strength throughout the country. The IU did particularly well in Lima, where it won the mayoral race and all of the races in the city's poor districts as well (Dietz 1985). These elections were widely viewed as a referendum on Belaúnde's performance and a precursor to the 1985 presidential contest.

In the 1985 campaign, Alán García emerged as the great hope for a new generation of APRA followers and for many other Peruvians. García won almost half the popular vote in a four-man presidential race, and APRA also dominated the newly elected Congress. The IU finished a distant second, but the Belaúnde government's administrative record was so dismal that the AP did not even compete in the elections. The 1986 local elections only reinforced APRA's electoral grip, giving it the mayoralty of Lima and a majority of the city's precincts, as well as numerous provincial mayoral and city council victories.

But after eighteen months of seeming economic success, the García government encountered many of the same problems as Belaúnde had, and with similarly disastrous political consequences. García's initial public approval rating, which approached 90 percent at times, fell rapidly as the economic miseries mounted, the policy failures multiplied, and the Sendero luminoso's campaign of violence spread throughout the Andean region and into urban Peru. The 1989 municipal and congressional elections reflected these difficulties. Ricardo Belmont, a television personality with no prior political experience, won Lima's mayoralty election, and a newly created center–right coalition called the Democratic Front (FREDEMO), led by the writer Mario Vargas Llosa, finished second in Lima, won numerous provincial elections, and gained a plurality of seats in Congress. With García's public approval rating now hovering in the teens, APRA lost all of the Lima precincts it won in 1986, and nationally it captured less than 20 percent of the vote. The left fared equally badly. As attention turned to the 1990 presidential elections, it thus appeared that a powerful center–right force, FREDEMO (Frente democrático) might be about to establish long-term electoral dominance.

During the first months of the 1990 election campaign, FREDEMO was the clear front-runner, and the most important question was whether Vargas Llosa could avoid a runoff election by taking a majority of the popular vote outright in the April election. But FREDEMO's campaign tactics and Vargas Llosa's draconian proposals for privatization of the economy and other economic shock treatments created much public unease, so that Alberto Fujimori, a little-known independent candidate, moved from the 5 percent level in public opinion polls three weeks before the election to finish a close second, with 31 percent, as compared with Vargas Llosa's 34 percent of the vote. A June runoff election was thereby required, and from it Fujimori emerged as the clear winner, with almost 60 percent of the popular vote.

Fujimori's election and Vargas Llosa's defeat stunned virtually all observers and pollsters, although Ricardo Belmont's win just a few months earlier might have been seen as a bellwether. Like Belmont, Fujimori was not a politician. Neither man had any connection with existing parties, and both ran campaigns that highlighted their independence and their supposed ties with ordinary Peruvians. However, Fujimori's victory depended at least as much on a call for voters to reject his opponent, Vargas Llosa, as for them to vote for him. The vote in the runoff election showed a remarkably clear correlation between social class and voting behavior, with the extent of support for Vargas Llosa declining directly with the voters' social status. In Lima in particular, Fujimori tapped a reservoir of votes from what is locally called Lima *cholo,* meaning low-income, mestizo, and Indian residents, as distinct from Lima *pituco,* the white, upper-class residents that had always dominated the electoral process through cooptation and control of the major parties and their candidates. Fujimori won by margins of three to two, two to one, and even three to one in Lima *cholo,* and because those areas have enormous populations, the margins he enjoyed in them more than offset Vargas Llosa's wins in Lima *pituco.* The same pattern appeared throughout the country, where Vargas Llosa went down to defeat almost everywhere.

Fujimori's victory has several implications. One concerns the low level of party institutionalization in Peru today. The inability of the parties that dominated electoral politics during the 1980s to cope with the protracted and deep economic crisis has greatly weakened them and contributed to the emergence of maverick, antiestablishment candidates and movements that play on the voters' desperation. Fujimori's surprise victory also implies increased elite disunity. Supported by fervent Protestant evangelicals, Fujimori incurred the distrust and hostility of elites affiliated with the Catholic church, and he is also regarded with suspicion by the military leaders who, it was rumored, prevailed on Vargas Llosa not to withdraw after he failed to win a majority in the election's first round, lest a Fujimori victory open the way to military intervention, which the generals themselves wanted to avoid. But third, Fujimori's victory, combined with Vargas Llosa's strong showing, implies the existence of a still somewhat incoherent and unmobilized center–right majority in the electorate, for neither of the two presidential candidates was even remotely left wing, at least in terms of his stated ideology. Upon taking power in July 1990,

Fujimori immediately announced a drastic economic austerity program that in many ways went beyond anything Vargas Llosa had proposed. The result was a dramatic rise in prices across the board and the onset of a deep recession. Most observers agreed that this program was essential; evidently, preinaugural meetings with leaders of the International Monetary Fund and the World Bank convinced Fujimori that he had no alternative. Nevertheless, the fact that he had campaigned on an antiausterity program left many of his supporters dismayed. Fujimori's initial appointments also startled almost everyone. For example, he gave several key cabinet posts to members of Belaúnde's AP and to members of the left, but he named no one from his own group, Cambio 90, to his cabinet. It was thus difficult to see in Fujimori's actions much prospect for the emergence of a stable center–right elite coalition of the sort that signals the beginning of elite convergence. Instead, the first six months of Fujimori's presidency showed signs of unpredictability and instability, especially in regard to elite cooperation and accommodation. The old elites were clearly defeated in the 1990 elections, and the consequence appeared to be continuing elite disunity accompanied by still wider disparities between Peru's haves and have-nots.

To summarize Peruvian political changes during the 1980s, it must be said that in a country in which virtually all earlier attempts at democratic politics were stillborn, the uninterrupted electoral politics of these ten years was impressive, all the more so when the country's desperate social and economic circumstances are taken into account. But as Sendero luminoso's powerful insurgency (which has resulted in well over eighteen thousand deaths) indicated, Peruvian democracy remains far from consolidated in the early 1990s. Indeed, given the many signs of economic collapse and the spread of violence, it is remarkable that the democratic regime continues to function, that the military has not again intervened, and that Sendero has not advanced even further. The parallels with Colombia are, of course, unmistakable (see Chapter 3). But unlike Colombia, no elite settlement has been achieved in Peru, and there is as yet no sign that an elite convergence is getting under way.

Conclusions

Evidence that an elite settlement took place in Peru during the late 1970s is not convincing. A democratic transition certainly began in 1978, and the democratic regime that subsequently emerged has displayed considerable staying power. Crucial to the transition was the truce that APRA and the military leaders worked out in 1977 and

1978. The discussions between Haya de la Torre and Morales Bermúdez that led to the election and convening of a Constituent Assembly, along with Bermúdez's statements that the military was willing to forget its past conflicts with APRA, indicated the military elite's recognition that a democratic transition could not occur without APRA's participation. APRA had historically been able to win at least a third of the popular vote in any election in which it was allowed to participate, and it was (and today still is) by far the best-organized party in Peru. Therefore, any idea that the military might turn power over to civilians while denying APRA a role was fanciful. For their part, APRA leaders, and especially Haya de la Torre, played exemplary roles in keeping the Constituent Assembly on schedule and in adopting moderate, frequently nonpartisan stances that contributed directly to the Assembly's success.

This cooperation between APRA and the military leaders must be seen as an important elite condition for Peru's democratic transition. But it fell short of an elite settlement as understood in this book. To be sure, the circumstances that gave rise to the cooperation were in some respects analogous to those that are conducive to settlements. There had been a costly, largely inconclusive conflict between these two major elites for a long time. By the late 1970s there was also something like a precipitating crisis, in the form of the military regime's failed economic policies, a rapidly deteriorating economy, as well as mass mobilization and a spate of violence associated with strikes and other protest actions. As in a settlement, moreover, the accord between APRA and the military elites was achieved with considerable speed on the basis of face-to-face negotiations between experienced and skilled leaders, principally Haya de la Torre and Morales Bermúdez. No formal, written agreement was struck, but a series of publicly conciliatory speeches by these and other key leaders of the two sides were widely reported. Finally, APRA's victory in the Constituent Assembly election and the decision that Haya de la Torre should lead the Assembly had the military leadership's consent. An at least tacit accord between APRA and the military was thus arranged, and it was the basis for much that followed politically.

Yet the accord was very limited in its scope. Although meetings between military leaders and the leaders of other parties, especially Belaúnde and other representatives of the right, did take place, they did not lead to anything resembling the military–APRA accord. The left-wing parties and the military had only fleeting exchanges, and even though the military allowed those parties to participate in the electoral process, neither side wanted to have much to do with the other. The decision by Belaúnde and the AP to boycott the Constituent

Assembly election was further evidence that there had not been a broad settlement. Finally, the accord between APRA and the military did not call for any concessions and compromises on specific principles or issues; rather, it amounted to a kind of "live and let live" understanding, which, important as it was to getting the transition under way, remained perhaps too vague and undefined to constitute a settlement.

What evidence is there that an elite convergence may have begun in Peru after the democratic transition? First, apart from the leaders of Sendero luminoso, the elites showed themselves willing to engage in electoral politics throughout the 1980s, and Sendero's refusal to do so has been denounced by all other left-wing parties. Thus, with the important exception of Sendero's insurgent stance, the basic condition for an elite convergence – a readiness among elites to contest for power in electoral terms – exists. But it is difficult to discern the formation of a winning center–right coalition that, by dominating electoral politics, might eventually force dissident left-wing elites to emulate the winning coalition in order to gain election to executive offices. On the contrary, the record of the 1980s suggests that fragmented, poorly institutionalized parties and/or movements remain ideologically disparate and without the capacity to dominate on a longer-term basis. As the electoral victories of candidates from outside the established elites and parties suggested during the late 1980s and in 1990, the fluidity of political alignments may in fact be increasing. On the other hand, and as noted earlier, the fact that these interlopers are identified with center–right positions that apparently resonate with an electoral majority may mean that there is a basis for a winning center–right coalition that might support elite convergence.

How then should we conceive of elites and democracy in Peru at the beginning of the 1990s? Given the strength and intransigence of Sendero, the national elite cannot be classified as other than disunified. Sendero's leaders obviously do not subscribe to the existing rules of the political game or to the worth of existing political institutions. Moreover, it is still an open question whether other elites on both the left and the right display such consensus and unity. Leftist elites have clearly been weakened by their internecine disputes, but there is no evidence to suggest that the left will not continue to adhere to democratic institutions and procedures. Insofar as right-wing elites (especially the military) are concerned, it is clear that the military has no appetite for resuming the responsibilities of government after the disillusionments it experienced between 1968 and 1980. Yet just how long military leaders will have faith in the democratic regime that they in part nurtured will in large part depend on how successful the

Fujimori administration is in implementing what are bound to be extremely difficult and politically explosive economic adjustment policies and in confronting the damage wrought by Sendero luminoso.

What of the democratic regime itself? Though democratic, the regime is obviously not stable. Not only is it attempting to fight off the Sendero insurgency, but it remains mired in deep economic crisis, and it has little public support. For example, a 1988 national survey asked some fifteen hundred mainly urban respondents about their perceptions of the regime in regard to the extent to which they (1) think that courts in Peru guarantee a fair trial, (2) believe that the basic rights of citizens are well protected, (3) take pride in Peru's political system, (4) regard the political system as the best possible one, and (5) feel that they should support the political system. On a seven-point scale on which answers 5, 6, and 7 represented support for or agreement with the questions, less than a quarter of the sample responded positively to any one of the five items. Together with the Sendero insurgency and the doubts about elite commitments to the regime, this abysmal level of public support strongly suggests an unconsolidated democracy.

Given the many problems that the country confronts, it is possible that discussions of elite settlements and convergences in Peru are the equivalent of rearranging the deck chairs on the *Titanic*. Yet the argument persists that without elite consensus and unity, there is little chance of overcoming these problems. All opinion polls during the 1980s indicated that the Peruvian public favored (by wide margins) civilian democratic rule over all other options. Thus, the effort to produce the elite configurations necessary to such rule must be seen as an end in itself. Peruvian elites made important progress toward this end during the 1980s. At the beginning of the 1990s, they have probably reached a decisive point. With the economy in virtual ruins, with Sendero knocking at the door, and with a new set of elected leaders taking government power, the only alternative to a further, possibly dramatic unification of elites operating the democratic regime appears to be the abyss.

References

Abugattas, Luis. 1987. "Populism and After: The Peruvian Experience." In *Authoritarians and Democrats: Regime Transition in Latin America*, ed. James Malloy and Mitchell Seligson. Pittsburgh: University of Pittsburgh Press.

Bourricaud, François. 1970. *Power and Society in Contemporary Peru*. New York: Praeger.

CIED (Centro de información, estudio y documentación). 1980. *¿El Voto perdido? Crítica y autocrítica de la izquierda en la campaña electoral de 1980*. Lima.

Clinton, Richard. 1970. "APRA: An Appraisal." *Journal of Inter-American Studies and World Affairs* 12: 280–97.

Cotler, Julio. 1986. "Military Interventions and 'Transfer of Power to Civilians' in Peru." In *Transitions from Authoritarian Rule: Latin America*, ed. Guillermo O'Donnell, Philippe Schmitter, and Lawrence Whitehead. Baltimore: Johns Hopkins University Press.

De Soto, Hernando. 1987. *El Otro sendero*. 6th ed. Lima: Instituto libertad y democracia.

Dietz, Henry. 1980. *Poverty and Problem-solving Under Military Rule: The Urban Poor in Lima, Peru*. Austin: University of Texas Press.

1985. "Political Participation in the Barriadas: A Re-examination and Extension." *Comparative Political Studies* 18: 323–56.

1986–7. "Electoral Politics in Peru, 1978–1986." *Journal of Inter-American Studies and World Affairs* 28: 139–63.

Gorman, Stephen, ed. 1982. *Post-revolutionary Peru: The Politics of Transformation*. Boulder, CO: Westview Press.

Handelman, Howard, and Thomas Sanders, eds. 1981. *Military Government and the Movement Toward Democracy in South America*. Bloomington: Indiana University Press.

Lowenthal, Abraham, ed. 1975. *The Peruvian Experiment*. Princeton, NJ: Princeton University Press.

McClintock, Cynthia. 1985. "Why Peasants Rebel." *World Politics* 37: 48–84.

McClintock, Cynthia, and Abraham Lowenthal, eds. 1983. *The Peruvian Experiment Reconsidered*. Princeton, NJ: Princeton University Press.

Malpica, Carlos. 1970. *Los dueños de Perú*. Lima: EDESA.

Morales Bermúdez C., Francisco. 1989. *Apuntes sobre autoritarismo y democracia*. Lima: Iberoamericana de editores.

Pease García, Henry. 1988. *Democracia y precariedad bajo el populismo aprista*. Lima: DESCO.

Pease García, Henry, and Alfredo Filomeno. 1980a. *Peru, 1978: Cronología política*, vol. 7. Lima: DESCO.

1980b. *Peru, 1979: Cronología política*, vol. 8. Lima: DESCO.

1982. *Peru, 1980: Cronología política*, vol. 9. Lima: DESCO.

Sanchez, Peter. 1989. "Elite Settlements and Democracy in Latin America: The Dominican Republic and Peru." Ph.D. diss., University of Texas at Austin.

Stephens, Richard H. 1971. *Wealth and Power in Peru*. Metuchen, NJ: Scarecrow Press.

9

Brazil's political transition

THOMAS BRUNEAU

The political transition from military to civilian government in Brazil culminated in free and hotly contested elections for the presidency in late 1989. These elections were the first direct presidential elections in twenty-nine years and followed two sets of virtually free elections for the Congress, state, and local governments, as well as the proclamation of a new and democratically formulated constitution in late 1988. In terms of the procedural definition of democracy, Brazil is clearly democratic. There is a profusion of political parties representing all sectors of opinion; elections are free and vigorously contested; adult suffrage is universal; and the rights of association and expression are in force.

If one were to use a substantive definition of democracy, however, Brazil would be found wanting, owing to extremes in the distribution of wealth and influence.[1] But substantive definitions of democracy are of limited value in empirical analysis in any case, and it is noteworthy that the lower classes in Brazil, for the first time in history, have access to numerous means of political representation and participation, including unions, interest groups, and political parties. The constitution of 1988 extended the vote to illiterates, which is unique in the history of Brazil, and it lowered the age of suffrage to sixteen. The candidate of the Workers' party (PT), Luis Inácio da Silva, or "Lula," himself from the lower class and running on a platform explicitly in favor of lower-class interests, received the second largest share of votes, 16 percent, among the twenty-two candidates in the November 15, 1989, elections, and he missed being elected president of Brazil in the December 17 runoff election by a mere 6 percent of the vote.

Despite the democratic format and functioning of contemporary Brazil, there remains some question regarding regime consolidation.

1 There is an abundance of literature on poverty and socioeconomic inequality in Brazil. For a thorough, and depressing, analysis see Jaguaribe et al. 1986.

This arises because of the tremendous socioeconomic disparities associated with the maldistribution of wealth and influence, because of the economic crisis epitomized by Brazil's $115 billion foreign debt and an inflation rate of 1,700 percent in 1989, and, most important, because of the background and nature of the democratic transition itself between 1974 and 1989.

Consonant with the analytical framework used in this volume, there is ample reason to be skeptical about the chances for democratic consolidation in Brazil. If elite consensual unity is indeed necessary for stable democracy, then although Brazil is currently a functioning democracy, this may turn out to be but another passing phase in Brazil's "experiment in democracy."[2] That is, democracy may be limited to the process of holding elections, providing group access, and producing a democratically constructed constitution. In the Brazilian case, there is as yet little or no evidence of a unification of Brazilian elites. None of the specified preconditions for an elite settlement can be found in the Brazilian experience, and it thus can be seen as something of a test case for the postulated relationship between elite settlements and democratic consolidation. If consensual unity is as crucial as Chapter 1 asserts, then Brazil's prospects are bleak, for whatever elite unity has existed seems to be decreasing with the entry of new political actors into the political system.

I argue in this chapter that there has been a democratic transition in Brazil, from a military to civilian regime, but one that has occurred without an elite settlement. I speculate that an elite settlement might have taken place if Tancredo Neves had not died in 1985. However, with his death and the assumption of the presidency by José Sarney, there was no pact amounting to a settlement. Rather, elites fragmented politically as mass mobilization increased and as President Sarney abused power in seeking to achieve his own personal ends. There could have been understandings (*entendimentos*), as they are typical of Brazil's sociopolitical history, but the facilitating conditions for an elite settlement were missing.

Most students of Brazil highlight its elitist character, with tremendous disparities between classes and regions. Some observers have called particular attention to the capacity of the political elites to conciliate their differences and to allow in emergent or contesting elites, providing that they conform to the rules of the game defined by those in power. As Francisco Iglesias summarizes Brazil's political history:

2 This is the subtitle of Skidmore's book on the last democratic phase, 1946 to 1964; see Skidmore 1967.

> "The government gives up a little and the contesting element also gives up a little, and they arrive at a transition by means of a transaction. In it the two sides seem to have discovered the common denominator; the fact is, however, that demands are only partially met, and the power of the establishment is further strengthened. Thus it can be said that conciliation is always antipopular. From independence in 1822 to the political conversations of 1984, the norm has been limited gains in which the people benefit little and the [established] power emerges strengthened in its structure, able to resist for several more years the pressures of protests. (Iglesias 1985, p. 221)

From this perspective, a degree of consensus and unity has existed among the Brazilian elites, but it rests on opposition to the entry of the masses; it is an antidemocratic consensus. The history of independent Brazil provides much support for this and little support for any other interpretation. Between independence in 1822 and 1889, the country was governed by a constitutional monarch; there was a very small political elite; and there were no structures for popular participation. Between the founding of a republic in 1889 and the first direct elections for the presidency with universal adult suffrage exactly one hundred years later, only the period between 1946 and 1964 might be considered democratic. The so-called Old Republic of 1889 to 1930 was characterized by minimal development of intermediary groups, control of regional oligarchies, and an extremely limited suffrage. Between 1930 and 1945, Brazil was under the control of Getulio Vargas, who ruled explicitly as a dictator for more than half of this period. During the "experiment in democracy" between 1946 and 1964, Brazil functioned as a democracy but one characterized by a restricted suffrage, low levels of political mobilization, corporatist patterns of interest representation, and strong authoritarian tendencies (see also Burns 1980). Although there were a number of factors involving personalities and institutions, probably the single most important reason for the military coup of 1964 was the fear of change. The entrenched elites, among which the military emerged as the key element, were unwilling to extend participation, under revised rules of the game, to new political actors such as rural and urban unions, leftist political parties, and student movements. What followed were two and a half decades of military rule with very little popular political participation, even though elections were held virtually throughout the period.

During its century as a republic, then, Brazil has functioned as a procedural democracy for a maximum of eighteen years. In sum, there is little democratic tradition in Brazil and certainly no instance of democratic consolidation. Despite this unimpressive political history, Brazil has recently undergone a democratic transition and is now a functioning democracy. In the process of the complex transition, has elite consensual unity been achieved and the grounds for a consolidated democracy laid? Let us begin to address this question with a brief review of the transition.

Liberalization and the transition

The transition was initiated in 1974 with President Ernesto Geisel's "decompression" or "opening" (see Bruneau 1983; Selcher 1986; Skidmore 1988). This followed a decade of military rule, preceded the impact of the oil shock, and took place when there was a high degree of unity in the armed forces and the regime more generally. The most plausible interpretation of Geisel's decision to open the regime views it as an attempt to broaden the basis of regime support. The opening followed the closed and dictatorial government of President Emilio Garrastazu Médici (1969–74) with its high rates of economic growth, grandiose projects, and its ominous Doctrine of National Security. It became reasonable to broaden support for the regime in the wake of the so-called economic miracle of 1968–74: Industrialization and economic growth having been achieved, the authoritarian regime was less valued by important economic groups, and there was concern that the state was too large and pervasive. At the same time, sectors of the middle classes and various institutions, such as the Catholic church and the Order of Brazilian Lawyers (OAB), were alienated by torture and other obvious excesses of the military government. The unpopularity of the regime was underscored by the results of congressional elections in November 1974 that went against the government party, the National Renovating Alliance (ARENA). The lone opposition party, the Brazilian Democratic Movement (MDB), won 16 of the 22 Senate seats contested and increased its representation in the Assembly from 87 to 160. President Geisel allowed the results to stand, but between 1974 and the end of his term in 1979 he tightly controlled the timing and agenda of the opening in order to placate a hard-line opposition in the armed forces, to avoid the MDB's control of Congress and, more important, of the electoral college, which the military regime used to certify the five generals who became presidents after 1964.

Central to the control of the opening was the government's use of *casuísmos* – arbitrary and individualized measures aimed at ensuring the predominance of ARENA, later renamed the Democratic Social party (PDS). The most important series of *casuísmos* were decreed in April 1977 in anticipation of the 1978 elections and again in November 1981 and June 1982 in advance of the 1982 elections (see Fleischer 1983). These many and changing controls rigged the electoral processes in order to maintain ARENA's, and then the PDS's, control of Congress despite the increasing popularity of the MDB (later renamed the Party of the Brazilian Democratic Movement, PMDB). President Geisel controlled the succession process internally in the armed forces, and the government-controlled electoral college certified Geisel's candidate, General João Baptista Figueiredo, as president with a commitment to continue the opening. Not precisely a *casuísmo*, but serving the same function, was the political party reform of November 1979 that abolished the two parties of ARENA and MDB and allowed the creation of additional parties. The result was as intended: a proliferation of opposition parties whose role had hitherto been played by the MDB. The effect of the *casuísmos* on the November 1982 election resulted in the PDS's taking 12 of the state governorships and 42 percent of the popular vote and placing 359 members in the electoral college. The PMDB took 9 governorships (in the most important states), 44 percent of the popular vote, and 269 members in the electoral college. The other three opposition parties – Democratic Workers' party (PDT), Brazilian Workers' party (PTB), and the Workers' party (PT) – won 1 governorship, took 14.5 percent of the vote, and gained 52 members in the college. The government's PDS, then, enjoyed a comfortable majority in the electoral college which chose the next president in January 1985.

Between the elections in November 1982 and late 1984, three processes developed and interacted that ultimately undermined the planned opening envisioned by President Geisel and assumed by President Figueiredo. First, the economy deteriorated rapidly, resulting in a major recession with productive capacity at a low 72 percent rate of utilization, inflation in excess of 200 percent per annum after 1983, and high levels of unemployment. Incomes for all but the most wealthy fell. Social manifestations of the economic crisis were the riots in São Paulo in May 1983 and the sacking of grocery stores in São Paulo and Rio de Janeiro in September 1983, as well as a sharp increase in crime. The second process was the emergence of a relatively cohesive opposition, composed of four parties as well as the church, the Order of Brazilian Lawyers, the Brazilian Press Association, and various popular movements, all demanding change and improvement. The PMDB translated these demands into a call for democratic elections, specifically direct presidential elections, to choose a government with enough popular support to confront the grave socioeconomic crisis. The PMDB also called for a new constitution to replace the military-imposed constitutions of 1967 and 1969 with their strongly authoritarian thrust. The initially controlled opening had thus stimulated the rebirth of civil society in a rapidly industrializing and modernizing Brazil and the emergence of political parties demanding greater roles.

The opposition could make its demands, but President Figueiredo still held the power to decide (buttressed by the unified armed forces), and the constitution stipulated indirect presidential elections via the electoral college in January 1985. As early as November 1983, however, Figueiredo began to show that he had lost whatever talent and interest he once possessed for politics. The third process that got under way thus involved Figueiredo's decreasing ability to control the timetable and agenda of the controlled opening. Of the three processes, the last seems the most critical because the president's apparent lack of interest, his ambiguous statements and actions, and his contradictory positions threw open the transition so that the opposition, and particularly Tancredo Neves of the PMDB, could capture the initiative in determining the timing and nature of the transition.

In November 1983, President Figueiredo stated publicly that he personally was in favor of direct elections but that it was not possible to reinstate them as his party would oppose such a move. At the end of the year, however, he relinquished control of the presidential succession to the PDS. Between early 1984 and the Democratic Social party convention in August of that year, the president equivocated on the selection procedure and his own party's likely candidate for election by the electoral college. The result was that of the half-dozen potential candidates, the one with the most unsavory reputation, ex-governor of São Paulo and federal deputy, Paulo Salim Maluf, tied up the party convention and became the PDS candidate for president. It was apparent that not even Figueiredo liked Maluf, and he was held in disrepute by large sectors of society and the political elite because he exemplified the most corrupt practices of the authoritarian regime. The choice of Maluf, and the equivocation and ambiguity by Figueiredo, resulted in a major split within the PDS: Fifty-two congressmen left it and founded the Liberal Front party (PFL). Among the founders of the PFL were Vice-President Aureliano Chaves, Senator Marco Maciel, an ex-president of the PDS, as well as other key figures in the Congress. Meanwhile, President Figueiredo and other key leaders of the government gave minimal support to Maluf.

Why did so many important members of the PDS desert the party? By 1985 the political transition had achieved a certain momentum, and many politicians felt that a liberal democracy was likely to emerge sooner rather than later. In a democracy, votes are the main currency, and getting them requires popularity among the public. It should be remembered that the Brazilian military regime never dissolved Congress or eliminated elections; rather, both were constrained and controlled by *casuísmos* throughout its rule. The theme of democratic legitimacy was maintained, but its implementation through direct elections and an independent Congress was held in abeyance while attention was focused on economic and security problems. By the late 1970s there was no longer a security problem, and the economy was proving intractable; if anything, the situation was worse by 1983 than it had been when the military took power in 1964. The government was able to continue to win elections and push their measures through Congress and the electoral college only by the most blatant form of institutional innovations embodied in the *casuísmos*.

The massive campaign led by the PMDB in early 1984 for direct elections of the president, the *"direitas ja"* campaign, brought more than one million people out on the streets of São Paulo and Rio, with commensurately large crowds in other cities; these were the largest demonstrations in the history of Brazil. Had the campaign succeeded and had direct elections been held in 1985, the key political actors thereafter would have been different, and the resulting transition also very different. But an amendment for direct elections fell 22 votes short of the required two thirds in the Assembly. In any event, it would not have passed in the overwhelmingly PDS-controlled Senate, one third of whose members had been appointed by the government in 1978. However, of the 298 votes in favor, some 54 were from the PDS, which showed that the party was already splitting in the face of popular pressure to complete the transition. The party's unpopularity became obvious to Jose Sarney and others in June 1984 with local elections in Santos, São Paulo, in which – in the first direct mayoral elections in many years – the PDS candidate came in last with only 3 percent of the vote. Thus, if politicians were going to have a future in a more democratic Brazil, it would not be with the PDS and its unpalatable candidate, Maluf.

After the failure of the PMDB-led campaign for direct elections, Tancredo Neves assumed the leadership of the transition process. In order to be able to use the instruments designed by the military regime to control the agenda and timing of the transition and to prevent the election of the PDS candidate, Maluf, there had to be an understanding with the military itself. Tancredo Neves met with ex-President Geisel to discuss the transition, and in November 1984 he had a series of meetings with General Walter Pires, minister of the army. An understanding was obviously worked out whereby there would be no revenge, as in Argentina, for the excesses of the military, and the armed forces would not impede the election of Tancredo. By this time the military wanted to get out of direct political involvement (see

Dreifuss 1986; Stepan 1988). By late 1984, hard-line military leaders, such as General Newton Cruz, commander of Brasília's military district, had been transferred to positions without troop commands, and by January 15, 1985, Tancredo Neves had the support of the armed forces for his presidency.

When the electoral college met on January 15, 1985, the authoritarian regime was clearly politically bankrupt. The military were unable to oppose Tancredo Neves; Maluf could hardly appear in public without being physically attacked; and public opinion polls indicated the Figueiredo government's low level of popularity. In a televised interview in late January 1985, President Figueiredo was bitter, frustrated, and hurt; he asked only that the Brazilian people forget him. The results of the meeting of the electoral college were 480 votes for Tancredo Neves and 180 for Maluf, with 26 either absent or abstaining. In order to consolidate the support of the PFL for the PMDB in what was termed the Democratic Alliance (AD), Jose Sarney became Neves's running mate. Following his election, Tancredo Neves formed a cabinet composed of thirteen members of the PMDB and four members of the PFL and PDS dissidents.

A tremendous amount of dialogue and conciliation was required to bring the political transition to the stage of electing Tancredo Neves in early 1985, and the bulk of the credit for this achievement belonged to Tancredo. Yet at the very beginning of Tancredo Neves's "New Republic," on the night before he was to take office as president on March 15, 1985, he was hospitalized. After five weeks, the seventy-four-year-old president-elect died on April 21 of intestinal problems and complications arising from seven operations for infections and internal bleeding. Brazil was traumatized by the personal suffering of Tancredo Neves, and the transition, which had earlier seemed so promising and sure, was now in doubt. The vice-president, Jose Sarney, took the oath of office and assumed the presidency.

The choice of Sarney as Tancredo Neves's running mate had been a matter of political expediency aimed at attaining additional votes. Sarney had been identified with military governments for most of the period since 1964; he was president of the PDS from 1979 until June 1984; and he had opposed the direct elections amendment that was the principal focus of the PMDB and politics in general in early 1984. If Tancredo Neves had lived and implemented his New Republic, substantial elite consensual unity might have been achieved. Indeed, this was how he had himself elected president: Tancredo Neves undoubtedly negotiated pacts with key elements in the military government, and by obtaining the support of virtually all the opposition he had established himself as the key figure in the democratic transition.

Unfortunately, none of the pacts he negotiated was made public. On his death, a new process of negotiation was initiated, but this time in public and involving a much less capable politician, Jose Sarney. As it was, Sarney became president in less than auspicious political and economic circumstances, and he proved unable to overcome them.

The Sarney presidency

The political dynamics of the Sarney presidency (May 1985–March 1990) did not include an elite settlement. Instead of moving Brazil's elites toward consensual unity, the Sarney presidency contributed to political disarray, uncontrolled popular mobilization, and delegitimation of his government. All was personalized, and little was institutionalized. The reasons included the following: the nature of the negotiated transition that emphasized continuity with the military regime, the political basis of support for the government, and the economic crisis. Sarney's pretensions and weaknesses aggravated these larger and more structural problems. That is, rather than overcoming political and economic problems, Sarney exacerbated them in an egotistical search for a respected position in Brazil's political history.

The nature of Brazil's negotiated transition had several implications. First, there was never a break with the past. If Tancredo Neves had lived, at least a figure of some stature from the opposition PMDB would have been president. But Sarney's assumption of the presidency signified the assumption of power by a longtime loyal, if relatively minor, figure from the old regime. Sarney was from the politically and economically unimportant state of Maranhao and was a member of the Congress that, during the military regime, was not a particularly important institution. He did not, therefore, come to the presidency with much prestige, and unfortunately, he did little to increase it.

While the military regime manipulated the laws and even the constitution via its *casuísmos*, at least formal legality was generally maintained during its rule. This was possible because the military elaborated a corpus of legislation to ensure stability, control, and demobilization. Except for a brief flurry of legislation in May 1985 that legalized the leftist parties, extended the vote to illiterates, and abolished indirect elections, the legislation that had buttressed the military regime remained intact (see Dallari 1986). This included measures regarding political parties and elections that encouraged weak parties and an overrepresentation of Brazil's more underdeveloped regions (see Lamounier and Meneguello 1985). Other still-binding laws made strikes illegal, maintained censorship, and provided for a heavy dose of the Doctrine of National Security, all of which discouraged democratic participation.

The continuity of the Doctrine of National Security is suggestive of another vital element of continuity: the position of the armed forces. Unlike Argentina or even Peru, the Brazilian military did not relinquish their positions in government because they had led the country to economic collapse or defeat on the military battlefront. Instead, the Brazilian military initiated the transition themselves, and it was to be seen to completion by Tancredo Neves in accordance with his negotiations with the military. The military thus came through the transition completely intact, but without the onerous demands and tensions of governing. They retained six positions in the cabinet; the National Information Service (SNI) maintained its presence throughout the government; and their 1979 proclamation of an amnesty that insulated them from prosecution for human rights abuses also held. Further, because President Sarney lacked a strong base of political support, he increasingly relied on the military, thereby augmenting their real, if somewhat hidden, power.

Initially Sarney maintained the cabinet chosen by Tancredo Neves. Following a cabinet shuffle in February 1986, there were six ministers who had been either PDS or ARENA governors during the military regime and two others who had served it loyally. This highlights the continuity with the previous regime and leads to a consideration of the political base of support for the Sarney government.

The Democratic Alliance fashioned by Tancredo Neves consisted of the PMDB and the PFL (which consisted of dissidents from the Democratic Social party). In the 1982 elections, the PMDB won 44 percent of the vote, versus 42 percent for the PDS. With the split in the PDS and the formation of the Democratic Alliance, the PMDB was thus the largest and most important party. Further, in line with recent electoral trends, it seemed likely to grow larger still. On the death of Tancredo Neves, many in the PMDB wanted Ulysses Guimaraes, the party head, to become president. But this did not happen because of the concern for establishing legitimacy by allowing the duly elected vice-president to take over. Nonetheless, Guimaraes did become president of the Chamber of Deputies. Thus Sarney held executive power that, under the 1967–9 constitutions, was tremendous, but Guimaraes and the PMDB held most of the power in the Congress. In a sense, the national government became a diarchy, with frequent conflicts and tensions between the president, who relied heavily on the military and civilian elements from the old regime, and the PMDB. This conflict did not, of course, promote stability or effective policymaking and implementation.

Brazil was in particular need of stability and effective policymaking owing to the serious economic crisis inherited from the old regime. The foreign debt was approximately $105 billion in 1985, and inflation was 250 percent by early 1986. Sarney's solution was the Cruzado Plan of late February 1986 which, on the basis of legislation enacted by the old regime, he decreed without even consulting with Guimaraes or other key figures in the PMDB. The Cruzado Plan sought to bring inflation under control by creating a new monetary unit, the cruzado, and by freezing wages, prices, and the monetary value of most transactions. The economic package worked for most of 1986 and resulted in a tremendous increase in the popularity of President Sarney and the PMDB because the package stimulated great increases in consumption. In the elections of November 15, 1986, the PMDB won twenty-two out of twenty-three governorships, as well as a majority in the Congress, which would also become the Constituent Assembly in early 1987. A few days after the elections, however, the Sarney government reneged on its promise to maintain the package, and prices shot upward rapidly. Two other economic plans were tried and failed, Brazil had a new cruzado, and now another cruzeiro, and inflation in 1989 was 1,700 percent and heading rapidly toward hyperinflation. All of the Sarney presidency, therefore, except the period from March to December 1986, was characterized by a serious economic crisis.

The initial years of the Sarney presidency did not foster elite unity. After the temporary exuberance resulting from the Cruzado Plan, the Sarney government lost all credibility, and the division between the president and the PMDB widened while a wide variety of other political actors emerged. It was in this context that Brazil formulated a new constitution. One might expect that the process of writing a new charter would bring elites together, but unfortunately it did not.

The politics of framing a constitution

We should note first that a new constitution was not necessary for a hypothetical elite settlement in Brazil. (Nor, as I am arguing, did a new constitution create a settlement.) In principle, the constitution of 1967, substantially amended by the military in 1969, could have been purged of its more authoritarian elements after 1985 and retained as the charter for a democratic Brazil. It was, however, in the long and complex political transition that demands for a new constitution emerged, and these demands reemerged when the transition took a different turn.

The MDB first focused seriously on a new constitution in response to the most egregious *casuísmo*, the so-called April Package of 1977. In that package President Geisel used his unchecked executive power to change the constitution in order to bolster his control over the political transition. This act dramatized for the opposition that the transition would at best be slow and hesitant. The MDB thus promoted a campaign for a Constituent Assembly, the first it had waged (outside election campaigns) since it was founded ten years earlier. The theme appeared in PMDB documents up to and including Tancredo Neves's speech upon being elected president on January 15, 1985. For Neves a new constitution would complete the transition from the military to a civilian regime.

In 1977, other organizations also in opposition to President Geisel and the military regime promoted the theme of a new constitution. It became the single most important aim in the push for a more rapid and profound political transition. In August 1977 the OAB published a document that advocated a return to a state of law. It continued to focus on this theme in opposing the regime. Also in 1977, the National Conference of Brazilian Bishops (CNBB), speaking for much of the Catholic church, published a document advocating a similar goal. A general consensus developed among the opposition regarding the need to replace the constitutions of the military regime with a new document, both in order to mark a break with military rule and to consolidate a new democratic regime.

Following Tancredo Neves's death and Sarney's inauguration, the need to make a break with the past by means of a new constitution seemed urgent. The new government, based on the Democratic Alliance of the PMDB and the PFL, appeared reasonably comfortable in using some of the authoritarian measures of the 1967–9 constitutions. However, in the context of the negotiated transition, the coming to power of Sarney and the PMDB, and the fear that little would be changed, other opposition elements, now working against the PMDB, began to concentrate on a constituent assembly as the only way of breaking with the past. These elements included the OAB, the CNBB, the PT, some unions, and a plethora of newly formed grass-roots movements. Many of these so-called popular movements came together in the umbrella Plenário pro-participação popular na constituinte, or Plenary, which was closely linked to the Catholic church. As one of its proponents stated:

"The convocation of a Constituent Assembly is, today, a natural and necessary consequence of the campaign [in 1984] for direct elections. It is necessary to complete this campaign and, mainly, to extend its goal. We want not only to elect the president of the republic directly but also to open spaces in order to begin a cycle of profound change in the economic and social policies of the regime and, mainly, to bring an end to the military regime itself. (Bicudo 1985, p. 186)

The Plenary and its component parts promoted political mobilization and the development of public awareness through publications, meetings, press campaigns, trips to Brasília, and pressure-group tactics. It made a number of demands regarding the election and composition of a Constituent Assembly in which the break with the past would be dramatized. These included the numbers of congressmen to be elected from each state, the residual authoritarian legislation still in force, the role of parties in elections, the use of referenda, and the role of a drafting committee. Taken together, the implementation of these five points would, according to the Plenary, encourage involvement in politics by the lower classes, put pressure on the Constituent Assembly for a document guaranteeing their interests, and allow for an accurate representation of interests (where numbers would count) in politics.

Despite a high level of mobilization and publicity, none of these demands was adopted. President Sarney proposed a bill to the Congress on June 28, 1985, that would amend the constitution and call a National Constituent Assembly composed of the two houses of Congress to begin meeting on January 31, 1987. The Congress passed legislation in accord with this bill whereby the Congress to be elected on November 15, 1986, would also serve as the Constituent Assembly. The states' representation was not changed; the authoritarian legislation remained; the candidates had to belong to political parties; and a proposal for use of the plebiscite was killed by the Congress. President Sarney established a drafting committee, the Commission Afonso Arinos, which met between mid-1985 and late 1986. Initially rejected by the Plenary, it was later criticized by conservatives when it presented its proposed constitution to President Sarney in September 1986. The draft was not only incredibly detailed, with 468 articles, but also nationalistic and populist. Among other things, the commission recommended a parliamentary system of government with a four-year presidential term.

The prospects for consolidating, through a new constitution, a political system recognizing the interest of broader sectors of the population appeared increasingly less promising. Virtually none of the proposals was adopted, and the overall purpose of the Constituent Assembly received little attention in the media, focused as it was in 1986 on the Cruzado Plan. In the elections on November 15, 1986, the Constituent Assembly was downplayed, and attention instead turned to the election of state governors. The PMDB won a majority of 302 seats in the 559 member Congress/Constituent Assembly; the PFL came in second with 135 seats. After the election and the demise of the Cruzado Plan, popular indignation exploded; the economic situation became even worse; and the frustrated Plenary and affiliated groups renewed their efforts to influence the new constitution. The Constituent Assembly began its work in this context after Carnival 1987.

Between February 1, 1987, and October 1988, the Assembly was the only focus of politics in Brazil. The final document of 245 articles plus 70 transitory articles was the result of 330 sessions, 70,000 amendments, and 14,000 speeches. The planned completion date was extended four times, and there were numerous major shifts in the orientation of various sections and finally of the whole document. A brief review of some aspects of the process will allow us to understand better the political dynamics and resulting changes.

The political scene was complicated and became even more so during the Assembly's deliberations. Sarney held executive power, but the PMDB had a majority in the Assembly and wanted a document that would have an immediate restraining effect on President Sarney. There was thus a built-in tension between the president and the Assembly, and conflicts between Sarney and Guimaraes (who was now president of the PMDB), the Chamber of Deputies, and the Constituent Assembly surfaced immediately. Sarney was overwhelmingly concerned about provisions governing his own tenure. The 1967–9 constitutions, as emended by *casuísmos*, stipulated the president's tenure at six years; Tancredo Neves had indicated he would govern for four as the last indirectly elected president, and Sarney had initially reiterated his predecessor's commitment. But with his popularity plummeting after the end of the Cruzado Plan, Sarney came out publicly on May 18, 1987, for a five-year term, presumably in order to give himself time to regain his lost prestige. From then on his main goal was to achieve a five-year term from the Assembly.

Unlike Portugal and Spain, no formal pact existed between the regime and the opposition. The "understandings" or pacts made personally by Tancredo Neves in effect died with him. The tenor of those understandings (it is assumed that there were several of them) was a matter for speculation and political battle (see Cardosa 1986; Fleischer 1988). The Assembly began with no prior documents or drafts, because Sarney chose to withhold the Commission Arinos document on the grounds that he disagreed with its proposals for a parliamentary system and a four-year presidency. Of the political parties, only the Workers' party had a draft – or for that matter had given any attention to the Assembly – of its purpose in elaborating the country's basic charter, before the Assembly's opening in February 1987 (see Coparato 1986).

In the unicameral Constituent Assembly, the PMDB and PFL – the "democratic alliance" that had been the vehicle of Tancredo Neves's election and the political basis of the Sarney government – had 436, or 78 percent, of the 559 seats. The remaining 123 seats were divided among the nine other political parties. The PMDB, however, had expanded tremendously and changed since entering government in March 1985. Consistent with the tradition of malleability and the lack of ideological and organizational coherence of Brazilian parties, it was wide open to new members. David Fleischer has demonstrated that the largest political grouping in the Constituent Assembly was not the PMDB but, in terms of 1977 political affiliations, ARENA, with 217 members. The number of those originally affiliated with the MDB was 212. Of the 298 PMDB members for whom data were available in 1987, 40 were from the PDS of 1983 and another 42 from the ARENA of 1979. The latter two parties had been the basis of the military regime. Thus instead of a majority of 54 percent in the Assembly, the PMDB could count on only 40 percent once these late entrants from the right were discounted (Fleischer 1988, p. 39). Even if Guimaraes were president of the PMDB and the Assembly, it would not ensure that he, much less Sarney, could be sure that the party would vote as he directed. This made the process more complicated and unpredictable.

After the November 1986 elections, the eruption of the economic crisis, the plummeting of Sarney's popularity, and the opening of the Constituent Assembly, the CNBB, the OAB, some unions, and other movements involved in the Plenary sought to define the agenda and then influence the Assembly. They still hoped to make a break by means of a new constitution. At a minimum, they turned public attention to the significance of the Assembly and the constitution it would write. Their efforts undoubtedly increased the attention that pressure groups would in any case have directed to the Assembly. Because the popular movements wanted change, others would have to become involved to secure what they already had. All groups and movements wanted their goals incorporated into the basic charter. This is particularly relevant, as it was clear from the beginning, from the Commission Arinos in 1986, that the new constitution would be long, detailed, and programmatic. It was expected to be at least as long as the Portuguese constitution of 1976 with its 312 articles. The Assembly's deliberations were as long, drawn out, and volatile as these prior considerations led one to expect.

The dynamics of the Constituent Assembly

In contrast with 1946 when a "grand committee" drafted a constitution in four months that an Assembly approved in another three, the Assembly in 1987 went into what David Fleischer termed a "total participation mode" (Fleischer 1989, p. 13). The 559 members were divided into eight committees by functional areas to take testimony and draft sections of a working document. Each committee was then further divided into three subcommittees. Another committee, the twenty-fifth, was created to systematize and integrate the final reports from the eight committees. Because of the influence of more progressive elements of the PMDB, and pressure by the popular movements, the process was extremely open. The committees were receptive to suggestions by all imaginable associations and movements; the debates were held in public; and provision was made for "popular amendments" in which an item would have to be considered by the twenty-fifth, or systematization, committee, if it were supported by three associations and received thirty thousand signatures. Ultimately there were 122 popular amendments that received twelve million signatures (see Coelho 1988). By June the eight committees had each combined their three subcommittee reports into final reports that then went to a ninety-member systematization committee. This committee was chaired by the venerable Senator Afonso Arinos, but the more powerful position of relator, or recording secretary, was held by Senator Bernardo Cabral of the PMDB. The committee enjoyed considerable autonomy and produced one working draft in July and another in September. It was dominated by the more progressive elements of the PMDB, aligned with Senator Mario Covas, and other parties with extensive contacts with the popular movements. In addition, the progressives were constantly present, whereas the committee's more conservative members had business interests away from Brasília and tended to be absent much of the time. Consequently, when the systematization committee presented the final draft of 351 articles in November, there were a number of items that were new, not to say radical, for Brazil. They included the adoption of a parliamentary system, a mixed electoral system, decentralization of substantial taxing powers to states and municipalities, increased powers for the Congress and diminished powers for the executive, guarantees of extensive labor rights and allowances for the expropriation of idle land, and the prohibition of public funds for private schools. Whereas future presidential terms would be set at five years, Sarney's was shortened to four.

The parliamentary system was to be adopted immediately upon promulgation of the constitution.

The change in the system of government and the decrease in his own tenure incensed Sarney, and the economic provisions mobilized business sectors against the draft. Under the rules adopted at the beginning of deliberations in February 1987, voting by the full Assembly on the systematization committee draft would be as follows: Preference would be given to their version before considering amendments, and only if their version were defeated or lacked the quorum of 280 would amendments be allowed. The opponents to the draft organized a conservative interparty coalition called the big center, or *centrão*. By bringing almost all of its members to Brasília in December, it gathered a sufficient number of votes to change the rules governing voting procedures. From then on, any amendment with more than the absolute majority of 280 signatures would take precedence in voting. Only if the amendment failed would the committee's version stand. In late January 1988, the Assembly began voting on the draft that was completed in June. A second stage, during which articles could be eliminated but none added, took place between July and September.

Whereas the systematization committee was fairly cohesive, the *centrão* was not. It contained not only more conservative parties, including the PFL and the PSD, but also approximately one hundred members of the (expanded) PMDB (see Schmidt 1988, p. 40). It was generally conservative but consensus depended on the issue at hand. Its heterogeneity meant that virtually every article had to be negotiated, and a majority could not be assumed on any given vote. Indeed, to complicate the process further, the PMDB was splitting apart at this time with the formation of the Brazilian Social Democratic party (PSDB), by seven senators and thirty-eight deputies, before the constitution was promulgated in October. In addition, the president of the PFL, Senator Marco Maciel, had already broken with Sarney. The fractured party system thus splintered even more, and lobbies of all types came to predominate in the Assembly.

The constitution of 1988

The final document reflected and reinforced the unstructured political process of elaborating it. President Sarney pulled out all the stops in cajoling, threatening, and buying votes to achieve a five-year term of office in a presidential system. He persuaded the military ministers to support him; he distributed government funds to allies; and he bought off others by assigning them radio and TV licenses. In two crucial votes on March 22, 1988, the first and only time that all 559 members were present and voting in the Assembly, the proposals for a presidential system and the five-year presidential term passed. The only agreement after that occurred in mid-May when a section on agrarian reform was defeated, though other extensive social and economic reforms were included in the constitution.

The constitution stipulates a fundamental redistribution of power. The executive, whose powers increased tremendously during the military regime, is weakened in relationship to Congress, and the central government is diminished in relation to the states and municipalities. Decree laws, which were the most common form of legislation during the military regime and which remained in force after 1985, must now be approved by Congress within thirty days. The Congress has extensive powers in economic areas such as modifying budgetary items and overseeing the process of economic decision making. Congress also must now approve all international agreements, including those on the debt. It also has oversight on the country's nuclear program. States and municipalities are to receive increased shares of tax receipts. And the federal government is restricted when creating new revenue sources and expanding the public-enterprise sector (see Foreign Broadcast Information Service LAT-88-233S, December 5, 1988).

The constitution includes provisions for improving human rights and social guarantees, with incredibly detailed sections on everything from censorship to maternity and even paternity leave. There also are provisions for a variety of instruments of popular participation, including initiatives, plebiscites, referenda, and popular vetoes. The overall tone of the constitution is nationalistic, populist, and statist. Foreign firms are not allowed to prospect or extract minerals from the subsoil, and those currently doing so have five years to cede majority control to Brazil. The concept of a "national company" with headquarters and directors in Brazil, or one whose principal capital owners are Brazilian, is defined with extensive advantages regarding access to a strictly defined national market and a variety of advantages over foreign firms. There are provisions regarding sports, Indians, the environment, and culture.

In reaction to the constitution's social and economic reforms, and particularly the redistribution of power and wealth between governments and the separation of powers, Sarney went on national television in late July 1988 and described the draft as a document that would bankrupt Brazil and make it ungovernable. He urged the Assembly to reject it, which would have pushed the process back to its beginning. The day after Sarney's speech, Guimaraes called for a vote on the first draft, which passed with a massive majority of 403 to 13. Voting was completed on the second draft by September, and the constitution was promulgated on October 5. By this time Sarney was politically isolated, his government consisting largely of PDS collaborators and some old friends.

The constitution in no way represents an elite settlement. Produced in over twenty months in the 559-member Constituent Assembly, it is notable for its scope, detail, and overall orientation. It provides something for everyone in Brazil, with the exception of poverty-stricken landless peasants. But it clearly encourages and presages an ongoing and open-ended process of conflict and negotiation that is unlikely to result in the elite consensual unity due its content and the manner in which it was framed.

Indeed, the constituent process itself was far from complete: Implementation of the constitution still required passage of approximately two hundred items of ordinary and complementary legislation. This process did not begin until late November 1988, forty-seven days after its promulgation, and by October 1989 only nine such laws had been passed by the Congress. This means that many elements of the constitution have yet to be implemented (*Jornal do Brasil*, October 1, 1989), and many important and basic issues have yet to be resolved: Article 2 of the transitory section, for instance, provides for a plebiscite on September 7, 1993, on the form (republic or constitutional monarchy) and system (parliamentary or presidential) of government! It is, in short, tentative, and crucial elements (such as the system of government) will continue to be fought over.

This lack of decisiveness in addressing key constitutional issues has been paralleled by behavior that has undercut progress toward institutionalizing essential political institutions, such as parties and the Congress itself. Even though the Constituent Assembly formally defeated a proposal for a parliamentary system, it substantially increased the powers of the Congress and reduced those of the executive. Thus, in actual practice, the powers of the Congress approximate those of some parliamentary or semipresidential systems. But even though the Congress now has power, it appears to lack the tradition, means, and possibly commitment to exercise such power responsibly. Congress took more than six months, for example, before it even got around to defining its internal procedures. Despite its size (559 members) and the tremendous expansion of its responsibilities, the Congress has a total of 55 staff experts – and none in the areas of national defense, nuclear energy, public health, or foreign relations. And for the first year during which the Congress functioned under the new constitution, it continued to operate according to traditional orientations stressing nepotism and financial favors.[3]

Similarly, neither the text of the constitution nor the constituent process itself did anything to strengthen the political parties, which could conceivably increase the ability of Congress to exercise its powers responsibly. The earlier legislation pertaining to the parties and the unrepresentative electoral system has remained more or less intact. And the parties have continued to fragment. The candidates of the five largest parties in the November 1986 elections (PMDB, PFL, PDS, PDT, and PTB) did not even receive enough votes to enter the second round of the presidential elections on December 17, 1989. The PMDB and PFL, the two main actors in the Assembly owing to their combined majority, came apart in attempting to choose candidates for the first round of the elections on November 15, 1989. Their candidates together received a total of 6 percent of the votes, whereas the parties of the two front-running candidates held a total of just thirty-nine congressional seats between them. And as the established parties fragmented, there was an explosion of new actors in politics, taking advantage of instruments for popular participation included in the constitution, in particular emphasizing direct access to the Assembly via popular amendments. And lobbies of all imaginable kinds, from religious associations to environmental groups to economic interests, have pressed their unaggregated demands on the legislature.

Finally, the constituent process did not definitively address the nature of civil–military relations, leading to considerable ambiguity concerning the proper political role of the military in the new democracy. Brazil's transition from a military to civilian regime may be unique in that the role of the armed forces has diminished minimally, if at all (see Goés 1988). This is related to the nature of the transition itself: The military came through the transition with their prestige intact and began a modernization program with the inception of the civilian regime. They lobbied effectively in the Constituent Assembly, and their prominence and role increased as President Sarney relied on them. They remain at the center of power, both in reality and in terms of the constitution. Article 142 stipulates, in part: "[The military's] purpose is to defend the fatherland, guarantee the constitutionally established powers and – upon the initiative of any of the said powers – law and order." This is essentially the same role that

3 For an extensive discussion of these points with examples, see "O Congresso fora de compasso," *Veja*, April 12, 1989.

the military has had since the founding of the republic in 1891. A Ministry of Defense was not created, and the National Security Council was merely replaced by a Council of National Defense, which is consultative. Their structures and representation in the cabinet were not diminished.

The 1988 constitution has had a mixed impact on democratization in Brazil. On the one hand, it includes many features that have encouraged the emergence of new forces attempting to influence policymakers. But on the other hand, it failed to create incentives for restructuring or disciplining the political parties or even for establishing a coherent state structure. There are thus more mobilized actors but not the political or institutional framework for their action. The presidential elections in late 1989 highlight this excessively fluid situation.

The presidential elections of 1989

The elections were the first direct elections for the presidency since 1960. As noted, they were the first ever with universal adult suffrage, which, in accord with the new constitution, included all persons sixteen years or older. Consequently, 82.1 million voters registered for the elections. After approximately six months of campaigning, twenty-two candidates remained in the race for the presidency. There had almost been twenty-three when, two weeks before the elections, a television personality who is extremely popular with the lower classes but who had no previous political involvement, declared his candidacy. Immediately before the election, however, the elections board disallowed his candidacy. The front-runners in the elections were Fernando Collor de Mello, with 28.5 percent of the vote, and Luís Inácio Lula da Silva, with 16.1 percent. In the runoff elections on December 17, Collor won with 53 percent of the valid votes.

Collor's candidacy epitomizes the malleability and the lack of institutionalization of the elites in the Brazilian party system today. He belongs to the third generation of a political family. He began his political career in the ARENA and later (like so many others) joined the PMDB. In March 1989 he switched to the tiny Youth party (the PJ, founded only in 1985), whose name he soon changed to the National Reconstruction party (PRN). The party has no ideology or identity, and its representatives take diverse and conflicting positions in Congress – indeed, Collor's platform included many statements that contradicted the positions of many of the party's twenty-three members in Congress. His opponent, Lula, represented a very different orientation, and it may be said that Lula's PT is currently the only "real" party in Brazil.

In response to Lula's strong second-place showing in the first round of the election, some factions in the Congress (including Ulysses Guimaraes), concerned that he might in fact win the runoff election, proposed establishing a parliamentary system. This was little more than a year after the constitution was proclaimed and almost four years before the plebiscite on this issue called for by the constitution. The fact that important political leaders in the new regime were willing to tamper with its basic political institutions (that they themselves had created), for purely partisan reasons, attests to the lack of consolidation of this new democracy.

Further evidence of the lack of elite consensual unity can be seen in the positions taken by major candidates in the presidential election. Although Lula and the PT may be said to be in tune with the new constitution, the winner, Collor, definitely is not. In the campaign he, and in fact most of the leading candidates, criticized sections of the new constitution. One of Collor's first appointments was that of justice minister, Bernardo Cabral, previously secretary of the systematization committee in the Constituent Assembly. In an interview in *Veja*, Cabral reported that there would have to be changes in the document, particularly in those sections defining relations between the president and Congress.[4] Apart from the lack of consensual support for key institutions of the new democracy, the disunity of Brazilian elites was manifested in the polarized positions of the two finalists in the presidential elections.

Though coming from opposite ends of the social and political spectrum, Collor and Lula share a lack of identification with the traditional elites they attacked in the campaign. But whereas Lula is supported by a "real" political party, Collor used a "party for rent" to get elected. Given the continuation of past legislation pertaining to elections and political parties and Collor's use of a party, it seems unlikely that a coherent party system will become institutionalized.

Conclusions

Brazil has undergone a complex and lengthy transition from military to civilian rule. Elections have been held for all levels of government, including the presidency, and a new constitution has been promulgated. There is no question that the country is currently functioning as a procedural democracy. There remains some doubt, however, whether Brazil's democracy will become consolidated. The reasons are not only the very serious economic crisis indicated by Brazil's high

4 *Veja*, January 24, 1990.

foreign indebtedness and hyperinflation (until its decreed elimination in March 1990) but also the fact that Brazil has gone through its transition with no elite settlement.

This does not necessarily imply that Brazil will come apart and collapse into military dictatorship. It seems likely that Brazilian democracy will continue on its haphazard and complex journey with much attention and energy devoted to political activities. But it is a democracy that faces great challenges. The radical economic package implemented by the Collor administration in 1990 presents one such challenge: It promised a radical restructuring of the economic system, with important political implications. It was the equivalent of the economic programs implemented in Germany and Japan immediately after World War II. In the view of most observers, if it fails, there will be extreme pressures on the political system for yet more change. Considering the nature of the political transition and the absence of an elite settlement, the country is now less able to deal with the pressures and the conflicts that arise. The ultimate consequences of the absence of consolidation remain to be seen.

The prerequisites for elite settlements?

This examination of the Brazilian case has been useful in underscoring the importance for achieving an elite settlement of several of the facilitating conditions set forth in Chapter 1. As I have argued, it is likely that some kind of settlement might have been achieved if Tancredo Neves had lived. Instead, the agreements he had reached with key political actors died with him, and his successor, Sarney, both lacked a political base and was incapable of the sophisticated negotiations required to create such a settlement. Thus, the personal characteristics of key elites are an important variable.

The writing of the new constitution presented a second opportunity for a political settlement, but because of the political and economic context and Sarney's actions, the opportunity was lost. It is important to note the marked procedural and structural differences between Brazil's constituent process and that of Spain (see Chapter 2). Unlike that in Spain, Brazil's party system was highly fragmented, greatly increasing the number of actors in the process. Decision making was further fragmented, and the number of participants increased by involving in that process eight different subcommittees rather than concentrating decision-making authority in the hands of a few (cf., the Spanish constitutional committee's seven-member *ponencia* and the handful of participants in the nocturnal negotiations of May 22, 1978). The highly unstable and personalistic nature of Brazil's political parties also served to undercut prospects for an elite settlement, insofar as it limited the capacity of key actors to bargain authoritatively. Conducting constitutional negotiations in public, rather than behind closed doors, contributed to the reluctance of elites to make concessions, as hypothesized in Chapter 1. Moreover, the extremely protracted transition and the subsequent constitutional negotiations also impeded any settlement, while giving rise to a progressive mobilization of various societal sectors. Finally, the absence of a sense of immediate crisis or of historical memories of costly and destructive conflict in the past meant that an important spur to such deliberations was lacking. Thus, the constituent process settled very little. Indeed, as a result of the political mobilization that occurred and of the unwieldy nature of the resulting document itself, there is probably less chance of an elite settlement today than there was before the process began.

References

Bicudo, Helio. 1985. "O verdadeiro caminho da democracia." In *Constituente e democracia no Brasil hoje*, ed. Raymundo Faoro. São Paulo: Editora brasiliense.

Bruneau, Thomas. 1983. "Transitions from Authoritarian Regimes: The Contrasting Cases of Brazil and Portugal." In *Constitutional Democracy: Essays in Comparative Politics*, ed. Fred Eidlin. Boulder, CO: Westview Press.

Burns, E. Bradford. 1980. *A History of Brazil*. 2nd ed. New York: Columbia University Press.

Cardoso, Senator Fernando Henrique. 1986. Speech. In *Folha de São Paulo*, May 19.

Coelho, Joao Gilberto Lucas. 1988. "O Processo constituinte de 1987." In *Constituinte: Questoês polêmicas*, ed. Vania Lomonaco Bastos and Tania Moreira da Costa. Brasília: Caderno CEAC/UNB.

Coparato, Fabio Konder. 1986. *Muda Brasil: Uma constutuição para o desenvolvimento democrática*. São Paulo: Editora brasiliense.

Dallari, Dalmo. 1986. "Entulho autoritário." In *Nova república: Um balanço*, ed. Barbara Freitag. São Paulo: L & PM editores.

Dreifuss, Rene. 1986. "Nova república. Novo exercito?" In *Nova república: Um balanço*, ed. Barbara Freitag. São Paulo: L & PM editores.

Fleischer, David. 1983. "Constitutional and Electoral Engineering in Brazil: A Double-edged Sword, 1964–1982." In *Wahlen und Wahlpolitik in Lateinamerika*, ed. Dieter Nohlen. Heidelberg: Esprint-Verlag.

1988. "From Non-competitive to Competitive Elections to the 1987/88 Constituent Assembly." Academia de humanismo christiano, Santiago, March 23.

1989. "The Impact of the 1988 Municipal Elections on Brazil's 1989 Presidential Elections." Institute of Interamerican Studies at the University of Miami.

de Goés, Walder. 1988. "Militares e política. Uma estratégia para a democracia." In *A Democracia no Brasil: Dilemas e perspectivas*, ed. Fábio W. Reis and Guillermo O'Donnell. São Paulo: Editora vertice.

Iglesias, Francisco. 1985. "Momentos democráticos na trajectória brasileira." In *Brasil, sociedade democratica*, ed. Helio Jaguaribe. Rio de Janeiro: José Elympio.

Jaguaribe, Helio, et al. 1986. *Brasil, 2000: Para um novo pacto social*. Rio de Janeiro: Paz e terra.

Lamounier, Bolivar, and Rachel Meneguello. 1985. "Political Parties and Democratic Consolidation: The Brazilian Case." Woodrow Wilson International Center for Scholars.

Schmidt, Benicio Viero. 1988. "Transição política e crise de governabilidade no Brasil." In *Constituinte: Questoês polêmicas*, ed. Vania Lomonaco Bastos and Tania Moreira da Costa. Brasília: Caderno CEAC/UNB.

Selcher, Wayne. 1986. *Political Liberalization in Brazil*. Boulder, CO: Westview Press.

Skidmore, Thomas. 1967. *Politics in Brazil, 1930–64: An Experiment in Democracy*. New York: Oxford University Press.

1988. *The Politics of Military Rule in Brazil, 1964–85*. New York: Oxford University Press.

Stepan, Alfred. 1988. *Rethinking Military Politics: Brazil and the Southern Cone*. Princeton, NJ: Princeton University Press.

10

Redefining the Portuguese transition to democracy

LAWRENCE S. GRAHAM

Within the context of the analytic framework developed for this book, the Portuguese case warrants particular attention. Seen from the vantage point of 1991, Portugal's current political leaders can look back over the last two decades with considerable pride. For in a comparatively short period of time and despite a previous history of nearly half a century of authoritarian rule (1926–74), followed by revolutionary upheaval (1974–6), they have successfully consolidated a democratic regime. Institutionally this particular regime can be characterized as a semipresidential, parliamentary system. Within it, displacing earlier patterns of personalist civilian and military rule, stable institutional roles have evolved in which the main participants are the president, the prime minister and his cabinet, and deputies serving in the National Assembly organized by party affiliation according to parliamentary blocs.

Yet if the definitions established in the first chapter are followed rigorously, it should be made clear that democratic rule has come to Portugal through neither elite settlement nor elite convergence. The revolution that swept across Portugal in 1974 destroyed the old order and left instead a badly divided country that has precluded either form of elite agreement. At the same time, these particular concepts of elite settlement and convergence provide a framework in which a sequence of events producing democratic outcomes can be captured in such a way as to bring a fresh perspective to the comparative analysis of democratization.

Since 1976 there have been in Portugal a series of partial settlements. Coming sequentially, these settlements have been little more than transitory agreements on procedures designed to limit conflict and to

The field research on which this chapter is based was supported by a travel grant from the University Research Institute of the University of Texas at Austin.

establish a modus vivendi among contending political forces. They began in the late 1970s and have extended to the 1990s. Often interpreted as a demonstration of instability and indicative of the failure of democratic principles to take root in Iberia, this institutional fluidity and constant reshuffling of political leaders has had the cumulative effect of producing a political environment in which procedural democracy has become the accepted medium through which radically different political agendas for state and society can be debated while political leaders have tackled, one at a time, policy issues of great import (see Wiarda 1989).

It is only now, as Portugal is entering the 1990s and this process is largely complete, that we can see the success of its elites in building a consensus on the desirability of democratic procedures in the midst of great social and economic disparities. For those who would argue that an essential prior condition in the consolidation of democracy is a certain level of socioeconomic development, we point out that this is a society that has long been subjected to considerable resource constraint, with marked divisions along class lines between elites and masses. In Portugal, the historic response to underdevelopment has been domination by certain elites, as well as mass emigration by socioeconomically disadvantaged groups (see Leeds 1984).

In order to defuse what had become an explosive situation as a consequence of revolution, since 1976 Portuguese leaders have, on their own, tried to work out quietly a new institutional arrangement while continuing to attract sufficient international support to finance economic transformations. If we are to capture the essence of these developments, it is not to foreign commentators that we must turn but, rather, to the Portuguese themselves and their analysis of their own new democracy. In contrast with the dearth of empirical social science research under the old regime, when the social sciences were often equated with "the sciences of the have-nots," a new generation of Portuguese scholars has come to the fore. Their writing is significant because of its new insights into the democratic transitions of other divided societies and because some of these scholars have also been active politically in building Portugal's new democracy. Let us, then, look at how they explain Portugal's achievement of democratic consolidation (see Coelho 1989).

In the context of both the new Europe that is emerging in the aftermath of the Marxist–Leninist collapse in the east and the Latin America that is in transition in the west – where really very few countries have been able to sidestep the military – the Portuguese experience is instructive for those committed to realizing democratic ideals in the midst of difficult circumstances. Crucial to understanding this experience in a comparative perspective is an awareness of how the collapse of the authoritarian regime (the Estado novo) caught everyone by surprise, as did the profundity of the revolution that followed in 1974 and 1975. Because Portugal was so close to armed conflict in late 1975, what warrants our attention is how those divisions that formed as a consequence of revolution have been transcended, gradually and pragmatically. Since 1976 the increasing elite convergence has replaced previous patterns of confrontation and conflict with democratic procedures as the most effective way to overcome past differences and to avoid repeating a history of factionalism, military insubordination, economic instability, social conflict, and recourse to authoritarianism.[1]

The Portuguese revolution

Forty-eight years of authoritarian rule came to an end in Portugal on April 25, 1974, when a small group of military officers, calling themselves the Armed Forces Movement (Movimento das forças armadas, MFA) seized power. In overthrowing the regime of Marcello Caetano, not only did they decisively intervene in mainland Portugal's politics, but they also became a catalyst for independence in its overseas territories. A power vacuum quickly developed into which a host of new leaders and groups rushed, each hoping to impose its own version of what the new order should be. The initial lineup produced a coalition government, known as the Junta of National Salvation and dominated by the military – senior officers who had joined the movement and junior officers who had carried out the coup. The head of the junta, General António de Spínola, sought to temper the revolution and build a new coalition of reformist officers and civilians tied to the old regime. His preference for a political democracy – in which established economic interests would be ensured a place in a Portugal committed to integration into the European Community and into a commonwealth that would bind the metropole and the colonies – directly conflicted with the revolutionary project that the MFA had in mind. Although the movement had begun as an internal military

1 For those not familiar with Portuguese political history and the past that current leadership groups have wished to transcend, it is important to understand that in their experience, authoritarian rule has not always been equated with political and economic stability. A major contribution in clarifying these dimensions is Wheeler (1986). The seven years of military rule, albeit equally authoritarian as Antônio de Oliveira Salazar's, that preceded the consolidation of the Estado novo (the civilian dictatorship dominant from 1934 until 1974) proved to be as unstable and volatile as the civilian regime it had replaced (the First Republic, 1910–26).

affair, dissatisfaction with the stalemate that had emerged in the wars to defend Portuguese colonial interests soon became more prominent as a focus for more revolutionary expectations. Earlier concerns – grievances over pay inequities and hostility to the government's attempt to resolve the shortage of field commanders by promoting into the officer corps soldiers with extensive field experience as platoon leaders – had convinced most of the younger officers of the ineptitude of old regime's bureaucrats. This perception, combined with the realization that the wars they were commanded to fight could not be won and with the idea that perhaps they should be as concerned with liberating the metropole as with defending the colonies, led to their conclusion that much radical change was necessary.

When it became apparent that Spínola and his supporters were moving quickly to galvanize popular support behind their project for national reconstruction, Lieutenant Colonel Otelo Saraiva de Carvalho and the MFA officers sharing his views took action to stop this mobilization by blocking a mass demonstration that conservatives were organizing for September 28. The consequence of Otelo's move was the removal from power of Spínola and his supporters. From this point forward, the MFA took the upper hand and reconstituted the government by bringing in officers with a much stronger, clearly revolutionary, commitment. Over the next six months, from early October 1974 through March 1975, the MFA consolidated its control of the military and the Portuguese state through a new government led by General Francisco da Costa Gomes as president and general António dos Santos Vasco Gonçalves as prime minister.

Seeking to halt what now had become a revolution that was mobilizing masses of citizens to action through the occupation of farms, factories, and vacant housing, Spínola once again acted, this time by organizing a coup on March 11. The MFA reacted quickly, and before Spínola and his supporters could gain a foothold, it secured control of all military bases and government agencies. With Vasco Gonçalves continuing in place as prime minister and presiding over a new, more radical cabinet of civilian and military officers, the government issued decrees nationalizing banks, insurance companies, and large-scale firms owned by Portuguese nationals. By the summer of 1975, social movements were under way throughout Portugal that brought mass mobilization to a level previously unknown in that country.

But at that very moment, when from the vantage point of Lisbon it looked as though the struggle for power at the top had coincided with the wide-reaching social revolution from below, the reaction was put in gear. In the north, citizens mobilized, surprisingly, against the revolution. When leftist military officers and civilian militants arrived in villages in the north during what became known as "the long hot summer of '75," they found themselves met not by enthusiastic supporters – as had been their experience in the south – but by angry groups of peasants. Determined to defend their small plots of land against the collectivization that had already taken place elsewhere, these peasants considered their traditional way of life to be under attack. In contrast with the landless agricultural workers of the south, faced with miserable working conditions on large estates, the northern landowning peasants rose up to defend their tightly knit farming communities built around family and church. By August, Portugal was at the brink of armed conflict between the proponents of revolution, concentrated in the center and the south, and those mounting a counterrevolution in the north and on the islands (the Azores and Madeira), with the latter as adamant in their opposition to radical change as were the former in its support.

By then it had also become apparent that the Gonçalvistas – the radical military officers and civilians constituting the government – were able neither to govern effectively nor to consolidate their power by themselves. Newly organized political parties, with leaders and followings, continued to press for freedom of the press and of assembly and for an alternative political model in which those in power would be sanctioned solely by their ability to win at the ballot box, through elections allowing people to express their preferences by voting rather than using force. Concerned about the reign of military and civilian radicals and fearing that a new authoritarianism of the left was replacing that of the right, social democratic forces within the military and civilian society were galvanized into action.

A new set of military leaders and civilians thus began to move to the foreground, first by forcing a reorganization of the Council of Ministers on September 19, 1975, and finally through a countercoup on November 25. The ministerial shake-up took place in the midst of considerable sparring between contending political forces based in both the polarized and contentious civil society and in what had become a hopelessly politicized military. The November 25 countercoup, successfully executed in a matter of hours, was a reaction to what military moderates perceived to be a final desperate attempt by the far left to incite military troops to insurrection by joining what the radicals hoped would become mass upheaval in key urban areas (Lisbon, Setúbal, and Porto).

Once the dust settled, it was clear that moderate military officers, led by General António Ramalho Eanes, were in command and were determined to reestablish order and to underwrite the consolidation of a civilian regime committed to democracy and free elections. From this point forward, political forces on the center and the right moved into the interim government, and preparations were made first to elect and convene a Constituent Assembly to write a new constitution and then, to select a new president. The outcomes of these processes were the April constitution and the June 1976 election of General Eanes as president of the republic.

All this, albeit in excessively brief form, is essential as a backdrop to understanding why Portugal's transition to democracy has been so extended and how divided the country had become as a consequence of revolution. Construction of a stable, democratic order thus required transcending the cleavages that emerged from this revolutionary turmoil (see Maxwell 1986).

Partial settlements as a vehicle for promoting elite consensus

Portugal's transition from the fluidity of the revolutionary situation surrounding the breakdown of institutionalized authoritarian rule in 1974, to the stability of a fully consolidated democracy in 1990, took fifteen years. Landmarks in this protracted transition are the two pacts between the armed forces and the political parties of April 11, 1975, and February 26, 1976; the constitution of April 2, 1976; and the constitutional revisions in November and December 1982 and in May and June 1989 (see Braga da Cruz 1986). Each of these agreements concentrated on the resolution of a significant issue dividing a particular set of political forces, excluded other significant actors, and set up transitory arrangements subject to redefinition once the key players had changed. It was not until the end of 1989 that all major actors in postauthoritarian Portugal accepted procedural democracy as the framework most appropriate to structuring and regulating Portuguese politics for the foreseeable future.

The first pact (I Pacto MFA–Partidos) was signed on April 11, 1975, at the high point of the revolution and in the context of a strong reaction to the failed countercoup of March 11 and a government determined to enact more radical policies. Yet even then, at the apex of power of radical military and civilian forces, it was clear that a plurality of political parties, representing various constellations of leaders and mass followings, had become an integral part of the new political scene. At no point was it possible for military and civilian radicals to consolidate power solely in their own hands, hence the need for a political accord. This first agreement, therefore, established a bifurcated governmental system in which civilian and military affairs were to remain separate. In the civilian sphere, representation was given to parties in a national assembly – the Assembly of the Republic

– while at the same time an attempt was made to institutionalize the political role of the military through the creation of the Assembly of the Armed Forces Movement. Far from a satisfactory solution to the institutional vacuum that had developed with the collapse of the Estado novo, this represented a tentative first step in redefining civil–military relations in post-1974 Portugal. It embraced the major players at the time: the military officers who had led the coup – the Armed Forces Movement (Movimento das forças armadas, MFA) – and the political parties that had come to the fore after the coup on April 25, 1974. The issue at this point was how to restructure civil–military relations, for without an accord between military and civilian leaders there could be no progress toward filling this institutional vacuum. Chaos, conflict, and uncertainty had been the results of the ill-defined relationships among the Junta of National Salvation (which intended to act as a self-appointed government), a competing civilian government with prime minister and cabinet, and the armed forces, especially those who had led the coup under the designation known as the Armed Forces Movement. Whereas the military officers in the junta and the MFA had sought to redefine politics on their own terms (albeit without achieving any consensus among themselves), by 1975 with the junta and the government redefined as the same collective executive organ, it also was clear that the political parties were and would remain important players. No less diverse ideologically, these parties also held considerable power given their ability to mobilize mass support. To avoid armed conflict, it was obvious that these contending elites would have to negotiate an agreement. Accordingly, the pact of April 11, 1975, established a framework within which politics could be conducted without bloodshed, at least for the time being.

The second pact (the II Pacto of February 16, 1976) was a response to the countercoup of November 25, 1975. In this agreement the MFA – now purged of its radical officers and dominated by those sympathetic to social democracy – recognized a single national assembly with elected political party representatives, committed the signatories to electing a president by means of universal and direct suffrage, and confined military influence to a Council of the Revolution in which counselors elected by the armed forces were given constitutional oversight authority. Although this pact resembled its predecessor in bringing together key military and civilian actors and persuading them to acknowledge that neither had the power to dispense with the other, its core constituency was quite different. Whereas the first pact had included committed revolutionaries as its key players – the left-wing of the MFA, the Portuguese Communist party (PCP), and other radical political groups – the second pact marginalized the military and civilian radicals and brought to the foreground social democratic forces within the military and the civilian parties. The failure of the revolutionary left to bring about mass insurrection on November 25, 1975, and the successful military countercoup led by General António Ramalho Eanes had decisively changed the course of the revolution. This second pact reflected that realignment and opened the way to negotiation of a new constitutional document that would establish a working relationship among the new political forces.

Continuing the practice of separately administering civilian and military affairs, the coordination of civil–military relations was confined to the presidency of the republic, with the president simultaneously acting as head of state and head of the armed forces. Subsequently, with the ratification of a new constitution in April 1976 and the election of General Ramalho Eanes as president two months later, support for these new arrangements was ensured by popular vote and reinforced by Eanes himself, who defined his role as guarantor of the constitution.

From 1976 until 1982, there was considerable uncertainty regarding Portugal's democratic politics. Seen from the vantage point of 1991, Portugal's new regime was unstable and tentative. The country was governed by a dual executive: a president, who had a national constituency and who was also head of the nation's armed forces, and a prime minister, who had a cabinet reflecting the majority political parties' alignments in the National Assembly. Gradually, however, the balance shifted toward civilian primacy. The principal players influencing this shift were General Eanes (as head of the armed forces), Mário Soares (as leader of the Socialist party, PS), Francisco Sá Carneiro (of the Social Democratic party, the PSD), and Diogo Freitas do Amaral (of the conservative Social Democratic center, CDS), plus members of their respective political entourages. Accommodation came first through the agreement among them that substantive legislation and control of the budget would be the exclusive domain of the government (i.e., the prime minister and the cabinet). Accountable to the National Assembly, the government would continue in office only as long as it could marshal majority support from Parliament. Over time, these party leaders also reached a second informal understanding that all cabinet members, including the defense minister, would be civilians.

Later, following Sá Carneiro's tragic death in November 1980 shortly after his victory in new National Assembly elections and following Eanes's election for a second term in December 1980, Eanes took the initiative in assuring political party leaders that as a second-term president he would cease to head the armed forces and would downgrade the influence of the Council of the Revolution. Accordingly, in early 1981, Eanes designated a full-time military officer as head of the armed forces' general staff and made it clear that the role of the Council of the Revolution would be limited to issuing advisory opinions to the president. Despite these revisions, however, civil and military affairs remained under separate jurisdictions, coordinated only through the presidency of the republic, and military oversight continued informally, with democratically oriented officers working in conjunction with like-minded civilian politicians as guarantors of the new system. At this juncture, the military still retained veto power over civilian actions, should politics take a sudden turn to the left or the right (see Ferreira 1989; Freitas do Amaral 1989).

Given this continued military role in Portuguese politics, the significance of the 1982 constitutional revisions should not be minimized. These reforms clearly acknowledged the primacy of elected civilian representatives and finally removed unelected (and therefore not democratically responsible) military officials from pivotal positions of power, thereby completing Portugal's transition to democracy, as that concept is defined by the demanding procedural ideal type set forth in Chapter 1. Thereafter, the constitution placed the nation's armed forces more clearly under civilian authority. This reform was the product of a carefully crafted accord among civilian and military elites. Through these negotiations and an accompanying public debate, the practice of separately constituted civilian and military affairs, begun in the first military–civilian pact in 1975, came to an end. The vehicles for accomplishing all this were two major changes in the constitution: (1) the abolition of the Council of the Revolution, coupled with replacement of its judicial review functions by a Constitutional Tribunal, and (2) the promulgation of a National Defense Law that became part of the nation's constitutional charter. Indicative of the extent to which the military would honor its commitment to Portugal's civilian leadership by subjecting itself to civilian control was President Eanes's stance on the final version of the law passed by the National Assembly. While disagreeing with clauses limiting the power of the president to select the head of the general staff and shifting military oversight authority to the government (i.e., the prime minister and the cabinet), Eanes accepted the National Assembly's vote on this matter. When the Assembly overrode his veto of the law, he did not reverse his position. Rather, both he and the heads of the armed services let it be known that though they disagreed with the language of the final law, they recognized it as legitimate and binding.

The fact that this accommodation took place at all, that an accord was worked out at this point, and that it was respected and implemented is no small accomplishment. Why this happened can be summarized as follows: An authoritarian regime had been overthrown by what was after all a military coup. What followed was a social and economic revolution led in large part by radical military officers, who, with equally radical civilian support, moved the country dangerously close to establishing an authoritarian socialist state. A military countercoup led by a different group of military officers, also in league with civilian counterparts, stopped that movement from proceeding leftward. Nonetheless, having closed off the possibility of left authoritarianism, these officers still supported the idea of writing into the new constitution a commitment to socialism as a goal of the Portuguese state. To ensure military guardianship of a democratic socialist state, the Council of the Revolution had been created to ensure that military oversight of civilian authorities would continue and to prevent politics from swinging to the right. All this had to be undone.

The first steps toward moderating these stances had already been taken by the military, and these actions were completed by the end of Eanes's first presidency, because of his determination to separate military and civilian affairs and his commitment to working with those officers who supported the idea of a professional military without the intense politicization of the preceding years. That action required first removing and isolating radical officers and, later, as the party-based government developed, accepting the fact that those officers most closely linked to political actions in the fall of 1975 would have to be marginalized. All this was in place by 1982, and it explains why the abolition of the Council of the Revolution was no longer a real issue.

Much more important in 1982 was getting a new defense law negotiated and approved. Matching the aforementioned changes within the military was a considerable evolution in the direction of party government, in which the party leaders within the government and the National Assembly, especially those in the PSD, the CDS, and the PS, had already acquired much experience in constituting governments and working within the framework of competitive politics. Despite Sá Carneiro's death in 1980, the conservative coalition aligning the PSD with the CDS (and a third minority party, Partido popular Monárquico, or the PPM) had held together, and it constituted the core of the initiative to work out a new national defense law that would sideline the military and establish a new framework for civil–military relations. Central to that endeavor was the defense minister at the time, Diogo Freitas do Amaral of the CDS. Although others from the PSD and the PS were certainly involved, his role was crucial to working out the initial accommodation, one that he personally guided in the negotiations among key party representatives and matched with equally important individuals on the military side. Without going into the details of this informal agreement and later attempts to ensure adequate legislative oversight of civil–military affairs through the National Assembly's Defense Committee, we should mention several other significant actors: Jaime da Gama (PS), Ricardo Bayão Horta (PSD–Freitas's successor as defense minister), and Defense Minister Mota Pinto's undersecretary of defense in the next cabinet, António de Figueiredo Lopes (also PSD).

Even then, after all the negotiations in the National Assembly, consultations between the parliamentary government and the presidency of the republic, and parallel discussions between each of these groups and senior military officers, implementing the law was not easy. Eanes only reluctantly relinquished his authority over senior military appointments and the right of service heads to determine their own commanders independently of the government. His support for civilian primacy had meant removing the armed forces' veto over civilian politics in the event of an outcome not to their liking. But it was clear that he and other senior military officers expected to retain control over internal appointments, and they viewed the presidency as a means of keeping the National Assembly's partisan politics out of military affairs. It was not until Prime Minister Soares came to blows with Eanes in July 1983 over the government's right to approve or disapprove the army head's appointment of a regional military commander that this issue was finally resolved. Faced with an institutional crisis and a personal standoff between president and prime minister, the principals (Eanes and Soares) ultimately resolved their differences by agreeing that members of the general staff of the armed forces (the Estado maior geral das forças armadas, EMGFA) would serve only when they held the confidence of both the government and the president. In the case of future appointments or dismissals below armed forces' heads, it was also agreed that the principle of reciprocity would be respected by president and prime minister; no such appointments would occur in the future without the concurrence of both (see Graham, forthcoming).

Thus, by the mid-1980s, with the PCP isolated on the left, with the Council of the Revolution gone, with the military accepting the new civilian arrangements, and with the PS and PSD both able to form governments on their own, Portugal had made enormous progress toward consolidating a democratic regime. When the PSD emerged from the 1987 elections with a clear-cut majority in the National Assembly, the stage was set for a final agreement that has contributed to democratic consolidation. This agreement was economic in nature, involving removal from the constitution of the Marxist-inspired commitments to socialism and the nationalization of private property. Although they go largely unnoticed in the framework of this book, such economic agreements in countries like Portugal are often as important as are informal political agreements. It must also be pointed out, however, that major changes in Portugal's economic doctrine probably could not have taken place until civil–military relations had been redefined and elite consensus regarding the procedures to be followed in resolving conflicts had been established.

The accord in question pertained primarily to the leadership of the Socialist and Social Democratic parties in the National Assembly, and the main player was Aníbal Cavaco Silva. Despite his 1987 electoral victory and the formation of Portugal's first majority government under the PSD's leadership, the Social Democrats could not achieve their goal of removing the constitutional commitment to socialism and reversing the nationalizations of 1975 without the cooperation of the PS. Earlier attempts in 1988 by the Cavaco Silva government to introduce labor reform legislation had generated the largest general strike in the nation's history, on March 28, and the strike made it clear that nothing could be achieved in this domain without the cooperation of the Socialists.

Negotiations between the parliamentary blocs of the two parties took place during the last half of 1988 and the first half of 1989. Eventually what emerged was a coalition of all the major parties, except the PCP. This coalition affirmed the country's commitment to a mixed market economy, and it authorized the government to move ahead with its project of privatizing the nation's banks and insurance companies. Through constitutional revisions executed in May 1989, the irreversibility of the nationalizations carried out at the high point of the revolution in 1975 was canceled by removing Article 83, the clause originally written into the constitution to lock in these changes. Subsequently, after much greater debate and the emergence of a slimmer majority made up of deputies affiliated with center and center–right political alignments, the government succeeded in convincing the National Assembly to ratify removal of the commitment to socialism, in Article 2 of the constitution.

Both changes were seen as prerequisites to Portugal's full entry into the European Community (EC) by the end of 1992, when all barriers to free trade must end, and to other economic changes that must be made to achieve integration into the EC. Despite the importance of these issues in Portugal's external alignments and in demonstrating support for the European Community, what is more significant is the symbolic effect of these revisions on domestic politics. By making these changes, the government has sent a clear signal to the private sector. Ending constitutional constraints on the private sector and opening up the nation's banks and insurance companies to domestic private ownership have given private-sector interests a major voice in the new order. The symbolic effect of these economic changes has been enormous, for at the heart of the grievances expressed in 1974, 1975, and 1976 was the issue of the distribution of economic resources, with the advocates of socialism arguing for a strong, state-regulated economy and the advocates of liberal democracy fighting for the creation of competitive market conditions that would enable Portugal's economic modernization and protect private property.

Thus, by 1989 one could claim that a consensus had been established among elites in Portugal regarding the desirability of consolidating a procedural democracy. The creation of this consensus required, first, spelling out a set of procedures for electing political leaders through full representation of diverse interests and, second, resolving major issues through public contestation and deciding on important legislation through majority vote by deputies in the National Assembly. The two MFA-party pacts and the 1976 constitution were partial agreements regarding issues of participation and representation. In contrast, the constitutional revisions of 1982 and 1989 resolved two major issues dividing elites and masses and preventing the consolidation of a democratic regime: removing the military from politics, thereby ensuring an end to the possibility of the armed forces' exercising a veto power over civilian actions, and ratifying a new public- and private-sector relationship enabling the development and consolidation of a market economy compatible with the European Community's norms and expectations.

At this writing, only one key player remains at the margins of the new regime: the Portuguese Communist party (PCP). Throughout the revolutionary era (1974–5), the transition to democracy (1976–81), and the consolidation of a democratic regime (1982–9), analysts have differed over the place of the PCP in Portuguese politics. Such conflicting assessments are central to conclusions regarding the stability or instability of the new regime (see Bruneau 1989; Gaspar 1990; Pereira 1989; Wiarda 1989). In my view, the acquiescence of PCP leader Alvaro Cunhal in accepting the changes in post–1975 Portugal – as the country has followed a democratic route in its political evolution, without breakdown and recourse to authoritarianism – testifies to the extent to which civilian and military leaders favoring procedural democracy have preempted the country's political space.

There should be no doubt, however, that at this time the PCP remains a semiloyal party that has unwillingly abandoned its earlier status as an antisystem political organization. If it is to survive in the future, I suspect that it, too, will find it necessary to modify both its ideology and its program. One indication that this is likely is the party's internal debates over tactics. During 1989 not only did discussions surface regarding the aging Alvaro Cunhal's successor, but also a new openness began to appear as the party debated the impact of changes in Eastern Europe on Portuguese politics and the need to gain greater voter appeal in national elections. Equally important have been the views of younger party leaders who link the party's survival as a force in Portuguese politics with abandoning orthodox Marxist–Leninist principles and redefining the party as democratic socialist organization. But as long as Cunhal is its leader, it is doubtful that the PCP will abandon its long-standing opposition to bourgeois democracy and capitalism. Despite the prospects of newer, younger leaders eventually rising to the top, Cunhal's continued domination of the party and its solid core of electoral support suggest that orthodox Marxist-Leninism will prevail over the foreseeable future.

But these developments within the PCP do not undercut the argument that there has been much convergence in Portugal among elites. For the time being, the PCP continues to work within the democratic parameters of the new regime because it has no alternative way to participate in politics and express its views on national issues. The longer the PCP acts in this fashion, the more likely it is that Cunhal's successors will redefine the party's place in Portuguese politics. The alignment of the PCP with the PS to ensure the election of an agreed-upon candidate in Lisbon's mayoral election in December 1989, and the success of this strategy, supports this argument. Without agreeing on goals or altering its ideological stance, the PCP continues to stand for elections and to work within the system to achieve its objectives. Once Cunhal has passed from the scene, it is likely that the PCP will associate itself more fully with the existing democratic regime.

The salient features of Portuguese democracy

There are four lessons to be learned in reexamining the Portuguese transition, especially if the Portuguese case is contrasted with South American cases and with the transitions under way in Eastern Europe.

First, throughout Latin America and continental Europe there is a concern with jurisprudence and the use of law to build system legitimacy. Generally speaking, U.S. scholars, especially social scientists, have considered such endeavors to be formalistic and more often obstacles to, rather than supports for, democratic consolidation. Recognizing that legalism can inhibit elite compromise and accommodation as much as it can facilitate it, there is a need to listen to the content of such debates in societies in which legal traditions and democratic ideals have not led to much success in building democratic regimes. In Portugal, the centrality of constitutional and legal issues in debates and discussions about democracy should be seen not as the residue of earlier formalistic studies of the state rooted in the juridical sciences. Instead, they manifest the concern of Portuguese elites with establishing the rule of law that led in the 1970s and the 1980s to the extensive discussions about the Portuguese constitution and the attention given to constitutional revision.

In a divided society, with great inequalities in class and other social conditions, concern with the rule of law in establishing an agreed-upon set of procedures for debating and resolving fundamental differences is essential to the process of building and consolidating democratic institutions. Replacing the legalism of the Estado novo to give legitimacy to a state that always remained illegitimate for major sectors of Portuguese society has required major experimentation and enormous adjustments among conflicting groups and interests. Over these last fifteen years, then, what must not be overlooked is the importance of this protracted discussion about which institutions and legal principles are to take precedence over individual interests and partisan goals. Through this discussion, a consensus has been reached on the use of the vote to determine majority representation, on the open contestation of major issues to express diverse interests in society, and on the use of parliamentary majorities to determine policy outcomes. Out of these debates has come a set of guarantees sanctioned by the force of law and designed to sustain commitment to democratic rule. Rather than viewing the constitution of 1976 as a fundamental charter, with fatal flaws because of its imperfect combination of socialism, democracy, and restrained capitalism, it is more important to recognize its role and the subsequent revisions in 1982 and 1989 as an essential part of an evolving body of democratic understandings and procedures that define the structures and principles that guide the new regime.

Second, the protracted nature of the Portuguese transition should not be seen as indicating the instability of democratic rule and the fragility of the country's new regime. Rather, it confirms the observation that the extent to which a new regime must simultaneously confront a variety of crises and differences weakens its prospects for survival. What has been occurring over the last fifteen years is a resolution, not simultaneously but sequentially, of the main issues dividing the polity.

Given the profundity of the revolution and the frequency with which previous political institutions collapsed, the first and most sensitive issue was civil–military relations. Between 1976 and 1986, various institutional arrangements were tried and abandoned until a consensus was reached among military as well as civilian leaders over the necessity of the military's disengagement from political power, even as guarantors of the new regime, and for civilian rule over all aspects of public policy. Accompanying these adjustments was an agreement on the desirability of competitive party politics and full representation within the National Assembly of the plurality of groups and interests that had emerged since 1974.

Once the military question was laid to rest, the next major item on the national agenda was economic modernization and the restructuring of the Portuguese economy so that it could become more productive and competitive in world markets. This issue has been the primary concern of the Cavaco Silva government since it was first constituted in 1987, and it will remain the dominant issue before the Portuguese public throughout the 1990s. In the process, issues of social policy and attention to the inequities in Portuguese society have been postponed, except for marginal adjustments designed to ensure continuation of civil accord in time of strikes and threats to the new social pact. Yet, if past patterns hold, as economic policies tied to accession and integration with the EC are ratified, attention to related social issues will increase.

Third, in societies with a long history of a politicized military and political instability broken only by periods of authoritarian rule, civil–military relations lie at the core of new political relationships, even when such issues are not discussed and dealt with publicly. Certainly, until 1982 there were open conflicts and debate over the appropriateness of military participation in politics. But it was not until the presidential election of 1986 and the withdrawal of all military candidates for this office that these issues were finally laid to rest. Since that time, it has also become clear that an agreed set of procedures has materialized concerning how civilian control over the military is to be exercised.

Although there is a body of scholarship that emphasizes civilian control of the military under the Salazar dictatorship, it is more accurate to refer to those controls as subjective and reflecting a conservative military hierarchy strongly committed to maintaining the Estado novo. Objective controls and the establishment of professional norms linked to an apolitical officer corps are post–1980 developments. Throughout the life of the Estado novo, the prospect of military insurgency from within the officer corps never disappeared. Today, however, the prospect that the military might reenter politics is as remote as it ever has been (see Wheeler 1979). In considering this change, it is essential to link the consolidation of democratic rule with the protracted settlement between military and civilian leaders in a series of accords extending from 1975 through 1986.

Fourth, it makes a great deal of difference to distinguish democratic transitions from democratic consolidations. My own conclusion regarding the Portuguese case is that consolidation is only just beginning and could not occur until, first, the autonomy of the military and the institutional separation of military affairs from civilian authority had ended and, second, the clauses in the constitution defending the nationalizations and the commitment to socialism had been removed. The latter issue was originally part of civil–military relations, as a major section of the officer corps, those who took power through the April 1974 coup, conceived of their role as guarantors of the original revolutionary changes. Once the military hierarchy had been reasserted and the principle of civilian authority accepted, then it was possible to deal with these economic problems through extended party debate, discussion, and logrolling. From the time Cavaco Silva took office in 1987, he saw his mandate as revising these constitutional clauses. The parliamentary debates over economic issues, between 1987 and 1988, and the final votes on specific clauses in the constitution, in May and June 1989, record how elite convergence in this issue was achieved. The Portuguese case has thus been what I regard as a *protracted elite settlement*, out of which a consolidated democracy is taking shape.

The centrality of civil–military relations in democratic transitions in Brazil and the Southern Cone countries of Latin America and the extensive economic problems in the Eastern European regimes make events and outcomes in Portugal since 1974 especially relevant. Thus, although the Portuguese experience is different from the other transitions in Southern Europe and Latin America discussed in this book, the issues raised in Portugal, the absence of a single overarching settlement, and the way in which the country has resolved its differences incrementally is far more significant than Portugal's small size and peripheral location on the European continent would suggest.

References

Braga da Cruz, Manuel. 1986. "A Evolução das instituições políticas: Partidos políticos e forças armadas na transição democrática portuguesa (1974–1986)." *Povos e culturas* 1:205–15.

Bruneau, Thomas C. 1989. "Portugal Fifteen Years After the April Revolution." *UFSI Field Staff Reports*, Europe. Indianapolis: Universities Field Staff International.

Coelho, Mário Baptista, ed. 1989. *Portugal: O Sistema político e constitucional, 1974–1987*. Lisbon: Instituto de ciências sociais, Universidade de Lisboa.

Ferreira, José Medeiros. 1989. "Um corpo perante o estado: Militares e instituições políticas." In *Portugal: O Sistema político e constitucional, 1974–1987*, ed. Mário Baptista Coelho. Lisbon: Instituto de ciências sociais, Universidade de Lisboa.

Freitas do Amaral, Diogo. 1989. "A Constituição e as forças armadas." In *Portugal: O Sistema político e constitucional, 1974–1987*, ed. Mário Baptista Coelho. Lisbon: Instituto de ciências sociais, Universidade de Lisboa.

Gaspar, Carlos. 1990. "Portuguese Communism Since 1976: Limited Decline." *Problems of Communism* 39:45–63.

Graham, Lawrence S. Forthcoming. "The Portuguese Military: Modernization and Changing Perspectives." In *Democracy and Foreign Policy*, ed. Kenneth Maxwell. Durham, NC: Duke University Press.

Leeds, Elizabeth. 1984. "Labor Export, Development and the State: The Political Economy of Portuguese Emigration." Ph.D. diss., Massachusetts Institute of Technology.

Maxwell, Kenneth. 1986. "Regime Overthrow and the Prospects for Democratic Transition in Portugal." In *Transitions from Authoritarian Rule: Southern Europe*, ed. Guillermo O'Donnell, Philippe C. Schmitter, and Laurence Whitehead. Baltimore: Johns Hopkins University Press.

Pereira, José Pacheco. 1989. "O Partido communista português e a esquerda revolucionária." In *Portugal: O Sistema política e constitucional, 1974–1987*, ed. Mário Baptista Coelho. Lisbon: Instituto de ciências sociais, Universidade de Lisboa.

Wheeler, Douglas L. 1979. "The Military and the Portuguese Dictatorship, 1926–1974: 'The Honor of the Army'." In *Contemporary Portugal: The Revolution and Its Antecedents*, ed. Lawrence S. Graham and Harry M. Makler. Austin: University of Texas Press.

1986. *A Ditadura militar portuguesa (1926–1933)*. Mém Martins: Publicações Europa–America.

Wiarda, Howard. 1989. *The Transition to Democracy in Spain and Portugal*. Lanham, MD: American Enterprise Institute.

11

The Dominican case

PETER M. SANCHEZ

On August 16, 1978, Antonio Guzmán was inaugurated as president of the Dominican Republic. Although such an event might be taken for granted in many countries, for the Dominican Republic it was the first time that political power was transferred peacefully from one president to another. Before the 1978 election, political office was determined more by force than by electoral procedures. Since that watershed election, the ballot box has determined the nation's political leadership, and irregular seizures of power have been nonexistent. In 1982, national elections were again held and, although there were some discrepancies, the political parties and the military accepted the results. The 1986 elections produced yet another peaceful transfer of power. The most recent elections, on May 15, 1990, were historically symbolic, juxtaposing two long-standing political rivals – Joaquín Balaguer, the incumbent, and Juan Bosch, a man who had been ousted by a military *golpe* in 1963. Although the elections were very close and there was some question of fraud, Bosch accepted his defeat, and Balaguer was inaugurated president for the fifth time since 1966.

The 1978 democratic transition thus represents an important and abrupt departure from traditional Dominican politics. Although political repression and irregular seizures of power had characterized the political climate of Dominican politics from the time of independence, since 1978 free and competitive elections have served as the vehicle for transferring political power. During a two-month period, from May to July 1978, the political environment progressed from military intervention in a tenuous democratic process to a situation in which the dominant political party and the military establishment allowed the opposition candidate, Guzmán, to assume the presidency. These important political changes present a good opportunity to test whether the elite settlement concept can help explain the Dominican democratic transition of

1978.[1] In looking at the transition, this chapter seeks to answer the following questions:

1. Did the Dominican elites indeed settle their long-standing differences in 1978, resulting in a significant change in elite behavior that led to the peaceful democratic transfer of power?
2. If an elite settlement did occur in 1978, did it exhibit the characteristics set forth in Chapter 1? That is, was there costly social conflict or a major crisis before the settlement? Was the accord characterized by speed, face-to-face secret negotiations, formal agreements, and informal forbearance among key elites? And finally, did the Dominican political elites have enough autonomy to reach important compromises?
3. Is there evidence that the 1978 settlement led to a transformation from elite disunity to consensual elite unity and the consolidation of a democratic regime? Did a settlement produce adherence to new rules of the game, resulting in the absence of significant challenges to the legitimacy of basic governmental institutions?

The politics of instability

Rafael Trujillo autocratically ruled the Dominican Republic from 1930 until his assassination in May 1961. Most scholars and journalists agree that the Trujillo dictatorship was one of the most brutally repressive in modern history. Essentially, Trujillo dominated the nation through his control of the armed forces. The dictator's legacy was therefore a politically active military that has often and willingly intervened in struggles for political power.

After the dictator's assassination, Joaquín Balaguer, Trujillo's nominal head of state, remained in that position until a *golpe* forced him into exile in January 1962, when the Council of State took control of the nation. While he was in power, Balaguer restored many civil liberties and nationalized the Trujillo family's vast landholdings, actions that subsequently enhanced his image. The Council of State that ruled after Balaguer's ouster acceded to Washington's urging and in December 1962 held the first free and honest elections in over thirty years.

Juan Bosch was elected president and was inaugurated on February 27, 1963. He was the leader of the Partido revolucionario dominicano (PRD or Dominican Revolutionary party), a social democratic party that he had established while in exile in 1939. The PRD won a commanding majority, 64 percent of the vote, as well as more than two

1 Much of the evidence in this chapter is derived from over twenty personal interviews with Dominican political and social leaders that were conducted in January 1989 in Santo Domingo.

thirds of the seats in both houses of congress. All political parties during the election called for the end of *trujillismo*; anything that had to do with the late dictator was anathema. The new democratic regime was short-lived, however, lasting only seven months. A military *golpe* in September 1963 ousted Bosch, who went into exile in Puerto Rico. The military thereupon discarded the progressive constitution and dissolved Congress.

Juan Bosch was overthrown primarily because he was perceived, by the most powerful sectors in Dominican society, to be a danger. With hindsight, we can say that in 1962 Bosch was not really a revolutionary but, rather, a democratic reformer. He was a writer, an intellectual who had strong ties with democratic reformers such as Rómulo Betancourt of Venezuela, Luis Muñoz-Marín of Puerto Rico, and José Figueres of Costa Rica. However, Bosch adopted "agitational" and "populist" political tactics that overstated his political stance (see Bell 1981; Martin 1966; Weston 1979).

In any event, Bosch's constitution, promulgated in April 1963, alienated the most powerful elites. Bosch himself characterized the constitution as "revolutionary" and as emphasizing "social justice and economic democracy." Those who opposed the constitution feared, or at least played on such fears, that it would eliminate private property, separate church and state, give too much power to the workers, and jeopardize the autonomy of the armed forces.

The labeling of Bosch's government as "Communist" by his opponents raised the United States' suspicions. To make matters worse, the U.S. ambassador, John Martin, had a very poor opinion of Bosch. Even though Martin concluded that the Communist influence in Bosch's regime was "surprisingly small," he described Bosch as "emotionally unstable" and "erratic" (Martin 1966, p. 11). In light of this intense and powerful opposition, it is not surprising that the Bosch regime lasted for only seven months. In 1962, only three years after the Cuban revolution, most of the Dominican elites, and their American counterparts, were not ready for a democratic reformer, especially one who was prone to inflammatory rhetoric. Consequently, they would not consider reaching an accommodation with Bosch.

A three-man junta, referred to as the Triumvirate, took control of the country after Bosch's ouster. Eventually it came to be dominated by Reid Cabral, a man who had almost no base of popular support. The Triumvirate was constantly under attack, but the United States supported it, as it promised to hold elections in 1965. Nevertheless, austerity measures during a period of economic troubles eventually brought down Cabral's Triumvirate, and the resulting power struggle led to civil war.

On April 24, 1965, a military *golpe* ousted the Triumvirate. Reflecting Cabral's lack of support, the *golpe* was sparked by a popular uprising partly instigated by a young PRD activist, José Peña Gómez. Peña Gómez took control of Radio Santo Domingo, the government radio station, and urged the masses to take to the streets in order to restore to power Bosch and his constitution. The PRD radicals had acquired weapons and were passing them out to anyone who would support their "constitutionalist" cause. Although there were only one thousand to fifteen hundred rebels on April 24, by the next morning there were several thousand (Bracey 1980, p. xiv). This social turmoil was enough to prompt the military to oust the Triumvirate and try to put down the Boschist insurrection.

On April 28, 1965, President Lyndon B. Johnson sent the U.S. Marines to the Dominican Republic to "protect U.S. citizens."[2] Eventually, about 22,000 U.S. troops occupied a zone in the Dominican capital of Santo Domingo, preventing the two warring factions – the "constitutionalists" and the "loyalists" – from engaging in major conflict. After intense U.S. lobbying, the occupation became an international venture when, on May 6, the Organization of American States (OAS) voted to establish an Inter-American Peace Force (IAPF) on Dominican soil.

The IAPF created a military stalemate in the conflict, so it became obvious that a compromise solution was the only way out of the impasse. After a failed attempt by the Johnson administration to negotiate an accord, the OAS established an *ad hoc* committee to resolve the conflict. The committee eventually facilitated a compromise between the two sides. A provisional government, acceptable to both sides, was put in place until a new government could be elected.

The 1966 election that resulted from this compromise did not, however, pave the way for the establishment of a consolidated democracy in the Dominican Republic. The main contenders were Juan Bosch, who returned from exile in September 1965, and Joaquín Balaguer, who founded the Partido reformista (PR or Reformist party) while in exile in 1962. In the elections, Balaguer received a substantial victory with 57 percent of the vote; Bosch received only 39 percent. Parties of the far right received 3.5 percent, and parties of the far left received less than 1 percent. Balaguer also won a substantial majority in both houses. Most evidence indicates that after the election Joaquín Bal-

2 Most analysts agree that President Johnson's principal concern was preventing another Cuban revolution. The administration became convinced that the "constitutionalists" were being infiltrated by Communists, even though reports from the embassy estimated that the Communist influence was minimal. Thus, the intent of the intervention was to halt the military gains made by the rebel forces.

aguer used the military to repress his opponents, especially the PRD. Haffe Serulle, former president of the Dominican Union for the Defense of Human Rights, stated in an interview that "many leftists who fought in the civil war were systematically killed by death squads in the years after the war." In fact, some estimates show that there were about one thousand political murders between 1966 and 1971. One noted expert on Dominican politics described the Balaguer government as "willing to use fraud and intimidation in order to remain in power." Such repressive measures helped Balaguer win the presidency in the 1970 and 1974 elections. But the PRD boycotted both elections, charging the government with violations of civil liberties and electoral fraud.

The moderation of Dominican elites

Although the PR under Balaguer's leadership maintained itself in power with military support, the PRD reached a point of internal crisis in 1973 when a personal and ideological rift pitted the patriarch Bosch against the younger activist and secretary general of the party, Peña Gómez.[3] It is believed that at this time Bosch became impatient with the dominance of Balaguer's PR and began to call for the PRD's radicalization. Although it is still uncertain whether Bosch fully supported a revolutionary route to power, the younger Peña Gómez was dead set against such a course. Bosch and Peña Gómez thus disagreed over basic political strategies. Whereas Bosch labeled electoral parties "traitors," Peña Gómez was quite willing to follow the electoral route to political power. The conflict between the two men was also personal in nature. Bosch, very much the caudillo, prevented all young leaders from overshadowing him. Peña Gómez was becoming too popular and too independent for Bosch's taste, and thus he attempted to isolate and undermine the younger, charismatic leader.

Toward this end, Bosch founded the Partido de liberación dominicana (PLD or Dominican Liberation party) in November 1973, hoping that most of the PRD militants would follow him. Unfortunately for Bosch, Peña Gómez inherited the PRD label and organization and retained most of its followers. What Bosch unwittingly did was to take with him the most radical militants of the PRD. Once the caudillo and many of his devoted and more radical followers were gone, "the

3 General Caamaño, the former constitutionalist leader, led a revolutionary expedition to oust the Balaguer regime in 1973. Bosch wanted the PRD to support the endeavor, but Peña Gómez urged moderation and wanted to distance the party from Caamaño's revolutionary exploits.

PRD reaffirmed its moderate position under the leadership of José Francisco Peña Gómez" (see Espinal 1986).

Immediately, Peña Gómez and the PRD leadership faced the important decision of whether to participate in the 1974 elections. The PRD, along with five other opposition parties, had signed the Acuerdo de Santiago (Santiago accord) as a means of unifying the opposition against the Balaguer regime in those elections. Only days before this took place, however, the PRD pulled out of the agreement, its leaders fearing that the opposition, as in 1966, would be repressed by Balaguer's military and that as a consequence violence would break out. Their fears were well grounded, as the military were very active in the 1974 campaign, openly placing red banners – the PR's color – on the soldiers' rifles. Once the PRD withdrew from the election, the accord disintegrated, and only one small party challenged Balaguer. With military assistance, the PR had again intimidated the opposition and held on to government office.

At this point, the PRD faced another major decision. Either the party would have to adopt Juan Bosch's more revolutionary posture, or it would become an acceptable, fully mainstream political force. Peña Gómez and other PRD leaders decided to detach themselves from any radical orientations or antiregime stance. This move terminated all remaining links between the PRD and Bosch's newly formed PLD, and it resulted in a complete political redirection of the once-revolutionary PRD.

In founding the PRD in 1939, Bosch was greatly influenced by other Latin American revolutionary parties, like the Partido revolucionario institutional (Institutional Revolutionary party) of Mexico, the Partido revolucionario cubano (Cuban Revolutionary party), and the Alianza popular revolucionaria americana (American Popular Revolutionary alliance) of Peru. These parties tended to be antioligarchic, egalitarian, and highly nationalistic, which usually translated into opposition to American imperialism. The PRD's revolutionary doctrine was initially directed against the Trujillo regime, and in 1949 and 1959 the party organized unsuccessful military attacks against the dictator.

Peña Gómez and other PRD leaders rejected this legacy and decided that instead of participating in a lost cause in the 1974 election, they would prepare the PRD to participate in the 1978 elections, a strategy that paid off handsomely. Essentially, Peña Gómez and other PRD leaders decided to make the party an "acceptable" political institution, not just to Balaguer, the PR, and military elites, but to Dominican businessmen, professionals, clergy, and the international community as well.

The first step was to organize the party's domestic support. The

PRD leaders realized that the party was little more than a band of intellectuals and political activists. Although many Dominicans supported or sympathized with the PRD and its goals, there were no strong links between the party leaders and the mass electorate. Thus, in 1974 the PRD leaders and activists began a nationwide effort to organize urban and rural syndicates, university students, and PRD youth clubs. A second step was to acquire international support. As early as 1972, some PRD leaders had begun to establish ties with U.S. political elites. The PRD in that year prepared a document for Senator Edward Kennedy that described the political repression carried out by the Balaguer regime. After 1974, Peña Gómez traveled extensively to the United States and Europe in an effort to legitimate his opposition party in the eyes of foreign political leaders. He attended the 1976 Democratic National Convention that nominated Jimmy Carter, and he developed strong personal ties with Senators Frank Church, William Fulbright, and Edward Kennedy. This enabled the PRD leaders to win the Carter administration's ear. Thus, Peña Gómez and Jacobo Majluta (who became the party's vice-presidential candidate) met on several occasions with U.S. State Department representatives to discuss the upcoming 1978 election. They insisted that if the PRD won it would need U.S. influence and support to check the Dominican military's power.

The PRD leaders also developed close ties with other nations of the industrialized West and with Latin American countries. In 1976 they obtained membership in the Socialist International (SI), thereby obtaining important political ties as well as economic and organizational support. Through SI membership, Peña Gómez and his party came to count Willy Brandt, Felipe González, and François Mitterrand among their supporters abroad, and they developed or enhanced ties with leaders of socialist parties in Latin America. In particular, Peña Gómez cultivated strong personal ties with President Carlos Andrés Pérez of Venezuela, who proved to be an important actor in the 1978 "transaction" that ended the electoral crisis.

Once the PRD leaders transformed their party into a mainstream political organization, they needed only to choose a viable presidential candidate. Although he was the chief engineer of the PRD's political transformation, Peña Gómez knew that he would not be accepted as president by the PR, many economic elites, and especially the military: His involvement in the civil war and his youthful radicalism worked against him. Another critical consideration was that Peña Gómez was a black man in a nation made up predominantly of mulattoes who had a deep-seated hatred for Haitians (or anyone who looked Haitian).

Peña Gómez, an astute politician, thus stepped aside to enable the party to select a more suitable candidate. The result, however, was a power struggle among three other top PRD leaders – Antonio Guzmán, Jacobo Majluta, and Jorge Blanco. After intense competition, the party convention selected Guzmán, who clearly represented the new, moderate PRD image. He was a wealthy landowner, had been a pivotal figure in the 1965 negotiations as a possible leader of the provisional government (and so he was acceptable to the United States), and had excellent ties with the Dominican business elite.

Through these pragmatic steps, the PRD became a strong political organization with mass domestic support and important international ties. By 1978 the PRD leadership had discarded all of its earlier radicalism. Naturally, this transformation invited criticism from parties on the left. Two days before the 1978 elections, Juan Bosch attacked his old party by calling the PRD a "rightist organization." After Guzmán was officially proclaimed the winner of the election, Narciso Isa Conde, the leader of the Partido comunista dominicano (Dominican Communist party) stated that Guzmán's government would be very similar to Balaguer's government. These criticisms were plausible because the PRD had won the support, or at least the acceptance, of the business elite. In a radio speech one week before the election, Peña Gómez pointed out that PRD relations with the business community were "better" than in 1963. He confirmed that although some businessmen still believed that the PRD was an extremist party, many of them "did realize that their interests and their sons' interests were guaranteed with the PRD." Thus, by 1978 "the PRD had a following that was by no means confined to manual laborers and the unemployed. Its spread was both vertical and horizontal: from the masses upward into the middle-classes and, more important still, from the towns outward into the countryside" (Bell 1981, p. 223).

The PRD was not the only party that showed signs of political moderation prior to the 1978 elections. Even though the PR was classified as a conservative and even reactionary political party, Balaguer was certainly no Trujillo, and even the PRD leaders seldom compared him with the ruthless dictator. On the contrary, during the 1960s and 1970s, right-wing forces had also shifted gradually toward the center. After Trujillo's death in 1961, the regime led by Balaguer exhibited important tendencies toward moderation. For example, Balaguer immediately reinstated civil rights, confiscated all of Trujillo's vast landholdings, and instituted a land reform program. But the chaos and uncertainty that followed Trujillo's death prevented the establishment of a stable and legitimate government, owing largely to the elites' disunity. Most of the elites at that time disagreed about what direction the nation should take and about the type of government it should have.

The civil war heightened these disagreements and led to a repressive regime. Yet even Balaguer's rule from 1966 to 1978 was but a pale shadow of Trujillo's tyranny. Even those PRD leaders who were persecuted between 1966 and 1972, thought of it as a *semidictadura* (semidictatorship). Balaguer's three governments, though repressive, allowed the opposition some degree of freedom, especially after 1974. Without such leeway, the PRD would not have been able to carry out its transformation between 1974 and 1978. In 1978, Balaguer even permitted the Communist party to participate in the national elections.

In addition to gradual political liberalization, in 1972 Balaguer instituted a land reform program. This new initiative could well have been a PRD program. In fact, Bosch has stated that he was deposed in 1963 for much less than what Balaguer enacted in 1972. Nonetheless, Balaguer's land reform program alienated many of the landed elite. Abortively in 1974 and then clearly in 1978, these disaffected elites had a moderate alternative – the PRD.

By 1978, other social organizations had moderated as well. Economic elites, professionals, intellectuals, and church leaders all urged the government to respect the elections. In 1962, most of the elites from these sectors (except perhaps the intellectuals) had been violently opposed to PRD rule under Bosch. One week before the 1978 election, Peña Gómez stated that democracy might now be possible in the Dominican Republic, for two reasons: First, business elites had more "progressive, democratic ideas," and second, church elites had become much more concerned with the condition of the lower classes. The PRD leader was simply recording the fact that a variety of traditionally conservative social forces in the country had become more moderate through the years.

The 1978 electoral crisis

The political environment preceding the May 16, 1978, elections was thus substantially more moderate than that in earlier elections. On several occasions, Balaguer and the military leaders assured the public that the outcome of the elections would be respected. Indeed, in March, Balaguer and Guzmán signed a "nonaggression pact." In an effort to reduce violence and ensure that the results would be respected, the two leaders agreed to refrain from agitation or violence and to accept the outcome without any retribution.

Despite these preelection assurances, the 1978 elections were marred by violence, military involvement, and electoral fraud. In April, the newsweekly *Ahora!* cited twelve different cases in which the opposition was subjected to political violence by the ruling party and the military. More important, on May 17, the day after the election, the National Police occupied the headquarters of the Junta central electoral (JCE or Central electoral board) and stopped the vote count. On the next day, Balaguer went on national television and announced that the vote count would resume and that the results would be honored. But the count then proceeded at a snail's pace, creating widespread suspicion. Indeed, the JCE was forced to hire foreign election specialists to verify the electoral results, as most Dominicans who were qualified would not accept this responsibility because they were afraid of reprisals. Nevertheless, on May 26 the JCE announced that Guzmán had won the election but that it was investigating charges of fraud brought against the PRD by the PR. When the official results were finally made public, on July 7, Guzmán was still the victor, but his party had lost four Senate seats, which happened to give Balaguer's party a majority there. Initially, the PRD had won control of both houses, but the JCE had overturned the results of four Senate races, giving the PR a sixteen-to-eleven edge in that chamber. Not only did this ruling give the PR an opportunity to block PRD legislation, but it also gave them considerable control over the judicial branch, as one function of the Senate was to select supreme court judges. The PRD's leaders protested the JCE's decision and brought their case to the supreme court, but it ruled that it did not have jurisdiction over electoral matters, and so the decision stood.

Why did the PR and the armed forces allow their traditional archenemy, the PRD, to take control of the presidency and the Chamber of Deputies, and why did the PRD accept a blatantly arbitrary decision by the JCE that took away their control of the Senate and judiciary? There is convincing evidence that the resolution of the 1978 electoral crisis was the result of a secret agreement among Balaguer, the military leadership, and Guzmán.

Just a few weeks before the JCE ruling, Guzmán met with Balaguer on three occasions, with military leaders on two occasions, and once with the U.S. ambassador. On May 30, Guzmán and Balaguer met, in Guzmán's words, to obtain a better "understanding" and to discuss the "transition of power." The meeting was conducted in private between the president and the president-elect. Guzmán characterized the discussion as "extremely cordial," stating: "We have established the base for a series of meetings and dialogues that we will celebrate in the future." One week later, on June 7, Guzmán met with the secretary of the armed forces, General Juan Beauchamp Javier, and other military leaders. Guzmán, who had requested the meeting, explained that the purpose of the encounter was to maintain good relations with the military, an "important sector." He regarded the meeting as "very cordial" and claimed that the interchange "was very beneficial and fruitful." Guzmán met with Balaguer a second time on June 8, following which Guzmán remarked, "I know that on August 16 I will take possession. The new government will take possession." He also revealed that Balaguer had authorized him to visit with the chief of the national police. Three days later, on June 11, Guzmán met with General Neit Nivar Seijas, the man who had initiated the electoral intervention. Before the meeting, Balaguer announced that he was giving the national police a pay raise. After the meeting, Guzmán stated that he had told Nivar Seijas that Balaguer had beaten him to the punch, as he would have done the same once he was inaugurated. Guzmán and Balaguer met for the last time on June 17. This time, unlike the previous meetings, the Balaguer regime released official photographs of an encounter that lasted one hour and twenty minutes. After the meeting, Balaguer stated that he was confident that the electoral crisis would be resolved; Guzmán added that the JCE would announce the official results of the election within eight to ten days. Guzmán also mysteriously told the press that he could not reveal details of the meeting, saying only that "there are things that I cannot reveal to anyone."[4] Finally, Guzmán met with U.S. Ambassador Robert Yost on June 20 for a brief fifteen minutes.

All indications thus are that Guzmán was certain after this round of meetings that he would be inaugurated president. On June 23, he visited the PRD's headquarters and urged the party militants to remain calm. He also told them that once the JCE announced its decision, "all will be normalized in the country." Guzmán's action strongly suggests not only that he was confident that he would be the next Dominican president but also that he knew of the JCE's upcoming decision.

The meetings just described are insufficient in themselves to conclude that an elite settlement was worked out by Guzmán, Balaguer, and the military, especially because the details of the meetings are not available. However, reactions to the arbitrary JCE decision by the PRD, the PR, and the armed forces, plus the revelations by relevant

4 All quotations regarding the series of meetings are from the Dominican newspaper *Listín diario*, the Dominican weekly magazine *El Nacional de ahora!*, and the Miami Spanish newspaper *Diario de las Américas*.

individuals, provide additional support for the assertion that a relatively comprehensive elite agreement had indeed been reached.

It seems that the Dominicans understand the importance of the JCE decision quite well, as they refer to it as the "historic decision" (*el fallo histórico*). But though historically important, the JCE's overturning of four senatorial contests was completely arbitrary. The PR claimed that in many precincts its supporters were kept off the computerized electoral rolls because of a conspiracy between the PRD and some JCE officials.[5] The PRD, on the other hand, argued that the rolls were not up-to-date because of the enormous voter turnout and that large numbers of PRD supporters had also been prevented from voting. The JCE, nevertheless, sided with the PR. The average abstention rate in the election had been 27 percent, but in four districts had been higher. The JCE therefore estimated the number of voters who had been unable to cast ballots in those four districts and gave the PR a percentage of that estimate (the percentage they had received in the election). This new total put the PR ahead of the PRD in all four cases. What was most arbitrary was that no other party received a percentage of the estimated abstention.

If the JCE's action was unusual, the reactions to it were even more so. Although the PR's attorney, Mario Vinicio Castillo, called the ruling "absurd," "antijudicial," and "unconstitutional," the presidential candidates reacted in a conciliatory fashion. On July 13, both Balaguer and Guzmán went on national television to discuss the JCE's ruling. Balaguer stated: "Even though [the decision] is monstrous in its judicial aspect, it is convenient for the country because it brings to an end a dangerous crisis." He also added that although some PRD leaders were criticizing the decision, they should remember that the PR and the PRD had signed a nonaggression pact that committed him to cooperate with the new government and the "necessary" reforms it would initiate, including land reform. Perhaps most significantly, he observed that the JCE's decision actually was "convenient" because President Guzmán would need an "independent political force" to counterbalance the radical forces within the PRD, an interesting comment from a man who had suppressed the political opposition for twelve years.

Guzmán and other PRD leaders, though certainly critical of the

5 Many have charged that in 1978 the JCE was replete with PRD sympathizers. Indeed, before 1978 the PRD had developed close ties with many JCE officials, and there are some indications that JCE officials had favored the PRD in 1978. To date, Joaquín Balaguer is convinced that the PRD robbed him of the presidency in 1978 through the manipulation of the JCE.

decision, also exhibited a great deal of restraint and moderation. To avert the possibility of chaos, Peña Gómez, in a radio speech aired on the night of the JCE ruling, called for "patience and calm" and urged party militants not to obey any orders that did not originate directly from the PRD's executive committee. In his July 13 address, Guzmán asked all Dominicans, especially PRD supporters, for "cordiality, tranquillity, and harmony." He also stated that the ruling should not detract from the "joy and satisfaction" of the PRD victory and that the decision was "worthy of being pardoned." In a radio speech on July 10, Peña Gómez stated that the *fallo* was unconstitutional but that the PRD's national executive committee had decided to accept it as "valid" so that it would not succeed in provoking the PRD "irresponsibly [to] send its masses into the streets." Thus, even though the PRD leadership criticized the decision rhetorically, it ensured that PRD militants would not repeat the capricious actions of 1965 that led to civil war.

Finally, the military and national police supported the decision wholeheartedly. On July 12, the armed forces and the national police promulgated a declaration signed by all officers of the rank of captain or above who supported the JCE decision. This declaration, published in the newspaper *Listín diario,* stated that the army, navy, air force, and national police "offered their unconditional support to the ruling decreed by the JCE," adding that the decision "could guarantee the continuation of peace . . . maintain the constitutional regime, and make possible the peaceful transition of power."

This overwhelming acceptance and support of the JCE's arbitrary decision lends credibility to the assertion that elites substantially agreed. If not, how else could we explain the unanimous support of an arbitrary decision by factions that only a month earlier were on the verge of serious conflict?

In addition to the unanimous acceptance of the JCE's *fallo,* political leaders who were involved in, or closely followed, the crisis almost without exception believe that an accord was reached. Some have provided details of the negotiations. According to these accounts, sometime in June when the PR was attempting to have the JCE annul the election, there was a secret meeting between a close friend of Balaguer, Guzmán's daughter (Sonia Guzmán), the U.S. political attaché, and an emissary sent by President Pérez of Venezuela. The purpose of this meeting was to resolve the political impasse. Two sources claim that President Pérez, a leader well aware of the importance of accommodating elites, introduced the idea of a "transaction" that would give presidential power to the PRD, while at the same time giving the PR control of the Senate. One observer close to

Balaguer and closely involved in the crisis claims that Sonia Guzmán agreed to this "transaction" on behalf of her father, because Antonio Guzmán preferred to have a Senate led by Joaquín Balaguer than by his party rival Jorge Blanco. This claim is made more credible by Balaguer's recent revelation of the bitter conflict between Guzmán and Blanco.[6] One observer, politically removed from both the PR and the PRD, believes that this transaction, even though "it could not be called democracy," was necessary for national stability.

Most PRD leaders, however, refrained from viewing the JCE ruling as a political transaction. Peña Gómez pointed out that Guzmán always denied that he struck a deal with Balaguer. He also argued that the *fallo* was Balaguer's decision and that Guzmán simply decided not to press the issue. The current PRD secretary general, Hatuey De Camps, characterized the *fallo* as the "greatest act of corruption in Dominican history." Finally, Winston Arnaud, secretary general of the PRD splinter group, La Estructura, called the *fallo* "a robbery." Although these men regard the JCE decision as an imposition by Balaguer, they recognize that Antonio Guzmán did in fact accept the transaction in order to avert social turmoil. Peña Gómez admitted that Guzmán decided not to contest the JCE ruling in earnest and that he gave orders to respect Balaguer once he was inaugurated as president. De Camps pointed out that the PRD was forced to deal with Balaguer and the military, as the alternatives were to accept the *fallo* or to face the possibility of another civil war. And Arnaud admitted that Guzmán told the PRD leaders that they should offer an "olive branch."

It is understandable that PRD leaders would hesitate to accept or admit that the electoral crisis of 1978 was resolved through a deal or transaction. After all, if true, such a solution would be considered by many to be antidemocratic. It is likely that those who reject this interpretation are themselves convinced that the *fallo* was not the result of a transaction but, rather, of political and military pressure brought on Guzmán by Balaguer and the antidemocratic generals. No one could argue that Guzmán was not under pressure to accept the *fallo*. However, it is also true that Balaguer and certain generals were likewise under extreme domestic and international pressure to hand power over to the PRD. Therefore, it can just as easily be argued by PR sympathizers that even though Balaguer believed that there had been fraud in the election, Guzmán forced him into transferring power by using pressure from the United States, the Socialist International, and numerous influential domestic groups. It is understandable, then,

6 See Balaguer 1988, pp.370–2. Blanco led a bitter, obstructionist opposition with his PRD followers in the Congress during Guzmán's presidency, 1978 to 1982.

that some PRD leaders perceive the *fallo* as an imposition rather than a transaction because the negotiations between Balaguer and Guzmán took place under a great deal of pressure and because Guzmán always denied that he had struck a deal. Nevertheless, the evidence strongly points to the existence of an explicit compromise among elites.

This reluctance to admit that a compromise was made is in line with the covert and delicate nature of elite settlements. Leaders who have previously experienced violent conflict necessarily come to the bargaining table with mistrust and apprehension. During the course of a settlement, negotiations among antagonistic elites are fraught with suspicion, and a provocation or confrontation may doom the process to failure. Thus, the continued willingness of the elites in such delicate circumstances to compromise depends heavily on their interpretation of events and their diplomatic skills. After an agreement is reached, moreover, it is doubtful that the elites will readily admit to their followers that they have made a pact with their former enemies.

In sum, the general consensus among key Dominicans is that the 1978 transfer of power could not have occurred without the transaction that gave the PR control of the Senate. For important political, military, and economic elites, this control was imperative for a peaceful transfer of power to the opposition, as it ensured that the PRD would neither carry out "risky social reforms" nor attempt to persecute judicially the PR or the military. Without those explicit guarantees, the power transfer probably could not have taken place.

The democratic aftermath

Unfortunately, Antonio Guzmán did not complete his term in office; he committed suicide on July 3, 1982. There is no indication, however, that his death was a political murder. Guzmán was in the presidential palace with his brother-in-law and bodyguards when he entered the bathroom and shot himself with his pistol. It is widely believed that he took his life during a period of intense depression, generated by his realization that many high officials in his administration were involved in corruption. Guzmán had always verbally attacked government corruption and vowed to end it. In fact, before his inauguration, in 1978, he stated that his "greatest dream" was to establish a government that was a "model of honesty." Balaguer has recently claimed that Guzmán's suicide was influenced by the fact that Guzmán's archrival within the PRD, Jorge Blanco, intended to carry out reprisals and persecutions against him, if he, Blanco, became the next president.

The elections of 1982 gave the PRD a second presidential victory, augmented by control of both houses of Congress. As Guzmán had feared, Jorge Blanco became the new president. The election also gave Juan Bosch nearly 10 percent of the vote, providing his PLD with nine seats in the Chamber of Deputies. Although there were no major complaints about the 1982 electoral proceedings, approximately twelve people died and several hundred were injured as a result of political violence. But former political hatreds had abated significantly. Thus, before the election the army chief of staff, General Manuel Lachapelle, stated that the left represented "no danger" to the nation and even that its participation in the election "might possibly enhance democracy." The military had also lost its fear of the PRD, and especially of Antonio Guzmán. In fact, by 1982 most military leaders wanted Guzmán to be reelected. One PRD vice-president confided that Guzmán "drank and rode horses" and, because of his landowning background, had a "feudal demeanor," but the military leaders liked and admired this behavior. Finally, and most important the most feared PRD leader – Peña Gómez – was elected mayor of Santo Domingo. The man who had helped instigate the 1965 civil war and whom many had labeled a Communist, even as late as 1978, was now part of the governing elite.

The elections of 1986 produced the second peaceful transfer of power to an opposition candidate, thus further enhancing the democratic process. Joaquín Balaguer, whose PR had merged with a smaller party in 1985, defeated Jacobo Majluta, the PRD candidate and vice-president under Guzmán. Perhaps the most important aspect of this election was its rebuff of the PRD's attempts to entrench itself as a hegemonic party like the PRI in Mexico. Not only did the PR victory spoil this effort, but Bosch's strong showing (over 18 percent of the vote and sixteen seats in the Chamber of Deputies) forced the PRD to negotiate with the PR. In fact, Balaguer held secret talks with the PRD after his inauguration in order to secure its support in Congress.

The 1986 elections were not devoid of problems. Six people died as a result of political violence during the campaign, and during the vote count Majluta claimed that the JCE favored Balaguer. Thereupon, two of the three board members, including the JCE president, resigned in protest, thus causing the vote count to be suspended. The controversy was resolved, however, when Majluta and Balaguer met and agreed on a government of "national unity."

Another important aspect of the 1986 elections was that Juan Bosch, who in 1978 had labeled the PRD's involvement in electoral politics as "treason," became much more supportive of electoral politics. Curiously, during the campaign, Bosch stated that Dominican capitalism had to be strengthened before socialism could succeed. Encouraged by his increasing electoral support – 10 percent in 1982 and 18 percent in 1986 – Bosch saw that moderation was the key to electoral victory.

The 1990 elections, although eventually deemed legitimate, were marred by allegations of vote fraud. Before them, fears abounded that Bosch could win the contest (polls showed him in the lead) and that the military and economic elites would not allow him to take office. But a high-ranking general involved in the Government of National Reconstruction[7] and labeled a rightist in 1965 by the Johnson administration candidly admitted that the threat of Communism in the Dominican Republic was no longer real. And in a press conference, Balaguer declared that if Juan Bosch won the 1990 elections, "he would personally celebrate it as a triumph of Dominican democracy."[8] Preelection polls predicted a Bosch victory. Thus, when early returns indicated that Balaguer had a slight edge, Bosch's PLD charged the government with vote fraud. The vote count was stopped after five days to retally the results under international scrutiny, including that of the former U.S. president Jimmy Carter. On June 11, 1990, the JCE delivered the final results, declaring Balaguer the victor, with a margin of only 25,000 votes. Balaguer's PR received 35.7 percent of the vote, with Bosch's PLD attaining a close 34.4 percent. International observers declared that the vote fraud was insufficient to alter the results, and Bosch accepted the JCE's tallies.

It appears, then, that democratic consolidation is well advanced in the Dominican Republic and that it rests on a considerable foundation of political stability. Leaders who had at one time resorted to violence have forsaken that tactic for peaceful electoral competition.

Conclusion: an elite settlement?

There is evidence that a settlement or a partial settlement among important Dominican elites came in 1978. Elite behavior changed dramatically in that year, and a political environment in which all political and military leaders respect the rules of the game and refrain from

7 The GNR was the government established by the "loyalists" soon after the civil war broke out.

8 All of the individuals that I interviewed believed that if Bosch were to win in 1990, he definitely should be allowed to take office. There were three basic reasons offered: because democracy should be preserved; because Bosch would not, and probably could not, make drastic reforms or changes; and because a civil war could break out if he were denied power. The lessons of 1965 have not been lost in the minds of Dominican elites.

challenging the regime by force was created. In concluding, I want to expand this interpretation by highlighting several discrepancies between the Dominican case and the idea of elite settlements as set forth in Chapter 1.

The historical preconditions that facilitate elite settlements – costly conflict and a new, major crisis – were certainly present before and during the events of 1978. From the time of Trujillo's murder in 1961 to the United States' intervention in 1965, the Dominican Republic was embroiled in a continuing political crisis. The repugnant features of Trujillo's regime had led the international community to virtually ostracize the country and had convinced some Dominican elites that a sweeping regime change was necessary. Bosch emerged in the power vacuum that followed Trujillo's death, but he was not trusted by other elites, who participated in his ouster. In turn, the Triumvirate that replaced him also became prey to the elites' distrust. The nation became divided into two violently antagonistic camps, eventually culminating in a costly but inconclusive civil war, in which some three thousand lives were lost. When foreign occupation abruptly halted the war, the elites had become tired of the killing, tired of constant political turmoil, and, finally, tired of having their national sovereignty challenged by occupying American forces. In general terms, then, many of the circumstances that can lead to a settlement among disunified elites were present in the Dominican Republic. But perhaps because the United States sided with the "loyalists" (the military and pro-Balaguer factions), Balaguer was in a position to dominate his political opponents, namely, the "constitutionalists" and the PRD. Under these circumstances, there could be no elite settlement: Balaguer had no incentive to compromise, as he had a virtual monopoly on political power.

Eventually, the Dominican elites reached another critical watershed. The 1978 electoral crisis had the potential to erupt – at least in the eyes of most political leaders – into another major conflict. Although it began when the military stopped the vote count, the 1978 crisis was really a crisis over *continuismo*. During his twelve-year rule, Balaguer had encouraged or allowed considerable political repression. By 1978, many elites had tired of his rule and sided with the newly moderate PRD. When the election showed that a majority of Dominicans wanted change, most elites indicated that they would not tolerate electoral fraud. Even segments of the military opposed those military leaders who wanted to deny Guzmán his victory. In fact, there was so much opposition to the electoral intervention that a majority of military officers feared that a *golpe* aimed at preventing Guzmán from taking office would precipitate another civil war. Fear of renewed civil strife was certainly a strong incentive for previously warring elites to reach a political compromise. Even Juan Bosch, a marginal actor in the 1978 crisis, argued that unless an accord was reached by all the "people and principal political forces affected by the crisis," the "crisis could enter into a state of decomposition." This kind of fear had been absent in 1965, and yet violence erupted; in 1978, memories of the civil war and fear that it might be repeated induced the elites to search for another way out.

Moreover, the manner in which the elites resolved the 1978 crisis closely parallels the processes associated with elite settlements. First, the crisis was resolved quickly. It began on May 17 when the military stopped the vote count, and it was effectively resolved by the time the JCE issued its decision on July 7, less than two months later. Second, there were many face-to-face, partially secret negotiations among the paramount leaders of the major elite factions. Guzmán met privately with Balaguer three times (recall that they also met before the crisis to sign a nonaggression pact), with military leaders twice, and with the U.S. ambassador once. For his part, Balaguer met regularly with military leaders during the crisis, most likely in order to understand exactly what was transpiring and to convince the military to resume the vote count. Additionally, military officers who were against a *golpe* met on several occasions to rally support for their cause and to organize their efforts. These meetings in turn generated many meetings within each elite faction. For example, when the JCE announced its decision on July 7, the PRD's national executive committee held an intensive two-day meeting. All of these meetings were, for the most part, secret. In fact, details of the discussions between Balaguer and Guzmán are still unknown to the public, and many of those who were intimately involved in the process still refuse to disclose what really took place in the June 1978 negotiations.

Third, experienced and paramount political leaders were the key actors. Balaguer had been president under Trujillo and for eight months after his death, and he had been elected president in 1966, 1970, and 1974. Guzmán was a critical player during the 1965 crisis, having been the prominent choice in the U.S.-led negotiations for a PRD-dominated government without Bosch. He served as minister of agriculture in Bosch's 1962 government, and he was Bosch's vice-presidential candidate in the 1966 election. But most important, as the leader of the PRD in 1978, he commanded the best-organized political party in the country. Finally, although the military was fragmented in 1978, the principal generals – Nivar Seijas, Beauchamps, and Pérez y Pérez – all were closely involved in the crisis negotiations.

Formal constitutional agreements were not reached in 1978, however. Before the election, Balaguer and Guzmán signed a nonaggression pact, and all military officers and national police officers above the grade of lieutenant signed a national declaration supporting the JCE's *fallo*. But no constitutional or other binding document was hammered out, and there are no written records (at least public) of the secret discussions that took place in June. The reason may be that a constitution acceptable to both sides was already in place and, perhaps more important, that the two major parties did not significantly differ on broad policy issues. In 1978, only two things had to be resolved in order for a stable democratic regime to emerge: the acceptance of a transfer of power to the opposition and the depoliticization of the military. Both were resolved in the June 1978 negotiations.

Forbearance and conciliatory behavior among elites was also clearly present during the crisis. The best example was the PRD's mild reaction to the JCE's ruling. The party lost control of the Senate because of an arbitrary decision, yet it accepted the decision and even took steps to ensure that its constituency did not react violently. As we have seen, both Guzmán and Penã Gómez exhibited a great deal of restraint and moderation when the *fallo* was made public. There was forbearance on the part of the PR and the military as well. First and most important, Guzmán was allowed to take office. Although this is common practice in democratic systems, an electoral transfer of power in the Dominican Republic was unknown in 1978, and most experts did not believe that Guzmán would last more than six months. Also, Guzmán removed military officers who supported Balaguer; such an action by a civilian leader before 1978 would have resulted in military intervention (as the experts predicted). But the PR and the military acquiesced in Guzmán's bold actions, and thus he was able to reform the military.

Thus, all three major elite factions made important concessions. The PRD's leaders, although convinced that they had won political power legitimately, nevertheless accepted the loss of a majority in the Senate and a concomitant loss of judicial power. The PR, although convinced that the PRD had perpetrated some sort of electoral fraud, nevertheless allowed it to take control of the presidency. And several important military leaders, although convinced that a PRD government would be dangerous for the country and contrary to their self-interests, nevertheless accepted a PRD victory and subsequent civilian control of the military institution.

The final condition that enabled political elites to reach a settlement in 1978 was a low and controllable level of mass mobilization. The Dominican Republic during the period in question was predominantly an agrarian society. In 1960, 67 percent of the labor force was in agriculture, and only 12 percent was in industry. Not much had changed by 1977: 58 percent remained in agriculture, with 16 percent in industry. In addition, only a small portion of the labor force (12 percent in 1977) was organized in trade unions. Under Trujillo's regime the only major political organizations were his Dominican party and the armed forces; he repressed all other groups. Even though mass mobilization increased greatly during the 1960s, organized labor and political parties were tightly controlled for twelve years under Balaguer. For example, from 1962 to 1965 an average of nearly fifty unions were being certified annually by the Labor Ministry. Between 1966 and 1977, however, the number dropped to just over twenty-five certifications per year. Moreover, labor organizations were significantly polarized and did not constitute a cohesive political force.

During the 1978 crisis, mass mobilization was kept in check by the PRD. Balaguer and the conservative military elites feared that a civil war could break out because they knew that the PRD's militants could mobilize a significant portion of the population. However, intense discussions within the PRD's national executive committee led to an appeal to party militants to remain calm. The party leadership did call for a "patriotic civic day's work in seclusion" (*jornada cívica de recogimiento patriótico*), on which people were asked to "reflect and pray" at home to protest the JCE decision that took four Senate seats away from the PRD. But the PRD leaders emphasized that the day of seclusion was not a national strike and that there were "no subversive intentions on the part of the PRD." Twenty-four hours before the event, Peña Gómez announced that the PRD's political commission had decided to cancel the observance, because it could be the pretext for the party's opponents to "unleash acts of violence." The PRD leaders' ability to control their militants thus gave them the leeway to negotiate a political settlement and subsequently to prevent their followers from rejecting or undermining it. And Guzmán's ability to reach a settlement with Balaguer and the military in the first place was greatly enhanced by the fact that just before the 1978 elections, the PRD's national executive committee had granted him "full powers to make the compromises that he deemed convenient."

Although a low level of mass mobilization resulting from the country's relative underdevelopment probably facilitated elite accommodation, the evidence suggests that equally important was the elites' ability to control mobilizations. The ability of the PRD leaders and Balaguer to control their supporters appears to have been crucial, especially because the 1965 civil war had demonstrated that there could indeed be considerable mass mobilization in the Dominican

Republic. This suggests that in developing societies the elite autonomy necessary for settlements must be rooted in well-organized political groups under the effective control of a few pivotal elites.

One can also argue that the events of 1978 were preceded, perhaps even were dependent on, a process of moderation following the upheavals of the 1960s. Most important, the PRD gradually abandoned the radicalism so prevalent in its early history. Although Bosch had founded a revolutionary party in 1939, by the time he was elected president in 1962, the PRD had become a more moderate political organization. Nevertheless, Bosch was overthrown primarily because he was still perceived to be a dangerous radical and because his constitution, promulgated in April 1963, had alienated most of the powerful sectors of the nation.

Bosch's overthrow reradicalized the PRD to the extent that it supported and carried out an armed uprising. The civil war led to bitter hatred between strong elements of the armed forces and the PRD leadership that prevented any sort of political settlement among the PRD, the PR, and the armed forces in 1966. With Bosch in exile, the subsequent repression carried out by the Balaguer regime turned the PRD into a "conspiratorial" political organization, especially between 1966 and 1970. In 1970, however, Bosch returned to the Dominican Republic and worked to reorganize and reorient the party. After Bosch left the PRD, Peña Gómez continued the process of transforming it into a more moderate mass-based political organization, gaining for the party much greater acceptance at home and abroad.

Meanwhile, under Balaguer's leadership, the PR also moderated by carrying out land reform and expanding civil liberties. All of this suggests than an elite convergence was under way before 1978, and it points to the possibility that the analytically distinct processes of elite settlement and elite convergence may, in reality, be intertwined.

One final observation is necessary. The Dominican case illustrates the importance of external pressures in an elite settlement. In 1965, the United States sided with the "loyalists," and the result was a proloyalist government that consolidated power with the help of the armed forces. In 1978, the United States pushed for free elections, and the democratic transfer of power was successful. We cannot conclude that U.S. intervention determined politics in the Dominican Republic. Nevertheless, the importance of U.S. influence compels us to guard against the idea that elite settlements and convergences are entirely internal matters. In countries like the Dominican Republic, foreign pressures can help propel or inhibit elite transformations.

References

Balaguer, Joaquín. 1988. *Memorias de un cortesano de la "era de Trujillo."* Santo Domingo: Editora corripio C. por A.

Bell, Ian. 1981. *The Dominican Republic.* Boulder, CO: Westview Press.

Bracey, Audrey. 1980. *Resolution of the Dominican Crisis, 1965: A Study in Mediation.* Washington, DC: Institute for the Study of Diplomacy, School of Foreign Service, Georgetown University.

Espinal, Rosario. 1986. "An Interpretation of the Democratic Transition in the Dominican Republic." In *The Central American Impasse*, ed. Giuseppe Di Palma and Laurence Whitehead. New York: St. Martin's Press.

Martin, John Bartlow. 1966. *Overtaken by Events: The Dominican Crisis from the Fall of Trujillo to the Civil War.* New York: Doubleday.

Weston, Charles H. 1979. "The Failure of the Democratic Left in the Dominican Republic: A Case Study of the Overthrow of the Juan Bosch Government." Discussion Paper no. 65. University of Wisconsin at Milwaukee, Center for Latin America.

12

Elites and democratic consolidation in Latin America and Southern Europe: an overview

MICHAEL BURTON, RICHARD GUNTHER, AND JOHN HIGLEY

This volume has analyzed the roles played by elites in recent transitions to democracy in Latin America and Southern Europe. Its thesis has been that the consolidation of a new democracy requires the establishment of elite consensus and unity, as well as extensive mass participation in the elections and other institutional processes that constitute procedural democracy. The primary focus has been on the elite variable because we regard this as logically and factually prior to the existence of regime stability or instability, to peaceful or disruptive mass mobilization and participation, and thus to the several types of democratic regimes that we have distinguished – consolidated, unconsolidated, stable limited, and pseudo-democracies. Elite consensus requires agreement on the worth of political institutions and on the rules of the political game that is played within and around those institutions. Elite unity involves formal and informal communication networks that encompass all or most elite groups and that enable them to defend and promote their interests through access to central decision-making processes. Historically, most national elites have lacked consensus and unity; the result has been unstable regimes switching between varieties of authoritarian rule and various forms of pseudo- or unconsolidated democracy, with shifts from one to another occurring through irregular power seizures by the groups that make up such disunified elites. For a disunified elite to achieve consensus and unity, there must be a fundamental transformation in elite orientation and structure. We have posited that such transformations take two basic forms: (1) sudden and deliberate settlements that precede or are coterminous with democratic transitions and that create stable limited democracies or lead directly to consolidated democracies and (2) more gradual convergences through a process of electoral competition in societies at relatively high levels of socioeconomic development, the eventual result of which are consolidated democracies.

All thirteen of the countries examined in this book had long histories of elite disunity and unstable regimes in which democracy, if practiced at all, was unconsolidated and subject to breakdown. Moreover, all thirteen countries have recently experienced, or are currently undergoing, new transitions to democracy. The basic research question for our collaborators has accordingly been whether elite transformations from disunity to consensual unity have occurred in these countries. Ancillary questions have concerned the forms that these transformations may have taken, the elite and mass conditions that spurred or hindered them, and the nature of the resulting democratic regimes.

Before setting forth an overview of the findings from our thirteen case studies, some methodological caveats are in order. At the several workshops and conferences that led to this volume there were numerous discussions about whether this or that group should be considered a "politically significant" elite, whether a particular national elite at a particular time was disunified or consensually unified, and whether a specific regime was consolidated or unconsolidated. Doubts were also expressed about whether political processes in Portugal, Costa Rica, and the Dominican Republic (among others) clearly constituted an elite settlement or an elite convergence. These discussions and doubts reflected the difficulty of trying to measure exact degrees of elite unity or disunity, regime consolidation, or whatever, as well as specifying the dividing lines between the categories central to our analysis. Such ambiguities are inevitable in the effort to typologize on the basis of variables that are, in reality, continuous. Nevertheless, we believe that in attempting to build theories about national elites and political regimes, there is no alternative to a categorical or typological approach. Too great an insistence on strict empirical precision threatens to create a methodologically induced immobilism. Obviously, more specification is desirable, and further application of our concepts will most likely reduce ambiguities. We think, in any event, that the application of these concepts to thirteen Latin American and Southern European countries has helped shed much light on the most crucial questions regarding the consolidation of their new democracies.

The assessments of our collaborators may be summarized as follows:

Country	*Elite transformation*	*Regime type*
Argentina	None	Unconsolidated democracy
Brazil	None	Unconsolidated democracy
Chile	Possible settlement 1989–90	Democracy, possibly consolidating
Colombia	Settlement 1957–8	Democracy, possibly de-consolidating
Costa Rica	Settlement/ convergence 1948–70	Consolidated democracy
Dominican Republic	Convergence/ settlement 1966–78	Consolidating democracy
Italy	Convergence 1963–78	Consolidated democracy
Mexico	Settlement 1929	Stable, limited democracy or inclusionary authoritarian regime?
Peru	None	Unconsolidated democracy
Portugal	Convergence 1983–9	Consolidated democracy
Spain	Settlement 1977–9	Consolidated democracy
Uruguay	Settlement/ convergence 1984–90	Consolidated democracy?
Venezuela	Settlement 1958	Consolidated democracy

It appears that elite transformations have occurred, or are occurring, in ten of the thirteen cases. Four countries experienced clear-cut elite settlements: Colombia, Mexico, Spain, and Venezuela. In the judgments of our collaborators, Costa Rica and Uruguay experienced partial settlements that were augmented by subsequent elite convergences, and there were also important indications of a settlement in Chile in 1989–90, though further evidence is needed before we can be certain. In three other countries, the elite transformations were predominantly convergences: the Dominican Republic, Italy, and Portugal. On the other hand, there is as yet no convincing evidence of elite transformations in Argentina, Brazil, or Peru. To the extent that these judgments (and the analytical scheme that informs them) are correct, the record of democratic consolidation in Latin America and Southern Europe in recent years is impressive: Eight countries have achieved consolidated democratic regimes; Chile may be moving in this direction; and Mexico may also be growing more democratic.

In this concluding chapter, we shall summarize the main findings about each country and raise questions that require further research or that suggest interpretations somewhat different from those of our collaborators. We shall also draw on the case studies to take stock of the scheme we advanced in Chapter 1.

Democratic consolidation via elite settlement

Two unequivocal instances of elite settlements directly resulted in consolidated democracies, in Spain and Venezuela. It is more doubtful that consolidated democracy resulted from the settlement that clearly took place in Colombia, and it is an open question whether Chile will constitute a fourth case in this category.

As one of the world's oldest states, Spain provides a classic illustration of the strong tendency for elite disunity and regime instability to persist over long periods. Previous efforts to move Spain in a democratic direction (e.g., in 1812, 1876, 1931) involved sharp breaks with preexisting regimes and their supporters, and at least partly for that reason, they failed, most dramatically in the bloody civil war of the 1930s. Richard Gunther points out that an exclusionary pact between Liberals and Conservatives in 1876 produced a stable limited democracy, but the unwillingness of entrenched elites to incorporate Socialist and other emerging elites during the years around the turn of this century led to the regime's overthrow in 1923. Thus, after Franco's death in 1975, it was quite conceivable that political instability would return. To be sure, rapid economic development and a modest liberalization initiated in the 1960s opened a path for a more evolutionary regime change. But that Spain followed this path was largely due to the collective elite memory of previous costly conflicts and to the emergence of able leaders, especially Adolfo Suárez and King Juan Carlos. After becoming prime minister in July 1976, Suárez proceeded, through a series of dialogues with key leaders followed by decrees that embodied their demands, to dismantle the Franquist regime, to build strong relationships with opposition leaders (most notably the PCE's Santiago Carrillo and the PSOE's Felipe González), and to set the stage for fully democratic Cortes elections in July 1977. The main business of this Cortes was to draft a constitution, which, as Gunther shows, was accomplished primarily in small groups containing representatives of all the important elites, except the Basques. At the same time, mass mobilization that might have provoked elites associated with the old regime was kept in check. Taken together, the constitution approved by the Cortes in October 1978 and the Basque and Catalán autonomy statutes of the following year amounted to an elite settlement. The steadfast defense of the democratic regime by all significant political parties in the face of an attempted coup in 1981 demonstrated the extent to which consolidation had been achieved, and the failure of that coup definitively laid to rest lingering fears of military threats to Spain's new democracy. All nationwide parties and the Catalán nationalist parties acknowledge the legitimacy of the constitutional monarchy and its basic institutions, and both the leaders and the supporters of these parties have behaved in accordance with the new democratic rules of the game. In Euskadi, a significant number of Basque nationalists have challenged the regime and called for secession, but in the last few years the number of Basques taking this stance has declined, and it appears that a process of convergence between Spanish and Basque elites is under way.

Venezuela had no significant experience with democratic politics before the 1940s. The Liberal and Conservative parties that were organized after independence in the 1820s were little more than vehicles for personalistic, usually violent power struggles, and they ceased to be a factor with the destruction of the Conservative party in the civil wars of the 1860s. Thereafter, until the 1940s, the country was dominated by a series of dictators. In 1945, Rómulo Betancourt, the leader of Acción democrática, the first successful mass-based party, and a group of mid-level military officers seized power and began constructing a modern democratic regime. But the heavy-handed and fairly radical way in which this was done alienated virtually all other elites, and the members of Betancourt's own junta received wide support when they overthrew him and his AD party in 1948. The Pérez Jiménez dictatorship that followed proved even more distasteful, however, and by the mid-1950s an increasingly broad coalition of party, business, labor, intellectual, and military elites was working toward his ouster, a settlement of previous conflicts, and a democratic transition. As the result of agreements reached at a secret New York City meeting in 1957 among leaders of the three major parties (AD, COPEI, and URD) and a prominent business leader, as well as discussions between members of this group and sympathetic military leaders, Pérez Jiménez was overthrown in early 1958, and a military–civilian junta took over while further elements of a settlement were worked out privately by party leaders. The outcome was several pacts that embodied compromises struck among previously warring elites, notably the Pact of Punto Fijo, the Declaration of Principles, and the Minimum Program of Government. An important feature of the settlement process was the disavowal of radical social and economic programs and the exclusion of the Communist party. As a consequence, the Communists, together with radical factions in the AD and URD, mounted a guerrilla insurgency during the 1960s. But by the end of that decade, these groups had been defeated and incorporated into competitive electoral politics as accepted left-wing parties. Since the settlement in 1958, six freely contested presidential and congressional elections have been held, and the opposition has won four of them. Serious economic problems triggered riots in 1989, but the regime's basic stability was not threatened. As in Spain, an elite settlement that was coterminous with a democratic transition led within a few years to a consolidated democracy.

Colombia's politics have historically been dominated by the Liberal and Conservative parties. During much of the country's history, relations between these parties alternated between periods of violent confrontation and periods of cooperation. Until the 1950s, the periods of cooperation always degenerated into violent confrontations because party elites regularly sought dominance over their opponents; cooperation and power sharing were merely expedients for ending episodes of violence. The elite settlement of 1957–8, codified in the National Front agreements, broke this cyclical pattern. Power-sharing mechanisms were more permanently installed and more strictly adhered to than ever before. Between 1958 and 1974, this meant the full sharing of congressional and appointive offices between Liberals and Conservatives, rotation of the two parties in the presidency, constitutionally mandated coalition governments, and the exclusion of all other parties. But even this arrangement did not prevent former dictator Rojas Pinilla from almost winning the 1970 presidential election as an alternative Conservative candidate. Beginning in 1974, presidential and congressional elections were opened to leftist parties and factions, some of which had led insurgencies, and they thus became fully competitive. In 1986, the Conservatives eschewed their constitutional right, as the party losing a presidential election, to offices in the cabinet, instead adopting the stance of a full-fledged opposition. In 1988, under a constitutional amendment, formerly appointive mayoral offices were opened to competitive elections, and fiscal changes increased the flow of resources to these and other local offices, making them more important. In the 1990 elections, the M-19 guerrilla group, having only two months earlier laid down its guns, participated as a legitimate political party and finished third in the presidential race, with 13 percent of the vote (1 percent ahead of the official Conservative candidate); and Liberal president-elect Gaviria kept his promise to give M-19 a cabinet post. In short, the initially narrow elite consensus and power sharing of the National Front period has been expanded impressively, and although expediency doubtless has been and remains a major motivation for this expansion, most elites now seem to be committed to cooperation and power sharing as ends in themselves. But as John Peeler forcefully reminds us, we cannot conclude that Colombian democracy is consolidated. At least two important insurgent groups remain in the field, waging war against the regime, and left-wing elites that have "come in from the cold" are subject to much violence and harassment by right-wing paramilitary groups. And over the last decade the capacity of drug traffickers to corrupt and intimidate elites and masses alike has presented the regime with a major challenge, though one, it should be noted, with substantial external causes. It may be, as Peeler points out, that "we are witnessing a process of deconsolidation, of slow-motion breakdown." Nevertheless, the survival and expansion of democracy in Colombia in the face of severe threats testifies to the watershed political effects of the 1957–8 elite settlement.

Whether Chile will become the latest instance of an elite settlement leading to a consolidated democracy remains to be seen. Marcelo Cavarozzi argues that the democratic transition of 1989–90 entailed a double-barreled settlement among all but the most extreme elites. First, all but intransigent Communists and radical Socialists on the left and die-hard supporters of Pinochet on the right agreed to abide by the outcome of the 1988 plebiscite on Pinochet's bid to retain the presidency for another ten years, and all agreed to drop their demands for his immediate resignation. Second, through prolonged negotiations, leaders of the Christian Democrats and moderate Socialists forged an electoral alliance for the 1990 elections and agreed to a power-sharing arrangement should they win those elections. This coalition, led by Patricio Aylwin of the Christian Democrats, won that election; the military regime accepted the results; and in May Pinochet vacated the presidency peacefully, though he was allowed to remain as commander in chief of the armed forces. Although this transition process exhibits many features that we regard as facilitating democratic consolidation, only the passage of time and/or the collection of additional data concerning the extent of elite consensual unity in Chile will enable us to reach a more definitive verdict on the regime's prospects for long-term stability.

Democratic consolidation via elite convergence

Elites in Italy, Portugal, and the Dominican Republic achieved consensus and unity, and the regimes they operated became consolidated democracies, through processes that predominantly involved convergence.

After nearly a century of disunity, interrupted only by the forced unity of the Fascist dictatorship under Mussolini, Italian elites came close to reaching a settlement in 1943–4 when almost all elite factions joined in the Anti-Fascist Alliance. But the unprecedented elite cooperation achieved during that period was based on the need to fight a common enemy – German occupying forces and the remnants of the Mussolini regime – and it collapsed in 1947 under the weight of competitive politics that pitted the proponents of capitalist and socialist political and economic systems against each other, both within Italy and in the larger world arena. Communist and Socialist elites were excluded from government power, and they formed a strong antisystem force on the left. The threat that they posed to the democratic regime gave it an unconsolidated character, but it also enabled the Christian Democrats to draw a clear line between "them and us" and, in alliance with smaller centrist and right-wing parties, to mobilize an electoral majority that gave them a virtually unshakable hold on government executive power. Eventually, in Maurizio Cotta's analysis, this dominant center–right coalition began a "more complicated game, balancing integration and exclusion," the most concrete manifestation of which was the incorporation of Socialist leaders into the governing coalition in 1963. Although this caused a split in the Socialist party and strengthened support for the Communists, it marked the start of a gradual convergence among Italian elites. Cotta makes the intriguing point that this convergence was not a simple linear process, because Italian society and politics were in some ways more polarized during the 1970s than during the 1960s. Nevertheless, there were further important steps in the convergence: the Communist leaders' condemnation of the Soviet Union's invasion of Czechoslovakia in 1968, the parliamentary reforms in 1971 that gave Communist deputies a more central role in setting the parliamentary agenda, and the 1976 agreements that brought the Communists into the parliamentary majority supporting the Christian Democratic–led government and that gave them a number of important parliamentary offices. Cotta observes that the 1976 agreements amounted to "public acknowledgment of the democratic reliability" of the Communists, and he suggests that given their scope, these agreements can be seen as approximating a settlement or as constituting the final step in the process of elite convergence. During the late 1970s, the cooperation of all important elites, and especially the Communists, in suppressing terrorism indicated widespread elite consensus and unity in support of the democratic regime. Finally, in 1983 the Christian Democrats abandoned their campaign tactic of labeling the Communists a threat to the regime, and this, together with the Communists' recent moves to change their name and to turn themselves into garden-variety social democrats, indicates that the democratic consolidation has been completed.

With a history of elite disunity and regime instability as long as Spain's, Portugal's transition to democracy during the mid-1970s and the subsequent consolidation of its democratic regime during the 1980s have been remarkable. The basis of the latter development appears to have been gradual elite convergence. The "revolutionary" turmoil that accompanied Portugal's democratic transition in 1975–6 left the military elite in so central a position, both constitutionally and in de facto power terms, that the new regime was only a pseudo-democracy. So long as the military-run Council of the Revolution existed, the powers it held departed significantly from procedural democracy and generated much uncertainty about the prospects for civilian rule. Both the disputed role of the military and the existence of an unreformed Marxist–Leninist Communist party, which maintained only a semiloyal stance toward the new regime, indicated elite disunity and probable regime instability. The military question was removed, however, and the challenge of the Communist party was greatly reduced, in a sequence of developments during the 1980s. As Larry Graham recounts this sequence, the elites agreed to adopt a constitutional reform that abolished the Council of the Revolution in 1982 and thus took a crucial step toward extricating the military from politics. The election of Portugal's first nonmilitary president in 1986 affirmed civilian control, as did understandings with the military high command about the extent of autonomous military decision making. By eliminating an official commitment to socialist goals, as well as asserting full democratic control of economic policymaking, a second round of constitutional reforms in 1989 assured right-of-center elites about long-term economic prospects and laid to rest all remaining doubts about the acceptability of the constitutional order. Only the semiloyal stance of the Communist party, which is still officially Marxist–Leninist and is led by an individual often accused of Stalinist inclinations, prevents the conclusion that an elite convergence of some ten years' duration has been completed. But if the Communists' electoral decline continues or if current debates within the PCP result in a public conversion to social democracy, then such a conclusion will be warranted. Most indications are, in any event, that the process has moved so far that a consolidated democracy now exists in Portugal.

In terms of experience with democratic politics, the Dominican Republic, like Venezuela a few years before, was essentially starting from scratch when the first steps toward democracy were taken after the assassination of Trujillo in 1961 and the overthrow of his regime in early 1962. Under U.S. pressure, democratic elections were held late in 1962, resulting in a strong victory for social democratic reformer Juan Bosch and his Dominican Revolutionary party (PRD). But Bosch's plans for reform quickly alienated military, economic, and church elites, who backed a coup seven months after he took office. Over the next two years, in the midst of growing economic problems, these elites became deeply polarized between a "constitutionalist" faction seeking to return Bosch to power and a "loyalist" faction committed to protecting traditional elite interests. The resulting civil war was terminated by U.S. military intervention, followed by an OAS-negotiated compromise between the warring factions that paved the way for democratic elections in 1966. Joaquín Balaguer and his new Reformist party (PR) soundly defeated Bosch and the PRD. By skillfully mixing genuine reforms with selective repression, while presiding over a period of substantial economic growth, Balaguer won the elections in 1970 and 1974. By 1978, the regime had been substantially liberalized, and the PRD – which Bosch left in 1973 in order to form the Dominican Liberation party – had moved toward the center under the leadership of José Peña Gómez. Reflecting the moderating political climate, Balaguer and Antonio Guzmán, the PRD presidential candidate, signed a nonaggression pact several months before the 1978 election, and business elites, professionals, intellectuals, and church leaders all urged the government to respect the election outcome. Nevertheless, a crisis arose when the PR and the military were accused of using violence against the PRD, the PR accused the PRD of fraud, and the national police temporarily suspended the vote count. Numerous private negotiations among Guzmán, Balaguer, and military leaders ensued. Finally, the central election board declared Guzmán the winner, but initial results showing that his PRD had also won a Senate majority were reversed, and Balaguer's PR emerged with a majority in the Senate that enabled it to check any radical government programs. Peter Sanchez's interviews with the principal elite actors suggest this standoff was agreed to in private elite negotiations, which he interprets as amounting to an elite settlement. Although the negotiations do indeed bear many earmarks of a settlement, the issues – namely, who would be the winners of the presidential and congressional elections – were much narrower than in typical elite settlements; the 1978 agreement, therefore, may be more accurately characterized as a partial settlement. As Sanchez also considers, one may instead interpret the Dominican case between 1966 and 1978 as a convergence of elites from the antidemocratic right and left toward a democratic center. This was largely guided by Balaguer – a De Gaulle–like figure who gradually led entrenched right-wing elites toward the center in a context of electoral politics – with considerable assistance from José Peña Gómez, who transformed the major opposition party into a moderate force; all with strong encouragement from the United States. In any event, the conciliatory behavior of elites in the 1978 crisis indicated that substantial consensus and unity had already been achieved. Since 1978, Dominican elites have continued to behave in this manner: Four national elections have been held, and there twice have been peaceful transfers of government executive power to opposition forces. No significant elite group has been excluded from participating in electoral politics, nor does any such group advocate an alternative to the democratic regime. Election-related violence and irregularities have declined with each successive election; mass participation is fairly extensive; and mass commitment to democracy appears rather widespread. One might nonetheless stop short of proclaiming the regime a consolidated democracy because Balaguer has been such a central force that it is not clear whether elite consensus and unity is sufficiently established to survive his passing. The 1990 electoral imbroglio, in which octogenarians Balaguer and Bosch finished neck-and-neck amid charges of fraud by both sides suggests that Dominican democracy is not yet consolidated (Hartlyn 1990).

Democratic consolidation via settlement and convergence

In the judgments of our collaborators, Costa Rica and Uruguay have achieved consolidated democratic regimes through a combination of settlement and convergence.

In Costa Rica, the aftermath of the civil war in 1948 can be viewed as being both a partial elite settlement and the start of a more gradual elite convergence. Following the war, an important agreement was reached between José Figueres, the liberal reformer and leader of the Army of National Liberation that won the civil war, and Otilio Ulate, whose victory in the presidential election had been denied by the incumbent president and conservative-turned-populist, Rafael Calderón, thus triggering the war. This agreement allowed Ulate, a conservative, to assume the presidency after an eighteen-month junta, headed by Figueres, which affirmed the social security and labor reforms enacted by Calderón during his presidency (1940–4) and instituted major new reforms such as abolishing the military, nationalizing banks, and increasing the state's role in economic affairs more generally. The scope of this arrangement in both inter-elite and policy terms is consistent with the idea of a settlement. However, Calderón and the forces he represented were excluded, and it was not until

1958 – after he had twice attempted to lead coups against the democratic regime – that Calderón was allowed to reenter competitive politics upon demonstrating his acceptance of the existing institutions. The Communist party remained proscribed, and it was not until 1970 that the Communists were informally allowed back into competitive politics, and only in 1975 was the constitutional ban on the Communists removed. John Peeler regards this gradual incorporation of dissident elites as an elite convergence. But as he also points out, starting in 1953 ten regular presidential elections were held, and as a result of them, executive power passed peacefully to opposition candidates a total of eight times. In effect, elites ranging from the moderate left to the moderate right repeatedly demonstrated their ability to win elections, and all antidemocratic forces had to reconcile themselves to this fact. One can thus argue that the Costa Rican democratic regime moved rapidly toward consolidation soon after the settlement-like agreement of 1948, or one can choose to view consolidation as being achieved only after dissident, mainly left-wing elites chose to play by the established rules of the game. In either case, the fact that the democratic regime weathered serious economic and foreign policy problems without much difficulty during the 1980s testifies to the existence of elite consensus and unity and to the consolidated character of Costa Rican democracy.

Before the coup of 1973, as Charles Gillespie points out, Uruguay was widely viewed as a stable democracy. There was considerable evidence to encourage this view: a strong democratic political culture, a history of civilian government that gradually encompassed extensive mass participation, a relatively large middle class, an ethnically and religiously homogeneous and well-educated population, and what was arguably the Western Hemisphere's first welfare state. Yet, attention to relations among Uruguayan elites might have produced a more cautious assessment. Alongside the tradition of parliamentary politics during the nineteenth century was a pattern of Colorado dominance that was periodically challenged by violent Blanco rebellions, the suppression of which necessitated short-lived military regimes. A decisive Colorado victory in the 1903–4 civil war put an end to those rebellions and left the Blancos as a junior partner in government for the next fifty years. There was no elite settlement, and the Blancos were simply incorporated on the Colorados' terms. In 1933, reactionaries in both parties backed a successful coup d'état. In the return to civilian government ten years later, there was again no sign of a settlement; instead, the structure of government was subject to frequent revision based on limited Colorado–Blanco pacts. By the 1960s, the narrowness and fragility of the Colorado–Blanco arrangement were increasingly obvious. Parties of the left, labor organizations, and intellectuals had no access to decision making; the role of the military was ill defined; and the structure of government executive power was the subject of much elite disagreement. As a long economic slide continued and as excluded groups made more and more trouble, Colorado–Blanco mistrust intensified, and the leaders of each party began courting the military. The military dictatorship of 1973–84, which occurred in the context of widespread but quite abstract and hazy commitments to democratic ideals and was combined with a steadily worsening economy, seems to have provided the sense of crisis and political learning that typically precede elite settlements. Gillespie believes that this was the significance of the Naval Club Accord in 1984 in which Colorado, military, and left-wing leaders engineered a democratic transition on the basis of understandings that guaranteed each of the three factions a secure place in the new democratic regime. Gillespie emphasizes that it was precisely the exclusion of the Blanco leadership, headed by Wilson Ferreira, that enabled the three elites at the Naval Club to persuade one another that their agreement was superior to some alternative in which the radicalized Blancos would necessarily play a large role. Even after the democratic transition agreed to in 1984 took place, it was nevertheless necessary to reincorporate the Blancos, maintain the military elite's tolerance of the new regime, and prevent radical leftist forces from upsetting the apple cart. Gillespie details the ways in which all three tasks were accomplished rapidly: through President Sanguinetti's quick acceptance of Wilson Ferreira's return as a major player, subsequent cooperation between the Colorados and Blancos in passing legislation, the Blancos' sponsorship of a "Law of Limitations" that gave the military amnesty for human rights violations during its rule, the military's acceptance of an amnesty for political prisoners, Sanguinetti's retention of military commanders from the last phase of the military regime, and the largely successful efforts of Communist leaders to control strike activity. As in the Costa Rican case, in order to explain the basis of democratic consolidation in Uruguay, one can choose between emphasizing the partial settlement of 1984 or the rapid convergence of excluded and disaffected elites after the settlement.

Unconsolidated democracies and the persistence of elite disunity

There is no convincing evidence of elite transformations in Argentina, Brazil, or Peru. Thus, the new democratic regimes in all three countries should be viewed as unconsolidated. It is impossible to identify any single reason that settlements did not occur in these countries in conjunction with their democratic transitions or that convergences have not (as yet) followed the transitions. But it appears that they shared certain features that distinguish them from the countries in which the settlements and convergences did occur.

First, like all the other countries studied in this book, Argentina, Brazil, and Peru had long histories of costly elite conflicts and unstable regimes. But at the time of the most recent democratic transitions in these three countries, the elites apparently did not feel that dramatic steps were needed to avert some widely feared outcome, such as civil war, social revolution, or a brutal dictatorship. The military regimes in Argentina and Brazil had effectively suppressed (in Argentina, virtually wiped out) radical leftist forces, and the reformist nature of the Peruvian military regime had substantially, if temporarily, stolen the left's thunder, leaving it in pieces. Second, because both the Brazilian and Peruvian military elites favored a democratic transition, whereas the Argentine military leaders had been totally discredited in the Malvinas fiasco, a *dictadura* was not a realistic threat in the three countries. This is not to say that the countries were free of crisis, for all three were in the throes of rapid economic decline. Clearly, other factors militated against elite settlements.

Perhaps the most crucial of these factors was the fragmented and largely uninstitutionalized nature of contending elites at the time that democracy was initiated. In none of the three countries was there a limited number of disciplined parties and other organizations whose leaders could reflect a range of interests while at the same time striking authoritative compromises. Tom Bruneau and Henry Dietz show that in Brazil and Peru, respectively, the constituent assemblies that wrote new constitutions were open, highly public arenas in which virtually the whole gamut of opposing interests in the two countries were forcefully articulated. These forums were not conducive to the private, relatively centralized bargaining processes that produce the kinds of major concessions and mutual guarantees necessary for elite settlements. In Argentina, no new constitution was written; there was simply an abrupt shift to electoral competition among parties that had been banned for seven years, were in disarray, and, as Marcelo Cavarozzi observes, were historically unaccustomed to the practice of restrained partisanship.

Given the absence of settlements in these countries, what are the chances that elite consensus and unity may yet be attained through convergences? The most plausible answer is "not good." Elite convergences have most clearly taken place only in countries at relatively high levels of economic development and in contexts of continuing economic growth, such as France, Italy, Japan, Portugal, and the Dominican Republic. The economies of Argentina, Brazil, and Peru were in terrible shape when their democratic transitions came about, and they have only gotten worse since. All three confront seriously declining living standards, huge foreign debts, massive unemployment, and hyperinflation. In these circumstances, there is probably no large, reasonably contented, moderate segment of the electorate that can be mobilized reliably by the kind of center–right elite coalition whose electoral dominance can force convergence. Instead, voting patterns in the three countries show a great deal of volatility, with a marked penchant for supporting untried outsiders who are untainted by past economic and other failures: Menem in Argentina, Fujimori in Peru, Collor or, had he not been disqualified, possibly a TV celebrity in Brazil. To be sure, the worldwide collapse of socialism as a viable alternative economic and political system probably reduces the depth of elite ideological polarizations in these and other countries with disunified elites, and to that extent convergences are perhaps more feasible than in the past. But there is as yet no indication in these countries that an attenuation of ideological polarities will produce the broad elite coalitions that are essential to stabilizing, and thus consolidating, democratic regimes.

Perhaps Argentina, Brazil, and Peru (along with other developing countries that have disunified elites operating unconsolidated democracies) will simply muddle along for an extended period until and if their economies improve and thereby make elite convergences more feasible. But it is also conceivable that in the face of intractable economic crises, the sort of military regime with a "foundation project" that Pinochet led in Chile could become an attractive alternative to many elites in these countries.

The conundrum of Mexico

The treatment of Mexico in this volume departs quite sharply from most existing analyses of that country's political record. By arguing that Mexico experienced an elite settlement in 1929, partial though it may have been, Alan Knight sheds much light on the reasons that Mexico's record has been so different from those of other Latin American and Southern European countries during most of this century. In a nutshell, Knight argues that the circumstances Mexican elites found themselves in at the end of the 1920s were highly propitious for a settlement: a legacy and memory of extremely costly conflicts; a sudden new crisis, in the form of Obregón's assassination, that clearly threatened the resumption of those conflicts; and the presence of a powerful and skilled leader, Calles, who found ways to bring the elites making up "the revolutionary family" together in 1928–9. Knight details the trade-offs that this elite settlement entailed, and he shows how it transformed an eminently disunified elite operating a highly unstable regime into a hegemonic formation presiding over a regime whose stability made it stand out from virtually all other Latin American and Southern European regimes during the next half-century. He goes on to discuss the steps by which elites that were initially excluded from the settlement were progressively incorporated during succeeding decades. The result, he argues, has not been a democracy, either consolidated or unconsolidated, but an "inclusionary authoritarian" regime.

In adopting this locution to characterize the Mexican elite and regime patterns, Knight echoes the widely held view that Mexico is a unique case among Latin American and, for that matter, other developing countries. As noted, Knight presents a novel, elite-centered explanation for this uniqueness. But his analysis fits uneasily into the framework that informs this volume. Knight's focus on an elite settlement as the origin and basis of Mexico's stable regime is, of course, wholly consistent with the framework. But he finds that none of the types of democratic regimes distinguished in the framework is applicable to Mexico, and he instead emphasizes the regime's authoritarian character. If one accepts, as Knight does and we do, that a settlement and its subsequent incorporation of dissidents has been the main feature of elite politics in Mexico, then in our framework it follows that the regime would be one of two types: a stable limited democracy or a consolidated democracy. As a characterization of the Mexican regime over the last sixty years, Knight contends that the latter can be dismissed out of hand. But whether it has approximated a stable limited democracy is, in our view, more open to debate. Recall that this type of regime requires an oligarchical context in which different elite factions that agree on the worth of institutions and the rules of the game simply take turns wielding power on the basis of regular but limited electoral competitions and through parliaments and other bodies that operate according to representative principles. The course of Mexican politics since the 1928–9 settlement is consistent with this pattern: After Byzantine negotiations and competition among different factions within the PRI, regular elections have ratified the ascendancy of different groups, whose governments have employed an interplay between the elected Congress and the strong executive branch, but with mass participation limited and tightly controlled throughout.

For Alan Knight and many other Mexican analysts, calling this regime pattern a stable limited "democracy" is obviously a stumbling block, and the regime's record for much of the period since 1928–9 certainly warrants such reluctance. A key question is whether, as in England during the eighteenth and nineteenth centuries or in Sweden during the nineteenth century, the oligarchical regime has gradually moved in a democratic direction. Grappling with the question, Knight acknowledges the spread of multiparty electoral competition in Mexico, especially during the past decade or two. But because of the PRI-directed campaigns of intimidation and electoral fraud that have pervaded these competitions, as well as other controls that the PRI continues to exert on political discussion and participation, he believes that the regime remains well short of even the minimal requirements of procedural democracy.

How the Mexican regime should be classified since 1928–9, and especially in recent years, is a question that cannot be resolved by definitional fiat. It is enough to spark further discussion by highlighting, as Knight's treatment in this book has done, the main feature of substantial elite consensus and unity in Mexico since 1929 and to pose the alternatives of viewing the regime as some form of stable authoritarian rule or as a stable limited democracy that has begun to move toward a more open democracy only very recently.

A theoretical stock taking

The experiences of the countries studied in this volume and summarized in this chapter are strong evidence that elite consensus and unity is the essential precondition for consolidated democracy. This is not a monocausal, elite-determinist explanation. Rather, the focus on elites, and more specifically on their understandings and interrelations, constitutes a summary variable that encompasses many of the forces that influence political outcomes in societies. Like Max Weber, we think of elites as the "switchmen of history." Concentrating on elite structures, orientations, choices, and actions is, therefore, a parsimonious way to confront the complex reality of multiple causation. Let us consider the many causes of democratic consolidation as we attempt to identify the circumstances that facilitate consensual unifications of previously disunified elites.

The existence of a democratic political culture has often been posited as an important precondition for consolidated democracy. Could it be that elite consensual unity is simply a by-product of such a culture? The studies here offer little support for this notion. Some of the countries we have classified as having consensually unified elites – Mexico, Venezuela, the Dominican Republic – had virtually no traditions of democratic rule that could have created a democratic political culture that in turn spawned elite consensus and unity. In some of the other countries whose elites are now characterized by consensus and unity – Spain, Portugal, Italy – previous experience with democratic politics had largely been confined to small political classes, and moreover, that experience lay in the distant past. Conversely, the countries of Latin America's Southern Cone had relatively extensive democratic traditions, yet we find no consistent relationship between the democratic political cultures that their traditions may have created and their extent of democratic consolidation today.

This does not mean that mass commitments to democratic norms are irrelevant to elite consensus and unity. Among the countries we explored, Uruguay had a comparatively strong democratic political culture. Although this did not prevent its democratic regime from breaking down in the early 1970s, Charles Gillespie believes that Uruguay's political culture facilitated the Naval Club's partial settlement of 1984. He reminds us that Uruguay's history of democratic politics was one reason that the military elites who seized control in 1973 tried to maintain civilian rule and at least the appearance of democratic processes, and it also helps explain the prodemocracy votes of large numbers of citizens in the crucial referenda and elections in Uruguay's democratic transition during the 1980s. Elsewhere, the proximity of countries to neighboring consolidated democracies – Spain's and Portugal's proximity to flourishing West European democracies, Mexico's current proximity to American democracy – can plausibly be said to generate mass cultural pressures for democratization at home. Democratic political cultures or, more precisely, mass pressures for democracy are undoubtedly conducive to a coming together of elites, but it is doubtful that they play any stronger causal role.

Neither do simple versions of modernization theory provide adequate explanations of when and why some elites have become consensually unified and others have not. The two classic instances of consensual elite unification – England in 1688–9 and Sweden in 1809 – occurred before modernization. The unification of Mexican elites in 1928–9 likewise came before or at the start of the modernization process. Elite unifications in Colombia and Venezuela occurred simultaneously in the late 1950s, but Venezuela was substantially more modernized than Colombia at that point. Meanwhile, several of the most modernized Latin American countries, especially Argentina but also Chile and Uruguay, did not experience elite unifications until very recently, if then.

This is not to say that levels of socioeconomic development are irrelevant to democratic consolidation. The close relationship between modernization and the mobilization of broad population sectors for active participation in politics has been well documented, and because widespread popular participation is an essential component of our definition of democracy, it is clear that achievement of a certain minimum level of socioeconomic development is an important if not necessary precondition for the existence of a democratic regime. Socioeconomic modernization is also directly related to certain elite unification processes, as we have argued. Specifically, elite convergences appear to depend on a relatively high level of development in which a majority of voters have stakes in the existing social and economic order and are disposed to vote against radical alternatives. We have also speculated that the current and serious economic problems in Argentina, Brazil, and Peru may inhibit elite convergences. But the evidence we presented indicates that there is no simple relationship between the extent of modernization and democratic consolidation.

Likewise, Marxist and neo-Marxist models fail to account for the elite unifications that have and have not occurred. One can find struggles between classes and class fractions in each of the nations studied here, but these have had no systematic impact on elite structures and interrelations, except in the broad sense that previously dominant upper-class elites everywhere have had to respond to demands for inclusion by elites representing peasants, workers, and middle classes. But whether, when, and how such inclusion has been achieved has not corresponded to any Marxist logic we can discern. Moreover, conflicts of other kinds – personal, inter- and intraorganizational, regional, ethnic, religious – have been at least as important to elite structures and interrelations as have class conflicts.

Without dismissing such structural variables, the framework and analyses in this book have concentrated on more specific, shorter-term, and contingent circumstances. Particularly in regard to elite settlements, this concentration seems warranted. As Alan Knight puts it in his analysis of the Mexican case, elite settlements depend heavily for their occurrence on "conjunctures" of circumstances and actors. There is no need to repeat the emphasis that our framework places on particular historical legacies of conflict, triggering crises, and the pivotal role of skilled and senior leaders in elite settlements; our collaborators greatly amplify these observations. But the case studies bring out several additional aspects of the circumstances in which elite unifications, especially settlements, are brought about.

The extent to which elites are fragmented is one of these aspects. Fragmentation can simply create too many elites with whom agreements have to be reached, a problem well illustrated by the Brazilian and Peruvian democratic transitions, as Tom Bruneau and Henry Dietz demonstrate. Moreover, if the fragmentation is great, elites wishing to settle disputes with their opponents may be constrained by the fear of being outflanked by more extreme elements. As Maurizio Cotta shows, this was a recurrent problem for core elites in Italy: Attempts at compromise by Liberals and Conservatives, and then by Liberals and Socialists, resulted in serious losses of mass support for more extreme elites on the right and left.

The extent to which elites are anchored in coherent and powerful organizations also significantly affects the prospects for unification and subsequent regime consolidation. Insofar as elites are not clearly acknowledged as valid interlocutors for their respective clienteles, the agreements they reach may not hold. In Brazil, for example, Tancredo Neves apparently reached agreements with leaders of the military regime that might have helped consolidate the emerging democratic regime. But Neves spoke for no very coherent force in Brazilian politics, and in any case, he kept the agreements secret and thus took them to his grave. Moreover, elites who lack confidence that their supporters will continue to back them in the reconciliation of long-standing differences may be reluctant to make concessions in the first place. This probably helps account for the inability of Alfonsín and the Peronist Renovación faction in Argentina to achieve a mode of cooperation, and it is well illustrated by the PNV leader who told Richard Gunther that he had no real intention of forming a Basque state but believed that he would lose his leadership position if he renounced Basque aspirations to self-determination.

The anchoring of elites in coherent and powerful organizations also affects their ability to implement agreements over the longer term. Examples are the Colombian government's inability to control elements of the army and the police that have polarized politics by violently attacking leftists, as well as the declining significance of APRA's agreements with the military as its share of the Peruvian electorate has shrunk. Conversely, the vital contributions to democratic consolidation made by well-disciplined Communist parties in Spain, Uruguay, and Italy in controlling and, at crucial points, demobilizing their supporters further attests to the importance of elites' anchoring in coherent and powerful organizations. It is also clear that this factor affects the elites' ability to engage effectively in secret negotiations, which has been a necessary feature of all elite settlements.

In the final analysis, however, a central conclusion of these studies is the great responsibility of national elites for achieving, or failing to achieve, the degree of consensus and unity necessary for the establishment and consolidation of democracy. Socioeconomic and culturally based mass cleavages and demands may make it difficult for elites to compromise, may contribute to their fragmentation, and may weaken the organizations that they lead. But we see little evidence to support classical elitist notions that the characteristics of mass populations constitute the major barrier to stable democracy. Overall, achieving consolidated democracy depends principally on the choices and skills of elites.

Much of the recent work on democratic breakdowns, transitions, and consolidations stresses this centrality of elite choices and skills. But many scholars question whether these elite processes can be captured in a coherent theoretical model. Writing about Latin America, James Malloy concludes that "there are no readily identifiable structural parameters that allow us to project – let alone predict – the outcomes" of recent democratic transitions, and he suggests that "one possibility – in fact, a probability – is that the basic cyclical swing between authoritarian and democratic modes will continue. Perhaps the region is trapped" (Malloy 1987, pp. 251, 256). In the concluding volume of their edited works on democratic transitions in Latin America and Southern Europe, O'Donnell and Schmitter note: "We did not have at the beginning, nor do we have at the end of this lengthy collective endeavor a 'theory' to test or to apply to the case studies and thematic essays in these volumes" (1986, p. 3). And in the prefaces to their volumes on Africa, Latin America, and Asia, Diamond, Linz, and Lipset state: "Rather than pursuing some new, elegant, 'parsimonious' model, we deliberately eschewed mono-causal and reductionist interpretations in favor of an exhaustive examination of all the historical, cultural, social, economic, political and international factors that might affect the chances for stable democracy" (1988–9, p. xiii).

Given the inadequacies of previous theories, such skepticism is understandable. But refusing to engage in theory building leads nowhere. Without the guidance of a theoretical model, scholarly analyses lack focus and a sound basis for judging whether a new democracy is consolidated. Research therefore tends to be idiosyncratic, noncumulative, and noncommittal about the future of new democratic regimes. Moreover, lacking a coherent model of the central determinants of democratic transition and consolidation, scholars have little to offer policymakers and concerned citizens who hope to promote democracy, and they are ill prepared to assign responsibility when democracy breaks down.

We certainly do not think that our theory, which emphasizes the importance of elite transformations to consensus and unity, has solved these problems. But we do think we have made a start. By asking whether elites have become consensually unified, we and our collaborators have drawn rather firm conclusions about whether and why the thirteen countries studied here are now consolidated democracies. In doing so, we have left ourselves open to being proved wrong by future events and future researchers. This we regard as the essence of the scientific enterprise.

A speculative postscript on Eastern Europe

What lessons from this study might be applied to an even more dramatic series of regime transitions than those we have examined – the collapse of the Eastern Bloc and the emergence of democracies, limited democracies, and more open authoritarian regimes in Eastern Europe and the Soviet Union? It would be presumptuous if not absurd to attempt to analyze these political developments in the closing pages of a book about Latin American and Southern Europe and in the absence of an adequate base of empirical data. No such effort will be made here. Nevertheless, some brief comments concerning similarities and differences among these varied processes of political change might usefully highlight the elite conditions and transformations that we regard as crucial to democratic stability. To date, most of the information disseminated by the Western news media about the East European upheavals focuses on burgeoning mass demands for democracy and, in some cases, national self-determination. But from the standpoint of this volume, the issue is whether the elites that have stepped from the revolutions of 1989 and under *perestroika* in the Soviet Union have the inclination and ability to reach a consensus about the democratic rules of the game and become unified around new democratic institutions, in short, whether the new or changed regimes in these countries will be operated by disunified or consensually unified elites.

In the most schematic of terms, there are three ways in which transformations into consensually unified elites might take place. Two of these have been explored at length in this volume: settlements and convergences. The possibility of a settlement presupposes that substantial disunity describes current elite relations in a country: elites deeply distrust one another; they are fundamentally at odds over basic political and economic questions; and so forth. Our case studies have examined the circumstances and processes that must then unfold in order for a settlement to take place. Alternatively, a convergence begins with the formation of a broad and moderate electoral coalition in an unconsolidated democracy whose electorate is relatively affluent and in which a majority of voters thus have a stake in the existing order. Fearing permanent exclusion from power, antisystem or semiloyal parties with radical political ideologies (e.g., the former Communist parties) adopt more centrist and democratic stands and work to project a moderate image. Crushing electoral defeats for Communist or formerly Communist parties in Hungary and Czechoslovakia at least make thinkable an eventual elite convergence in those countries.

A third way in which elite consensual unity might be achieved has no parallel in Latin America or Southern Europe. This involves a more or less direct transformation from the prerevolutionary configuration of elite ideological unity to a new consensual unity. In this scenario, elites that have survived the upheavals of the past few years remain anchored in the bureaucratic state and other organizations that were the basis of their earlier power, even though they no longer adhere to a single (Marxist–Leninist) ideology in their public utterances. Having abandoned such ideological unity, these surviving elites nevertheless continue the practice of respecting one another's places, privileges, and political needs. Meanwhile, new elites interact cooperatively with elite survivors of the old regimes in order to avoid economic collapse, civil strife, and other calamities. Recriminations for earlier failures and misdeeds are downplayed, and the basic condition of elite structural unity continues, albeit in an increasingly consensual rather than ideological form and involving more diverse elite groups than before.

Whether and by what processes such elite transformations take place varies, depending on a range of contingencies that must be analyzed in each national case. Although we wish the countries of Eastern Europe well in their efforts to establish consolidated democracies, a cursory overview of the economic, political, and social-structural variables on which this volume has concentrated suggests that these tasks will indeed be daunting. First, we have observed that recognized elites must feel relatively secure in their leadership positions at the head of coherent and organized social groups: A lack of stable organization can lead to fragmentation; elite insecurity can impede the concessions necessary for compromise resolution of divisive issues; and unless elites are acknowledged as valid interlocutors for their respective groups, any agreements they reach with their opponents will not hold. A substantial difference between the former regimes of Latin America and Southern Europe, on the one hand, and those of Eastern Europe and the Soviet Union, on the other, is that many of the latter attempted systematically to crush autonomous secondary organizations or subordinate them to state control. Although such efforts have been more successful in some countries (e.g.,

Romania) than in others (e.g., Poland), everywhere they have retarded or prevented the emergence of stable, secure elites at the head of institutionalized and competitive secondary groups. This fundamental difference between postauthoritarian and posttotalitarian transitions (see Linz and Stepan, forthcoming) means that pluralistic elite configurations that are normally regarded as prerequisites for democracy (let alone consolidated democracy) are generally absent. Even where a secondary organization was conspicuously successful in emerging and surviving despite repression (e.g., Solidarity in Poland), the lack of viable competing organizations, in combination with the unchallengeable status of a single leader (Lech Walesa being roughly analogous to the fathers of their countries who led many former African or Asian colonies to national independence), are hardly conducive to the competitive processes that lie at the heart of democracy.

Second, the economic problems confronting most of Eastern Europe and the Soviet Union are severe and, at a minimum, appear to rule out the prospects for stable prosperity that we have argued facilitates the elite convergence process. Not all of the countries we have surveyed have enjoyed prosperity for protracted periods: Indeed, some (e.g., Peru, Argentina, and Brazil) have experienced economic crises that have undermined unconsolidated democratic regimes in the past. But none of those countries has faced the challenge of simultaneously restructuring their political and their economic systems from the ground up. Not only is economic restructuring likely to impose a considerable burden on new democratic or newly liberalized authoritarian institutions in Eastern Europe, but even if this restructuring succeeds, the resulting redistributions of wealth and economic power are likely to have destabilizing consequences, as a plethora of new groups and elites appear while others decline. The forging of elite consensual unity under these circumstances will be enormously difficult.

Third, the international dimension is likely to have a more direct and decisive impact on these transition processes than in most of the countries we examined. Although our analysis has looked at domestic political processes, we clearly acknowledge the importance of international influences, which are alluded to in various chapters: U.S. intervention in the Dominican Republic and U.S. interference over a long period in Mexican affairs; the impact of the cold war on Italian political alignments during the late 1940s; the exposure of Spain and Portugal to West European democratic models for emulation, coupled with aspirations of dominant elites in both countries to qualify for admission to the European Community; the impact of fluctuating world petroleum prices on Venezuelan politics; the possibly destabilizing effect of the U.S. demand for cocaine on Colombian society; and so on. But in no case is the impact of foreign powers on political developments as great as in Eastern Europe. Indeed, before the Soviet proclamation of the "Sinatra Doctrine" (indicating that East European countries were free to liberalize in their own way), the wave of democratization that swept across Eastern Europe in 1989 was virtually unimaginable. Following the Soviets' withdrawal from Eastern Europe, direct foreign influence has been reduced. But its legacy continues to have a substantial impact on the character of domestic politics. It appears to have resulted, for example, in delegitimizing socialism (at least of the maximalist variety) and stigmatizing leftist politicians as lionizing simplistic conceptions of capitalism that had disappeared from Western Europe and North America in the early twentieth century.

Finally, with one limited exception, none of the countries we have considered here has faced micro-nationalist challenges remotely comparable to those confronting the Soviet Union, Yugoslavia, and even Czechoslovakia. In the one country we surveyed in which a democratic transition took place in a multinational society – Spain – the result was a violent struggle between a Basque minority seeking national self-determination and a state defending its territorial integrity and the interests of the majority of Basques who wished to remain within Spain. When we consider that only about one quarter of the population of a region containing less than a tenth of the population of Spain was capable of mounting a violent proindependence campaign for more than a decade, we can appreciate the plight of countries that contain numerous and very populous minority groups.

The elites of Eastern Europe and the Soviet Union certainly have their work cut out for them, and the most sober appraisal must be that elite disunity, and thus endemic regime instability, beckons. But the failure of most political observers to predict the course of *perestroika* in the Soviet Union and the sudden downfall of Communist regimes elsewhere in the region caution against a confident prediction. Elites are sometimes capable of overcoming the most dire challenges and, even, of transforming themselves and the regimes they operate in quite unforeseen ways. Whether the Soviet and East European elites will transform themselves in the direction of the consensus and unity necessary for consolidated democratic regimes is, in our view, the main political and analytical question that bears watching during the next few years.

References

Diamond, Larry, Juan J. Linz, and Seymour Martin Lipset, eds. 1988–9. *Democracy in Developing Countries*. Boulder, CO: Lynne Reinner.

Hartlyn, Jonathan. 1990. "The Dominican Republic's Disputed Elections." *Journal of Democracy*, Fall, pp. 92–103.

Linz, Juan J., and Alfred Stepan. Forthcoming. "Democratic Transition and Consolidation in Southern Europe (With Reflections on Latin America and Eastern Europe)." In *The Politics of Democratic Consolidation in Southern Europe*, ed. Nikiforos Diamandouros, Richard Gunther, and Hans-Jürgen Puhle.

Malloy, James. 1987. "The Politics of Transition in Latin America." In *Latin American Politics and Development*, ed. Howard J. Wiarda and Harvey F. Kline. Boulder, CO: Westview Press.

O'Donnell, Guillermo, and Philippe Schmitter. 1986. *Transitions from Authoritarian Rule: Tentative Conclusions About Uncertain Democracies*. Baltimore: Johns Hopkins University Press.

Index